LIBERATION IN OUR HANDS

LIBERATION IN OUR HANDS

Part Three:
The Ultimate Goals

A series of oral discourses by
Pabongka Rinpoche Jampa Tenzin Trinley Gyatso

Transcribed and edited by
Yongzin Trijang Rinpoche Losang Yeshe Tenzin Gyatso

Translated by
Sermey Khensur Lobsang Tharchin
with Artemus B. Engle

Mahayana Sutra and Tantra Press
Howell, New Jersey

Mahayana Sutra and Tantra Press
112 West Second Street
Howell, New Jersey 07731

Library of Congress Cataloging-in-Publication Data
(Revised for vol. 3)

Liberation in our hands.

Translation of: Rnam grol lag bcaṅs su gtod pa'i man ṅag zab mo tsaṅ la ma nor ba mtshuṅs med chos kyi rgyal po'i thugs bcud byaṅ chub lam gyi rim pa'i ñams khrid kyi zin bris gsuṅ rab kun gyi bcud bsdus gdams ṅag bdud rtsi'i sñiṅ po śes bya ba bśugs so.

Includes bibliographical references and index.

Contents: v. 1. Preliminaries — v. 2. Fundamentals—v. 3. The Ultimate Goals.

1. Tsoṅ-kha-pa Blo-bsaṅ-grags-pa, 1357–1419. Lam rim chen mo. 2. Lam-rim. I. Khri-byaṅ Blo-bzaṅ ye-śes-bstan-'dzin-rgya-mtsho, 1901–1982. II. Tharchin, Sermey Geshe Lobsang, 1921– . III. Engle, Artemus B., 1948– .

BQ7950.T754L3613 1989 294.3'923 88–63954

ISBN Number: 0-918753-12-0 (V.3)

Cover: *Tangka* painting of the future Buddha, Maitreya (Courtesy of First Kalmuk Buddhist Temple, Howell, New Jersey).

CONTENTS

DAY FOURTEEN:
CONTEMPLATING THE SUFFERING OF SAMSARA

(Kyabje Pabongka Rinpoche opened the discourse by reciting two verses from a prayer by the great dharma king Je Tsongkapa that begin: "Please bless me to recall that body and spirit are as fragile/ As a water bubble . . ."[1] Following that, he briefly described the preliminary exercise of how to correct one's motivation and also went over the list of topics that had already been covered. Then he explained, once again, the instructions on karma and its results, which represent the actual means of achieving happiness in future lives.)

b. Training the mind in the levels of the path that are held in common with persons of moderate capacity

This section has two parts: (1) developing the aspiration to achieve liberation, and (2) establishing the nature of the path that leads to liberation.

i. Developing the aspiration to achieve liberation

The first part also has two divisions: (1) contemplating the general suffering of samsara, and (2) contemplating the specific types of suffering of samsara.

1) Contemplating the general suffering of samsara

By relying on the stages of the path that are held in common with persons of lesser capacity [248b] we can develop the moral practice that avoids committing the ten nonvirtuous deeds. This will allow us to escape temporarily from the suffering of the lower states and find a rebirth in one of the happy states.[2] We should not, however, be satisfied with achieving such a result. This is like a criminal whose punishments have been reduced for a while through the intercession of some influential person, but who is still sentenced to die in one month. While he may escape daily whippings and

[1] *Basis of All Virtues* (T: *Yon tan gzhir gyur ma*), vv. 3–4. The two verses state: "Please bless me to recall that body and spirit are as fragile/ As a water bubble, and that dissolution by death comes quickly;/ Bless me also to acquire the firm conviction that white and black karma/ Follow in death like a body and its shadow—/ So that I may always maintain/ The mindfulness that abandons/ Even the most subtle wrongdoing/ And pursues good deeds of every kind." For a translation of the complete prayer, see Part One, Appendix C, pp. 263–265.

[2] S: *sugatiḥ*, T: *bde 'gro*. Birth as a human or as a god.

other tortures, he has not escaped the ultimate penalty of being executed. Similarly, unless we free ourselves from samsara permanently, one day our good karma will definitely run out and we will have to return to the lower states. This is described in a verse from *Engaging in Bodhisattva Activities*:

> They came to the happy states again and again,
> And enjoyed delightful pleasures here continually.
> Then they died and fell back to the lower states,
> Where the suffering is long-lasting and severe.[3]

Therefore, if we want to put an end to future suffering, we must free ourselves permanently from samsara. In order to accomplish this, we must first generate the aspiration to achieve liberation, an attitude that I am now going to explain as part of the instructions relating to persons of moderate capacity.

There are two ways of developing this attitude: one is based on contemplating the nature of the Four Noble Truths and the other on contemplating the Twelve Limbs of Dependent Origination.

The term *liberation*[4] means to become free from a state of bondage. For example, when a person who had been tied up with a rope or some other kind of restraint is able to gain his release, we say that he is liberated. Similarly, samsaric bondage is a condition that occurs in relation to our "afflicted grasping heaps"[5] and the ropes by which we are bound are karma and the mental afflictions. The essence of this bondage is that our heaps are continually forced to be reborn by karma and the mental afflictions. The

[3]S: *Bodhicaryāvatāraḥ*, ch. 9, v. 157. In Bibliography, see listing under *Śāntideva*.

[4]S: *mokṣaḥ*, T: *thar pa*. In this usage, it serves as a synonym for Hinayana nirvana.

[5]S: *sāsravopādānaskandhāḥ*, T: *zag bcas nyer len gyi phung po*. Buddha taught that the individual is essentially a collection of five heaps (S: *skandhāḥ*, T: *phung po*): (1) form, (2) feeling, (3) conception, (4) compositional factors, and (5) consciousness. The term "afflicted" here is a somewhat loose rendering of a technical expression that literally means "related to the outflows" (S: *sāsravaḥ*, T: *zag bcas*). "Outflow" (S: *āsravaḥ*, T: *zag pa*) is a synonym for the mental afflictions. Vasubandhu explains that the mental afflictions are "outflows" in that they cause the mind to flow out toward objects (*Commentary to the Treasury of Higher Learning*, S: *Abhidharmakośabhāṣyam*, in explanation of ch 5, v. 40 of the root text). He also explains that the expression "related to the outflows" applies to all impermanent, caused entities, with the exception of the Truth of the Path, because of their capacity to cause the mental afflictions to become stronger (*Treasury of Higher Learning*, S: *Abhidharmakośa-kārikā*, ch. 1, v. 4). The term "grasping" (S: *upādānam*, T: *nye bar len pa*) in the expression "grasping heaps" (S: *upādānaskandhāḥ*, T: *nye bar len pa'i phung po*) is another synonym for the mental afflictions. It is meant to indicate that desire and the other mental afflictions cause us to grasp at sense objects and other entities. Thus, "grasping heaps" refers to the impure heaps that are produced by karma and the mental afflictions. See below, pp. 40–41, for three interpretations of the expression.

place where our heaps are reborn is the three realms[6]—that is, the desire realm and so on. The types of existence into which they are reborn are either the five states of transmigration[7] or the six classes of beings.[8] And [249a] the forms of rebirth they can take are the four known as birth from a womb and so on.[9] Since the essence of our bondage is that our heaps have to be reborn, liberation should be understood as becoming free of that condition.

Generally speaking, the term *samsara* means "to wander about," taking birth everywhere from the Peak of Existence[10] to the hell called Unrelenting Torment.[11] Those of you who have not studied Buddhist philosophy think the word *samsara* means the homes where you live or the regions that are inhabited by the six classes of beings. But this is just an accepted usage of the term, not its true meaning.

The opinions of scholars vary on the exact meaning of samsara. For instance, some hold that it means the condition of being born again and again. However, I prefer the definition of the Supreme Conqueror Kelsang Gyatso, who described samsara as the continuum of rebirths that is experienced by the afflicted grasping heaps. Therefore, we will achieve liberation from samsara when we put an end to the series of rebirths that is caused by karma and the mental afflictions.

In order to gain his freedom from prison, a prisoner must first want to be released. But he won't develop this desire unless he thinks about the disadvantages of being in prison. Similarly, we will not strive to practice the methods for achieving liberation from samsara unless we gain the desire to be liberated. And the way to develop the desire for liberation is to cultivate aversion for samsara. This point is described in the *Four Hundred Verses*:

[6]S: *dhātuḥ*, T: *khams*. They are: (1) the desire realm, (2) the form realm, and (3) the formless realm.

[7]S: *gatiḥ*, T: *'gro ba*. The five are: hell beings, hungry ghosts, animals, humans, and gods.

[8]T: *'gro ba rigs drug*. This classification differs from the five states of transmigration only in that it divides the category of gods into demigods (S: *asuraḥ*, T: *lha ma yin*) and gods (S: *devaḥ*, T: *lha*). The demigods are a group of celestials who are jealous of the gods and are constantly doing battle with them in an attempt to usurp their power and wealth (see below, pp. 33–34).

[9]The four are: (1) birth from a womb, (2) birth from an egg, (3) birth from warmth and moisture (e.g., insects, worms, and the like), and (4) spontaneous or miraculous birth (S: *upapādukaḥ*, T: *brdzus te skye ba*). The latter category refers primarily to the way in which hell beings and many of the gods are born. Such beings are born with fully developed bodies.

[10]S: *bhavāgraḥ*, T: *srid pa'i rtze mo*. This is the fourth and highest level of the formless realm. As the name implies, it is the most lofty of all the domains in samsara.

[11]S: *avīciḥ*, T: *mnar med*. The most severe of the eight hot hells. See Part Two, Day Eleven, pp. 150–151.

The wise also fear the celestial states
As much as they do the hells.[12]

This aversion is developed by contemplating the suffering that occurs in samsara. The Buddha taught two methods for contemplating that suffering: the Four Noble Truths and the Twelve Limbs of Dependent Origination. Of these two teachings, [249b] I shall begin by explaining the Four Noble Truths.

The first turning of the dharma wheel took place in Varanasi, where the Blessed One taught the noble group of five with these words: "O monks, this is the noble truth of suffering; this is the noble truth of the origin of suffering; this is the noble truth of the cessation of suffering; and this is the noble truth of the path." This discourse is known as the turning of the dharma wheel in which the four truths were taught in three phases and twelve aspects.[13] The term "truth" here means that which exists exactly as the Noble Ones[14] perceive it.

If the Buddha had wanted to teach the Four Noble Truths in the order that cause and effect naturally occur, he would have taught the truth of the origin of suffering first. However, the reason that he reversed this order and began with the truth of suffering is because he wanted to teach the Four Noble Truths in the order that a practitioner should cultivate them. He taught the truth of suffering first so that we might develop aversion for those objects whose nature is suffering. This is because we will not develop a desire to abandon the causes of suffering until we generate disgust for that suffering.

[12]T: *Bzhi brgya pa*, ch. 7, v. 14. In Bibliography, see listing under *Āryadeva*.

[13]In the first phase (S: *parivartam*, T: *lan*), Buddha described the essential nature (S: *svarūpam*, T: *ngo bo*) of the four truths by declaring that he had realized the following: "This is the noble truth of suffering; this is the noble truth of the origin of suffering; this is the noble truth of the cessation of suffering; and this is the noble truth of the path leading to the cessation of suffering." In the second phase, he described the goal to be accomplished (S: *kartavya-rūpam*, T: *byed pa*) relative to each of the four noble truths by declaring he had gained the knowledge that "this noble truth of suffering is something that should be realized; this noble truth of the origin of suffering is something that should be abandoned; this noble truth of the cessation of suffering is something that should be made manifest; and this noble truth of the path leading to the cessation of suffering is something that should be practiced." In the third phase, he described the completion of these goals (S: *pariniṣṭhārūpam*, T: *'bras bu*) by declaring he had gained the knowledge that "the truth of suffering has been fully realized; the truth of the origin of suffering has been abandoned; the truth of the cessation of suffering has been made manifest; and the truth of the path leading to the cessation of suffering has been fully practiced." These twelve statements about the four noble truths represent their twelve aspects (S: *ākaram*, T: *rnam pa*).

[14]S: *āryaḥ*, T: *'phags pa*. A practitioner who has achieved a direct realization of ultimate reality and reached the Path of Seeing in any of the three vehicles. In so doing, he transcends the state of an "ordinary being" (S: *pṛthagjanaḥ*, T: *so so skye bo*). See also Day Eight, note 66.

We must also develop a desire to achieve freedom from suffering and its causes[15] before we will strive to practice the path that will bring about such freedom.

These four truths are the principal objects that practitioners who wish to attain liberation must abandon and adopt. In the *Higher Science of the Mahayana*, the exalted Maitreya used similes to explain a variety of points. As one verse in particular states, we must first come to understand our suffering condition so that we can eliminate the causes of that suffering:

> An illness should be discerned, the cause of the illness removed,
> Good health should be achieved, and medicine should be taken.
> So, too, with suffering, its cause, cessation, and the path; [250a]
> They should be realized, abandoned, achieved, and pursued.[16]

Thus, when we experience an illness, we must learn its cause and then take the medicine that will remove it.

The Great Fifth[17] used water as an analogy to describe the order in which the truths were taught. (Kyabje Pabongka Rinpoche explained that in this example the order of the truths is compared to an experience in which a person is first soaked by water while lying comfortably on a spot of ground. Then, after learning where it came from, he develops the desire to block the water.)[18]

We must then develop the desire to free ourselves from the cause of suffering before we will start to practice the method that will liberate us from the illness that is the truth of suffering. In order to develop that desire, we must investigate the cause of our suffering. However, that step depends upon our first recognizing that we are in fact experiencing suffering. As Je Rinpoche declared:

[15]"Freedom from suffering and its causes" is a reference to the noble truth of cessation.

[16]S: *Mahāyānottaratantraśāstram*, ch. 4, v. 52. In Bibliography, see listing under *Maitreya Nātha*.

[17]That is, the Fifth Dalai Lama, Ngawang Losang Gyatso (T: *Ngag dbang blo bzang rgya mtso*, 1617–1682).

[18]*Mañjughosha's Oral Instruction* (T: *'Jam dpal zhal lung*), pp. 72–73 (ff. 36b–37a). The passage reads: "For example, suppose we are sitting one day on some dry spot and water suddenly comes pouring over us, soaking our clothes and the cushions we are sitting on. The discomfort of this cold sensation is like the truth of suffering. If we investigate where the water came from and determine its origin, this is like the truth of the origin of suffering. When we free ourselves from the sensation of cold [caused by the water], this is like the truth of cessation. Finally, if the means we use to free ourselves is to dig a trench so that we can divert the water, this is like the truth of the path." In Bibliography, see listing under *Ngag dbang blo bzang rgya mtso*.

We cannot develop a true aspiration to achieve
liberation
Without contemplating intently the disadvantages of
the truth of suffering.
Nor can we gain an understanding of the way to cut
samsara's root
Without contemplating how the origin of suffering
perpetuates samsara.
So hold dear cultivating renunciation and disgust for
cyclic existence,
Along with gaining knowledge of what binds us to
samsara.[19]

Each of the four truths also has four aspects. The four that relate to the first noble truth are: (1) impermanence, (2) suffering, (3) voidness, and (4) lack of self.[20] The four that relate to the second noble truth are: (1) cause, (2) origination, (3) contributing factor, and (4) source.[21] The four that relate to the third noble truth are (1) cessation, (2) peace, (3) goodness, and (4) deliverance.[22] And the four that relate to the fourth noble truth are: (1) path, (2) rightness, (3) attainment, and (4) leading to deliverance.[23]

[19] *Brief Stages of the Path* (T: *Lam rim bsdus don*), vv. 19–20.

[20] (1) The impure heaps are impermanent (S: *anityam*, T: *mi rtag pa*) in that they arise and pass away from moment to moment; (2) they are characterized by suffering (S: *duḥkham*, T: *sdug bsngal ba*) in that they are disagreeable in nature; (3) they are void (S: *śūnyam*, T: *stong pa*) in that they are not associated with a self; and (4) they are selfless (S: *anātman*, T: *bdag med pa*) in that they do not constitute a self.

[21] (1) General craving for the self is the root cause (S: *hetu*, T: *rgyu*) that produces the impure heaps. This is analogous to the way a seed is the cause of a fruit. This aspect is an antidote for the erroneous view that the heaps have no cause. (2) The continuous and general craving for rebirth is the main factor in the origination (S: *samudayaḥ*, T: *kun 'byung ba*) of the impure heaps. The analogy for this aspect is the way in which a fruit is brought forth by the preceding stages in a plant's development, such as those of the sprout and so forth. This aspect is an antidote for the view that the heaps are brought into being by a single, permanent cause, such as a divine creator. (3) The particular form of craving for rebirth is the contributing factor (S: *pratyayaḥ*, T: *rkyen*) in the arising of the impure heaps. That is, the particular form of craving that a person has for rebirth becomes a determining factor in the type of suffering that is manifested in that rebirth. The analogy for this aspect is the various functions that a field, water, fertilizer, and so forth fulfill in producing fruit. This aspect is an antidote for the erroneous belief that the world was created by the will or premeditated thought of a divine creator. (4) Craving for conception is the source (S: *prabhavaḥ*, T: *rab skyes*) or proximate cause from which the impure heaps arise. The analogy for this is the way in which a flower is the proximate cause from which fruit arises. This aspect is an antidote for the erroneous belief that causation is a process in which a pre-existent essence undergoes transformation.

[22] (1) The third noble truth describes a condition of cessation (S: *nirodham*, T: *'gog pa*) in that the bondage of samsaric existence has been brought to an end; (2) a state of peace (S:

The afflicted grasping heaps experience three types of feeling:[24] pleasurable, painful, and neutral. Of these, we only recognize as suffering those afflicted feelings that are painful. This is known as the suffering of suffering.[25] For the most part, we are unaware of the two other forms of suffering.[26]

Therefore, we are like the tantric practitioner [250b] who once said to his wives: "I have the ability to go to the knowledge-holders' realm,[27] but if I did it would cause you great hardship." Later, when he was ill and near death, his wives reminded him: "O Tantric Practitioner, you told us that you had the ability to go to the knowledge-holders' realm but that you did not want to cause us hardship." To this the tantric practitioner could only reply, "If only I had the power, I would much rather stay here with you, my wives, than go to the realm of knowledge holders."

As in the story of Acharya Manu,[28] we also tend to think it is quite pleasant here in samsara, and remain attached to it without realizing its suffering nature.

śāntam, T: *zhi ba*) in that it is free of all suffering; (3) a state of goodness (S: *pranītam*, T: *gya nom pa*) in that it is unsurpassed; and (4) a state of deliverance (S: *niḥsaraṇam*, T: *nges par 'byung ba*) in that one who attains it will never return to samsaric existence. Of these, the third aspect in particular is an antidote for the belief that the pleasure experienced in one-pointed states of mental composure represents liberation and the fourth aspect is an antidote for the belief that liberation is not permanent.

[23](1) The fourth noble truth describes the path (S: *mārgaḥ*, T: *lam*) that leads to the cessation of suffering. This aspect is an antidote to the belief that there is no true path. (2) This truth is characterized by rightness (S: *nyāyaḥ*,T: *rigs pa*), in that it represents a system of proper conduct. This aspect is an antidote for the belief that something that is actually a form of suffering constitutes the true path. (3) This truth is a means of attainment (S: *pratipad*, T: *sgrub pa*), in that it leads definitely to the attainment of liberation. This aspect is an antidote for the belief that some other form of practice represents the true path. (4) This truth is described as leading to deliverance (S: *nairyāṇikaḥ*, T: *nges par 'byin pa*), in that it brings about permanent deliverance from samsaric existence. This aspect is an antidote for the belief that the path does not bring permanent deliverance.

[24]S: *vedanā*, T: *tsor ba*. This is the second of the five heaps.

[25]S: *duḥkhaduḥkhatā*, T: *sdug bsngal gyi sdug bsngal.*

[26]The other two are: (1) the suffering of change (S: *pariṇāmaduḥkhatā*, T: *'gyur ba'i sdug bsngal*) and (2) the suffering of conditional existence (S: *samskāraduḥkhatā*, T: *khyab pa 'du byed kyi sdug bsngal*). See below, pp. 38–40, for a discussion of the three types of suffering.

[27]T: *rig 'dzin zhing*. Tantric term for a Buddha realm.

[28]A brief account of this story appears in the *Ornament of Losang's View: An Instructional Treatise on Training One's Mind in the Mahayana Practices* (T: *Theg pa chen po'i blo sbyong gi khrid yig lo bzang dgongs rgyan*), p. 173: "Long ago, there was a certain artisan named Acharya Manu, who was staying at Radreng Monastery in order to help construct an image of Atisha. Once, during a certain full moon, it was noticed that he had begun to cry. When asked why he was crying, he replied, 'I was thinking about my homeland and how this is a time when my whole family is playing many different games.' Then he was asked, 'Well, if you could choose between achieving Buddhahood right now and being able to meet your wife, which one

In addition to realizing the truth of suffering, we must understand that the cause of our suffering is the truth of origination; then we must abandon this cause. The truth of the origin of suffering has two aspects: the origination brought about by karma and the origination brought about by the mental afflictions.

The truth of cessation is the condition or result of having achieved a separation from suffering.[29] The truth of the path is the means by which the truth of cessation is achieved. That is to say, the way to achieve the truth of cessation is by practicing the truth of the path.

There are various instructions to help us to realize the truth of suffering. The *Great Treatise on the Stages of the Path* presents separate topics for contemplating eight, six, and three types of suffering. Of these, the eight sufferings are specific forms of suffering that humans experience, while the three sufferings are related to the suffering of conditional existence.[30] So I shall discuss here the topic of the general suffering of samsara in terms of the following six sections: (1) the defect of being uncertain, (2) the defect of providing no satisfaction, (3) the defect of having to discard one's body again and again, (4) the defect of having to be reborn again and again, (5) the defect of having to fall from a high position to a low one again and again, and (6) the defect of having no companion.

a) The defect of being uncertain

Although we might take birth and live for a time in one of the happy states, no matter where we are born in samsara we can never escape what is essentially a condition of suffering, [251a] because the happiness of samsara is completely unreliable. For example, the relationships that we have with others of being a friend, enemy, father, mother, and the like can become reversed from one life to another.

There was once an elderly householder who regularly ate fish from a pond behind his house. When he died, he was reborn as a fish in that very pond. Because his wife was so attached to her family, she was reborn as a

would you choose?' And he is said to have answered, 'I would choose my wife.'" In Bibliography, see listing under (*Tse mchog gling yongs 'dzin*) *Ye shes rgyal mtsan*.

[29]Although the truth of cessation is referred to as a "separation result" (S: *visaṃyogaphalam*, T: *bral ba'i 'bras bu*), it is not a true result because it is not an impermanent entity produced by a cause. Though it is achieved on the basis of the path in which we achieve a direct realization that there is no real self, its nature is that of an uncaused and permanent condition, described as the destruction of the factors that permit the mental afflictions to arise.

[30]The point being made here is that this section addresses samsara's general suffering. Because the eight types of suffering mainly represent human suffering, they are explained later as part of the suffering experienced by that specific type of being (pp. 20–33). The three types of suffering are described at the very end of the discussion on suffering (pp. 38–40).

dog in the same household. The family son, meanwhile, killed another man for committing adultery with his wife. Because of his lust for the son's wife, this enemy was reborn as her son.

Some time later, the son caught and killed the fish that his father had become. While the son was eating its flesh, his mother the dog was gnawing on the leftover bones. So the son began to beat the dog. At the same time, the son was holding in his lap the child that formerly had been his enemy. Upon witnessing this scene, Shariputra declared:

> Eating his father's flesh, a son beats his mother
> And holds in his lap the enemy that he killed.
> A wife, likewise, gnaws on her husband's bones.
> These circumstances of samsara are laughable.[31]

A verse in the *Letter to a Friend* also states:

> A father becomes a son, a mother becomes a wife,
> And one who was an enemy becomes a friend.
> Because the opposite of this can occur as well,
> There is no certainty whatsoever in samsara.[32]

Although we act as though someone who is a friend or an enemy will always remain so, these relationships are not permanent. Even in the same lifetime, someone who was a friend at first can later become an enemy; likewise, an enemy can become a friend.

The same can happen with wealth. Someone who was once rich can have his wealth stolen by an enemy and become poor. Examples such as these clearly show how our circumstances [251b] are constantly changing with each passing moment.

(Kyabje Rinpoche then told us in great detail the story of the householder Shrija.)[33]

In this story, Shrija witnessed a number of scenes, including one in which a snake slithers in and out of a woman's mortal remains; a second in which a large tree is being eaten by many insects; a third in which a man is being

[31]Quoted in the *Quick Path* (T: *Myur lam*), f. 53a. A slightly different version of this verse, along with an explanation of the events, appears in the *Great Sutra on the Distinctions of Karma* (S: *Mahākarmavibhaṅgasūtraḥ*), pp. 198–199. However, this source associates the incident with Maudgalyayana rather than Shariputra. See also Part Two, Day Eleven, p. 174, where this story is also referenced.

[32]T: *bShes pa'i spring yig*, v. 66. In Bibliography, see listing under *Nāgārjuna*.

[33]This story appears in the *Sutra of the Wise and the Foolish* (T: *mDzangs blun zhes bya ba'i mdo*), ch. 16.

assaulted by a large group of hungry ghosts, each with the head of a different kind of animal; a fourth in which the carcass of a sea monster is as tall as a mountain and so large that it can even obscure the sun.

Maudgalyayana explained to him that the body in the first scene was that of a woman who had great attachment for her own body. Likewise, the insects in the second scene had been a group of persons who carelessly and improperly used wood that belonged to the sangha. The man in the third scene was someone who had been a hunter in a previous life. And the carcass in the fourth scene was from one of Shrija's own former lives.

The latter birth was the result of an incident that occurred long ago. A certain king was asked by his ministers how a criminal should be punished. Absorbed in a game of chess, the king simply replied, "Punish him according to the law." And so the man was executed.

After he had finished his game, the king asked what had happened to the criminal. Despite his deep remorse at being told by the ministers that the man had been killed, the king was reborn as a sea monster for his misdeed of having the criminal put to death.

Much later, a group of merchants were sailing across the ocean when they came upon this sea monster and were about to be swallowed by it. But when the monster heard the frightened merchants loudly crying out the words for taking refuge in the Buddha, he closed his mouth and eventually died of starvation. His remains were then carried to the beach by *nagas* that lived in the ocean.

This series of births in which Shrija was first a king, then [252a] a sea monster, and finally a human being again illustrates samsara's uncertain nature.

b) The defect of providing no satisfaction

Moths are destroyed by their attachment to visible form, deer by their attachment to sounds, flies by their attachment to foul smells, and elephants by their attachment to tactile sensations.[34] Indulging in the pleasures of samsara is much the same for us. Like drinking salty water, no matter how much we experience we are never satisfied.

[34]This remark can be traced to a verse found in a short work by Vasubandhu entitled *A Presentation of the Disadvantages of the Five Sense Objects* (T: *'Dod pa'i yon tan lnga'i nye migs bshad pa*). The verse, which Je Tsongkapa quotes in his *Great Stages of the Path* (T: *Lam rim chen mo*), pp. 392–393 (ff. 180b–181a), states: "The five of the deer, elephant, moth, fish, and fly/ Are each destroyed by one of the five sense objects./ If a being can be destroyed by just one sense object,/ Why not a person who constantly indulges in all five?"

For example, a person who has only one or two *sang*[35] of money will think to himself, “I wish I had ten *sang*.” But if he gets ten, he’ll wish he had a hundred, and if he gets a hundred, he’ll wish he had a thousand. So, no matter how much he actually has, he never feels satisfied.

A verse from the *Extensive Cosmic Sport* says:

> O King, no matter how many divine pleasures
> And fine human enjoyments there might be,
> If a single person were to acquire them all,
> He would be unsatisfied and still want more.[36]

The story of King Mandhatar illustrates how someone can fail to be satisfied even after experiencing vast human and divine pleasures.[37] Though he ruled the four continents together with several celestial realms, in the end he fell back to the southern Jambudvipa continent when his merit was exhausted. With his final words, he declared that there is no greater fault than having insatiable desires.

If we rule one country, we want to rule two. No matter how much power we have, we are never satisfied. However great our wealth, we want still more and feel a need to intently pursue the objects of these desires.

If we remain unsatisfied with the things we have, [252b] no matter how much wealth or how many possessions we accumulate, we will be no different from those who have none. There was once a pauper in India named Surata, who found a priceless gem and declared he would give it to the most needy person. He then offered it to King Prasenajit, saying, “You are the poorest of all men because you are never satisfied with what you have.”[38]

A person who is satisfied with what he has is rich, even though he may lack material wealth. As the *Letter to a Friend* states:

> Be satisfied with what you have. By remaining satisfied,
> You will be truly rich, though you may lack material wealth.[39]

[35] T: *srang*. A unit of Tibetan currency that at the time was roughly equivalent to ten U.S. dollars.

[36] S: *Lalitavistaraḥ*, ch. 16, v. 23.

[37] A brief Tibetan account of King Mandhatar (T: *nGa las nu*) can be found in the *Sutra of the Wise and the Foolish* (T: *mDzangs blun zhes bya ba'i mdo*), ch. 46. A longer Sanskrit version is in *Divine Narratives* (S: *Divyāvadānam*), ch. 17.

[38] Surata was a great Bodhisattva teacher. This incident is described in the *Sutra of Questions Posed by Surata* (T: *Des pas zhus pa'i mdo*).

[39] T: *bShes pa'i spring yig*, v. 34.

Drogön Tsangpa Gyare also said:

> In the gatehouse of one who knows satisfaction, there sleeps a rich person who is keeping guard; but those who have great desires do not notice him.

Thus, by never being satisfied with what we have, our desires will know no bounds.

(Kyabje Rinpoche concluded by saying that not being able to remain satisfied and having insatiable desires are among the worst faults that a person can have.)

c) The defect of having to discard one's body again and again

No matter what kind of body we acquire, it is not trustworthy. As the *Letter to a Friend* declares:

> After attaining extremely great celestial pleasures,
> Including the blissful nonattachment of Brahma's realm,
> You return again to the continuous suffering
> Of being kindling for the fires of Unrelenting Torment.
>
> After attaining the status of the sun and moon,
> In which your body lights up the entire world,
> You return again to that pitch-black darkness
> Where you cannot even see your outstretched arm.[40]

Although we have acquired the bodies of Brahma and Shakra countless times, this has brought us nothing of lasting value. We had to take birth again in places like the hell called Unrelenting Torment, and in circumstances where we were the lowest of servants [253a].

On occasion, we were born as the deities of the sun or the moon, and the light from our bodies illuminated the world with its four continents. But then we had to pass away from those states, only to be reborn in the darkness between worlds where a person cannot even see his own arm when he stretches it out or draws it back.

In the past, we have possessed every form of human or divine wealth that there is. There isn't any object we could point to and say, "I haven't possessed that before." But no matter how much wealth we have had, none of it has ever proved reliable. We have been born before in the celestial realms,

[40]Ibid., vv. 74–75.

where we could spread diamonds on the ground as seats to sit on. Many times we enjoyed living in houses that were made of nothing but precious gems. Yet now we find that we must make do with sitting on such things as animal hides. We gain nothing by being born as the god Shakra if we just end up becoming poor again.

Another verse from the same work states:

> After long enjoying the pleasures that come from
> Touching the breasts and hips of celestial maidens,
> Again, in the hells, you feel the horrible touch
> Of those devices that grind and sever and slash.[41]

(Kyabje Rinpoche explained how in the past we have taken birth in the celestial realms and long enjoyed the pleasurable company of celestial maidens. But after passing away from there, we were reborn in the hells, where we were surrounded by terrible guards and had to undergo tremendous suffering. Likewise, although we have drunk the gods' nectar of longevity many times, eventually we had to leave those divine realms and be reborn in the hells where we drank molten iron.)

Previously, we have achieved the status of a wheel-wielding monarch in which we ruled over many hundreds of thousands of subjects and possessed the seven articles of royal authority.[42] Yet nothing remains from that period; [253b] we have nothing of value to show for it now. Instead, as I mentioned before, those pleasures only caused our desire to increase. And since they never gave us any lasting satisfaction, we were driven to accumulate bad karma so that we could continue to indulge our desires. As a result, we ended up having to go back to the lower states. Such are the disadvantages of samsaric existence.

My own guru, my precious lord and protector, used to tell the story of a lama who was asked for a final instruction as he was about to pass away. The lama answered by repeating over and over: "Samsara's activities have no value."

In the same way, we too must realize that no matter what kind of birth and no matter how much material wealth we may achieve here in samsara, we always return to our former ordinary condition and never gain anything of real value. We were born in the past many times as a wheel-wielding monarch. Even the shoes we wore then were more valuable than all the wealth found in this world. Yet none of the wealth we possessed at that

[41] Ibid., v. 70.

[42] T: *rgyal srid sna bdun*. They are: (1) a wheel, (2) a jewel, (3) a queen, (4) a minister, (5) an elephant, (6) a horse, and (7) a military commander.

time has been of any real benefit to us. When someone is traveling along that perilous road of the intermediate state, it makes no difference whether he had previously been a king or a beggar. Neither one has an easier time of it; their experiences are the same. Therefore, we must exercise great care in our actions. As Chen-ngawa said: "Lord Tönba, no matter what kind of body I obtained over the course of beginningless time, never before was I able to practice Mahayana dharma as I now can. Therefore, I must practice with great effort."[43]

d) The defect of having to be reborn again and again

Several lines from the *Letter to a Friend* declare:

> If we tried to count our maternal lineage with pellets
> of soil
> The size of juniper berries, the entire earth would not
> suffice.[44]

The text *Dispelling Grief* also states:

> Not even all the water in the oceans
> Can equal the amount of molten copper
> That you have had to drink
> Over and over in the hells.[45]

[254a] In all the past lives when we were born in the hells, each of us has drunk more molten copper than all the water contained in the great oceans of the world. But unless we can stop the continuous cycle of rebirth in samsara, we will have to drink an even greater amount than we already have.

Another verse states:

> The amount of filth that you've eaten
> When born as a dog or a pig
> Would form a mass much greater in size
> Than Meru, king of mountains.[46]

[43]Quoted in the *Great Stages of the Path* (T: *Lam rim chen mo*), p. 321 (f. 145a). Chen-ngawa Tsultrim Bar (T: *sPyan snga ba Tsul khrims 'bar*) said this to his teacher Dromtönba (T: *'Brom ston pa rGyal ba'i 'byung gnas*), who was Lord Atisha's principal disciple in Tibet.

[44]T: *bShes pa'i spring yig*, v. 68.

[45]T: *Mya ngan bsal ba*, f. 33a. In Bibliography, see listing under *Aśvaghoṣa*.

[46]Ibid., f. 33a.

Although the amount of filth each of us has eaten in our past lives as dogs and pigs would create a mountain even greater in size than Mt. Meru, we will have to eat an even greater quantity in the future unless we bring samsara to an end.

The same work again says:

> Not even the oceans could hold
> All the tears your eyes have cried
> When, in this samsaric realm,
> You were parted from friends.[47]

In the past, when we had to be separated from our parents, children, relatives, and so on, each of us has cried more tears than all the water contained in the great oceans. And unless we can bring an end to our future samsara, we will have to cry an even greater quantity of tears.

Yet another verse declares:

> If all the heads you've had severed
> While doing battle were piled up,
> They would rise even higher
> Than Brahma's realm.[48]

If someone were to pile up all the heads each of us has had severed by our enemies in the past when we were fighting in battles, they would reach higher than Mt. Meru. And we are certain to lose an even greater number in the future unless we put an end to samsara's continuous cycle of rebirth.

> If all the filth you have eaten in hunger
> When you were born as a worm [254b]
> Were put into the vast ocean of milk,[49]
> It would be completely filled.[50]

If someone were to deposit into the great outer ocean all the dirt and filth that each of us has eaten in the lives when we were born as worms living in mud, the ocean would not be able to contain it all. Although we have

[47] Ibid., f. 33a

[48] Ibid., f. 33a.

[49] Here the term probably refers to the whiteness of the ocean's foam. Indian mythology also speaks of a sacred ocean of milk churned by the gods to produce the nectar of longevity.

[50] Ibid., f. 33a.

already eaten that much dirt, we will have to consume an even greater amount in the future unless we free ourselves from samsara.

Nagarjuna also said:

> While everyone has drunk more milk
> Than the four oceans, the samsaric person
> Who follows the ways of ordinary beings
> Has far more still to drink.[51]

All of us have taken birth in samsara so many times in the past that we have drunk more milk from our mothers' breasts than there is water in the four great oceans. But unless we are able to stop samsara's cycle of rebirth, we will have to drink a much greater quantity in the future.

Earlier, during the instructions for persons of lesser capacity, I explained how to reflect on the fear and suffering that is experienced each time we die and are reborn in the lower states.[52] But if there is that much fear and suffering in just one death and rebirth, then certainly we will have to experience a tremendous amount in the countless deaths and rebirths that await us in the future.

(Kyabje Rinpoche concluded with the following point. Right now, we are frightened at the mere sight of a scorpion. Yet each of us has actually taken birth as a scorpion so many times that just the bodies from our scorpion births would create a mountain the size of Meru. And unless we can bring samsara's cycle of rebirth to an end, we will have to be born as scorpions an even greater number of times in the future.)

e) The defect of having to fall from a high position to a low one again and again

A verse from the Vinaya scriptures declares:

> All accumulations are lost in the end;
> Everything that rises eventually falls [255a];
> All coming together ends in separation;
> Every living thing ultimately must die.[53]

[51]*Letter to a Friend* (T: *bShes pa'i spring yig*), v. 67.

[52]See Part Two, Day Eleven.

[53]The verse also appears in the *Collection of Uplifting Sayings* (S: *Udānavargaḥ*), ch. 1, v. 22.

All accumulated wealth eventually is lost. Anything that rises to a high position ends up falling again. Everything that comes together eventually undergoes separation. Everything that is born ultimately must die. These conditions are described as the "four ends of composed things."[54] This instruction teaches that every kind of well-being we achieve in samsara always ends up being lost. As Geshe Sangpuwa[55] said, "It is troubling to consider the many ups and downs we experience in samsara."[56]

What's more, no one is able to keep all the things he worked long and hard to acquire—such as a house and other property. One way or another, we eventually lose them. They might be taken away by an enemy, or the owner himself might simply die. Even you and I, who have gathered here as guru and students, will definitely have to go our separate ways after a few years or so. As the Supreme Conqueror Kelsang Gyatso wrote, "Even a person of high birth before long can become a servant who must endure being kicked."[57]

The *Letter to a Friend* also states:

> Having been Shakra, worthy of the world's veneration,
> You fall back to the earth by the force of karma.
> And having been a wheel-wielding, universal monarch,
> You return as the lowest of servants in samsara's round.[58]

Those who achieve such exalted positions as becoming the gods Brahma or Shakra eventually fall. Even the more modest positions we can achieve in this human realm have no real value. As Je Gungtangba wrote:

> If you climb too far, going ever higher
> In the dead tree of position and fame, [255b]

[54]T: *'du byas kyi mtha' bzhi.*

[55]T: *dGe bshes gSang phu ba*, fl. late 10th–early 11th centuries. An early Kadampa teacher whose name literally means "the person from Sangpu." Sangpu is in the lower part of Kyishö (T: *sKyid shod*), which lies downstream from Lhasa along the Tsang River. Geshe Sangpuwa built a monastery there in the year 1073 on the instructions of Lord Atisha, whom he served for some ten years. This disciple was also known as Ngok Lekbey Sherab (T: *Ngog legs pa'i shes rab*).

[56]This statement is quoted in Je Tsongkapa's *Great Stages of the Path* (T: *Lam rim chen mo*), p. 321 (f. 145a).

[57]This line is from a poem by the Seventh Dalai Lama Losang Kelsang Gyatso, entitled *Falling Rain of Well-being and Happiness: A Poem of Praise and Supplication Unto the Arya Who is the Embodiment of Great Compassion* (T: *'Phags pa thugs rje chen po la bstod cing gsol ba 'debs pa phan bde'i char 'bebs*), v. 19. In Bibliography, see listing under *Blo bzang bskal bzang rgya mtso*.

[58]T: *bShes pa'i spring yig*, v. 69.

> You'll get hurt when a weak branch breaks;
> So you're better off staying near the trunk![59]

This kind of misfortune doesn't only happen from one life to the next; everything in our current life is uncertain as well. For instance, a king sometimes ends up being imprisoned.

(Kyabje Rinpoche concluded this section by describing events that took place during the time of Desi Sang-gye Gyatso.[60] The Desi, or chief minister, established many new policies in the Tibetan government and was a person of very great wealth, authority, and knowledge. In the end, however, he was beheaded after a long-standing dispute with Hlasang Khan.[61] His severed head was left for many days at Tri Bridge in Tö because no one had the courage to claim it. Sang-gye Gyatso's family, including his mother and other relatives, were also forced into exile and left destitute. Some time later, Hlasang Khan went to war against the Jungar Mongols and was himself killed.)

f) The defect of having no companion

When we emerge from the womb at the very beginning of this life, we are completely alone. Throughout this life, we experience illnesses and other kinds of suffering alone. In the end, we also must face death alone, like a strand of hair that is plucked from a lump of butter. No one accompanies us at any of these times. As *Engaging in Bodhisattva Activities* declares:

> A living being is born all alone
> And, indeed, quite alone he also dies.

[59]In *Miscellaneous Didactic Poems, Including "A Guide to the Jewel Island: Advice for Studying the Sutra and Tantra Scriptures"* (T: *mDo sngags kyi gzhung la slob gnyer byed tsul gyi bslab bya nor bu'i gling du bgrod pa'i lam yig sogs bslab bya sna tsogs kyi skor*), p. 112. In Bibliography, see listing under (*rJe Gung thang pa*) *dKon mchog bstan pa'i sgron me.*

[60]T: *sDe srid Sangs rgyas rgya mtso*, 1653–1705. *Desi* (T: *sde srid*) was the title of the chief political administrator in the Tibetan government, a position established during the time of the Fifth Dalai Lama. It was abolished some eighty years later. Sang-gye Gyatso was appointed *Desi* three years before the Fifth Dalai Lama's death and continued in power for more than twenty years. The more temporary position of regent or *Gyeltsab* (T: *rgyal tsab*) was established in 1757 following the death of the Seventh Dalai Lama. The person who filled it acted in place of the previous Dalai Lama and held the position until the next Dalai Lama was discovered and was old enough to assume power.

[61]T: *rGyal po lHa bzang*. Hlasang Khan was the chief of the Qoshot Mongols and the grandson of Gushri Khan. Gushri Khan was largely responsible for establishing the Fifth Dalai Lama in power in 1642.

When no one else will share his misery,
What use are loved ones who merely hinder?[62]

Je Tsongkapa also wrote in a verse:

Enjoying samsara's fortunes never brings lasting
satisfaction;
They are the source of all suffering and unreliable.
Please bless me to realize these defects . . .[63]

These lines teach that there is no genuine happiness or success to be found anywhere in samsara. [256a] Nor will we ever be able to find a friend upon whom we can always rely.

(Kyabje Rinpoche concluded by making the following point. After reflecting on the above instructions that explain how much suffering we have experienced in samsara and how endless samsara can be, we should be overcome by a feeling of great weariness. There is no need, however, to give much thought to such issues as whether samsara in general is endless or not. Rather, each of us should resolve to find a way of terminating our own individual samsara. And, as he explained earlier, the only way we can terminate our own individual samsara and bring our suffering to an end is by gaining the ability to halt samsara's continuous cycle of rebirth.)

2) Contemplating the specific types of suffering in samsara

This topic is divided into two sections: (1) contemplating the suffering of the lower states, and (2) contemplating the suffering of the higher states.

a) Contemplating the suffering of the lower states

The first section was covered earlier during the instructions for persons of lesser capacity. Moreover, the effect of having already contemplated the suffering of the lower states is that we become like a person with a hangover who is disgusted at the thought of drinking any more beer.[64]

[62]S: *Bodhicaryāvatāraḥ*, ch. 8, v. 33. This verse is also quoted in Part Two, Day Ten, p. 132.

[63]These lines are from the prayer known as *Basis of All Virtues* (T: *Yon tan gzhir gyur ma*). See Part One, Appendix C, p. 264.

[64]This image is found in *Mañjughosha's Oral Instruction* (T: *'Jam dpal zhal lung*), p. 73 (f. 37a). The Fifth Dalai Lama writes there: "Because the practitioner already developed a genuine realization of the nature of the three lower states earlier when he was meditating on the instructions for a person of lesser capacity, he is like a person who has become quite ill from drinking beer and is feeling nauseous. Since such a person will be disgusted by the mere sight of beer,

b) Contemplating the suffering of the higher states

This section is in three parts: (1) contemplating the suffering of humans, (2) contemplating the suffering of demigods, and (3) contemplating the suffering of gods.

i) Contemplating the suffering of humans

This topic is presented in seven parts: (1) the suffering of birth, (2) the suffering of old age, (3) the suffering of sickness, (4) the suffering of death, (5) the suffering of being separated from desirable things, (6) the suffering of having to encounter undesirable things, and (7) the suffering of seeking, but not being able to acquire, the things that we desire.

(1) Contemplating the suffering of birth

Some of you might think, "While the lower states may contain the suffering that was described earlier, wouldn't I have less suffering if I were born as a god or a human being?" Once a being is born in samsara, he will experience suffering and only suffering, even if he acquires a physical form in one of the higher states. While all of us here have been born as human beings, the only thing that can give our life meaning is for us to practice dharma. In reality, a human being's life is filled with great suffering.

Various factors, including the foul conditions in the womb, have caused us to forget everything about the way we suffered earlier, during the period of birth[65] [256b]. Even so, we will have to undergo all that suffering again whenever we succeed in obtaining a human rebirth.

A sentient being goes through five stages of development[66] from the moment it enters the womb until it emerges at birth. A distinct type of suffering is experienced during each of these periods, as well as each time a

he does not have to consider any of its specific qualities, such as its bitter and unpleasant taste. This situation can also be described by the saying: 'When a horse gallops, flowers are crushed.' Therefore, the practitioner does not commit any error if he does not specifically meditate again here on the suffering that comes from being born in the three lower states."

[65]In the present context, the term "birth" refers to the period that begins at the first moment of conception, when the intermediate-state being enters the womb, and continues until just after the newborn infant has emerged from the womb.

[66]The first four stages are associated with each of the first four weeks of gestation. During the first stage (S: *kalalam*, T: *mer mer po*), the fetus is the consistency of whey; in the second (S: *arbudam*, T: *nur nur po*), it is like curds or coagulated oil; in the third (S: *peśī*, T: *ltar ltar po*), it is shaped like a tiny iron spoon; and in the fourth (S: *ghanaḥ*, T: *mkhrang gyur*), it is like a pestle. The fifth stage (S: *praśākhā*, T: *rkang lag 'gyus pa*), which begins during the fifth week, marks the point at which the body begins to form limbs and develop into a human form.

new part of the body is formed. At the very beginning, when the mind consciousness first enters the material made up of the mother's egg and the father's sperm, the body is nothing more than a tiny mass having the consistency of yogurt. When the mind enters there, we experience an intense suffering that feels as if we are being boiled in a great cauldron in one of the hells.

Later, when the fetus begins to form the five bulges that will eventually become the head and the arms and legs, we experience pain that is like being tortured on a rack by having our limbs pulled apart. As each of these protrusions continue to develop, we feel greater suffering.

The mother's activities also cause us to experience many different kinds of suffering. For instance, when she drinks something hot, it feels like we are being boiled in a hot spring. When she moves around, it feels like we are being tossed around by the wind. When she lies down, it feels like a huge mountain is pressing down on us.

A verse from the *Letter to a Disciple* states:

> Having entered that hellish abode of the womb—
> Foul smelling, packed with great quantities of filth,
> Exceedingly narrow, and cloaked in thick darkness—
> One endures great suffering, with limbs all curled up.[67]

Suppose someone put us inside an iron pot filled with all kinds of filth and then, after sealing the lid securely, left us there for a day. This would surely be unbearable; yet we must remain inside a mother's womb—narrow, dark, and packed with foul-smelling impurities—[257a] for a period of nine months and ten days.

At the end of that time, five different ideas[68] arise in the mind—including the desire to leave the womb, which is brought on by the impression that it is such a disgusting place. But as we emerge from the womb, it feels like the body is being forced through an extruding die[69] and, so again, we experience intense suffering. As the *Letter to a Disciple* says:

> Then, in due course, one is somehow born—
> As if being squeezed in a powerful sesame press.[70]

[67]S: *Śiṣyalekhaḥ*, v. 19. In Bibliography, see listing under *Candragomī*.

[68]The five ideas are: (1) the womb is a filthy place, (2) it smells bad, (3) it is like a prison, (4) it is dark, and (5) you feel the desire to escape from it.

[69]T: *'jur mig*. A metal block containing small conical holes through which metal, or other ductile material, is extruded or drawn.

[70]Ibid., v. 20.

After we are born, we experience many sensations that completely terrify us. Our skin is so sensitive that it is compared to that of a cow that has been flayed alive. No matter how soft the bed on which we are laid, it feels as if we have been thrown into a pit filled with thorns. When the air blows against our body, it feels as if we are being slashed with a sword. When our mother picks us up and carries us, it can seem as terrifying as when a hawk swoops down and snatches a baby bird. Because any knowledge we may have gained in past lives becomes obscured, we come into the world without the slightest wisdom or other virtuous qualities. We must relearn even such simple acts as eating, lying down, walking, and sitting.

Don't meditate on the suffering of birth as if you were watching someone else undergo these experiences. You should imagine, as vividly as possible, that you are experiencing these various kinds of suffering right now. Also generate the firm conviction that you will have to undergo them when you take birth in the future. To contemplate this topic in even greater detail, refer to the sutra called *Teaching Nanda about Entry into the Womb*.[71]

(Kyabje Rinpoche then made several concluding remarks about this topic. For instance, he said that some people think we don't need to reflect on the suffering of birth, since it is an experience that is over and done with. However, until we put an end to the samsara that awaits us in the future, we will have to undergo even just the suffering of birth an endless number of times. This alone should be something that we find unbearably disturbing.)

(2) Contemplating the suffering of old age

A verse from the sutra called *Extensive Cosmic Sport* declares:

> Old age makes a beautiful body turn ugly [257b].
> Old age steals your radiance, strength, and power.
> Old age robs you of happiness and brings contempt.
> Old age steals your vitality; old age brings death.[72]

Old age brings many forms of suffering, including loss of physical beauty, loss of physical strength, loss of the senses, loss of the ability to enjoy pleasurable objects, and loss of the life force.[73] Old age causes our

[71]T: (*'Phags pa*) *dGa' bo mngal na 'gnas pa bstan pa zhes bya ba theg pa chen po'i mdo*. This scripture is found in the *dKon brtzegs* section of the Kangyur. See listing in Bibliography.

[72]S: *Lalitavistaraḥ*, ch. 13, v. 85.

[73]These five aspects of old age are mentioned in the *Great Stages of the Path* (T: *Lam rim chen mo*), p. 312 (f. 140b). Their source is Asanga's *Compendium of Elucidations* (T: *rNam par gtan la dbab pa bsdu ba*), ff.163b–164a. In Bibliography, see listing under *Asaṅga*.

sense faculties and our intellect to degenerate gradually. Our body becomes bent like a bow. We lose our vitality. It becomes difficult for us to stand up and sit down. Our bodies become ugly—for instance, our hair turns white, our skin becomes wrinkled, and so on. It is as if we have taken birth in a different life altogether.

As Je Mila sang:

> One, you stand up as if you're pulling a stake from the ground.
> Two, your gait looks like someone that's stalking a bird.
> Three, you sit down like a load falling from a pack animal's back.
> When this group of three has made its appearance in you,
> O Granny, saddened by the loss of your illusory body . . .[74]

A few lines later, the song continues:

> One, your outer skin is shriveled and covered in wrinkles.
> Two, your inner bones protrude from wasted flesh and blood.
> Three, in between you are dull witted, speechless, deaf, blind, and confused.
> When this group of three has made its appearance in you,
> O Granny, your angry, wrinkled face is an image of ugliness . . .

All these points illustrate the disadvantages of being in samsara.

The Kadampa Geshe Kamapa[75] said:

> It's a good thing that old age comes on little by little. We could not bear having it come all at once.[76]

It would be unbearable if we went to bed tonight as a radiant and healthy young man or woman, only to wake up the next morning with dim senses, an aged, worn-out body, and so on [258a]. Therefore, we must practice

[74] *Hundred Thousand Songs of Milarepa* (T: *Mi la ras pa'i mgur 'bum*), p. 118. (In the English edition, see vol. 1, p. 138. Note that the translation given here differs significantly from Garma C.C. Chang's rendering.) These lines appear in the chapter entitled "The Meeting with Peldar Bum, a Female Disciple from Geba Lesum in Chung."

[75] T: *Ka ma pa Shes rab 'od*, 1057–1131. See *Lives of the Lamrim Teachers*, vol. 1, pp. 445–446.

[76] Quoted in the *Great Stages of the Path* (T: *Lam rim chen mo*), p. 313 (f. 141a).

dharma right now, before the sense faculties, intellect, and body have deteriorated. In the future, we will be overwhelmed by the suffering of old age. Our bodies will be transformed and it will seem as though we have been born into a different life. How will we practice dharma when our faculties have become weak and we can't even get up or sit down?

Gungtang Tenbey Drönme[77] wrote about this in the following verses:

> Old age transforms me like the holy water
> Sprinkled on the head in an initiation.
>
> These hairs, white as a conch shell, didn't come
> Because my impurities have been washed away.
> They are arrows of spit cast by the Lord of Death
> That have fallen on me like a frost.
>
> My forehead has deep lines like a horn's growth rings;
> These aren't the fleshy folds of a plump young child.
> Time, the envoy, drew them to keep count
> Of the many years that have gone by.[78]

Several verses later he continues:

> These drops of mucus that fall from my nose
> Are not an ornamental string of pearls.
> They are the ice of a bright and splendid youth
> That has been melted by the sun's burning heat.
>
> This row of teeth that has fallen out
> Is not caused by new teeth wanting to grow in.
> It's the putting away of the tools for eating,
> Since the work of chewing this life's meals is nearly done.[79]

---

[77]T: *rJe Gung tang pa dKon mchog bstan pa'i sgron me*, 1762–1823. Gungtang, an area in southwestern Tibet near the Nepalese border, identifies the region that the Gelukpa scholar Könchok Tenbey Dröme was from.

[78]*Conversation with an Experienced Old Man* (T: *Nyams myong rgan po'i 'bel gtam*), p. 285.

[79]Ibid., p. 285.

Again, a few verses later:

My shriveled face with its bad complexion
Is not a monkey mask that I've put on.
My borrowed youth has been taken back,
Revealing this ugliness as my true color.

The constant shaking motion of my head
Is not because I'm chiding others' work.
I have been struck with the stick of mortality
And my brain is vibrating with unbearable pain.

This body bent over as I walk on the road [258b]
Is not because I'm looking for a lost needle.
It's the manner of one who has dropped the jewels
Of his youth and lost his keenness of wit.

I have to use all four limbs when I get up;
But I don't do this to mimic a cow.
It's because my arms have to lend assistance
To legs that cannot hold up my body.

It's not from being angry with my friends
That I fall with a thud when sitting down.
The cord of my exuberant mind has snapped,
Along with the rope of my youthfulness.

When I totter along with an unsteady walk,
This isn't the haughty gait of a prominent man.
The burden of my age has become so heavy
That I can no longer keep my balance.

It's not from greediness for wealth
That my hands tremble back and forth as they do.
It is my fear that the Lord of Death
Will suddenly snatch away all that I own.

It's not because of stinginess about food
That I eat and drink in such small amounts.
This aged person fears that he will succumb
Because his stomach's digestive fires are weak.

I don't wear such light, comfortable clothing
To show off how little I need to wear.
Because my body has lost its inner strength,
Even my clothes have become a burden.

When I sigh deeply and exhale long breaths,
I'm not blowing mantra-whips[80] for someone.
This labored coursing of my breath is a warning
That it wants to disappear into the sky.

I'm not just being foolish and impulsive
When I change everything I plan to do.
I've been seized by the demon of old age
And have lost all my power of self-control.

It's not an act of haughty disregard
When I forget everything I'm supposed to do.
All my body's faculties have deteriorated;
Lost are memory, intellect, and knowledge [259a].[81]

As these verses reveal, the Lord of Death has turned our hair white and given us wrinkles in order to show that we are marked for death. Old age brings many other forms of suffering as well, such as the apprehension that is caused by our fear of death.

(3) Contemplating the suffering of illness

A verse from the *Extensive Cosmic Sport* declares:

Just as the great snows and winds of late winter
Steal the vitality of grasses, shrubs, forests, and herbs,
So, too, does sickness steal the vitality of all beings,
And weaken their bodies, faculties, and strength.[82]

Many different kinds of suffering are associated with illness, including these: the body changes from its natural state of good health; physical pain and mental distress keep us in a state of great discomfort; we no longer feel

[80]T: *sngags lcag brdeg pa*. Certain yogis have the power to cure an illness or drive away an evil spirit by blowing on the afflicted person as they recite mantras.

[81]Ibid., pp. 286–287.

[82]S: *Lalitavistaraḥ*, ch. 13, v. 87.

any desire to enjoy pleasurable objects; we are compelled to endure unpleasant objects; and we experience great mental distress when we realize that we have to give up our life force.[83]

When overcome by illness, even someone in the prime of life collapses on his bed, having lost all his physical strength and vitality. This is described in the verse that contains the line, "The body loses strength, the nose and mouth become dry, and the lips curl up . . ."[84]

(Kyabje Rinpoche noted that an even more extensive way to practice this topic is to recall each and every illness there is, and then contemplate all the various kinds of suffering we would have to undergo if we contracted them. We should reflect how the pain of a terminally ill person can be so severe that he is unable to say any final words of instruction to those he is leaving behind. Rinpoche concluded by describing how young Prince Siddhartha was moved to go forth in search of liberation after he saw an old man, a sick person, and a dead body, and then meditated on the nature of their conditions.[85])

(4) Contemplating the suffering of death

A verse from the *Extensive Cosmic Sport* declares:

> Death, passing away, decease, time's final act—
> It separates us forever from everything we hold dear [259b].
> There's no coming back, no way to meet again;
> Like leaves fallen from a tree or a river's flowing current.[86]

Death brings final separation from all cherished and excellent things—our possessions, relatives, attendants, even our bodies. At the moment of death, we also experience intense suffering and great mental anguish.

83 *Compendium of Elucidations* (T: *rNam par gtan la dbab pa bsdu ba*), f. 163b. These conditions are also cited in the *Great Stages of the Path* (T: *Lam rim chen mo*), pp. 313–314 (ff. 141a–141b).

84 *Plea for Deliverance from the Treacherous Path of the Intermediate State* (T: *Bar do 'phrang grol gyi gsol 'debs*), v. 8. In Bibliography, see listing under (*Paṇ chen*) *Blo bzang chos kyi rgyal mtsan*. The verse actually describes what it is like to be in the throes of death. The full verse states: "When the earth, water, fire, and air elements successively dissolve,/ The body loses strength, the nose and mouth become dry, the lips curl up,/ The body's warmth disappears, and the breath becomes rapid and loud,/ Please bless me to develop a powerful virtuous mind."

85 See *Extensive Cosmic Sport* (S: *Lalitavistaraḥ*), ch. 13–15.

86 Ch. 13, v. 89.

As mentioned earlier during the topic of recalling death, the *Sutra of Instruction for a King* teaches us that when death comes, there is no way of avoiding it.[87]

(5) Contemplating the suffering of being separated from things that we like

This suffering comes from being separated from persons like our gurus, disciples, parents, relatives, and friends, whom we love and cherish so much that we cannot bear to be apart from them even for the length of time it takes to drink a cup of tea. It also comes from losing our positions of status and influence, as well as our wealth, possessions, and so forth.

This type of suffering can occur in many other ways as well. For instance, it can be experienced by monks or nuns if they lose their morality. Moreover, whenever we experience such misfortune, we shouldn't think that it is undeserved. It is a sign of the kind of existence that is intrinsic to all samsaric beings.

(6) Contemplating the suffering of meeting with disagreeable things

The expression "disagreeable things" refers to anything that we don't like. This type of suffering comes in endless varieties, such as meeting with an enemy and being beaten, robbed, or otherwise harmed by him; meeting with and experiencing the torment of an illness; meeting with and then being driven mad by a harmful spirit; becoming the object of a legal proceeding; being punished by a king; or being confronted by a thug.

Whenever we encounter misfortune, we are thrown into a state of turmoil that brings great physical and emotional distress. But this is an intrinsic fault of samsaric existence. For instance, all the hardships that a donkey experiences, such as having to endure sores on its back [260a], being forced to carry heavy loads, and so on, are simply an inherent element of its karma; they aren't some kind of unnatural occurrence. As Geshe Potowa said:

> Once you take birth in any of the six classes of beings, none of the suffering that you experience—whether illness, death, or the like—is a random or improper occurrence. The person who becomes ill was meant to become ill. The person who dies was meant to die. This is an essential quality of samsara. This is its very nature. As long as someone remains in samsara, he

[87] See Part Two, Day Ten, p. 119.

> is subject to this condition. If this upsets us, we must abandon having to be reborn. And the way to do that is by abandoning its cause.[88]

(Kyabje Rinpoche concluded by saying: If we don't want to experience samsara's suffering, we must practice the method that will liberate us from it.)

(7) Contemplating the suffering of seeking, but not being able to acquire, the things that we desire

This is the type of suffering that we experience when we ignore cold, heat, fear, weariness, and the like because we are hungry and thirsty, or because we are trying to pursue a means of livelihood. For instance, if you ask a lord[89] to help you in connection with some important cause, in the beginning you feel much apprehension and put forth great effort in hopes of achieving your goal. And if your efforts should end in failure, the disappointment would bring you great suffering.

Some of you may think that farmers have a good life because their land brings them wealth. But a farmer endures nothing but suffering. For example, he gets up at dawn to begin work. Then, all day long, he trudges through the dirt while being burned by the sun and battered by the wind [260b]. From the time he plants his seeds in the field until he gathers in the harvest and places it in his storage bin, he must worry about all the things that could damage his crops, such as frost, hail, fungus, drought, and so on. He also suffers the constant worry that, despite all his work, his crops will be ruined.

Those who are farmers may think that merchants are the ones who have it good. But a merchant must leave behind his parents, wife, and children—that is, his entire family—and risk his life traveling to some far-off land. Even at night he doesn't relax and sleep soundly. He must cross mountain passes, rivers, steep gorges, and the like. Despite all these efforts, some merchants not only fail to make any profit, they even end up losing the wealth they used to start their business. Or they may have to endure the suffering of having enemies, bandits, or thieves steal everything they have, including their very lives.

[88]Quoted in *Great Stages of the Path* (T: *Lam rim chen mo*), pp. 317–318 (ff. 143a–143b). The original source for the passage is probably the *Commentary to the Blue Manual* (T: *Be'u bum sngon po'i 'grel pa*), p. 201. In Bibliography, see listing under *lHa 'bri sgang pa*.

[89]T: *dpon po*. The term "lord" refers to a person of high rank who typically had large land holdings and controlled the lives of many serfs.

Those who are destitute have to endure the suffering of having nothing—no money, no wealth, no possessions. Even when a beggar finds a meal, he has to worry, "After I eat this today, what will I have tomorrow?" And so, troubled by this thought, he goes off in search of more food. Yet he may well have to experience the suffering of not being able to find any.

Even if someone is wealthy, this can become its own form of suffering. A rich man who enjoys great wealth and property can experience the suffering of not being able to protect the fortune he has accumulated. It can be taken from him in a variety of ways: beggars ask for charity; people ask for loans; and those in positions of power can confiscate his wealth. Even cats and mice become his enemies when they try to make off with his goods.

A rich person faces other types of suffering as well. One is the fear that he might lose his entire fortune. Another is the bother of constantly being approached with requests for help.

Those who support themselves through manual skills, such as carpenters and tailors, also have their unique forms of suffering. For instance, their wages or other compensation can be inadequate to provide food and clothing. They have to worry that others will not be pleased with their work. They must cope with pride, jealousy, and the like [261a]. They even suffer from having to worry that a mere stick of wood or a scrap of cloth will be stolen by a thief, or that they themselves will not be able to obtain these materials.

Even though many of us are monks and nuns who have left the householder state, we can still fail to develop a pure dharma practice through not being able to develop the virtues of having few wants and being satisfied with what we have.[90] If this happens, even performing rituals and other forms of worship in the homes of householders will bring us suffering.

When a lord looks over his serfs, he may think they are happy; but in fact they know only suffering. Their food is tasteless and their clothes are tattered. They are compelled to use up whatever money they have to pay taxes and fulfill their *oolak* service,[91] all the while having to endure verbal abuse, beatings, and other mistreatment. Some servants are forced to travel up into highlands, down into valleys, and everywhere in between, without being given time even to eat their food. Others must pay taxes and fines, as

---

[90]Vasubandhu describes the opposites of these two virtues as follows: "to be dissatisfied (S: *asaṃtuṣṭiḥ*, T: *chog mi shes pa*) means to be unhappy because the things that one does have are considered inferior in quality or insufficient in quantity. To have great desire (S: *mahecchatā*, T: *'dod chen*) means to crave things that one does not have, and to want them to be of the best quality or in great quantity" (*Commentary to the Treasury of Higher Learning*, in explanation of ch. 6, v. 6). See also Part Two, Day Seven, p. 20, and accompanying note 69.

[91]T: *'u lag*. A traditional system in which serfs performed work on behalf of a landowner in return for housing and the right to work a plot for their own benefit.

well as endure severe punishments and other hardships, even though they don't have any *tsamba*[92] to eat. In short, servants worry day and night, and must spend their entire lives burdened by overwork and misery.

Serfs think that their overlord has a good life; but that is not true either. As the *Four Hundred Verses* declares:

> For high persons, suffering is mental;
> Those who are low suffer physically.
> Every day the world is harmed
> By these two kinds of suffering.[93]

Though someone might be the great king of a country, virtually all the troubles and controversies in the land are brought before him and he must bear the burden of the entire country's suffering. Among the various difficulties he must worry about are that his enemies might defeat him, that he will not maintain good relations with his allies, that the country's laws will not be obeyed, and that he will lose his power. Even we monks and nuns, [261b] who eat only one meal a day at noon, must work hard to perform our many tasks.

In short, as the saying goes: "If your wealth is as big as a horse, your suffering will also be as big as a horse." For example, whenever you meet someone—no matter who they are—the conversation always starts out very pleasant. But after you begin to feel more relaxed, all you do is chatter on about one another's problems. As the Supreme Conqueror Kelsang Gyatso declared:

> No matter whom you look at—high person or low,
>   monk or layman, man or woman—
> They differ only in their clothing, outer appearance,
>   and manner.
> Everyone is truly the same in having to live out his
>   life in misery.
> 'Tis sad, the image of beloved friends who share
>   this common lot.[94]

[92]T *rtzam pa*. A Tibetan staple consisting of barley grain that has been roasted and then ground into a meal.

[93]T: *bZhi brgya pa*, ch. 2, v. 7. In Bibliography, see listing under *Āryadeva*.

[94]*Collected Works*, vol. 1, p. 484. This verse is from an untitled poem that the author refers to as "A Song of Images That Deeply Sadden the Mind" (T: *Sems gting nas skyo ba'i snang glu*). In Bibliography, see listing under *Blo bzang bskal bzang rgya mtso*; the work is listed under this descriptive phrase.

It is only in our clothing and outer appearance that we differ. All of us are fundamentally the same in the way we have to experience suffering. We all encounter many problems with the places we live in, with our property, and with the people we know. Even if we find an excellent place to stay, the best of friends, and more than adequate wealth, the true nature of these things is still suffering. We can change our servants, disciples, and friends a hundred or a thousand times; they will continue to cause us nothing but trouble. We will not find anyone with whom we are truly compatible. This is a sign that no matter whom we associate with, everyone is just a companion in suffering.

No matter what we try to enjoy, including a mere cup of tea, it always gives us nothing but suffering. No matter where we stay, even in a monastery, it is always a place that brings nothing but suffering [262a]. For instance, we might start out living at a monastery. If we become unhappy there, we move to an isolated hermitage hoping that might be a better place. When we don't like it there either, we go on a pilgrimage. When we don't enjoy that any longer, we decide to go back to our homeland. This kind of restlessness is part of samsara's defective nature.

Whenever we talk with someone, all we hear is a constant complaining about the troubles we have to undergo in pursuit of the three main concerns: food, clothing, and reputation. This is another of samsara's bad qualities.

(Kyabje Rinpoche concluded by noting that the above remarks are an introduction to the suffering of humans. Without the benefit of such an explanation, we run the risk of thinking that all our suffering is caused by external factors, such as the places where we live or the friends that we have. We may also think that samsara exists in some place that is far removed from where we happen to be. But such views are mistaken. We must realize that all the suffering described earlier is rooted in samsara. It is all part of samsara's defective nature. And until we escape from samsara, no matter where we go we will only find the same kind of endless suffering that we have experienced in the past.)

ii) Contemplating the suffering of demigods

Some of you might wonder, "Would I find happiness if I were reborn as a demigod?" But if you were reborn as that type of being, you would experience nothing but suffering. As the *Letter to a Friend* states:

> Demigods have great mental suffering, because
> By nature they resent the gods' prosperity.

And though intelligent, they can't perceive Truth
Due to an innate obscuration of this birth state.[95]

The realm of the demigods lies just beyond the inner seas at the base of Mt. Meru [262b].[96] They reside in four cities named Radiant, Moon Garland, Beautiful Place, and Immutable. Despite their great distance from the god realms, these cities are located directly under them, as if they were the next floor down in a building.

The demigods possess only a fraction of the gods' splendor and generally are not as powerful as the gods. In addition, because the gods steal their most beautiful women and have much greater treasures, such as the nectar of longevity, the demigods are forever tormented by the fire of jealousy. We know how painful the jealousy is that humans feel when their enemies acquire even a modest amount of wealth. Imagine, then, how unbearable it must be for a demigod to ponder the great riches of the gods.

Eventually, when the demigods' resentment becomes too great, they set out to do battle with the gods. But the demigods' weapons will kill a god only when its body is chopped in half. The gods, on the other hand, have such weapons as the divine elephant Airavana, who can catapult great boulders with a mere swing of his trunk. And their weapons will kill a demigod whenever a vital part of the body is struck. Therefore, the demigods always suffer ultimate defeat and only rarely win a battle.

We know how terrified humans become when two armies of equal strength go to war against one another. Why, then, wouldn't the demigods also experience great fear when they do battle with the gods? Surely they feel immeasurably great terror.

(Kyabje Rinpoche described how, during war, male demigods experience the suffering of having to fight continuously until they are killed. He also told us how female demigods experience great suffering as well, even while they remain at home. When they gaze into a lake called All-Seeing, they can watch all the battles in which their men are defeated and killed [263a].

Finally, although demigods are intelligent, their birth state is affected by a karmic obscuration that prevents them from being able to perceive Truth[97] during their lifetimes.)

[95]T: *bShes pa'i spring yig*, v. 102.

[96]The canonical source for the instruction on the demigods (S: *asuraḥ*, T: *hla ma yin*) is the *Sutra on Well-Composed Recollection* (T: [*'Phags pa*] *Dam pa'i chos dran pa nye bar bzhag pa*), in the *Mdo mang* section of Kg. vol. 23 (*'a*), ff. 11a–81a.

[97]"To perceive Truth" means to attain a direct realization of ultimate reality. A practitioner who does so becomes an *arya* and achieves the first of the four fruits that eventually bring one to the state of *arhat*. See also Part One, Day Four, p. 123, note 10.

iii) Contemplating the suffering of gods

Some of you might think, "Well, maybe the gods are happy." But gods of the desire realm experience various types of suffering, including events relating to their death; becoming discouraged by the greater splendor of other gods; and having to undergo being cut, slashed, killed, and banished.

The first of these sufferings refers to the signs that a god experiences just before he dies. Some of these signs are described in the *Letter to a Friend*:

> The body's complexion becomes unattractive;
> There is dislike for one's seat; flower garlands wilt;
> The apparel becomes sullied; and the body
> Begins to perspire, which it never did before.
>
> These five omens foretelling death in the heavens
> Appear to the gods of the celestial realms.
> They are like the ill-fated signs that announce death
> To earth-bound humans when they are about to die.[98]

In all, there are ten signs that a god can experience when his death is imminent. Five are the main signs: his body loses its brilliance; he feels uncomfortable sitting on his throne; his flower garlands wilt; his clothing becomes soiled; and his body begins to perspire. The other five are secondary signs: his body becomes less radiant; after bathing, water droplets cling to his body; his clothing and ornaments emit unpleasant sounds; he closes his eyes; and his mind remains fixed on a single object.[99]

When a god experiences these signs that death is near, he goes off to some secluded spot and suffers for a period of seven days, writhing like a fish in the sand and wailing loudly. It should also be understood that the length of a day varies in the different heavens of the desire realm. For instance, seven days among the Maharajika gods is equivalent to three hundred and fifty human years [263b].[100]

[98]T: *bShes pa'i spring yig*, vv. 99–100.

[99]Kyabje Rinpoche's list of main signs corresponds to the one that appears in Nagarjuna's verses. Other sources, such as Vasubandhu's *Commentary to the Treasury of Higher Learning* (S: *Abhidharmakośabhāṣyam*, Skt. edition, p. 405), differ in only one of the main signs. In place of "the body's complexion becomes unattractive," Vasubandhu's list states: "his body gives off an unpleasant odor."

[100]In each of the next five heavens, a day lasts twice as long as in the one before. Thus, in the Heaven of the Thirty-three (S: *Trāyastriṃśaḥ*, T: *Sum cu rtza gsum*), a day lasts a hundred human years; therefore, this seven-day period would go on for seven hundred human years. In Yama (T: *'Thab bral*), a day lasts two hundred years; so this period of suffering would be for

The gods are also known as "three-timers."[101] This name refers to the fact that they have knowledge of three events: (1) the former deed that caused them to be born as a god, (2) the nature of their present situation, and (3) where they will go after they die. Thus, when the gods are about to die, they know the kind of circumstances they will experience in their next life.

During the course of their lives, however, these gods fail to generate even a single virtuous act motivated by such attitudes as renunciation or compassion. Renunciation is a mental state that must be cultivated before trying to develop compassion. We develop renunciation by reflecting on the suffering that we ourselves experience in samsara. Then we use that awareness of our suffering to develop compassion by contemplating how others also experience the same kind of suffering.

Instead of doing virtuous acts, the gods spend their current lives enjoying the fruits of merit they accumulated in the past. Here's an example that shows why the amount of merit that the gods squander is so great. If we wear a shawl that cost us ten *sang* instead of one that cost just one *sang*, we are using up the fruit of merit that is ten times as great. And since the kind of pleasure experienced in the divine realms is so exquisite, the amount of merit that the gods consume during their lives is also extremely great. This is why we should heed the saying: "This life is a time for accumulating merit, not for using up the fruit of our merit."

Because most of the gods are reborn into the lower states in their next life, that realization causes them to experience extraordinarily great suffering. When they become aware that rebirth in the lower states means losing all the happiness associated with their celestial abodes, their divine bodies, their wealth, their friends, and the like, they experience a mental anguish that is said to be sixteen times greater than the suffering of the hells.

We humans undergo suffering and mental torment when we die in a state of uncertainty about the kind of future life that awaits us. But the gods are fully aware that they will be reborn in the lower states. So they cry out in anguish, "Alas, Garden of Manifold Chariots!"[102] and so forth. A god who

one thousand four hundred human years. In Tushita (T: *dGa' ldan*), a day lasts four hundred years; so the suffering would go on for two thousand and eight hundred years, and so on. See also Part Two, Day Eleven, p. 152 for a comparison of the life spans in the hot hells and the heavens of the desire realm.

[101] S: *tridaśaḥ* or *tridivaḥ*, T: *skabs gsum pa*. The general meaning of the original Sanskrit terms is something more like "god of the [heaven of] three times ten" or "god of the triple heaven." Apparently there is another interpretation from which the Tibetan equivalent is derived. Our English translation is based on the Tibetan, in order to better fit the explanation that Kyabje Rinpoche gives.

[102] S: *Caitrarathavanam*, T: *Shing rta sna tsogs tsal*. This is one of four celestial gardens in the Heaven of the Thirty-three. The gods cry out the name of this and other marvelous sites because they have to leave them behind. The Garden of Manifold Chariots is described in a

experiences the signs of his approaching death [264a] is completely ostracized by the other gods and goddesses. By refusing even to look at him and avoiding him as if he were already a corpse, they force him to remain by himself.

The one who is soon to depart calls out in a pitiful voice to those gods who were formerly his friends: "Come and sit with me for a while. I long to see you now, for I am about to set out on a long journey to the next world, where I shall be reborn into the most desperate of circumstances."

Most of these former friends will not even look at him. The more steadfast ones, however, while keeping their distance will use the tip of a long pole or some other object to place flowers on his head. Then they utter this prayer: "After leaving here, may you be reborn in the world of humans. May you accumulate merit there and then be reborn once again as a god." But this only adds to the departing god's grief and causes tremendous suffering.

In addition to these experiences, lesser gods become discouraged and suffer great mental torment when they see the great splendor and wealth of other gods who possess more merit. When gods do battle with demigods, they experience such suffering as having their limbs cut or slashed, and sometimes are even killed. There are other types of suffering as well, for instance when more powerful gods expel weaker ones from their domains.

Beings who are reborn as a god in either of the two higher realms[103] will not experience the suffering of the omens that foreshadow their death. Nevertheless, they do experience the suffering of conditional existence.[104] They are also subject to the mental afflictions and other obscurations. And since they have no ultimate control over either their continued existence or their death, [264b] they must undergo the suffering of these imperfect conditions. As the *Declaration on the Accumulations* states:

> Beings in the form and formless realms
> Transcend the suffering of suffering.
> Rapt in the bliss of concentration,
> They remain unchanged for kalpas.

section from one of the seven original treatises on Higher Learning called *Instruction on the Nature of the World* (T: *'Jig rten gzhag pa*), ff. 32b–34b.

[103] The Buddhist universe is comprised of three domains: the desire realm, the form realm, and the formless realm. The gods of the higher realms are those who reside in either the form realm or the formless realm. All the previous descriptions of the gods are of those who inhabit the six divine levels of the desire realm. The desire realm also includes the three lower states, as well as the regions inhabited by humans and demigods.

[104] See p. 39 for a discussion of this type of suffering.

But even that is not true freedom;
One day they will fall from there.[105]

When beings are first reborn in the formless realm, they simply reflect, "Now I have been reborn." Then they enter a state of one-pointed concentration that lasts for many kalpas. Finally, they die and fall to a lower existence. This represents a kind of suffering in which beings lack the power to continue living in a blissful state.

During their time in that divine state, gods use up whatever merit they accumulated in past lives and also fail to accumulate any new merit. Therefore, after they die, they are reborn in a lower state of existence. And since they failed to use their discriminating wisdom during their previous life,[106] they also return as beings that are extraordinarily dull-witted.

Sometimes these beings mistake their state of mental absorption for true liberation. So at the time they enter these meditative states, they believe they have achieved ultimate liberation. Later, when they realize that they are going to take birth again, they reject the idea that liberation even exists. This negative thought[107] then causes them to be reborn in the hell of Unrelenting Torment. Thus, being born in the higher realms turns out to be nothing more than a temporary period of self-deception. Such an existence is like dangling over the open mouth of a cauldron in one of the hells. An old beggar who lives in the human realm and spends his time reciting the *Mani* mantra[108] has a better life.

The Supreme Conqueror Kelsang Gyatso declared:

The three realms that we call samsara are a house
of blazing iron.
Wherever we go in the ten directions [265a], we will be
burned by suffering.

[105]T: *Tsogs kyi gtam*, vv. 27–28. In Bibliography, see listing under *Vasubandhu*.

[106]Because their minds are completely absorbed in one-pointed concentration.

[107]Denying the existence of liberation is one form of wrong view (S: *mithyādṛṣṭiḥ*, T: *log lta*); see also Part Two, Day Thirteen, pp. 252–253. Because the gods generate this thought at the critical moment of their death, it causes them to be reborn in hell.

[108]The six-syllable mantra of Avalokiteshvara, the deity who is the embodiment of all the Buddhas' compassion: *Om mani padme hung*.

Though it torments the mind, this is truly the world
we experience.
'Tis sad, the image of having to wander in such
an awful place.[109]

No matter where we are born in samsara—from the highest point at the Peak of Existence to the lowest hell of Unrelenting Torment—we find nothing but suffering. It is as though we live in a six-story house built of blazing hot iron.

Long ago during a famine, a child asked for some *tsamba*. He was repeatedly offered turnips prepared in a variety of ways, but he refused to take any of them. Instead, he complained, "Those are still turnips!"[110] Thus, no matter where we are born, the nature of our lives is suffering; the only thing that changes is the kind of suffering that we experience. We are like members of a club in which everyone has a share of the same unfortunate condition.

(In short, Kyabje Rinpoche noted, we are all continually tormented by the three types of suffering. Then he concluded this discussion on suffering with the following explanation of the three types of suffering.)

Those samsaric experiences that we currently think of as pleasurable are actually a form of suffering. This is also true of the experiences that we think of as neutral.

All the pleasurable sensations that samsaric beings experience are like the temporary relief that is felt when a painful boil is bathed in cool water. They are known as the suffering of change,[111] because when they come to an end they give rise to suffering once again. The different kinds of consciousness and secondary mental states that accompany afflicted[112] pleasurable sensations, as well as the objects associated with the afflictions that produce pleasurable sensations when the mind focuses on them, are also part of the suffering of change [265b].

Although a boil is not extremely painful when it first forms, it is still uncomfortable. A boil in this condition—that is, when it is neither soothed by cool water nor aggravated by hot water—is a metaphor for all afflicted neutral sensations. These sensations, as well as the consciousness and

[109]"A Song of Images That Deeply Sadden the Mind" (T: *Sems gting nas skyo ba'i snang glu*), *Collected Works*, vol. 1, p. 487. In Bibliography, see listing under *Blo bzang bsKal bzang rgya mtso*.

[110]This story appears in Je Tsongkapa's *Great Stages of the Path* (T: *Lam rim chen mo*), pp. 373–374 (ff. 171a–171b).

[111]S: *pariṇāmaduḥkhatā*, T: *'gyur ba'i sdug bsngal*.

[112]The term "afflicted," as it is being used here, is a loose translation of the technical term "related to the outflows" (S: *sāsrava*, T: *zag bcas*). See note 5 above.

secondary mental states that accompany them, along with the objects perceived by these mental states, represent the suffering of conditional existence.[113] These afflicted entities make up the suffering of conditional existence because they have the all-pervasive defect of being governed by past karma and mental afflictions and they contain the seeds of future suffering and mental afflictions.

A painful boil that is splashed with hot water will cause particularly intense pain. This is a metaphor for afflicted sensations that are painful. All such sensations—those that harm both the mind and body—together with all the accompanying forms of consciousness and secondary mental states, as well as the objects perceived by them, represent the suffering of suffering.

Therefore, all the experiences that we normally think of as unpleasant make up the suffering of suffering, while those that we mistakenly believe are truly pleasant make up the suffering of change. A sign that the latter experiences are not truly pleasurable is the fact that if they go on for too long, they eventually bring on suffering again. The reason we wrongly believe the suffering of change to be pleasurable is that it occurs at a time when one painful experience is gradually disappearing and another one is gradually beginning.

For instance, if we stay in the shade too long, we begin to feel cold [266a]. When we move into the sunlight, at first we experience a sensation that seems pleasurable. But it isn't truly pleasurable. If it were, the pleasure we feel by sitting in the sun should get stronger as time goes on, just as a painful experience increases the longer it lasts. However, this is not what happens. After we have been in the sun for a while, this experience also becomes unpleasant, and so we decide to go back into the shade again. The reason we don't notice any suffering when we first go into the sun is because, in the beginning, it is small and only grows a little at a time.

Another example is what happens if we walk a long distance. After we have walked a while, we get tired and sit down to rest. When we do, the rest seems pleasurable at first, because the more intense discomfort of standing up is gradually disappearing while the discomfort of sitting down is only beginning. It isn't that there is no suffering present when we first sit down to rest; it's just that the suffering inherent in the act of sitting down has not yet become apparent.

After we have sat for some time, the suffering of that experience does become evident. So we get up and say, "It's time to start walking again." This time, the suffering that developed from sitting for so long is the greater pain that disappears slowly, while the suffering of standing up becomes the

[113] S: *saṃskāraduḥkhatā*, T: *khyab pa 'du byed kyi sdug bsngal.*

lesser pain that is not evident right away. As the treatise *Four Hundred Verses* declares:

> A growing pain does not
> Become reversed in the way
> That a growing pleasure
> Is seen to become reversed.[114]

The afflicted grasping heaps make up the suffering of conditional existence because their very existence is the source of all suffering. In short, the reason we have to endure all the suffering of samsara is because we have taken on these afflicted grasping heaps. Thus, the burning fire and freezing cold of the hells are experienced when we take on the afflicted grasping heaps of a hell being [266b]. The hunger and thirst of a hungry ghost are experienced when we take on these same grasping heaps in the form of a hungry ghost. Similarly, if we take on the body of an animal like a donkey, we automatically become a vessel for experiencing such forms of suffering as having to carry heavy loads and endure being whipped with a stick.

Thus, every kind of suffering we experience—from the prick of a thorn to the most unbearable of pains—derives from the fact that we have taken on these grasping heaps. For instance, if a naked man takes a load of thorns onto his bare back, his suffering will not let up until this burden is removed. Likewise, until we free ourselves of the burden of the afflicted grasping heaps, there will never be a moment when we are not being tormented by one form of suffering or another.

(Kyabje Rinpoche then told the story of how the householder Shrija entered the order of Buddhist monks, and how Maugalyayana, acting as Shrija's preceptor,[115] caused him to develop renunciation by taking him to the seashore and showing him bones and the corpse of his previous life.)

The compound *grasping heaps* can be interpreted in three different ways. The first point to understand is that the term *grasping* is a synonym for the mental afflictions. Thus, according to the first interpretation, the expression *grasping heaps* is a compound in which the result is referred to by its cause. This means that the grasping heaps are the heaps that arise from the former mental afflictions. This is like the compound *bramble fire*, which describes the source—brambles—of a particular fire.

[114]T: *bZhi brgya pa'i tsig le'ur byas pa*, ch. 2, v. 12. In Bibliography, see listing under *Āryadeva*.

[115]S: *upadhyāyaḥ*, T: *mkhan po*. The main functionary in the ritual for conferring Buddhist vows. See also Part Two, Day Eight, pp. 26–27. This story appears in the *Sutra of the Wise and the Foolish* (*mDzangs blun zhes bya ba'i mdo*), ch. 15.

The second interpretation explains the compound as a case in which an object is referred to by the entity to which it is related. Thus, the grasping heaps are the heaps that are subject to the mental afflictions. This is like the expression *king's man*, which describes a person who is subject to the king [267a].

The third interpretation explains the compound as a case in which the cause is referred to by its result. Thus, the grasping heaps are the heaps that give rise to the mental afflictions. This is like the compounds *medicine tree* and *flower tree*, which describe trees that produce medicinal fruit and flowers, respectively.

Once again, these heaps represent the suffering of conditional existence because they are always associated with the defects of suffering and the mental afflictions. Even though there may be occasions when we are not experiencing any overt pain, as long as we possess these heaps, they will very soon create many different kinds of suffering for us to endure. Therefore, the suffering of conditional existence pervades every moment of our experience and is the root of the other two forms of suffering. Because these heaps are the vessel for experiencing suffering in this life and the basis that produces suffering in future lives, they are the worst kind of suffering.

(Kyabje Rinpoche summed up the discussion by making the following point. The term *samsara* should be understood to mean the continuous cycle in which karma and the mental afflictions force us to take on the burden of the afflicted grasping heaps as we are reborn again and again, from the highest point at the Peak of Existence down to the hell of Unrelenting Torment. Since samsara is defined as an element of these very afflicted grasping heaps, the way to generate aversion for samsara is by cultivating aversion for the afflicted grasping heaps. Moreover, we will never be able to develop genuine disgust for samsara until we generate disgust for the suffering of conditional existence.

Kyabje Rinpoche ended the discourse by explaining all the instructions a second time, going over them in moderate detail.)

DAY FIFTEEN: CONTEMPLATING THE ORIGIN OF SUFFERING AND ESTABLISHING THE NATURE OF THE PATH THAT LEADS TO LIBERATION

(Kyabje Rinpoche began by quoting the following verse composed by the great teacher [267b] Aryadeva:

> This ocean of suffering
> Has no limit whatsoever.
> O fool, you who are mired here,
> Why are you not terrified?[1]

Then, after briefly describing the preliminary exercise of correcting one's motivation, he went over the list of topics that he had already covered on previous days. He also explained again the instructions for generating the wish to become liberated from samsara. Next, he gave the following brief description of how to meditate on them.)

The preliminary activities and other general points are the same as I explained before.[2] After that, visualize your divine guru seated on the crown of your head, and reflect on the suffering of samsara. During the time between meditation periods, you should read scriptures that describe samsara's defects, such as the *Sutra on Well-Composed Recollection*.[3]

There is a standard for determining whether or not you've developed true renunciation. You must feel disgust toward any form of samsaric happiness, power, or wealth you may encounter. You should think: "These are false and misleading, and actually a form of suffering." When you become upset at the suffering caused by a few samsaric problems, such as being criticized or blamed for something, this can bring a temporary state of mind known as "goose-bump renunciation";[4] however, this is a mere imitation of the true attitude.

[1]*Four Hundred Verses* (T: *Bzhi brgya pa*), ch. 7, v. 1. In Bibliography, see listing under *Āryadeva*.

[2]This is a reference to the six preliminary practices (T: *sbyor ba'i chos drug*), which are done prior to meditating on any of the main topics of the Lamrim teaching. See Part One, Days Four through Six.

[3]T: (*'Phags pa*) *Dam pa'i chos dran pa nye bar bzhag pa*.

[4]T: *nges 'byung spu sud*. A colloquial expression that refers to a naive kind of renunciation in which a person initially thinks and acts as if he is genuinely moved by the understanding that all samsara is suffering. Like goose bumps, however, this feeling can quickly fade as one is confronted by the challenges of everyday life.

By the very fact of being born in samsara, the actual nature of all our experiences is never anything but suffering. So if we want to escape having to experience suffering in the future, we must stop the continuous succession of rebirths. Renunciation, then, means the desire to gain release from samsara because of the aversion that is felt for its suffering nature. It is also described as the aspiration to achieve liberation. As Je Tsongkapa declared:

> If, after meditating this way, you never feel
> Even a moment's wish for samsara's prosperity [268a]
> And you seek liberation constantly both day and night,
> This marks the attainment of renunciation.[5]

Je Rinpoche is also reported to have said that whenever anyone prepared a fine seat for him or showed him respect or courtesy, he would experience an uncontrollably strong sense of renunciation and think to himself that all such things are impermanent and forms of suffering. He also noted that he had felt this attitude for a long time.[6]

Thus, no matter how much samsaric prosperity we might see, it must only serve to make our aversion that much stronger. When we are about to die, there is a tendency to become unhappy as we recognize that we are going to be separated from our friends, our wealth, and other pleasures of this life. This is referred to as "shallow impermanence"[7] and it comes from our attachment to the temporary pleasures of this life.

It is extremely important that we pursue the methods for developing genuine renunciation. Our ultimate goal is to achieve Buddhahood. To achieve Buddhahood, we must develop enlightenment mind; and to develop enlightenment mind, we must gain compassion. Likewise, to gain compassion, we must cultivate the awareness that all sentient beings are our mothers. All these spiritual awarenesses must be pursued in order, one after the other. Renunciation is developed by meditating on the samsaric suffering that we ourselves experience. Compassion is developed by meditating on how this same suffering is experienced by others. Thus, even for the

[5] *Three Principal Elements of the Path* (T: *Lam gyi gtzo bo rnam gsum*), v. 5.

[6] These remarks closely paraphrase a statement recorded by Khedrup Je in his biography of Je Tsongkapa entitled *The Entry Point for the Faithful: An Account of the Marvelous and Wonderful Spiritual Life of the Great Reverend Guru Tsongkapa* (T: *rJe btsun bla ma tzong kha pa chen po'i ngo mtsar rmad du byung ba'i rnam par thar pa dad pa'i 'jug ngogs*), p. 37 (near end of section 3). Though Khedrup Je records the words as though Je Tsongkapa uttered them himself, we do not present them here as a direct quote since they are not reproduced verbatim. In Bibliography, see entry under *mKhas grub rje* (*dGe legs dpal bzang*).

[7] T: *sna thung gi mi rtag pa*.

spiritual practices of a person of great capacity,[8] it is essential that we meditate on the instructions for developing renunciation.

Particularly in the present context of the instructions for a practitioner of moderate capacity,[9] it should be recognized that renunciation is one of the principal elements of the path.[10] After developing this attitude, any virtuous act we do serves as a cause for achieving liberation. However, until we generate at least a contrived form of this principal element of the path [268b], our virtuous acts will almost always do nothing more than perpetuate the wheel of samsara. The only exception is those acts that rely on the power of an extraordinary "field."[11]

It is a serious mistake not to try hard to practice the three principal elements of the path. If we ignore them, no matter how much we try to practice such profound teachings as meditating on the psychic channels and winds or a tutelary deity, or reciting mantras, our efforts will not even move us in the direction of the paths that lead to liberation and the omniscience of a supreme Buddha. Therefore, for the time being, we should stop the useless exertions of trying to practice those teachings that everyone considers to be so profound. It is crucial that we first strive as hard as we can to practice the three topics of renunciation, enlightenment mind, and correct view.

ii. Establishing the nature of the path that leads to liberation

This section has two parts: (1) contemplating the origin of suffering and how the process of samsara is set in motion, and (2) the actual explanation of the path that leads to liberation.

[8]T: *skyes bu chen po.* The Lamrim teachings are a body of instructions associated with three types of practitioner: those of small, moderate, and great capacity. A practitioner of great capacity is one who generates enlightenment mind and pursues the supreme goal of Buddhahood in order to benefit all sentient beings. See also Part One, Day One, note 14. The main instructions for practitioners of great capacity are taught in Days Sixteen through Twenty-four.

[9]T: *skyes bu 'bring.* Motivated by renunciation, a practitioner of moderate capacity pursues the goal of liberating himself from samsara.

[10]T: *lam gyi gtzo bo.* Je Tsongkapa defined the essence of the Lamrim teachings in terms of three principal elements: renunciation, enlightenment mind, and the correct view. See Part One, Day One, note 46.

[11]For a discussion of different types of field, see Part One, Day Five, note 101. The reference here is to a field of virtue (S: *guṇakṣetraḥ*, T: *yon tan gyi zhing*). Part Two, Day Twelve, p. 215 presents a scriptural passage describing how a virtue performed relative to a Buddha acts as a cause for attaining perfect enlightenment regardless of its motivation.

1) Contemplating the origin of suffering and how the process of samsara is set in motion

This part also has three sections: (1) how the mental afflictions arise, (2) how the mental afflictions cause us to accumulate karma, and (3) how we die and are reborn.

a) How the mental afflictions arise

This section is made up of four topics: (1) identifying the mental afflictions, (2) the order in which the mental afflictions arise, (3) the causes of the mental afflictions, and (4) the disadvantages of the mental afflictions.

i) Identifying the mental afflictions

There are two traditions about where the topic entitled "Contemplating the origin of suffering and how the process of samsara is set in motion" should be included in the outline of the teachings. One tradition places it in the previous section.[12] In this teaching, I shall follow the traditions associated with the *Easy Path* and the *Quick Path*, which include it in the topic called "Establishing the nature of the path that leads to liberation."

Through contemplating the previous instructions on samsara's general and specific defects, we can develop an aversion for samsara [269a]. This attitude should then develop into the desire to achieve liberation, at which point we must investigate what the causes of samsara are. After learning samsara's cause, we must try to bring it to an end.

There are two aspects to the truth of the origin of suffering: karma and the mental afflictions. Karma is what compels us to endure the burden of the grasping heaps. Karma itself, however, is generated by the mental afflictions. All the immeasurable amount of karma that we have accumulated in the past would remain like unwatered seeds unless the mental afflictions of craving and grasping[13] acted upon them in the form of cooperating factors. Thus, karma alone does not have the power to bring about rebirth. Even if we had no past karma, the mental afflictions would immediately cause us to accumulate new karma and, therefore, in due course, to take on the samsaric heaps of a future life. As the *Extensive Treatise on Knowledge* declares:

[12]That is, within the topic entitled "Developing the aspiration to achieve liberation."

[13]Craving (S: *tṛṣṇā*, T: *sred pa*) and grasping (S: *upādānam*, T: *len pa*) form the eighth and ninth limbs of the twelve-part teaching on dependent origination. They activate the past karma that determines the rebirth one will have in the next life. See below, p. 77.

> Those who overcome craving for existence
> Cannot create any further karma, because
> They have terminated the cooperating factor.[14]

The same work also states in a later verse:

> . . . because they[15] will arise again
> With the continued existence of craving.[16]

Therefore, the mental afflictions alone are the root cause that produces rebirth in samsara.

The term "mental affliction"[17] refers to those entities whose very occurrence immediately causes a person's mind to become agitated and undisciplined. It is important that we learn to identify the mental afflictions. If we fail to do so, we will not know how to apply an antidote to them because we won't be able to recognize the object to which that antidote should be applied. This is like trying to kill an enemy with an arrow when we don't even know what he looks like.

The topic of identifying the mental afflictions can be divided into two parts: [269b] (1) identifying the root mental afflictions, and (2) identifying the secondary mental afflictions.

Identifying the root mental afflictions

As the *Treasury of Higher Learning* states, there are six root mental afflictions:

[14] S: *Pramāṇavārttikam*, ch. 2, vv. 195–196.

[15] "They" refers here to karma and the body. This section of the root text addresses a prevalent view that rebirth has three principal causes: craving, karma, and the body. In fact, v. 274 refers to rebirth as "that which has three causes." Dharmakirti argues that craving alone is the necessary and sufficient cause for rebirth. He points out that there can be no rebirth in the absence of the single factor of craving ("Even with the continued existence of karma and the body,/ 'That which has three causes' cannot arise/ Because of the absence of a single factor—/ Just as a sprout cannot arise without a seed." vv. 274–275). Likewise, he declares in the lines quoted here that the continued existence of craving is sufficient to bring about the accumulation of new karma, and that this will necessitate taking on a new body in the next life.

[16] Op. cit., ch. 2, v. 276.

[17] S: *kleśaḥ*, T: *nyon mongs*.

The six attachments[18] are the root of existence.
They are desire, anger, pride, and ignorance,
Along with the views and doubt.[19]

Desire

The first of the six root mental afflictions, desire, arises when we perceive as attractive such objects as wealth, another person's body, food, drink, and so on. It is a state of mind that focuses on such an object and then does not want to be separated from it.

Because the mental afflictions other than desire are somewhat easier to overcome, they are like dirt stains on a piece of cloth. Desire, however, is like a grease stain. When grease comes in contact with cloth, it is especially difficult to remove because it penetrates into the fabric and then spreads out over a wider area. Similarly, when desire gives rise to attachment and craving toward a particular object, it creates in us the longing to see, touch, or otherwise have closer contact with that object. The mind seems almost to become embedded in the object as our craving for it grows continually stronger, making desire especially difficult to overcome.

A line from a prayer declares that we are "bound in samsara's prison by the shackles of craving for pleasure."[20] This identifies desire as the root

[18]The term being translated here as "attachment" (S: *anuśayaḥ*, T: *phra rgyas*) is a technical term that is synonymous with the more familiar "mental affliction" (S: *kleśaḥ*, T: *nyon mongs*). The verbal root from which it derives means "to adhere closely" to something. The Tibetan translation, literally "that which grows in a subtle manner," seems to have been formulated on the basis of several classical interpretations of the term (see verse cited below). Thus, the English translation—"attachment"—should be understood in the literal sense and not as a synonym for affection or desire. Vasubandhu describes the term in his *Treasury of Higher Learning* (S: *Abhidharmakośakārikā*, ch 5, v. 39): "They are called 'attachments'/ Because they are minute and follow closely after,/ Because they grow stronger in two ways,/ And because they attach themselves." *Aṇavo nugatāś caite dvidhā cāpyanuśerate/ Anubadhnanti yasmācca tasmād anuśayāḥ smṛtaḥ. Anuśerate* ("grow stronger") is glossed in Yashomitra's subcommentary as meaning "to obtain growth" (S: *puṣṭim labhante*) or to "obtain a stable resting place" (S: *pratiṣṭhām labhante*).

[19]S: *Abhidharmakośakārikā*, ch. 5, v. 1.

[20]Composed by Je Tsongkapa, the work is known popularly as the *Prayer to be Reborn in Sukhavati* (T: *bDe smon*). Although this prayer is often included as a separate work in modern prayer collections, it actually forms part of a larger work that describes Buddha Amitabha's paradise in detail and explains the causes, method, and benefits of praying to be reborn in Sukhavati. This practice, which forms the essence of the tradition known as Pure Land Buddhism, is based largely on the *Sutra That Describes Sukhavati Paradise* (S: *Sukhāvatīvyūhaḥ*). In Bibliography under listings for Je Tsongkapa's works, see *bDe ba can gyi zhing du skye ba 'dzin pa'i smon lam zhing mchog sgo 'byed* (*Opening the Door to the Supreme Buddha Field: A Prayer To Be Reborn in Sukhavati Paradise*).

factor that prevents us from developing aversion for samsara. Thus, we must recognize desire as the principal force that keeps us bound in samsara.

The antidote for desire is to practice meditating on ugliness.[21] One way to meditate on ugliness involves contemplating the image of a corpse in various stages of decay—for instance, one that is covered in blood, one that is dismembered, one that is swollen, or one that has been reduced to a heap of bones.[22]

[21]S: *aśubhabhāvanā*, T: *mi sdug pa bsgom pa*. In his *Listeners' Levels* (S: *Śrāvakabhumiḥ*, pp. 202–207), Asanga describes this practice in terms of six categories, of which only the first one, "the ugliness of impurities" (S: *pratyaśubhatā*, T: *mi gtzang ba'i mi sdug pa*), is discussed here. Asanga further distinguishes between inner impurities and outer impurities. Meditation on inner impurities consists of reflecting on one's own body as comprised of thirty-six impure substances (see note 23). This practice is intended as an antidote for attachment to one's own body. Meditation on outer impurities consists of reflecting on a corpse in any of various states of decay, and is described as an antidote for sexual desire. Other sources that address meditation on ugliness include Vasubandhu's *Commentary to the Treasury of Higher Learning* (S: *Abhidharmakośabhāṣyam*), commentary to ch. 6, vv. 9–11; Shantideva's *Compendium of Training* (S: *Śiksāsamuccayaḥ*), ch. 4, pp. 44–50; and Arya Vimuktisena's *Commentary to the Ornament of Realizations* (T: *mNgon par rtogs pa'i rgyan gyi 'grel pa*), ch. 1, ff. 21b–22b.

[22]Various canonical sources mention nine forms of unattractiveness. Only four are mentioned here: (1) The image of a body covered in blood (S: *vilohitasaṃjñā*, T: *rnam par dmar ba'i 'du shes*) is an antidote for attachment to a body that has been made to look more beautiful with ornaments. (2) The image of a dismembered corpse (S: *vikṣiptakasaṃjñā*, T: *rnam par 'thor ba'i 'du shes*)—that is, one in which the arms, legs, and head are detached—is an antidote for attachment to the gracefulness of the limbs and other lesser appendages of another person's body. (3) The image of a swollen corpse (S: *vyādhmātakasaṃjñā*, T: *rnam par bam pa'i 'du shes*) is of a body's shape in a ruined condition and is an antidote for attachment to the shape of a body. (4) The image of a corpse that has been reduced to a heap of bones (S: *asthisaṃjñā*, T: *rus gong gi 'du shes*) refers both to bones that are still joined together and to single bones. One meditates on it as an antidote for attachment to a body having excellent teeth and other bones. The remaining conceptions are as follows: (5) The image of a worm-infested corpse (S: *vipaḍumaka-* or *vidhūtaka-saṃjñā*, T: *rnam par 'bus gzhig pa'i 'du shes*)—that is, of a body whose inner parts have been hollowed out by various burrowing worms—is an antidote for attachment to a body's firmness. (6) The image of a putrid corpse (S: *vipūyakasaṃjñā*, T: *rnam par rnag pa'i 'du shes*) refers to one that oozes pus from various places. The practitioner meditates on the foul odors of such a corpse as an antidote for attachment to a body that has been embellished with the fragrance of garlands, perfumes, and the like. (7) The image of a blue corpse (S: *vinīlakasaṃjñā*, T: *rnam par sngos pa'i 'du shes*) is one that focuses on the discolored skin of a decaying corpse as an antidote to attachment for a body's good complexion. (8) The image of a gnawed corpse (S: *vikhāditasaṃjñā*, T: *rnam par zos pa'i 'du shes*)—that is, one that has been chewed here and there by dogs, jackals, and the like—is meditated on as an antidote to attachment for the breasts and other fleshy parts of a body. (9) The image of a charred corpse (S: *vidagdhakasaṃjñā*, T: *rnam par tsig pa'i 'du shes*) is one in which the charred skin and shrunken shape of a burned corpse is meditated on as an antidote to attachment for the shape and complexion of a body. These descriptions are taken from Arya Vimuktisena's *Commentary to the Ornament of Realizations* (T: *mNgon par rtogs pa'i rgyan gyi 'grel pa*), ff. 21b–22b (in Skt. edition, pp. 22–23).

When the object of our desire is another person, we should contemplate that individual as a sack full of thirty-six impure substances.[23]

If we crave meat and other food, we can reduce this desire by reflecting on the unattractiveness of the causes of the food and by reflecting on how sentient beings are killed as part of the process of obtaining food [270a].[24]

Anger

Anger, the second of the root mental afflictions, is a feeling of malice directed toward sentient beings or inanimate things, a harshness of mind that wishes to harm. It is a mental state that becomes extremely hostile whenever an unwelcome object, such as an enemy, is perceived.

When we allow anger to flare up, it causes us great harm. It is like a blazing fire in the way it destroys our virtue-roots. Anger is also what causes us to commit such acts as killing and beating others.

Nowadays, some people refer to anger with such nice-sounding expressions as: "Our lama has a wrathful nature." This shows that they don't consider anger to be a fault. However, anger is very harmful. Among the mental afflictions, none has the power it does to destroy our virtue-roots. It is also especially harmful because it is one of the main causes that sends us to the lower states. These points are made in passages like the following:

> There is no evil like anger,
> And no austerity like patience.[25]

[23]The following list of substances appears in Asanga's *Listeners' Levels* (S: *Śrāvakabhūmiḥ*, p. 203): (1) hair of the head, (2) body hair, (3) fingernails and toenails, (4) teeth, (5) skin irritations, (6) impurities (perhaps ear wax and such things as the mucous secretions that form at the corners of the eyes), (7) skin, (8) flesh, (9) bones, (10) tendons, (11) blood and lymph vessels, (12) kidneys, (13) heart, (14) liver, (15) lungs, (16) small intestine, (17) large intestine, (18) stomach, (19) rectum, (20) spleen, (21) feces, (22) tears, (23) sweat, (24) saliva, (25) snot, (26) oily body fluid, (27) watery body fluid, (28) bone marrow, (29) fat, (30) bile, (31) phlegm, (32) pus, (33) blood, (34) brain matter, (35) cerebral membrane, and (36) urine. As the previous note states, these objects are often meant as an antidote for attachment toward one's own body. However, as Kyabje Pabongka Rinpoche does here, other sources also counsel reflecting on these objects as a method of overcoming sexual desire.

[24]Asanga's *Listeners' Levels* (*Śrāvakabhūmiḥ*, pp. 74–81) lists a range of disadvantages relating to food. Those that deal with unattractiveness include reflecting how the pleasing appearance that food has when it is still on your plate quickly disappears after it is chewed and swallowed. You should also reflect how food is absorbed into the body in order to nourish such impure substances as flesh, blood, bones, skin, and so on. Another point is how food produces such unattractive waste as urine and feces. A different category of disadvantages addresses the hardships that one must undergo in the effort to acquire food or the money to obtain food.

[25]*Engaging in Bodhisattva Activities* (S: *Bodhicaryāvatāraḥ*), ch. 6, v. 2.

Another poem includes the line: "Anger is the weapon that destroys the life force of the higher states."[26]

In explaining how anger destroys one's virtue-roots, we must recognize several distinctions regarding the subject who shows anger and the object toward whom that anger is shown.[27]

[In addition to recognizing the nature of anger], we must practice the various antidotes to anger, such as cultivating patience. I will have more to say about that later, when I discuss the six perfections.[28]

(Kyabje Rinpoche also mentioned that in some situations it is appropriate for a teacher to beat a student as a form of punishment. But, in doing so, the teacher must not allow himself to become angry and must be motivated only by a desire to benefit his student.)

Pride

The third root mental affliction is pride. Pride is a kind of swelling up of the mind that occurs with regard to all sorts of objects, both good and bad. It can come through perceiving yourself as having great power, wealth, or spiritual knowledge; being from a better family than others; having superior intelligence or a pure moral practice; and sometimes even just by thinking that you have an excellent voice or great physical strength [270b].

When we look down from a high mountaintop, everything appears small and insignificant. Similarly, a person's mind becomes filled with pride when he holds himself as supreme and others as lower than him. Pride develops when we let the mind take on such an air of superiority. We can generate pride in relation to the most insignificant of objects and for the smallest of reasons.

[26] *Prayer to be Reborn in Sukhavati* (T: *bDe smon*). See note 20 above.

[27] Je Tsongkapa addresses the question of what it means for anger to destroy virtue-roots both in his *Great Stages of the Path* (T: *Lam rim chen mo*), pp. 550–555 (ff. 259b–262a), and in his *Elucidation of the Underlying Intent: An Extensive Commentary to the Introduction to the Middle Way* (T: *dBu ma la 'jug pa'i rgya cher bshad pa dgongs pa rab gsal*), pp. 107–116 (commentary to ch. 3, v. 6 of Chandrakirti's root text). In both cases the discussion centers around a number of scriptural passages that describe how a moment of anger can destroy a great amount of virtue, even as much as one could accumulate over a period of a hundred or a thousand kalpas. Among the issues that Je Tsongkapa discusses are these: (1) What kind of person is being described in the various scriptural passages? For instance, must both the individual who expresses anger and the object of his anger be Bodhisattvas? How does a different level of spirituality between subject and object alter the gravity of the act? (2) Does anger destroy every type of virtue, or are there certain types that it cannot destroy? (3) What does it mean for anger to "destroy" virtue? For instance, does anger prevent virtue from producing a desirable result quickly, or does it permanently destroy its ability to ever produce a desirable result?

[28] See Day Twenty, pp. 216–224.

It is difficult for a proud person to gain any spiritual knowledge. The early Kadampa teachers had several sayings that illustrate this point. One was: "See for yourselves! Does the vivid greenness of spring start in the high mountaintops, or does it come first in the low valleys?" They also used to say: "The water of knowledge cannot fill the bladder of pride."[29]

Even though a guru may teach someone who has great pride, the dharma will not benefit him. Therefore, the antidote for pride is to reflect on the great diversity of the constituents[30] in order to recognize all the subjects about which we are ignorant. More specifically, we must overcome our pride by contemplating how each part of our body, from the top of the head to the bottom of the feet, contain a great many inner and outer entities that we know nothing about.

Ignorance

The fourth root mental affliction is ignorance. The Tibetan word for ignorance is *ma rikpa*. It is formed by attaching the negative prefix *ma* to the word *rikpa*, which means "knowledge." This is like adding *not* to the verb *see* to make the phrase *not see*, or adding *not* to the verb *know* to make the phrase *not know*. The term *ma rikpa* or ignorance, then, means something like "not seeing," "not knowing," or "not being clear."

Ignorance is like the black murkiness we experience when we close our eyes or like being unable to see objects that are covered in darkness. It is a state of bewilderment concerning such subjects as the Four Noble Truths, karma and its results, and the Triple Gem. It can even mean [271a] the inability to see objects that are too far away for ordinary beings to perceive. Finally, ignorance is the root of all the mental afflictions.

[29]T: *rnga rgyal gyi sgang bu la yon tan gyi chu mi 'brub*. The word *sgang* also means a "hilltop." Since the straightforward meaning of *'brub* is "to inundate," this allows for an alternate reading: "The water of knowledge cannot flow up over the mountaintop of pride."

[30]S: *dhātuprabhedaḥ*, T: *khams kyi rab tu dbye ba*. Buddhist literature contains several classifications involving the term "constituent" (S: *dhātuḥ*, T: *khams*). The one being referred to here includes these six items: (1) earth, (2) water, (3) fire, (4) air, (5) space, and (6) consciousness. The practice of meditating on the six constituents as an antidote for pride is described in Asanga's *Listeners' Levels* (*Śrāvakabhūmiḥ*, pp. 211–218). The four physical elements are differentiated in terms of inner and outer forms. The description of the inner earth and water elements in particular corresponds exactly to the thirty-six substances mentioned in note 23. The constituents of space and consciousness are contemplated as elements within the makeup of the practitioner. The section concludes: "When a person who has a strong tendency to develop pride contemplates the diversity of the constituents, he frees himself from the notion that his body is comprised of a single mass and acquires an awareness of its unattractiveness. This prevents him from becoming puffed up; it weakens his pride and purifies his mind of that type of mental activity."

Some Buddhist philosophers, including Chandrakirti and Dharmakirti, held that the perishable-collection view[31] and ignorance are not distinct entities. They described the perishable-collection view as a form of ignorance. Others, such as Asanga and his brother Vasubandhu, held that ignorance and the perishable-collection view are different. According to them, the difference between the two minds can be explained using the analogy of the coiled rope that is mistaken for a snake. The perishable-collection view is like the erroneous belief that the rope is a snake. Ignorance, on the other hand, is like the cause of that erroneous belief—that is, the darkness that falls at dusk and prevents you from clearly perceiving the nature of the coiled rope.

Doubt

The fifth root mental affliction is doubt. It should be understood as the uncertainty about whether such things as the Four Noble Truths, the Triple Gem, and karma and its results actually exist or not, as well as the uncertainty about what their nature might be.

Doubting the authenticity of the Triple Gem keeps us from being able to generate spiritual realizations. This is described in the following verse by the Lord of Conquerors Je Gendun Drup:

> Save me from the threat of that vicious fiend of doubt,
> Who travels freely through the sky of bewilderment
> Wreaking havoc on those who seek sure knowledge
> And attacking the very life force of liberation.[32]

Doubting the truth of karma and its results keeps us from achieving rebirth in the higher states, while doubting the authenticity of the Four Noble Truths keeps us from achieving liberation. These reasons show why doubt is so harmful.

This concludes the explanation of the five mental afflictions that do not constitute views.

[31] S: *satkāyadṛṣṭiḥ*, T: *'jig tsogs la lta ba*. This is one of the five erroneous views that make up the sixth root mental affliction (see below). It is described as the false belief in an "I" and "mine." The object wrongly being perceived as an "I" is a substantially real and independent self. The objects wrongly perceived as "mine" are those entities that are mistakenly identified as forming parts of the fictional self—such as one's body and mind—or those external objects over which this self is believed to exercise ownership or control.

[32] Je Gendun Drup (T: *rJe dGe 'dun grub*, 1391–1474) was a direct disciple of Je Tsongkapa and was recognized retroactively as the first in the line of Dalai Lamas. We were unable to identify the source of this verse.

The five afflicted views

The sixth root mental affliction includes five mistaken views: (1) the perishable-collection view, (2) the extreme view, (3) the view that one's own beliefs are supreme, (4) the view that inferior ethical practice and asceticism are supreme, and (5) wrong view.

The perishable-collection view

The perishable-collection view[33] [271b] is a type of afflicted awareness that forms the notion of an "I" and "mine" on the basis of the collection of perishable heaps.

If someone either harms or helps us—for example, by expressing praise or scorn—we typically react by thinking, "Why did that person do this to me?" Such a thought is related to the belief that the "I" appearing strongly from deep within the mind really exists in the manner that it presents itself to us. This belief is the perishable-collection view and it is the root of all samsaric troubles.

(Kyabje Rinpoche then made this further point. The perishable-collection view is generated by all ordinary beings, even ants and other insects. For instance, if we touch a bug that is crawling along the ground with a blade of grass, it immediately becomes frightened and thinks, "Something bad is happening to me." Then it curls up in a ball and pretends to be dead. After a little while, it will turn around and quickly crawl away in the opposite direction. This behavior is caused by the perishable-collection view.)

The extreme view

The extreme view[34] mainly occurs in relation to that very "I" or self that is wrongly perceived by the perishable-collection view to be real. One aspect of the extreme view holds that such a self is permanent, unchanging, eternal, truly existent, and so forth. The other holds that, after one dies, that self ceases to exist. While this view is principally held by non-Buddhists,

[33]The phrase "perishable collection" in the perishable-collection view (S: *satkāyadrstiḥ*, T: *'jig tsogs la lta ba*) is a synonym for the five heaps (S: *skandhaḥ*, T: *phung po*) of: (1) form, (2) feelings, (3) conception, (4) compositional factors, and (5) consciousness. These heaps represent a "collection" (S: *kāya*, T: *tsogs*) of five types of entities that are "perishable" (S: *sat*, T: *'jig*) in that they are impermanent and only exist for a moment. For a more detailed explanation of the perishable-collection view, see the topic "the key point of determining the object to be refuted," Day Twenty-two, pp. 274–282.

[34]S: *antagrāhadṛṣṭiḥ*, T: *mthar 'dzin pa'i lta ba*. The extreme view has two forms: one believes in an eternalistic extreme (S: *śāśvatāntaḥ*, T: *rtag pa'i mtha'*) and the other in a nihilistic extreme (S: *ucchedāntaḥ*, T: *chad pa'i mtha'*).

we Buddhists also generate a form of the extreme view when we believe that entities are truly existent or that they don't exist at all.

The view that one's own beliefs are supreme

The view that one's own beliefs are supreme[35] is a type of afflicted awareness in which an individual regards as supreme any of three mistaken views that have already been explained—the perishable-collection view, wrong view,[36] and the extreme view. It can also arise in relation to one's own heaps,[37] which are the objects upon which those mistaken beliefs are based.

The view that inferior ethical practices and asceticism are supreme

The view that inferior ethical practices and asceticism are supreme[38] is the belief that practices such as standing continually on only one leg, sitting near five fires, and impaling oneself on a trident represent a means of achieving liberation. Another example is the view that dressing in an animal pelt represents a supreme form of spiritual practice [272a].

Also, some persons who gain a small amount of clairvoyance become confused when they realize that they were born as a dog in their previous life. Motivated by a desire to be reborn as a human being, they howl like dogs and practice various other kinds of dog-like behavior. Believing this kind of practice to be a supreme form of spiritual asceticism, they engage in base forms of physical and verbal conduct. This view also includes the

[35]S: *dṛṣṭiparāmarśaḥ*, T: *lta ba mchog tu 'dzin pa.*

[36]Wrong view (S: *mithyādṛṣṭiḥ*, T: *log par lta ba*) is one of the ten nonvirtuous karmic paths that was explained in Part Two, Day Thirteen, pp. 252–253. This view is described again here.

[37]Many sources point out that this view is not exclusively the belief that any one of the three views identified here are supreme; it can also occur in relation to one's heaps. The annotated edition of Je Tsongkapa's *Great Treatise on the Stages of the Path* (T: *Lam rim mchan bzhi bsgrags ma*, p. 452) identifies the latter type as the belief that one's afflicted five heaps represent the means of attaining purification and deliverance (T: *dag grol gyi rgyur 'dzin pa*). (This work is listed in the Bibliography under the full title: *The Bright Lamp of the Mahayana Path: A Commentary in the Form of Interlinear Notes by Four Scholars on Difficult Points in the Incomparable Lord Tsongkapa's Great Stages of the Path to Enlightenment* [T: *mNyam med rje btzun tzong kha pa chen pos mdzad pa'i byang chub lam rim chen mo'i dka' ba'i gnad rnams mchan bu bzhi'i sgo nas legs par bshad pa theg chen lam gyi gsal sgron*].) This description accords well with what Vasubandhu states in his *Commentary to the Treasury of Higher Learning* (*Abhidharmakośabhāṣyam*, p. 773): "The view that one's own beliefs are supreme is a view in which inferior entities are regarded as supreme. What are inferior entities? All the afflicted entities (S: *sāsrava*, T: *zag bcas*; see Day Fourteen, note 5 for an explanation of this term). They are inferior in the sense that they are objects that are abandoned by *aryas*."

[38]S: *śīlavrataparāmarśaḥ*, T: *tsul khrims dang brtul zhugs mchog tu 'dzin pa'i lta ba.*

belief that cultivating such base practices is the principal means of attaining deliverance from samsara.

Wrong view

The principal form of wrong view is the belief that there is no such thing as the Triple Gem, the Four Noble Truths, or karma and its results. Other examples take one of two forms: either they posit the existence of entities that *do not* exist or they deny the existence of entities that *do* exist. For instance, certain non-Buddhists claim that the world was created by ten incarnations of Vishnu.[39] The Samkhyas[40] classify all entities into twenty-five categories, and claim either that they are created by primordial matter[41] or the deity Ishvara.[42] These are examples of wrong view that attribute causality to objects that *do not* exist. Other traditions deny the existence of entities that *do* exist.[43]

Thus, the six root mental afflictions or "attachments"[44] are made up of the above five mental afflictions that are not views, along with the five views taken together as one.

(Kyabje Rinpoche concluded this section by saying that we must learn to apply the appropriate antidote when any of these mental afflictions arises in the mind. However, [272b] ignorance causes all the other mental afflictions and also operates wherever they do. This is described in the following lines from the *Four Hundred Verses*:

> Like the body faculty in the body,
> Ignorance is present everywhere.[45]

Because of these qualities, ignorance is particularly difficult to recognize; I will explain more about it later.)

[39]T: *Khyab 'jug.*

[40]T: *Grangs can pa.*

[41]S: *pradhānaḥ*, also *mūlaprakṛtiḥ*; T: *spyi gtzo bo*, also *rtza ba'i rang bzhin.*

[42]T: *dBang phyug.*

[43]The classic Indian nihilist tradition was the Charvaka or Lokayata school (T: *'Jig rten rgyang 'phen pa*), which denied the existence of past or future lives, karma and its results, a mind distinct from the body, and an omniscient being.

[44]See note 18 above for the meaning of "attachment" (S: *anuśayaḥ*, T: *phra rgyas*) as it is being used here.

[45]T: *bZhi brgya pa*, ch. 6, v. 10.

ii) The order in which the mental afflictions arise

All six of the root mental afflictions arise from the belief in real or self-existent entities[46] and from the perishable-collection view. Therefore, according to the Buddhist schools that regard the perishable-collection view as a type of ignorance, that view is identified as the root of all karma and the mental afflictions. According to the schools that regard ignorance and the perishable-collection view as distinct, ignorance alone is explained as the principal cause.

The position of the Madhyamaka Prasangika School is that the perishable-collection view is the root of all the other mental afflictions. Moreover, this view has two forms: conceptual[47] and innate.[48] Of these, the innate form is the ultimate cause. The innate form of the perishable-collection view also has two aspects: belief in a self-existent "I" and belief in a self-existent "mine." Of the two, the belief in a self-existent "I" is more fundamental.

This belief arises, for instance, when someone says something good about us. As we react with thoughts like: "That was a nice thing to say about me," the distinct image of an "I," or subjective self, develops deep within the mind. Once this object appears, the perishable-collection view holds it as self-existent and real. Then we perceive such a self as the enjoyer of what we experience. This causes us to develop attachment toward the self and animosity toward others. We also generate desire toward those who benefit us, anger toward those who harm us, and ignorance toward those we consider as neutral. This is described in the following verse from the *Extensive Treatise on Knowledge*:

> When there is a self, the conception of "other"
> will occur.
> The distinction between self and other brings attachment
> and hatred.
> Through being completely entangled with these two,
> All adversity comes into being.[49]

[46]S: *ātmagrāhaḥ*, T: *bdag tu 'dzin pa*. In the Madhyamaka or Middle Way School, this belief is identified with ignorance (S: *avidyā*, T: *ma rig pa*).

[47]S: *parikalpitaḥ*, T: *kun brtags*. The conceptual form of the perishable-collection view is any belief in an independently real self that is based on mistaken reasoning. For example, the classic non-Buddhist view is that the self is a permanent, single, and independent entity. Its permanence means that it is not perishable—more specifically, it is not subject to arising and passing away. Its singularity means that it is an indivisible unity—an entity without parts that is not subject to change. Its independence means that it controls the five heaps.

[48]S: *sahajaḥ*, T: *lhan skyes*.

[49]S: *Pramāṇavārttikam*, ch. 2, v. 221.

The *Introduction to the Middle Way* similarly states:

> Seeing with the mind that all mental afflictions
> and adversity [273a],
> Without exception, originate from the perishable-
> collection view . . .[50]

Another verse from this latter work also says:

> ...(Beings) who first become attached to the
> self by believing in an "I,"
> Then generate desire for objects by regarding
> them as "mine . . ."[51]

So the root of the six attachments is ignorance and, in particular, the perishable-collection view. It is the foundation upon which the other mental afflictions such as desire, hatred, and doubt arise. These mental afflictions, in turn, bring about the accumulation of karma. And the combination of these two factors is what causes us to wander continuously in samsara.

The root of samsara, then, is the innate belief in an independently real self, a form of ignorance known as the perishable-collection view. Therefore, if we want to permanently abandon all the mental afflictions, we must strive to generate the antidote to the erroneous belief that the self and all other entities are self-existent. And the antidote to this ignorance is the wisdom that realizes all entities are not self-existent.

The wisdom that realizes entities are not self-existent is like a singularly pure medicine that has the power to cure a hundred different illnesses. As the *Four Hundred Verses* declares:

> Therefore, by destroying ignorance
> All the mental afflictions are destroyed.[52]

[50]T: *dBu ma la 'jug pa*, ch. 6, v. 120.

[51]Ibid., ch. 1 v. 3. The full verse states: "I make homage to the compassion felt toward beings/ Who first become attached to the self by believing in an 'I,'/ Then generate desire for objects by regarding them as 'mine,'/ And who are completely without freedom, like a revolving water-wheel."

[52]T: *bZhi brgya pa*, ch. 6, v. 10.

The *Sutra on the Ten Bodhisattva Levels* also declares:

> All the misdeeds that occur in the world arise from the belief in self-existent entities. They are not committed by those who rid themselves of this belief.[53]

Nevertheless, until we gain the realization that will rid us of this belief, we must practice the methods that temporarily remove the mental afflictions by suppressing them. An important element of this practice involves putting a stop to the causes of the mental afflictions.

iii) The causes of the mental afflictions

There are six factors that make it possible for the mental afflictions to arise: (1) basis, (2) object, (3) social interaction, (4) discourse, (5) habit, and (6) attention.

Basis

The basis for the arising of the mental afflictions is the existence of their seeds—that is, their latent capacity to arise again. For instance, if we are unable to remove the seed of an illness, even very insignificant factors such as the wrong kind of food will cause it to arise again. Similarly, because of the existence of their seeds, mental afflictions [273b] will immediately arise in our mind whenever the appropriate conditions are present. This is the sense in which the mental afflictions are said to have a basis or potentiality for coming into being.

Object

The second factor that causes the mental afflictions to arise is a suitable object. The object can be attractive, unattractive, or it can take other forms as well. When we come into contact with such an object, a mental affliction will arise because we have not abandoned its seed. This is described in a verse from the *Treasury of Higher Learning*:

> The causes of the mental afflictions are complete
> When the attachments have not yet been abandoned,

[53]S: *Daśabhūmikasūtram*, p. 31.

When a suitable object is situated close by,
And when one's attention operates improperly.[54]

Therefore, we must make every effort to distance ourselves from such objects. One of the reasons that monks and nuns stay in monasteries and hermitages is so that they can separate themselves from unsuitable objects. For the time being, at least, those of us who are novice practitioners can best avoid generating the mental afflictions by not letting ourselves see such objects. Therefore, we should do everything we can to keep away from them.

A number of texts from the Mind Training tradition state that it is more important to avoid having contact with unsuitable objects than it is to apply an antidote to them. A verse from a work by Gyel-se Tokme[55] also states:

By avoiding unsuitable objects, the mental afflictions
gradually decrease.
By overcoming distraction, virtuous actions naturally
increase.
By maintaining clarity of mind, a sure understanding of
dharma will arise.
Remaining in solitude is a practice that sons of the
Victorious Ones follow.[56]

(After citing these passages, Kyabje Rinpoche emphasized the importance of avoiding objects that cause us to develop the mental afflictions and of dwelling in a place that is favorable to dharma practice.[57])

Social interaction

Social interaction refers to the distractions that come from associating with bad people. This is an activity that we should avoid.

[54]S: *Abhidharmakośakārikā*, ch. 5, v. 34.

[55]T: *rGyal sras thog med bzang po dpal*, 1295–1369. A Sakya teacher renowned for the strength of his enlightenment mind who transmitted the Kadampa Mind Training instructions to Je Tsongkapa's teacher Rendawa Shönu Lodrö (T: *Re mda' ba gZhon nu blo gros*, 1349–1412). See *Lives of the Lamrim Teachers* (T: *Lam rim bla ma brgyud pa'i rnam thar*), vol. 2, pp. 839–928. In Bibliography, see listing under *Ye shes rgyal mtsan*.

[56]*Thirty-seven Practices of the Sons of the Victorious Ones* (T: *rGyal ba'i sras kyi lag len so bdun ma*), v. 5.

[57]"Staying in a favorable place" (T: *mthun pa'i yul na gnas pa*) is the first of six requisites that a practitioner must cultivate or rely upon in order to develop quiescence. See Day Twenty-one, pp. 234–235.

Drinking beer, playing games, engaging in conversation that increases the mental afflictions, and so on are activities that keep us tied to this life. These are all caused by keeping bad company. Therefore, we should not listen to such people and we should not let ourselves become influenced by them [274a].

If we fall under the influence of a bad person, we will generate the mental afflictions and engage in improper activities. For example, there were two men who lived in the Gyel region of Penbo.[58] One of them was a beer drinker; the other wasn't. The one who drank beer went to Radreng,[59] where he met several Kadampa *geshes*.[60] The one who didn't drink beer went to Lhasa and fell in with bad friends. When the two met some time later, they learned that because of the people they had associated with the one who used to drink beer no longer did, while the other—who previously had not been a beer drinker—now was.

Some people refer to stinginess with such euphemisms as "thriftiness" and describe someone who is full of hatred as being "wrathful" or "short-tempered"; but, in fact, these are serious faults. A student who follows a so-called "thrifty" teacher—that is, one who clings to wealth and other possessions—will himself become very stingy. The same is true if one follows a teacher who is angry by nature.

Because it is very easy to pick up the habits of bad friends, we must avoid such persons. But almost everyone these days is a bad friend in the sense of being preoccupied exclusively with the affairs of this life. Since we can't avoid contact with everyone, it is important that we exercise great care and avoid becoming too closely involved with others.

For instance, long ago there was a land in which all the inhabitants drank a potion that made them experience the same hallucination. The only person who did not suffer from this delusion was the king. As a result, everyone else accused the king of being crazy. Nowadays, dharma practitioners do not fit well into ordinary society [274b]. However, that is not so bad, since we are supposed to be cultivating the three principles of banishment, entering, and attainment.[61]

[58]T: *'Phan po*. A region north of Lhasa.

[59]T: *Rva sgreng* is the site of the first Kadampa monastery, established by Dromtönba in 1057. Destroyed during the Cultural Revolution, its ruins lie about 60 miles north of Lhasa on a hill overlooking the Kyichu River.

[60]T: *dge bshes*. Tibetan equivalent for a term that means "spiritual teacher" (S: *kalyāṇa-mitram*).

[61]T: *bud snyegs thob gsum*. This is a reference to the last three precepts of the instruction called the Ten Jewels of Ultimate Commitment (T: *Phugs nor bcu*; see Part Two, Day Ten, note 29). "Banishment" is shorthand for the precept called "Banish yourself from the ranks of men." This means that we should remove ourselves from the ranks of persons who are mainly

When a bad friend tries to give us advice, we should ignore him and make ourselves like the neck of an old yak.[62] We can accomplish this by practicing the Kadampa instruction known as the Ten Jewels of Ultimate Commitment, which includes these precepts: (1) send ahead of you the diamond that makes you invulnerable, (2) set behind you the diamond that frees you from inhibitions, and (3) keep beside you the diamond of wisdom.[63]

Advice

The fourth factor is to receive bad advice. This can occur through reading the kinds of books that will cause you to generate the mental afflictions. These include stories like the epic *Gesar of Ling*, and treatises or manuals that deal with erotic practices. These will only serve to increase and strengthen your desire, hatred, and ignorance.

We should read instead the biographies of the great spiritual beings, since reflecting on their accomplishments can serve to plant the seeds of liberation in our mind.

Congregating with others and talking about topics that will increase our desire and hatred—such as politics, war, women, and legal disputes—also will cause us to develop the mental afflictions.

concerned with this life. We should regard thoughts about this life's happiness as an enemy to our spiritual practice and adopt a behavior that is at odds with the values of all worldly people. Because of this, ordinary society will look upon us as crazy. "Entering" refers to the precept called "Enter the ranks of dogs." This means that we should give up all interest in food, clothing, and reputation and accept any hardships we may encounter—such as hunger and thirst—in our pursuit of the dharma. "Attainment" is an allusion to the precept called "Attain the ranks of the gods." This means that we should give up all interest in worldly affairs and go into solitude, seeking to complete our practice and achieve the most divine of all states—Buddhahood—even within this lifetime.

[62]That is, we should remain unyielding to the influence of bad friends and resolute in our pursuit of a genuine spiritual practice.

[63]These are the fifth, sixth, and seventh precepts of the instruction. "Send ahead of you the diamond that makes you invulnerable" means that a practitioner should not let parents, relatives, friends, and the like persuade him to put off practicing the dharma. Instead, he should go into solitude at a hermitage with a mind that is like a diamond in its unshakably firm commitment to a pure dharma practice. "Set behind you the diamond that frees you from inhibitions" means that the practitioner should not be concerned with what others might think of him. He should remember that trying to please those who are mainly concerned with this life is a source of many faults and an obstacle to dharma practice. "Keep beside you the diamond of wisdom" means that the practitioner should not abandon any spiritual activity he may have begun and should renounce forever all the useless concerns of this life. Then, with a firm commitment to the dharma, he should devote his whole life to spiritual practice.

Habit

As Shang Rinpoche said, "Impressions left by the mind's bad habits are like rolled-up papers."[64] That is, even when we are distracted, bad mental states like desire and hatred enter our mind spontaneously, because we are so strongly accustomed to generating the mental afflictions.

The degree to which we develop the mental afflictions in this life is also determined by how habitual they had become in past lives. Some persons develop great desire or hatred toward even insignificant objects. For instance, people who are easily angered [275a] cannot even bear to have someone look at them the wrong way. The only thing we can do about these tendencies is apply the appropriate antidote and try as hard as we can to stop ourselves from continuing to act in such a way.

Attention

The sixth factor, attention,[65] refers specifically to improper attention, which is the activity of repeatedly ascribing to objects the kinds of qualities that lead us to develop desire, hatred, and the rest.

An example of an object that produces desire might be a piece of clothing. Improper attention toward it would be to think again and again how nice its color is, how beautiful its shape is, how good the weave is, and so forth.

A typical object that generates hatred is an enemy. Improper attention would be to think over and over, "This person harmed me by doing this and that," and, "Then later, he also did this and that to me."

These two examples show how improper attention operates toward attractive and unattractive objects. Another situation is when we think about someone, "Even though this person practices dharma, he still experienced various kinds of suffering and misfortune. So, I don't believe there is such a thing as karma and its results."

Because we will develop some form of the mental afflictions whenever the above factors are present, we must do everything we can to prevent them from occurring. If we don't apply any antidote, our mental afflictions

[64]T: *shog dril.* Secular papers such as government documents are typically stored by rolling them up and placing them in cubbyholes or on open shelves.

[65]Attention (S: *manaskāraḥ*, T: *yid la byed pa*) is one of five mental states (S: *caittaḥ*, T: *sems byung*) that accompany all moments of consciousness. It is defined in Buddhist Abhidharma literature as the turning or directing of the mind toward an object. Its main function is to cause the mind to continue holding an object. Improper attention (S: *ayoniśomanaskāraḥ*, T: *tsul bzhin ma yin pa yid la byed pa*) is the form of this mental state that causes the mind to engage objects in an erroneous manner and leads to the arising of mental afflictions.

will grow stronger and stronger. On the other hand, by applying the proper antidote they will gradually diminish. Therefore, we must try very hard to cultivate the antidotes to the mental afflictions.

iv) The disadvantages of the mental afflictions

As the following two verses from the *Ornament of Mahayana Sutras* declare, there are many disadvantages associated with the mental afflictions:

> The mental afflictions destroy you,
> They destroy beings, and destroy morality.
> They bring dejection, material loss, loss of protection,
> As well as the Master's reproach.
>
> You become subject to conflict and disrepute.
> In the future you are reborn in inopportune states.
> Losing what you've attained and not yet attained,
> You will undergo great mental suffering [275b].[66]

(Kyabje Rinpoche then described how the mental afflictions are a source of many detriments. For instance, when the mental afflictions arise, they cause the mind to take on a nonvirtuous nature; they cause the mind to grasp its object in a mistaken way; they cause their seeds or potentialities to become strengthened; they cause all similar mental afflictions—such as desire and hatred—to be generated continually; they cause us to perform those misdeeds that are condemned by great spiritual beings and that bring unhappiness in both this and future lives; and they lead us farther away from both liberation and the omniscience of supreme enlightenment. As a result of these and other factors, such as making us fall away from virtuous activities, the mental afflictions cause us to bring ruin both to ourselves and to others.[67]

[66]S: *Mahāyānasūtrālaṃkāraḥ*, ch 17, vv. 25–26. When clearly understood, these two verses reveal a great many instructions. Two excellent explanations are Sthiramati's commentary to the root verses (T: *mDo sde rgyan gyi 'grel bshad*), vol. 47 (*tzi*), ff. 61a–63a, and the annotated edition to Je Tsongkapa's *Great Treatise* (T: *Lam rim mchan bzhi sbrags ma*), vol. 1, pp. 455–456.

[67]The source for the disadvantages (S: *ādīnavaḥ*, T: *nyes dmigs*) listed in this paragraph is the first section of Asanga's *Levels of Yoga Practice* (T: *rNal 'byor spyod pa'i sa*), known as the *Manifold Levels* (T: *Sa mang po pa*), Tg. vol. 48 (*tsi*), ff. 87b–88a. This section is also cited in Je Tsongkapa's *Great Treatise on the Stages of the Path* (T: *Lam rim chen mo*), pp. 337–338 (ff. 153a–153b).

The mental afflictions destroy our moral practice. They also reduce the honor and material goods we might otherwise receive. They cause the Buddhas and dharma protectors to reproach us.

The mental afflictions lead some to bring suffering to themselves and others by causing them to engage in killing. In relation to this life, they ruin our reputation by involving us in litigation and other disputes. In relation to future lives, they cause us to be reborn in remote lands, the lower states, and other inopportune circumstances.[68])

So whenever these mental afflictions occur, we must immediately recognize them as our worst enemies and try to overcome them. As *Engaging in Bodhisattva Activities* declares:

> Even if all the gods and men
> Were to become my enemies,
> They still could not make me enter
> The fires of Unrelenting Torment.
>
> Yet the mighty foe of the mental afflictions
> Can hurl me instantly into a place
> That, if it were to touch Mount Meru,
> Would not even leave ashes behind [276a].[69]

There is no greater enemy than these mental afflictions. By being conciliatory, we can appease an ordinary enemy and persuade him not to harm us. But if we are conciliatory toward our mental afflictions, they will only continue harming us.

The mental afflictions created all the suffering we have ever experienced in the past, including being burned in the hell of Unrelenting Torment. These same mental afflictions are also the torturers that will cause us to experience more of samsara's suffering in the future. So they are the worst enemy we have in all the three realms.

The former Kadampa teachers had this saying:

> The way to train yourself toward the mental afflictions is to stand with your shoulder pointed toward them[70] and try to harm them as much as possible. Toward sentient beings, however,

[68]The eight inopportune circumstances are described in Part Two, Day Nine, pp. 73–76.

[69]S: *Bodhicaryāvatāraḥ*, ch. 4, vv. 30, 31.

[70]T: *zur bstan*. Literally "show a corner"; that is, stand sideways like a fighter who is preparing to defend himself against an opponent.

> you should be open to them[71] and try to help them as much as possible.

Geshe Ben also said:

> My only practice is to stand at the entrance to the fortress of my mind holding the spear of antidotes. If they[72] try to be aggressive, I become aggressive. If they ease up, then I ease up.

So we must regard the mental afflictions as our worst enemy, and immediately apply the appropriate antidote whenever they arise.

b) How the mental afflictions cause us to accumulate karma

There are two basic types of karma: volition and acts that are produced by volition. The first of these is described in the *Compendium of Higher Learning*: "What is volition?[73] It is the mental activity that shapes the mind. Its function is to propel the mind toward objects that are virtuous, nonvirtuous, or indeterminate."[74] Two examples of volition are: (1) the state of mind that moves you to decide to utter harsh speech, and (2) the mental activity that drives and urges you while you are actually uttering harsh speech [276b]. The acts that are produced by volition are those physical and verbal acts that are motivated by volition.

The *Treasury of Higher Learning* describes karma as follows:

> It is both volition and what that [volition] creates.
> Volition is the activity of the mind;
> What it creates are physical and verbal acts.[75]

The mental afflictions produce three types of karma: nonmeritorious deeds, meritorious deeds, and invariable deeds. Nonmeritorious deeds, such as killing and the like, are accumulated out of attachment to the affairs of this life. These deeds cause us to be born in the lower states.

[71] T: *mthil bstan*. Literally "show the innermost part"; that is, adopt a benign and unthreatening posture.

[72] The mental afflictions.

[73] S: *cetanā*, T: *sems pa*.

[74] S: *Abhidharmasamuccayaḥ*, pp. 5–6. In Bibliography, see listing under *Asaṅga*.

[75] S: *Abhidharmakośakārikā*, ch. 4, v. 1.

Meritorious deeds are accumulated from a concern for achieving the happiness of the desire realm in future lives. These deeds cause us to be born in the desire realm, either as a human being or as a god.

Invariable deeds are of two types. The first, deriving from dissatisfaction with the pleasures of external sense objects, is the act of absorbing oneself in the inner pleasure associated with one-pointed concentration. This type of invariable deed can bring results ranging from rebirth as a god in the first absorption level to rebirth as a god in the third absorption level. The second type of invariable deed derives from dissatisfaction with even the pleasure associated with one-pointed concentration, and is accumulated through an attraction to the sensation of equanimity. It can serve as a cause for taking birth as a deity in the fourth absorption level or any of the levels beyond that.

Both meritorious and nonmeritorious deeds are forms of projecting karma[76] that produce rebirth in the desire realm. They are also deeds whose results can vary. For example, even though someone has entered a type of intermediate state[77] that precedes rebirth in one of the hells, a lama can—through the power of ritual, mantras, and so forth—change this intermediate state and enable the person to be reborn in one of the pleasurable states. Thus, Drom Rinpoche said:

> If all the *upasakas* of Radreng combine the wealth they use for making offerings into a single fund, it will help those contributors to accumulate virtue even after they have died [277a].

(Kyabje Rinpoche explained this to mean that a person who has died and is still in the intermediate state can benefit greatly if virtuous activities are performed and paid for with money from a fund to which he had previously contributed.)

The reason the projecting karma that brings rebirth in the two higher realms[78] is called invariable karma can be explained as follows. For instance, if we accumulate karma that has the capacity to produce rebirth in the first absorption level of the form realm, that karma can only cause us to be reborn in the first absorption level of the form realm. It cannot cause us

[76]T: *'phen byed kyi las*. A projecting karma is one that has the power to "project" you (i.e., cause you to be reborn) into a particular kind of rebirth in a future life. See Part Two, Day Thirteen, p. 263.

[77]The intermediate state that one enters following death has different forms. Each one is specific to the type of rebirth that one is about to take. See the discussion in the next section.

[78]T: *khams gong ma*. That is, the form and formless realms.

to be reborn in any other level, such as the second absorption level. As the *Treasury of Higher Learning* declares:

> Merit is good karma of the desire realm.
> That of the higher realms is invariable,
> Because the ripening of the karma
> In those levels does not vary.[79]

(Kyabje Rinpoche concluded by saying that unless we are motivated by one of the three principal elements of the path,[80] all our deeds, no matter what they may be, will remain causes that perpetuate samsara. But if a deed is motivated by aversion for the three realms, it could not serve as a cause for anything but liberation. On the other hand, even though we renounce our attachment to this life and practice dharma by cultivating quiescence in some hermitage, if we do so without being motivated by the renunciation that aspires to achieve liberation or one of the other principal elements of the path, the most we could accomplish would be to accumulate causes that bring rebirth in the form or the formless realms. Therefore, for anyone who wants to practice true dharma, it is crucial to seek an instruction that is complete and unerring.)

c) How we die and are reborn

This section consists of three parts: (1) how death occurs, (2) how death is followed by entrance into the intermediate state, and (3) how rebirth occurs at conception.

i) How death occurs

The main factors that cause death are: (1) exhaustion of one's life force, (2) exhaustion of one's merit, and (3) not to have abandoned the perilous conditions. In relation to this last category, the sutras describe nine perilous conditions.[81]

[79]S: *Abhidharmakośakārikā*, ch. 4, v. 46.

[80]T: *lam gyi gtzo bo rnam gsum*. That is, renunciation, enlightenment mind, and correct view.

[81]The source for this section is Asanga's *Levels of Yoga Practice* (T: *rNal 'byor spyod pa'i sa*), Tg. vol. 48 (*tsi*), ff. 8b. Also drawing on this material in his *Great Stages of the Path* (T: *Lam rim chen mo*), pp. 345–346 (ff. 157a–157b), Je Tsongkapa writes: "Death caused by exhaustion of one's life force means to die when the life force projected by one's former karma is totally depleted. This is death that comes at the appropriate time. Death caused by exhaustion of one's merit means, for instance, to die from the lack of any means of subsistence." For the

When a person is about to die, his consciousness activates the karma that will propel him into his next birth. The factors that activate a person's karma are the limbs called "craving" and "grasping."[82]

As for the manner in which these factors activate karma, [277b] craving is the feeling of attachment that we develop toward our bodies as we approach death and think, "I am going to be separated from this body." An example of grasping is the desire for warmth that we develop if we are destined for birth in one of the hot hells.

The object that these two factors activate is the most powerful among all the many black and white deeds that we have accumulated in the past. If our black and white deeds are of equal strength, then craving and grasping will activate the type that we performed most habitually. If we are equally habituated to both types, then they will activate a deed that we performed at an earlier time.[83]

The moment of activation is that time just before we die, when we recall—or another person causes us to recall—some virtuous or nonvirtuous object and then react by developing a state of mind such as faith, compassion, desire, or hatred, and so on, for as long as we can maintain coarse conceptions. At the actual moment of death, the mind enters a very subtle state in which all coarse conceptions have ceased. At that time, the mind cannot maintain a conscious awareness of either a virtuous or a nonvirtuous object; therefore, it takes on a morally indeterminate[84] nature.

In short, if we can develop a state of mind such as faith at the time of death, then we will activate a virtuous deed. This is why it is crucial to generate a virtuous state of mind just before we die, because that is when we activate the deed that will determine our next life. Even though someone may have been a dharma practitioner who always performed virtuous acts, he will activate a nonvirtuous deed if he becomes angry when he is about to

nine perilous conditions, Asanga remarks that the following list is taken from a sutra but does not identify it: (1) eating food in improper amounts, (2) eating unwholesome food, (3) eating food before one has digested a prior meal, (4) being unable to expel undigested (literally "uncooked") food that remains in the stomach, (5) being unable to retain cooked food (perhaps unable to "keep down" food so that nutrients might be absorbed into the body), (6) not taking medicine properly, (7) not knowing what is good and bad for one's health, (8) going about at inappropriate times, and (9) not following a pure spiritual life.

82These are the eighth and ninth limbs of the twelve-part teaching on dependent origination. See below, p. 77.

83For a discussion of the type of karma that ripens first, see Part Two, Day Eleven, pp. 142–143. As explained there, a deed "performed at an earlier time" means a definite karma that will ripen some time after the life immediately following the one in which it was performed.

84The Buddha declared that acts motivated by virtuous states of mind have favorable karmic results and that acts with nonvirtuous motivations have unfavorable results. Those acts which he did not specify as having either favorable or unfavorable results are understood to be morally neutral and are called indeterminate (S: *avyākṛtam*, T: *lung du ma bstan pa*).

die. As a result, it will be a nonvirtuous deed that ripens, and he will end up being reborn in the lower states. Using the same reasoning, the opposite result can also occur for a person who continually performed evil deeds during his life.

Various things that occur as a person is dying can be examined to determine whether a person is going to be reborn in the higher states or lower states. For instance, if a person will be reborn in the higher states, his body heat begins to disappear from his lower extremities and then gradually collects in his heart. If he will be reborn in the lower states, the opposite occurs; that is, his body heat begins to disappear from his upper extremities and then gradually collects in his heart. Another sign of where a person will be born is the intensity of suffering that he experiences as his "vital points are cut." "Cutting a vital point"[85] [278a] means for a vital part of the body to cease functioning.

(Kyabje Rinpoche then told us how some persons experience hallucinations at the time of death, such as having a huge quantity of tea stacked on top of them, or being crushed by a crowd of men. He explained that some time ago, a minor official in the government's treasury office had stolen some tea. As a result, just before he died he experienced the inauspicious hallucination of being crushed under many boxes of tea. Kyabje Rinpoche also related how a landholder from Tsang who was passing away experienced a horrifying vision during which he cried out, "I'm being crushed by a large group of men!"

On the other hand, those who lead a virtuous life can experience auspicious signs. For instance, there was once a beggar who was sitting at the side of the road seeking alms. As death approached, he began having visions of a palace and white light. Kyabje Rinpoche also described how an old woman from Chusang[86] who had always recited the *Mani* mantra experienced auspicious visions as she was about to die. Such signs are premonitions that sometimes come to a person before he dies.)

ii) How death is followed by entrance into the intermediate state

At the very moment that the "death state" is ending, a person is also entering the state in which one's form corresponds to the "antecedent state."[87]

[85] S: *marmacchedaḥ*, T: *gnad gcod pa*.

[86] T: *Chu bzang*. An area about five miles from Sera Monastery, where many retreat facilities are located.

[87] See the *Commentary to the Treasury of Higher Learning* (S: *Abhidharmakośabhāṣyam*) in explanation of ch. 3, vv. 10–13. Four states of existence are described there: (1) the intermediate state (S: *antarābhavaḥ*, T: *srid pa bar ma*), which is the five heaps of a person that exist following his death at the end of one life and before the moment of conception at the

This process is compared to the way one side of a scale falls at the same time that the other side rises. In the state immediately following death, one takes on a physical form that is similar to the type of being one is going to become in one's next life. Thus, "antecedent state" refers to the heaps of the life into which one is about to be reborn. The expression literally means the state of existence that is antecedent to the death state.

Some people who misunderstand this expression say that it means the recently deceased person who is in the intermediate state has the same form as he did in his previous life. They also suggest that they can pass messages to, and receive replies from, this being. But these are false claims made by charlatans.

(Kyabje Rinpoche then told us that although it is possible to see such figures, they are not the spirit of the departed person. They are actually demons [278b] who have taken on the form of the deceased person in order to deceive common persons. In connection with this, Kyabje Rinpoche related the story of how Jetsun Milarepa liberated a certain Bön householder who had recently died.[88])

An intermediate state being is born with all its sense faculties intact, possesses supernormal wisdom,[89] and is naturally endowed by karma with miraculous powers. Because of this, it is able to travel unimpeded almost anywhere except through holy places and the womb.

The bodies of intermediate state beings that are going to be born in the hells, as hungry ghosts, animals, or as humans and gods of the desire realm look like a charred stump, water, smoke, and pure gold, in that order. The body of an intermediate state being that is going to be born in the form realm is white in color. There is no intermediate state for beings that are reborn in the formless realm.

beginning of the next life, (2) the birth state (S: *upapattibhavaḥ*, T: *skye ba'i srid pa*), which is the five heaps at the moment of conception in a new life, (3) the antecedent state (S: *pūrvakālabhavaḥ*, T: *sngon dus kyi srid pa*), which is the five heaps from the first moment after conception until the last moment before death, and (4) the death state (S: *maraṇabhavaḥ*, T: *'chi ba'i srid pa*), which is the final moment of the five heaps at the end of a life.

[88]This account appears in the chapter titled "Aiding a Dead Man's Spirit with the Hook of Compassion and Placing Sister Peta on the Path to Enlightenment" (T: *gZhin don thugs rje'i lcags kyu dang sring mo pe ta byang chub la bkod pa*, Tib. edition pp. 583–591) from the *Hundred Thousand Songs of Milarepa* (T: *Mi la ras pa'i mgur 'bum*). In Garma C.C. Chang's translation, see vol. 2, ch. 54, "The Salvation of the Dead," pp. 615–623. In Bibliography, see listing under *gTsang smyon He ru ka*. A reference to this incident also appears in Part Two, Day Eleven, p. 172.

[89]S: *abhijñā*, T: *mngon par shes pa*. The main one possessed by an intermediate state being is the divine eye, which enables it to see great distances.

Intermediate state beings that committed nonvirtuous acts in their former lives look like the darkness of the night sky. Those who performed virtuous acts look like a white cloth or a moonlit sky at night.[90]

(Kyabje Pabongka Rinpoche concluded by saying that there are many explanations about the duration of an intermediate state being's lifespan. When it is said to last seven days, this is probably meant in the way time is measured in the realm in which that being will have its future life. If the intermediate state being is unable to find a place to take birth within seven days, it undergoes a small death.[91] These small deaths can be experienced as many as seven times.)

iii) How rebirth occurs at conception

This topic deals with the way a sentient being is conceived into the birth state, and the explanation given here refers specifically to birth from a womb.[92] First, the intermediate state being mistakenly perceives what is actually the semen and egg of its prospective parents as the parents-to-be themselves, engaging in sexual intercourse. Variously developing both desire and aversion, it races there only to find itself in the presence of what appears as either the male or female sexual organ. Angered by this, the intermediate state being dies and is conceived into the birth state.[93]

[90]The description in this paragraph appears in Asanga's *Levels of Yoga Practice* (S: *Yoga-ācārabhūmiḥ*), p. 19. It can be taken as a variation of what is said in the previous paragraph, which is based on a passage found in the sutra called *Teaching Nanda about Entry into the Womb*. Both accounts appear in Je Tsongkapa's *Great States of the Path* (T: *Lam rim chen mo*), p. 350 (f. 159b).

[91]That is, the intermediate state being dies and is reborn again, all within the intermediate state.

[92]As distinct from the descriptions for birth from an egg, birth from warmth and moisture (e.g., the birth of worms and insects), and miraculous birth (e.g., hell beings and some gods).

[93]This paragraph is an abbreviated version of the description found in Asanga's *Manifold Levels* (T: *Sa mang po pa*), vol. 48 (*tsi*), ff. 12a–12b. To help the reader better understand the instruction, we provide additional detail from that passage: Through the power of karma, an intermediate state being only perceives sentient beings of the same class as the one into which it is about to be reborn. Thus, it develops a desire to see and interact with such beings. This is what causes it to approach the place where it will take birth. As the intermediate state being draws near, it mistakenly perceives what is actually the semen and egg of a couple who engaged in sexual intercourse as the couple themselves. This perception causes the intermediate state being to become sexually aroused. If it is to be reborn as a female, it will generate desire to have intercourse with the male that it sees. If it is to be reborn as a male, it generates desire toward the female. As it approaches the pair, an intermediate state being that is to be born as a female wants the female figure to go away. Similarly, an intermediate state being that is to be born as a male wants the male figure to go away. Following this, the intermediate state being that is to be born as a female perceives itself alone with the male figure, and the one that is to be born as a male perceives itself alone with the female figure. Then, as it draws closer still, it

The above explanations complete the section of the outline called "Contemplating the origin of suffering and the process by which samsara is perpetuated," as taught in the *Middling Stages of the Path*,[94] the *Easy Path*, and the *Quick Path* [279a].

Contemplating the origin of suffering and how the process of samsara is set in motion according to the teaching on dependent origination

The *Great Stages of the Path* also presents instructions for contemplating the origin of suffering and how the process of samsara is set in motion based on the twelve-part teaching on dependent origination. I shall now explain these instructions as they are presented in *Mañjughosha's Oral Instruction*.

If I were following the structure of my own outline for a Lamrim teaching,[95] the above instructions would suffice as a short presentation of the topic entitled "Contemplating the origin of suffering and how the process of samsara is set in motion." However, for some individuals—particularly those who have studied Buddhist philosophy—it is also beneficial to contemplate this topic from the perspective of the teaching on dependent origination.

(Then Kyabje Rinpoche told us how, at the direction of the Master, a king from Magadha sent a painting depicting the Wheel of Life to a king named Rudrayana who lived in a remote land.[96] The painting was offered in response to an earlier gift that King Rudrayana had made to the king from Magadha. After examining this painting, King Rudrayana developed aversion for samsara.

Kyabje Rinpoche further mentioned that Geshe Puchungwa[97] trained his own mind using the teaching on dependent origination, and also used it to

perceives itself in the presence of just the male or female sexual organ. This angers the intermediate state being, causing it to die and immediately be reborn in the next life.

[94]T: *Lam rim 'bring*. This is an alternate name for Je Tsongkapa's *Shorter Stages of the Path* (T: *Lam rim chung ngu*).

[95]See Appendix G.

[96]The Wheel of Life (S: *bhavacakraḥ*, T: *srid pa'i 'khor lo*) is a drawing that depicts the Buddha's teaching on dependent origination. The story of how this drawing came into being is told in the "Rudrayana Narrative" chapter found in *Divine Narratives* (S: *Divyāvadānam*, ch. 37). The painting was sent by Buddha Shakyamuni's royal patron, King Bimbisara of Rajagirha. For the Tibetan version of the story, see *Expounding the Discipline* (T: *'Dul ba rnam par 'byed pa*), in *'Dul ba* section of Kg., vol. 8 (*nya*), ff. 147a–189b (section 70). An abridged English translation can be found in *King Udrayana and The Wheel of Life*, pp. 1–81. For this English version, see listing in Bibliography under Sermey Khensur Geshe Lobsang Tharchin.

[97]T: *dGe bshes Phu chung ba*, 1031–1107. Puchungwa Shönu Gyeltsen (T: *gZhon nu rgyal mtsan*), an early Kadampa master, was a disciple of Dromtönba for 11 years and a lineageholder

instruct his disciples in the stages of the path for persons of lesser and moderate capacities.)

The Twelve Limbs of Dependent Origination

Now I shall explain how to contemplate the origin of suffering and the disadvantages of samsara based on the Twelve Limbs of Dependent Origination. Among the various reasons for presenting this instruction, the main one is to enable the practitioner to develop strong aversion for samsara.

The Master taught this instruction in the *Rice Stalk Sutra*[98] with the passage that begins:

> [Dependent origination means:] When that is present, this comes about. Because that occurred, this arises. That is to say, the compositional factors are conditioned by ignorance . . .

The first limb: ignorance

The first of the twelve limbs of dependent origination is ignorance. This is the root cause of our wandering in samsara. Where wisdom apprehends that both the person and phenomena lack any substantiality, ignorance [279b] holds that they possess a self-existent nature and are, therefore, real. Thus, the term "ignorance" refers to the state of mind which apprehends objects in a manner that directly opposes the way transcendent wisdom apprehends them. It is a state of confusion like blindness.

There are two kinds of ignorance: ignorance about karma and its results, and ignorance about ultimate reality.

The second limb: compositional factors

Compositional factors are like the act of doing work. Motivated by ignorance, we perform the karma that creates the heaps of a future life. Thus, ignorance about karma and its results serves as the motivation for performing

of the Kadampa esoteric teachings known as the Sixteen Drops. See *Lives of the Lamrim Teachers* (T: *Lam rim bla ma brgyud pa'i rnam thar*), vol. 2, pp. 972–984.

[98]S: *Śālistambasūtram.* This is a principal Mahayana source for the doctrine of dependent origination. Its name derives from an incident described at the beginning of the scripture. Shariputra approached Maitreya and reported to him that the Buddha, after gazing at a rice stalk, had recently remarked: "O monks, whosoever sees dependent origination sees the dharma. And whosoever sees the dharma sees the Buddha." Shariputra then asked Maitreya to explain what the Buddha's statement meant. The remainder of the sutra consists of Maitreya's exposition on dependent origination.

nonmeritorious deeds. Similarly, ignorance about ultimate reality serves as the motivation for meritorious karma and invariable karma.[99]

The third limb: consciousness

There are two aspects of the consciousness limb: consciousness during the causal stage and consciousness during the result stage. The first is consciousness when it is marked by the traces of the deeds that make up the limb of compositional factors. The second is consciousness at the moment of conception when the birth state[100] has come into being.

For example, when a person is motivated by ignorance to take another being's life, an imprint or trace[101] of that deed is implanted in the mind at the very next instant after the one in which the karmic path is completed. A person's mind at the moment this imprint is established represents the causal stage of the limb of consciousness. When a person is later reborn in one of the hells through the power of that deed, the moment at which his consciousness is conceived into the birth state of a hell being represents the result stage of the limb of consciousness.

Every nonvirtuous deed has the ability to generate many rebirths in the lower states. By the same reasoning, a single meritorious deed or a single invariable deed can also generate many rebirths in the higher states [280a].

The way a karmic imprint taints or becomes fixed in the mind is similar to the way oil is absorbed into sand or a seal becomes fixed onto paper. If this imprint is later activated by the limbs of craving and grasping, its power to generate a result is awakened.

The fourth limb: name and form

In terms of a womb birth, the four heaps of feeling, conception, compositional factors, and consciousness are the name portion of this limb. After consciousness enters the mixture of sperm and egg, the physical component of the embryo goes through several stages of development, known as *kalalam*[102] and so on. This physical component is the form portion of the

[99] See earlier section called "How the mental afflictions cause us to accumulate karma," pp. 66–68 for a description of nonmeritorious, meritorious, and invariable karma.

[100] See above, note 87.

[101] S: *vasanā*, T: *bag chags*.

[102] *Kalalam* (T: *mer mer po*) is the name for a human fetus during the first week of gestation, during which it is the consistency of whey. See Day Fourteen, note 66, for a description of several other stages.

limb. This limb of dependent origination is also known as "the limb that, according to circumstances, is comprised of name and form."[103]

The fifth limb: the bases

This limb begins at the point when the six inner bases[104] of the eye, ear, nose, and tongue have formed, and lasts until just before the three elements of object, faculty, and consciousness converge, allowing the particular form of an object to be discerned. (Kyabje Rinpoche noted that the body sense faculties and the mind faculty already exist at the first stage of fetal development, called *kalalam*.)

In the case of spontaneous birth in either of the two lower realms, both the limb of name and form and the limb of the inner bases are achieved at the same time.[105]

For beings that are born in the formless realm, the fourth limb consists only of the name component. In addition, the limb of the inner bases consists only of the mind faculty. Thus, beings of the formless realm possess neither the form component in the fourth limb of dependent origination nor any of the five physical sense faculties that otherwise would be present in the fifth limb.

The sixth limb: contact

Once the inner bases have formed, the three elements of object, faculty, and consciousness are able to converge and make contact. This leads to the discernment of attractive, unattractive, or neutral objects, which marks the dependent origination limb called contact.

[103]The phrase "according to circumstances" (T: *ci rigs pa*) means that since a being born in the formless realm has no physical body, in that instance this limb would consist only of the name portion and would not include form.

[104]S: *āyatanam*, T: *skye mched*. The six inner bases (the five sense faculties and mind) and the six outer bases (the five sense objects and mental objects) are the main causes of the six consciousnesses. For example, eye consciousness arises in dependence on the inner basis of the eye and the outer basis of a visible object; ear consciousness arises in dependence on the inner basis of the ear and the outer basis of a sound, and so on.

[105]"Lower two realms" means the desire realm and the form realm. In spontaneous birth (S: *upapādukaḥ*, T: *brdzus te skye ba*; see also Day Fourteen, note 9), a being is born all at once—that is, with all his limbs and faculties intact and fully formed. As there is no fertilization of an egg in spontaneous birth, the being that is born in this manner does not proceed through stages of fetal development. This is why the limb of name and form and the limb of the bases both occur at the same time.

The seventh limb: feeling

Through the influence of contact, there arises, according to the particular circumstances, one of three types of feelings: pleasant, unpleasant, or neutral. For example, through making contact with an attractive object, [280b] there arises a pleasurable feeling.

The eighth limb: craving

In response to a pleasurable feeling, there arises the craving of not wanting to be separated from that sensation. In response to a painful feeling, there arises a craving for separation—that is, the desire to be separated from that painful sensation. In response to neutral feelings, there is a craving that wants to avoid having that sensation come to an end.

The statement that "craving arises through the conditional factor of sensation" should be understood to mean that craving is generated on the basis of feelings that are associated with ignorance. This is because, in the absence of ignorance, craving would not occur even when feelings are present.

The ninth limb: grasping

Grasping is the desire and attachment for objects that occurs when craving grows stronger. There are four kinds of grasping: (1) "grasping at objects of desire" is the attachment to sense objects; (2) "grasping at views" is the attachment to the inferior views other than the perishable-collection view; (3) "grasping at inferior conduct and asceticism" is the attachment to inappropriate moral practices that develop from inferior views and the attachment to inferior ascetic practices; and (4) "grasping at belief in the self" is the attachment to the belief that entities are truly existent and, in particular, attachment to the belief that the perishable collection of the heaps are associated with a real self.

The tenth limb: existence

Existence refers to a change in the karma that occurred in the limb of compositional factors. The karma of that limb leaves its imprint in a sentient being's consciousness. In the present limb, that imprint is activated by the limbs of craving and grasping, and acquires the power to produce the body of a future life.

The eleventh limb: birth

Birth is the first moment of conception, when a being's consciousness enters any one of the four birth states. It comes about on the basis of the karma that was imbued with the power to produce a future life when it was activated by the limbs of craving and grasping.

The twelfth limb: old age and death

After a sentient being is born, the two elements that make up the twelfth limb—old age and death—gradually appear. Old age is the process in which the heaps [281a] gradually change and mature. Death refers to the discarding or destruction of a related continuum of heaps.

A condensed classification of the twelve limbs

After clearly understanding the classification of dependent origination into twelve limbs as described above, we must learn the manner in which the limbs can be condensed into these four categories: (1) projecting limbs, (2) producing limbs, (3) projected limbs, and (4) produced limbs. The first two of these categories include the limbs that are causes and the latter two those that are results.

Projecting limbs

The projecting limbs are made up of the first two of the dependent origination limbs—that is, ignorance and compositional factors—as well as one aspect of the third limb—consciousness.

Of these, ignorance is like a person who plants seeds. Compositional factors—that is to say, the karma that is produced by ignorance—are like seeds.

The consciousness limb is made up of two aspects: consciousness when it is acting as a cause and consciousness when it is a result. The one that applies here is the causal stage of consciousness. This aspect of consciousness is like the act of planting seeds in the ground; that is, when a person accumulates karma, the imprint of those deeds becomes embedded in his mind.

Producing limbs

There are three producing limbs: craving, grasping, and existence. The two limbs of craving and grasping awaken a karmic imprint, imbuing it with the power to generate a result. Thus, they are like the act of nurturing a seed. Craving, in particular, is like the nurturing action of water and fertilizer, while grasping resembles that of warmth and moisture.

The limb of existence is karma that has been activated by craving and grasping, and thus is certain to bring forth the heaps of a particular being's next life. This condition is analogous to a seed that has been given the power to generate a sprout by the action of such factors as water, fertilizer, moisture, and warmth [281b].

Projected limbs

The projected limbs include four of the twelve dependent origination limbs, as well as one aspect of a fifth limb. They are name and form, the bases, contact, feeling, and the result stage of the consciousness limb. The result stage of the consciousness limb was explained earlier in the description of each of the twelve limbs.[106]

Produced limbs

The category of produced limbs consists of two of the twelve limbs of dependent origination. One is the dependent origination limb called birth, which is represented by the very first moment at which a being is conceived into a new life. It is also known as the birth state.[107] This is like the sprout that arises from a seed.

The other member of this category is the two aspects of the limb of dependent origination called old age and death.

The number of lives in which the twelve limbs occur

The number of lives in which a complete twelve-limb cycle of dependent origination occurs can be illustrated using several examples. The first is a situation in which a sentient being is reborn as a deity. Due to ignorance about the nature of ultimate truth, a being accumulates karma that will cause him to be reborn as a deity. More specifically, he accumulates the type of karma whose result will be experienced after having taken birth.[108] Once this deed has been accumulated, its trace or imprint becomes established in

[106]See above, p. 75.

[107]See note 87.

[108]S: *upapadyavedanīyam*, T: *skyes nas myong bar 'gyur ba*. One of three types of "definite" karma, it is the type that ripens in the very next lifetime. See also Part One, Day Six, note 4, and Part Two, Day Thirteen, p. 265.

his consciousness. His aspiration to be born as a deity, which he expresses through prayer and in other ways, represents the limb of craving. Continually generating this aspiration in an even stronger manner is the limb of grasping. The limb of existence occurs just before this being dies, when craving and grasping activate his former deed and turn it into a cause that is certain to bring about his rebirth as a deity.

In this example, all six causal limbs of dependent origination—that is, the three projecting limbs and the three producing limbs—are completed within this being's current lifetime. Similarly, all six result limbs of dependent origination are completed in his very next life, when he is reborn as a deity. Specifically, the six result limbs are the four projected limbs of name and form, bases, contact, and feeling, along with the two produced limbs of birth, and old age and death. Thus, here a twelve-limb cycle of dependent origination reached completion within a period of two lifetimes.

Now take a sentient being that is reborn in the lower states. This time, the sentient being is motivated by ignorance about karma and its effects, which leads him to accumulate a nonvirtuous deed. The remaining points from the previous example, such as how craving and grasping activate a deed and so on, should be understood as taking place in the same way here.

Thus, when examined in the context of a single deed, [282a] it is not possible for a complete cycle of dependent origination to occur within one lifetime. The shortest time period in which it can occur is two consecutive lifetimes.

On the other hand, if the process is prolonged because craving and grasping do not activate a deed within the same lifetime that it was performed, the cycle of twelve limbs will be completed within three lifetimes. That is, the three projecting limbs will occur in one life, the three producing limbs in a second life, and the four projected limbs together with the two produced limbs in a third life.

For example, suppose someone accumulated a nonvirtuous deed in his present life. Having done so, an imprint of that deed is deposited in his mind, which has the potential to cause him to be reborn in the lower states. But as he reaches the end of this life and is about to die, he generates a virtuous state of mind, either through the aid of a lama or by some other influence. This enables him to activate a deed that will cause him to be reborn as a human being. And so he does take birth as a human in his next life. At the end of this second life, however, the limbs of craving and grasping cause him to activate the nonvirtuous deed that he performed in his previous life. So this time he is reborn in the lower states.

It can also be understood from this example that many lifetimes can occur between the projecting and producing limbs associated with one particular cycle of dependent origination. Nevertheless, the intervening lives are not counted as part of that cycle, because they form part of their own cycles of dependent origination. Thus, the shortest period of time it can take to complete all the limbs in one cycle of dependent origination is two consecutive lifetimes. Likewise, the greatest number of lives it can take is three. In short, a full cycle can never occur more quickly than over the course of two lifetimes; nor can it ever take more than three lifetimes to complete.

So as each limb of dependent origination produces the one that follows it, we are forced to endure in an ever-repeating cycle all the suffering of birth, old age and death, and the rest. Moreover, as we experience the result stages of one particular deed's cycle of dependent origination, we also continue to generate a great variety of new deeds that represent the causal stages for still other cycles of dependent origination.

Each limb of old age and death arises from a related limb of birth that comes before it. Likewise, all the other intervening limbs follow the limbs that precede them. Ultimately, though, we come to a limb of compositional factors that is produced by a particular limb of ignorance [282b]. Thus, while the wheel of samsara is kept turning as each limb of the series continues to generate the next limb, the root cause of this process is ignorance alone.

Lord Nagarjuna declared:

> From the three, two arise. From the two
> There come seven; from the seven again
> Come the three. So does this very wheel
> Of existence turn round and round again.[109]

The three limbs that are mental afflictions cause the two limbs of karma to arise. The two limbs of karma, in turn, bring about the seven that represent suffering. Those seven limbs then bring about the three mental affliction limbs again, causing the cycle to be repeated. In this way, the wheel of existence turns endlessly, perpetuating the wheel of suffering as well.

On the other hand, by practicing the path that reverses and thus stops the cycle of dependent origination, we can put an end to all our suffering. This begins with the step that is described in these words: "By terminating ignorance, the compositional factors are terminated." The instruction continues with all the remaining limbs until it reaches the final step: "By terminating birth, old age and death are terminated."

In short, the Twelve Limbs of Dependent Origination can be classified into three categories: (1) karma, (2) mental afflictions, and (3) suffering. The

[109] *Verses on the Essence of Dependent Origination* (T: *rTen cing 'brel bar 'byung ba'i snying po'i tsig le'ur byas pa*), v. 3.

three limbs of ignorance, craving, and grasping are the mental afflictions. The two limbs of compositional factors and existence are forms of karma. And the seven remaining limbs are suffering. As Lord Nagarjuna declared:

> The first, eighth, and ninth are afflictions;
> The second and tenth are karma;
> The remaining seven are suffering . . .[110]

The three limbs mentioned in the first line identify our motivation. The two limbs in the second line stand for the physical and verbal deeds that we do. Similarly, the limbs mentioned in the third line represent the experiences that we undergo.

Conclusion

Contemplating the Twelve Limbs of Dependent Origination in both the forward and reverse order [283a] is one way to meditate on the general nature of suffering in samsara. Through this practice, we can generate the desire to be liberated from samsara, an attitude that is like a prisoner's desire to be liberated from prison. Gaining this desire marks the attainment of renunciation.

2) The actual explanation of the path that leads to liberation

Once we gain the desire to achieve liberation, we must train ourselves in the path that leads us there. This topic is made up of two sections: (1) the type of human form that we need to escape from samsara, and (2) the type of path that we must practice to escape from samsara.

a) The type of human form that we need to escape from samsara

After contemplating the disadvantages of samsara as described earlier, we should recognize that the essential characteristic of samsara—both the external world and the beings that inhabit it—is impermanence. Impermanence is the condition in which everything perishes immediately, without lasting more than an instant. All entities are like the moon's fluttering reflection on the surface of water that is being stirred by the wind.

Similarly, we should recognize that all the pleasures and wealth in samsara provide little benefit and are actually quite dangerous, like the shade cast by the hood of a cobra.

[110] Ibid., v. 2.

We should also realize that we will have to endure suffering incessantly no matter where we are born among the five classes of beings. Someone trapped in a burning house or an inmate living in a prison would view his condition with horror and loathing, and want desperately to gain his freedom. We must cultivate the desire to free ourselves from samsara until it has this kind of intensity and becomes an uncontrived spiritual realization.[111]

Once we have developed such a desire to achieve liberation, we should investigate what causes samsara. This will lead us to discover that it has two causes: karma and the mental afflictions. We will also learn that, of these two, the mental afflictions are the main cause, and that ignorance, in particular, is the root cause.

Then we must strive to practice the methods that destroy that root cause. We must also understand that the ideal time for turning back samsara is now, because we possess a [283b] human form endowed with all the attributes of leisure and fortune, and we have the opportunity to practice the three Buddhist trainings within the spiritually pure life of a monk or nun. As Potowa described, this very physical form is the one that surpasses all others:

> During all the time we have spent wandering in samsara in the past, it did not stop on its own. Nor will it stop on its own now. Therefore, we have to make it stop ourselves. And the time for doing so is now, when we have achieved the qualities of leisure and fortune.[112]

b) The type of path that must be practiced to escape from samsara

In order to eradicate the root of samsara, we must destroy the ignorance that is our lack of understanding about ultimate reality. The principal form of this ignorance is the innate belief that the self is real and exists independently. This belief is the true root of samsara; therefore, it is the entity we must completely eliminate. Although we may be able to temporarily weaken

[111]T: *blo bcos ma ma yin pa*. The practitioner's aim in meditating on all the Lamrim topics, from serving a spiritual teacher up to generating enlightenment mind, is to achieve uncontrived spiritual realizations through practicing analytic meditation. In this instance, the goal is to generate an uncontrived form of renunciation. See Part Two, Appendix F for a description of analytic meditation. Page 330, in particular, describes the three stages that a practitioner must go through before he can develop uncontrived spiritual realizations.

[112]Quoted by Je Rinpoche in the *Great Stages of the Path* (T: *Lam rim chen mo*), p. 375 (f. 172a). The original source for the passage is probably the *Commentary to the Blue Manual* (T: *Be'u bum sngon pa'i 'grel pa*), p. 199. In Bibliography, see listing under *lHa 'bri sgang pa*.

the mental afflictions through other antidotes, we will never be able to permanently destroy them if we fail to uproot this ignorance.

Only one mind can overcome the innate belief that the self is an independently real entity. No other virtuous mind has this power. It must be a mind that directly opposes the way the innate belief in a real self holds its object. Only the wisdom that realizes entities have no independent reality can realize that the self lacks any inherent essence. This wisdom apprehends the self in the exact opposite of the way that the belief in an inherently real self does. Therefore, we must gain the wisdom that realizes entities have no independent reality if we want to eradicate the innate belief in an independently real self. Without this wisdom, every other virtuous mind we try to develop will only support the belief that entities are self-existent. No other virtuous mind can counteract this erroneous belief.

In order to gain this wisdom correctly, we must develop the superior training of one-pointed concentration;[113] for the former cannot be gained without first developing the latter. For example [284a], to cut down a tree, we need both a sharp axe and a pair of firm shoulders to wield the axe. Without a sharp axe, we cannot cut into the tree's trunk. And without firm shoulders, we won't be able to make the axe strike the tree in the same spot. This point is also explained using the analogy of looking at wall paintings at night, for which one needs a lamp with a flame that is bright and not disturbed by the wind.

The wisdom that realizes the insubstantiality of entities is like a sharp axe, or like a bright lamp that illuminates the way things are. This very wisdom is what cuts the tree of believing in self-existence and enables us to see accurately the ultimate nature of things.

These two analogies also describe how we need to develop the steady one-pointed concentration that keeps the mind from experiencing even the slightest form of inner distraction. In the first analogy this concentration is like the pair of firm shoulders that are needed to wield the axe of wisdom. In the second analogy, concentration is compared to a lamp whose flame is not disturbed by the wind.

It is also true that in order to gain steady one-pointed concentration free of inner distractions we must develop the superior training of morality,[114] because that is what frees the mind from coarse outer distractions.

[113]S: *adhisamādhiśikṣā*, T: *lhag pa ting nge 'dzin gyi bslab pa*. Buddha taught three superior trainings: morality, concentration, and wisdom. They are superior in the sense of exceeding the trainings taught in other spiritual traditions.

[114]S: *adhiśīlaśikṣā*, T: *lhag pa tsul khrims kyi bslab pa*.

These points are succinctly stated in a verse that appears in the treatise called *Essential Nature of the Levels*.[115] The verse is one in a series that the Buddha utters in response to a question posed by Brahma. It says:

> He who has very firm roots
> Delights in calming the mind
> And will gain the view of the *aryas*
> While removing those of the unrefined.

The phrase "view of the *aryas*" refers to the insight[116] that realizes the true nature of all things is emptiness. This realization is the antidote to the false belief that entities are self-existent. To achieve this insight [284b], we must first achieve quiescence. But without cultivating the training of morality, we will lack a necessary cause for achieving quiescence.

The *Letter to a Friend* states:

> Even if your head or clothes suddenly
> Caught fire, you should forgo putting it out.
> Strive instead to terminate rebirth;
> There is no other more exalted goal.
>
> Through ethics, wisdom, and concentration
> You must achieve nirvana—the stainless, peaceful,
> And subdued state; ageless, deathless, endless;
> Beyond earth, water, fire, air, the sun and moon.[117]

As these lines indicate, the main practice for a person of moderate capacity is the three superior trainings. If I were not going to present the instructions that relate to a person of great capacity, it would be proper to explain all three of the trainings at this point in the teachings. However, what I am teaching here is the method of leading disciples on the path that is held in common with persons of moderate capacity, not the actual path for persons

[115] S: *Bhūmivastu*, T: *Sa'i dngos gzhi*. The eleventh section of Arya Asanga's *Levels of Yoga Practice* (S: *Yogacārabhūmiḥ*), entitled the "Level of practice that derives from contemplation" (S: *cintāmayībhūmiḥ*, T: *bsam pa las byung ba'i sa*), is made up of three parts, each one comprising a set of verses or canonical material that is accompanied by prose commentary. The middle portion, called "Verses on the intended meaning" (S: *ābhiprāyika-arthagāthā*, T: *dgongs pa'i don gyi tsigs su bcad pa*), consists of 51 verses covering a variety of points that relate to the three Buddhist trainings. The verse cited here is number four.

[116] S: *vipaśyanā*, T: *lhag mthong*. See Day Twenty-two.

[117] T: *bShes pa'i spring yig*, vv. 104–105.

of moderate capacity.[118] And since the two trainings of concentration and wisdom will be explained during the topics of quiescence and insight[119] as part of the teachings for persons of great capacity, it is customary for the instructions that are presented here to emphasize the training of morality.

The *Letter to a Friend* states:

> Morality was declared the foundation of all virtue,
> Like the earth that supports all things moving and
> unmoving.[120]

Since morality is the foundation of all virtue, it is very important that we maintain a pure moral practice. In fact, morality is the very root of the Buddha's teaching and we will receive many benefits by practicing it well. But we will also suffer terrible consequences if we fail to practice it well [285a].

As relates to the benefits of practicing morality, we should understand that the very existence of the Buddha's teaching depends on whether or not the Pratimoksha[121] system of morality is being maintained. The teaching can only be said to exist in that place where there are *bhikshus*[122] who are upholding the Vinaya code. This is true even if Bodhisattvas who practice tantra live in that area.

The *Aphorisms on Individual Liberation* states:

> When I have entered nirvana,
> This will be your teacher.[123]

Thus, since the moral practice that you develop in your mind should be regarded as a substitute for the Master himself, you should both cherish it and guard it well.

Of the three trainings, it is particularly difficult for us to practice the trainings of concentration and wisdom right away, because we are beginning practitioners. But the morality of the Pratimoksha system is a form of the

[118]This distinction is explained in Part Two, Day Ten, pp. 98–100.

[119]These two topics are taught in Days Twenty-one through Twenty-three.

[120]T: *bShes pa'i spring yig*, v. 7.

[121]T: *so sor thar pa*. This system of moral practice is taught in the Listeners' vehicle. It includes several levels of vows for monks and nuns, as well as precepts for laypeople. Mahayana practitioners who have taken the Bodhisattva vows are also encouraged to keep some form of these vows.

[122]T: *dge slong*. That is, fully ordained Buddhist monks.

[123]S: *Prātimokṣasūtram*. f. 2a. "This" refers to the Vinaya teachings.

cognitional teaching[124] that we can definitely practice and develop in our mind right now. This is why the existence of the Buddha's teaching is said to depend on the sangha. The Pratimoksha also serves as the foundation or "vessel" in which the two higher systems of vows[125] are kept.

The act of preserving the teaching doesn't only mean to expound the dharma while seated on a teaching throne. We are also preserving the teaching when we keep our vows properly. When we listen to and contemplate the scriptural dharma, we are preserving the scriptural teaching. And when we keep pure the morality we have agreed to keep, we are preserving the realized teaching. Moreover, of the three classes of vows, it is the Pratimoksha vows that we can be most confident of practicing well.

A line from a sutra declares that "a moral [285b] *bhikshu* is radiant."[126] Another scripture gives a similar description of the extraordinary qualities of being a monk:

> Wherever there are *bhikshus* who uphold the Vinaya, that place is radiant and filled with light. It should be viewed as a place where I am not absent. It is a place about which I feel no need to be concerned.[127]

Here in the snowy land of Tibet there is one thing we possess that other countries do not. Yet this one thing is the only true root of well-being and happiness, both short term and long. It is the teaching of the Buddha.

Religious buildings, a large following, or bright temple decorations are not what determine whether the Buddha's teaching is flourishing in a particular region or not. The sole determining factor is the presence of the root of the teaching—the Pratimoksha system of morality.

If an individual monk cannot keep the Pratimoksha vows purely and allows the training of morality to disappear from his own mind, then no matter how widely the teaching is flourishing in the world, that monk's personal teaching has disappeared.[128]

A person can derive more benefit by cultivating morality during a degenerate age than he does by worshipping all the Buddhas of the three times

[124] S: *adhigamadharmaḥ*, T: *rtogs pa'i chos*. See Part One, Day Three, pp. 70–71, and Part Two, Day Twelve, p. 203 for an explanation of this term.

[125] That is, the Bodhisattva vows and the tantric vows.

[126] *The Sutra on Well-Maintained Morality* (T: *Tsul khrims yang dag par ldan pa'i mdo*), in *mDo mang* section of Kg., vol 26 (*la*), f. 196b.

[127] We were not able to identify the source of this passage.

[128] See Part Two, Day Nine, p. 78 for a similar reference to the idea of the "disappearance of an individual's personal teaching" (T: *bstan pa sgos nub tu song ba*).

during the six periods of the day and night. This point is made in the *King of Concentrations Sutra*:

> A person of pure mind may honor countless myriads
> Of Buddhas with food, drink, parasols, banners,
> And garlands of lights for as many tens of millions
> Of kalpas as there are grains of sand in the Ganges.
>
> Yet one can gain much greater virtue than this
> By practicing a single precept day and night,
> At a time when the holy dharma is in decline
> And the Sugata's teaching is reaching an end [286a].[129]

The scriptures also declare that more benefit is gained by practicing morality for a single day in this world during the time of the Buddha Shakyamuni's teaching than by practicing morality for an entire kalpa in the Buddha Rajeshvara's divine realm, which lies in a northeasterly direction. They further state that more benefit is gained by keeping a single precept of moral practice during these times than by keeping all the precepts during the early period of a kalpa. In short, it is greater virtue to practice morality than to worship many Buddhas for tens of millions of kalpas.

Another scripture declares that "a person who possesses morality will meet with a Buddha at a time when he appears."[130]

We should not view our twice monthly recitation[131] merely as an examination to see if the leader can recite the sutra from memory, nor as an exercise to recite the precepts. The purpose of this ritual is to remind monks and nuns about their vows. Therefore, all of you should reflect on the meaning of the words recited during the ceremony and practice carefully, so that you will stay within the boundaries of the precepts you have taken.

The words from one of our prayers says: [May the virtue I have accumulated here . . .] "long bring glory to the essence of [Venerable Lord Losang Drakpa's] teaching."[132] Another has this refrain: "May the Conqueror

[129] S: *Samādhirājasūtram*, ch. 35, vv. 3–4. These verses are also cited in Je Tsongkapa's *Great Stages of the Path* (T: *Lam rim chen mo*), p. 388 (f. 177b).

[130] *The Sutra on Well-Maintained Morality* (T: *Tsul khrims yang dag par ldan pa'i mdo*), f. 196b.

[131] This is a reference to the sangha's twice-a-month confession ritual (S: *poṣadhaḥ*, T: *gso sbyong*).

[132] This is from the *Hundred Deities of Tuṣita* prayer (T: *dGa' ldan lha brgya ma*). The complete verse states: "May the virtue I have accumulated here/ Greatly benefit the teaching

Losang's teaching continue to flourish."[133] But first of all we should make the essence of this teaching flourish in our own mind.

As to the disadvantages of not cultivating morality, a verse from the *Sutra of What a Monk Should Hold Dear* declares:

> Some people's morality brings happiness;
> Some people's morality brings suffering.
> He who is moral is happy;
> He who is immoral suffers.[134]

The following passage from the *Sutra on Well-Maintained Morality* also describes how we will have to experience suffering for many hundreds of thousands of lives if we fail to cultivate morality:

> O monks, it would be better for you to lose your lives and perish than to let your morality [286b] degenerate and be destroyed. Why? Losing your life and perishing only brings your present existence to an end. But if you allow your morality to degenerate and be destroyed, you will have to experience the great misfortune of losing your spiritual lineage and giving up happiness for ten million lives.[135]

Several verses from *Expounding the Discipline* also declare:

> One who takes lightly and transgresses even slightly
> The teaching of the compassionate Master
> Will be subjected to suffering because of that,
> Just as cutting a reed thicket damages a mango grove.
>
> In this world a person can sometimes violate
> The king's great edict and not receive any punishment.
> But a person who transgresses the Sage's word
> Will be born as an animal, like the *naga* Elapatra.[136]

[133]This refrain appears in the last line of every verse from the prayer called the *Teaching of the Conqueror Losang* (T: *Blo bzang rgyal bstan ma*). In Bibliography, see listing under *dKon mchog bstan pa'i sgron me*.

[134]T: *dGe slong la rab tu gces pa'i mdo*, in *mDo mang* section of Kg., vol 26 (*la*), f. 195a.

[135]T: *Tsul khrims yang dag par ldan pa'i mdo*, ff. 196a–196b.

[136]T: *'Dul ba rnam par 'byed pa*. These lines appear in the opening verses of the text.

In this world, when a person violates the word of a great and powerful king, sometimes he is punished and sometimes he escapes punishment. But a person who transgresses the precepts established by the compassionate Master will always have to face retribution. (Kyabje Rinpoche then told us the story of the *naga* Elapatra.[137])

The infraction that caused the monk to be reborn as the *naga* Elapatra was simply that he showed disregard for a precept of the *payantika* class.[138] And since we monks show disregard for many of the more serious precepts—such as those in the *parajika*, *samgha avashesha*, and the *sthula* classes of vows—what kind of being are we likely to end up as in our next life [287a]?

We might not be able to practice in any extensive way those other teachings that are considered so profound and powerful; but by properly observing our vows of a novice or a fully ordained monk,[139] we will be carrying out the very practice that qualifies us to be recognized as members of the sangha.[140] This is also what it means to be preserving or maintaining the teaching.

Leaving aside the advantages of keeping the vows of a novice or fully ordained monk, the Vinaya scriptures, the *Sutra of the Wise and the Foolish*, as well as other texts, record incidents from the past that show how even

[137]See *Expounding the Discipline* (T: *'dul ba rnam par 'byed pa*), in *'Dul ba* section of Kg., Vol. 10 (*tha*), ff. 418a–427b (end of section 24). The *naga* Elapatra had been a monk in a previous life, during the time of Buddha Kashyapa. This monk was a meditator who lived in a cave. Whenever he left the cave, he would brush his head against a branch that hung down in his path. Irritated by this, one day he cut down the branch. As he did so, the monk disdainfully questioned the Buddha's precept against cutting the limbs of trees. This act caused him to be reborn as a repulsive-looking *naga* who had growths on each of his seven heads in the shape of the tree from which he had previously cut a branch.

[138]T: *ltung byed 'ba' zhig*. A group of vows that relates to 90 infractions.

[139]A novice monk (S: *śramaneraḥ*, T: *dge tsul*) observes only 10 precepts; a fully ordained monk (S: *bhikṣuḥ*, T: *dge slong*) observes 253.

[140]The term *sangha* (S: *saṁghaḥ*, T: *dge 'dun*) is generally understood to mean the religious community of Buddhist monks and nuns. In the case of ordinary persons—that is, non-*aryas*—the sangha consists of any group of at least four morally upstanding, fully ordained monks. The *arya* sangha is anyone, whether a single person or group of people, who has achieved a direct realization of emptiness. In the case of the Listeners' and the Solitary Realizers' vehicles, this would be any follower who achieved any of the four fruits of the path (See Part One, Day Four, note 10). In the case of the Mahayana Sutrayana tradition, it would be any Bodhisattva *arya* who has achieved any of the ten Bodhisattva levels. And in the case of the Tantrayana, it would be all the *dakas*, *dakinis*, and dharma protectors who have achieved a direct realization of emptiness. The term *gendün* (T: *dge 'dun*), which is the Tibetan equivalent for sangha, is also given the following literal interpretation: The syllable *ge* (T: *dge*) refers to the ultimate virtue (T: *dge ba*) of nirvana, and the syllable *dün* (T: *'dun*) refers to the aspiration or desire (T: *'dun pa*) to achieve that goal. Thus, *gendün* or sangha is the community of ordained Buddhist followers who are intent upon achieving the ultimate virtue of nirvana.

householders can derive great benefit through keeping such precepts as those of the *upavasa* vow,[141] which is observed for only twenty-four hours. So those of you who are householders should make every effort to observe as carefully as possible either the *upavasa* or the *upasaka*[142] vows. The latter vow, in particular, can be taken in several forms, including keeping four, three or even just one precept.[143]

In addition to householders, monks and nuns should also take the Mahayana *poshadha* vow[144] and keep it as carefully as possible. Among the

[141]T: *bsnyen gnas kyi sdom pa*. A twenty-four-hour vow in which the practitioner abstains from these eight activities: (1) killing; (2) stealing; (3) having sexual intercourse; (4) lying; (5) drinking alcohol; (6) wearing perfumes, garlands, or ointments; as well as dancing, singing, or playing music; (7) sitting on a high seat; and (8) eating food after the noon hour. See also Part Two, Day Thirteen, note 76.

[142]T: *dge bsnyen gyi sdom pa*. The most common form of the *upasaka* vow requires abandoning these five activities for life: (1) killing, (2) stealing, (3) sexual misconduct, (4) lying, and (5) drinking alcohol.

[143]Six levels of the *upasaka* vow are recognized: (1) *upasaka* who practices one precept (e.g., abandoning killing), (2) *upasaka* who practices several precepts (e.g., the two precepts of abandoning killing and stealing), (3) *upasaka* who practices most of the precepts (i.e., either three or four of the five precepts mentioned in the previous note), (4) *upasaka* who practices all the precepts (i.e., all five precepts), (5) *upasaka* who practices celibacy (i.e., while practicing all five precepts, observing complete celibacy instead of just abandoning sexual misconduct), and (6) *gomi upasaka* (i.e., a person who keeps the eight *upavasa* precepts for life).

[144]T: *teg chen gso sbyong*. This vow is similar to the *upavasa* vow of the Pratimoksha system in that both practices involve keeping the same eight precepts for one full day. There are, however, a number of significant differences: (1) The *upavasa* vow can be received from anyone who posseses the *upasaka* vow or higher. The Mahayana *poshadha* vow (known more widely by the Tibetan name for the vow: *tekchen sojong*) must be received from a person who possesses the Mahayana vows, or a practitioner can take it by himself in front of a Buddha image and other objects representing the Triple Gem. (2) Monks and nuns may not take the *upavasa* vow, for it would cause them to lose their life-long vows if they accepted a vow that lasts only one day. However, monks and nuns may take the Mahayana *poshadha* vow, because of the unique Mahayana qualities that distinguish it from their Pratimoksha vows. (3) The motivation for taking the *upavasa* vow is the desire to attain liberation from samsara. The motivation for taking the Mahayana *poshadha* vow is at least a contrived form of enlightenment mind. (4) The ritual for the *upavasa* vow, which is based on the Vinaya scriptures, begins with taking refuge and then a repetition three times of the pledge to observe the eight precepts. The wording of the Mahayana *poshadha* ritual mentions how the Buddha practiced when he was still on the path. Then the practitioner agrees to keep the eight precepts as an act that is modeled on the Buddha's own spiritual practice. Moreover, he asserts that he does so with the aim of achieving complete enlightenment. (5) The Mahayana *poshadha* vow requires the practitioner to abandon eating meat for one day; the *upavasa* vow does not. (6) The result of the *upavasa* vow will vary depending upon the motivation with which it is taken. If taken with a motivation based on the Hinayana vehicle, it will bring the result of the Hinayana path. If taken with a Mahayana motivation, it can bring the result of the Mahayana path. However, the Mahayana *poshadha* vow will definitely bring the result of ultimate enlightenment, as long as the practitioner does not lose his motivation to achieve enlightenment. These points are mentioned in a work entitled the *Staircase Leading up to the Palace of Great Enlightenment: A*

reasons for its great value is the fact that this practice only needs to be observed for twenty-four hours, and therefore we should be able to keep it purely.

We often talk as though we know all about the three trainings, even though we haven't been able to practice even a shadow of the latter two trainings. On the other hand, since we can actually practice morality by keeping the Pratimoksha vows, this is the training that we should try hardest to cultivate. Moreover, in order to practice this training successfully, we must close the "doors" that cause us to commit moral transgressions.

There are four such doors, of which the first is lack of knowledge about the precepts. Lack of knowledge is a door that leads to moral transgressions because by not knowing what precepts we are supposed to keep, we won't know whether we have violated them or not. The method of closing this door is [287b] to learn about the precepts to the best of our abilities, through studying the major works on the Vinaya teachings, condensed explanations of the precepts, concise instructions on the three fundamental Vinaya practices,[145] or the summaries of the topics that appear at the end of each section in the Vinaya scriptures. At the very least, we should be able to name all the precepts we are required to keep.

Disrespect is a second door that leads to moral transgressions. Therefore, we must show respect toward the Master, toward the moral rules he established, and toward our companions who are pursuing a spiritual way of life. We must especially revere the morality training we have developed in our own mind and regard it as though it were the Master himself. We must never treat the Pratimoksha discipline as unimportant; indeed, after the passing of the Master, it stands as a substitute for him.

To have strong mental afflictions is a third door that leads to moral transgressions. A person who has a strong tendency to develop any of the mental afflictions is more likely to commit moral transgressions. Therefore, we should identify which of our mental afflictions stands out above the rest and then cultivate its antidote. For example, if we want to overcome an enemy in battle, we would first try to defeat the strongest members of the opposing force—such as the bravest fighters or the main leader.

Concisely Worded Ritual for Taking the Mahayana Poshadha Vow (T: *Theg chen gso sbyong gi sdom pa len pa'i cho ga nag 'gros su bkod pa byang chen khang bzang 'dzegs pa'i them skas*), which was composed by Yongzin Trijang Rinpoche (T: *Yongs 'dzin khri byang rin po che*), one of Kyabje Pabongka Rinpoche's main disciples. In Bibliography, see listing under his ordination name *Blo bzang ye shes bstan 'dzin rgya mtso*.

[145]T: *gzhi gsum bslab bya*. The three fundamental practices of monks and nuns are: (1) observing the twice-a-month confession ritual (S: *poṣadhaḥ*, T: *gso sbyong*), (2) staying in retreat during the rainy season (S: *varṣavāsana*, T: *dbyar gnas*), and (3) the ritual for terminating the rainy-season retreat (S: *pravāraṇaḥ*, T: *dgag dbye*).

Persons with strong desire should meditate on the ugliness of the physical body. This includes reflecting on the body as a bag of filth, and contemplating such images as a blood-splattered corpse, a swollen corpse, a worm-infested corpse, a corpse that is nothing but bones, and so on.[146]

The antidote for hatred is to meditate on loving-kindness.

The antidotes for pride are to reflect on sickness, old age, and death; on the samsaric defects of being uncertain and of having to fall from a high position to a low one again and again, and so on;[147] as well as on [288a] the diversity of the constituents.[148] The latter practice, in particular, consists of meditating on such topics as the heaps, the constituents, the bases, the faculties, and the various sensations of the body. This brings the realization that since we don't know even a small portion of all the entities that make up our own individual existence, we must know even less about the things that lie beyond ourselves.

The antidote for ignorance is to meditate on dependent origination. Finally, the general antidote for all the mental afflictions is to meditate on the correct view about the nature of emptiness.

Lack of mindfulness[149] is the fourth door that leads to transgressions. Therefore, in all our activities of walking, standing, lying down, sitting, eating, drinking, and so on, we must cultivate the recollection[150] that enables us to remain aware of the correct practices we should be trying to pursue and the improper activities we should be trying to abandon. In addition to this, we must continually examine our three doorways[151] to determine whether or not we have become tainted by any transgression. This is the method of closing the doors that produce moral transgressions.

[146]See above notes 21–23.

[147]These samsaric defects are described in Day Fourteen.

[148]S: *dhātuprabhedaḥ*, T: *khams kyi rab tu dbye ba*. See note 30 above.

[149]S: *pramādaḥ*, T: *bag med pa*. Lack of mindfulness is the mental state in which a person fails to guard his mind from desire, hatred, ignorance, and laziness, and fails to cultivate the virtuous states that constitute their antidotes. It serves as a support for the increase of nonvirtue and the decline of virtue.

[150]S: *smṛtiḥ*, T: *dran pa*. Recollection is the mental state that does not allow the attention to be drawn away from an object that has been previously experienced. Its function is to prevent one from being distracted.

[151]Body, speech, and mind are the three means of performing deeds.

If we inadvertently become tainted by any transgressions despite having tried to practice recollection, vigilance,[152] and a sense of shame[153] and modesty,[154] we should attend regularly the monks' semimonthly *poshadha* ritual and confess them there.

Certain Vinaya scriptures state that we must atone for such transgressions as those of the *sangha avashesha* class by observing the three disciplinary acts of abiding in probation,[155] paying homage to the sangha,[156] and being released from penance.[157] However, according to the tradition established by Gyelwa Ensaba[158] and his followers, a monk can completely purify himself of the *sangha avashesha* transgressions, as well as all those violations that are less severe, through regretting the wrongdoing he committed and strongly resolving not to commit them again.

[152]S: *saṃprajanyam*, T: *shes bzhin*. The mental state in which one examines and maintains a constant awareness of one's activities of body, speech, and mind. See also Part Two, Day Nine, pp. 69–71.

[153]S: *hrīḥ*, T: *ngo tsa shes pa*. Moral shame is defined as the feeling of embarrassment and apprehension about engaging in wrongdoing for reasons that relate to oneself or the dharma. An example of a reason relating to oneself would be when a person thinks, "I am trying to follow a high moral standard and I know that it's wrong to commit bad deeds. Therefore, I cannot let myself do such an act." An example of a reason relating to the dharma would be when a person has misgivings about doing a bad deed because he fears it will bring an unfavorable karmic consequence, or because he recognizes that it will bring harm to another person. The function of this mental state is to provide support for restraining oneself from committing bad deeds.

[154]S: *apatrāpyam*, T: *khrel yod pa*. Modesty is defined as the feeling of embarrassment or apprehension about engaging in wrongdoing for reasons that relate to others. An example of a reason relating to others would be when a person recognizes that a particular act is viewed as reprehensible by society at large, and fears the reproach of others if they should learn that he had committed such an act. Like the sense of shame, the function of modesty is also to provide support for restraining oneself from committing bad deeds.

[155]S: *parivāsaḥ*, T: *spo ba*. An act of contrition observed in varying degrees of severity that requires the transgressor monk to vacate a position of honor and occupy a lowly position.

[156]S: *mānāpyam*, T: *mgu bar bya ba*. A disciplinary action in which the transgressor monk must pay homage to the sangha by performing various acts, such as sitting in less honored positions, sweeping, and the like.

[157]S: *āvarhaṇam*, T: *dbyung ba*. A formal rite in which the transgressor is reinstated to a position of good standing after having completed his penance.

[158]T: *dBen sa pa*, 1505–1566. Known as Gyelwa Ensaba—the Conqueror Ensaba—his ordination name was Losang Döndrup (T: *Blo bzang don grub*). An extraordinary yogi of the Gelukpa tradition who is recognized as having achieved the ultimate goal of complete enlightenment during his lifetime. Although not usually counted as one of the Panchen Lamas, he is identified as having been the previous incarnation of Losang Chökyi Gyeltsen, the figure most often referred to as the First Panchen Lama. See *Lives of the Lamrim Teachers* (T: *Lam rim bla ma brgyud pa'i rnam thar*), vol. 2, pp. 2–57. In Bibliography, see listing under (*Tse mchog gling Yongs 'dzin*) *Ye shes rgyal mtsan*.

We present-day monks cannot practice morality the way the incomparable Atisha and the great Jamgön Tsongkapa and his spiritual sons did. That is to say, we cannot keep each and every one of our vows so carefully that we never become tainted by even a minor transgression. We must, however, guard against the four root transgressions[159] as well as drinking alcohol, [288b] and we must do so with such conviction that we would sacrifice our lives rather than commit any of them.

The Pratimoksha vows are taken in the presence of a preceptor, an instructor, and several members of the sangha.[160] So when a monk confesses an act that is both a bad deed[161] and a violation of one of his precepts, he must do so before members of the sangha. While he may be able to purify himself of a bad deed by confessing it in private when he is alone, this type of purification does nothing to expiate the karmic obstacle caused by having violated a precept.

Among the transgressions, it is wrong to have little concern when we are unable to follow all the rules that relate to such minor precepts as accepting water [to rinse the mouth after eating], taking off our shoes [before entering a temple or sitting on a mat], or wearing clothing with sleeves. Leaving aside the categories of expulsory offenses and *sangha avashesha* precepts, we set a bad example that greatly harms the teaching when we fail to observe such minor precepts as the ones just mentioned. We should also make every effort to do such practices as the sanctioning rituals that relate to the precepts of the *naisargika payatika* class.

In the everyday world, we must gather together many things—such as butter, salt, meat, and so forth—just to prepare tea or a noontime meal. Similarly, if we want to achieve a favorable physical form in our future lives, we cannot practice only a portion of the necessary factors such as observing morality, cultivating generosity, and the like. Therefore, in addition to maintaining a pure moral practice, monks and nuns must also cultivate generosity and other related practices to the best of their abilities.[162]

[159]These are also known as the four expulsory offenses (S: *pārājikaḥ*, T: *phas pham pa*): (1) killing a human being, (2) stealing, (3) having sexual intercourse, and (4) professing superhuman powers.

[160]Preceptor (S: *upadhyāyaḥ*, T: *mkhan po*) and instructor (*ācāryaḥ*, T: *slob dpon*) are the two main functionaries who preside over a monk's full ordination.

[161]S: *pāpam*, T: *sdig pa*. "Bad deed" here is meant in the sense of an act that is innately wrong (S: *prakṛtisāvadyam*, T: *rang bzhin gyi kha na ma tho ba*), as distinct from an act that is wrong in the sense of having been prohibited by the Buddha (S: *pratikṣepanasāvadyam*, T: *bcas pa'i kha na ma tho ba*). Many of the monks' precepts contain both elements, while others—such as eating food after midday—are moral transgressions in that they violate rules that the Buddha established. See also Part Two, Day Thirteen pp. 261–262 for a discussion that relates to this distinction.

[162]See Part Two, Day Nine, pp. 85–87, and Day Thirteen, pp. 267–270.

Some people view the Pratimoksha Vinaya as a form of practice best suited for those of dull faculties. They believe that practitioners of the highest abilities and sharpest faculties don't need to follow such a restrictive code of conduct. Instead, they may pursue the swift path of the secret mantra tradition, which transforms the three poisons into elements of the path [289a].[163] In effect, they are espousing the kind of wanton behavior that has no regard whatsoever for the training of Pratimoksha morality. But a tantric practitioner who has taken the Pratimoksha vows must observe the precepts carefully. This is supported by a passage from the *Tantra of Questions Posed by Subahu*:

> Except for the outer signs[164] and rituals, the householder
> Who practices mantra should also practice purely
> All the remaining elements of the Pratimoksha morality
> Which I, the Conqueror, have taught in the Vinaya.

The *Mañjushri Root Tantra* also declares:

> The Lord of Sages did not say that an immoral person
> Would achieve the attainments of the mantra teaching,
> Or that he would even travel in the direction
> Of the path that leads to the city of Nirvana.
>
> How could such a low and foolish person
> Ever achieve the goal of the mantras?
> How could such an immoral person
> Ever reach a happy state in the future?
>
> If he cannot reach either the higher states
> Or the status of transcendent happiness,
> How much less could he achieve the goal
> Of the mantras taught by the Conqueror.[165]

(Kyabje Rinpoche then described how some persons spend their whole lives trying to meditate on the mind's essence, without first having developed any renunciation, enlightenment mind, or correct view. His point was that such efforts will not produce anything of real value. In connection with

[163]T: *dug gsum*. The expression "three poisons" refers to the three mental afflictions of desire, hatred, and ignorance.

[164]That is, the wearing of a monk's or nun's robes.

[165]S: *Mañjuśrīmūlakalpaḥ*, ch. 11, vv. 86–88.

several further comments, he noted that the most that kind of practice could accomplish would be to accumulate invariable karma.[166] Then, after reviewing all the material covered during the day, he concluded the discourse.)

[166]Invariable karma could not bring any higher result than rebirth in the form or the formless realms. This point is also made above on pp. 67–68.

DAY SIXTEEN:
THE BENEFITS OF ENLIGHTENMENT MIND

(As is customary, the day began with a recitation of relevant passages from the texts on which this teaching is based.[1] Following this, Kyabje Rinpoche explained the introductory topic of how to correct one's motivation. As part of this discussion, he quoted the verse by the great dharma king Je Tsongkapa, which begins: "Moreover, if that renunciation is unsupported/ By true enlightenment mind . . . ,"[2] to point out the need for developing enlightenment mind in addition to renunciation [289b]. Then, after noting the list of topics that he had already covered in previous days, Kyabje Rinpoche went over all the material that forms the section of the outline called: "Establishing the nature of the path that leads to liberation."[3]

Among the main points covered in this review were these: Karma is the force that causes us to wander continuously in samsara. Karma itself is produced by the mental afflictions. Among the mental afflictions, the root cause of karma is ignorance. In order to eradicate ignorance, we must develop the training of superior wisdom. However, because we must complete the trainings of morality and concentration before we can develop wisdom, morality should be regarded as the foundation of all spiritual knowledge. When we are cultivating the antidotes to the mental afflictions, we should begin by generating each mental affliction. Then, after we have identified the nature of each mental affliction, we can start cultivating its antidote. This method enables us to recognize, even when we have become distracted, that we have generated a particular mental affliction.)

c. Training the mind in the levels of the path that relate to persons of great capacity

This portion of the teaching is made up of three sections: (1) establishing that enlightenment mind is the sole means of entering the Mahayana path, along with a presentation of its benefits; (2) how to generate enlightenment

[1]T: *rtzis bzhag gnang*. In this practice, the teacher recites from memory passages from the topic that is about to be taught, after which the listeners repeat, also from memory, those passages that were just recited.

[2]*Three Principal Elements of the Path* (T: *Lam gyi gtzo bo rnam gsum*), v. 6. The entire verse states: "Moreover, if that renunciation is unsupported/ By true enlightenment mind, it will not serve as a cause/ For attaining the perfect happiness of unsurpassed enlightenment./ Therefore, discerning ones should generate supreme enlightenment mind." In Bibliography, see listing under *(rJe) Tzong kha pa*.

[3]This is the subject that was taught during Day Fifteen.

mind; and (3) how to train oneself in the Bodhisattva practices once enlightenment mind has been generated.

i. Establishing that enlightenment mind is the sole means of entering the Mahayana path, along with a presentation of its benefits

Motivated by the attitude of renunciation, as explained in the teachings that relate to persons of lesser and moderate capacities, a practitioner can achieve the limited goal of escaping from samsara and attaining his own liberation through practicing the three superior trainings. However, we should not be satisfied with achieving this result, because it does not represent the elimination of all the objects that must be abandoned nor the attainment of all the spiritual knowledge that must be achieved. Since it brings only a partial fulfillment of our own and others' interests,[4] [290a] we would have to go back and start at the beginning of the Mahayana path. As *A Compendium of the Perfections* states:

> Abandon the two vehicles that are powerless
> In the ways of accomplishing the welfare of the world;
> Enter instead the vehicle of the King of Sages,
> A path that is taught from compassion and seeks only to
>   benefit others.[5]

Geshe Potowa also declared that [failing to enter the Mahayana path from the outset] is like having to cross the same river twice:

> Clothes shouldn't be lifted twice to ford a river once.
> Enter the Mahayana path from the very beginning.[6]

In addition, when an *arhat*[7] goes into the final mental absorption and passes away into the sphere of peace, he enters a state of inconceivably great

[4]Our own interests (S: *svārtham*, T: *rang don*) are fulfilled by permanently abandoning all the mental obscurations and by attaining the ultimate knowledge of Buddhahood. The interests of others (S: *parārtham*, T: *gzhan don*) are accomplished by attaining a Buddha's physical body, which alone has the complete ability to lead all sentient beings to ultimate happiness.

[5]S: *Pāramitāsamāsam*, ch. 6, v. 65. In Bibliography, see listing under *Āryaśūra*.

[6]These lines are from the *Blue Manual* (T: *Be'u bum sngon po*), a verse text composed by the Kadampa teacher, Geshe Dölpa Marshurpa Sherab Gyatso (T: *dGe bshes Dol pa dMar zhur pa Shes rab rgya mtso*). The lines quoted here appear on p. 203 of a commentary to the root text (T: *Be'u bum sngon po'i 'grel pa*) written by Hla Dri Gangpa (T: *lHa 'bri sgang pa*).

[7]T: *dgra bcom pa*. One who has attained liberation from samsara by eradicating all the mental afflictions.

bliss. His intention upon entering this state is never to arise from it again, and he remains absorbed in this mental equipoise for many kalpas. In fact, during the time he spends there another being who is living in the hells could gain a human rebirth possessing leisure and fortune,[8] enter the Mahayana path, and achieve ultimate enlightenment. Since anyone who enters this state greatly prolongs the length of time needed to attain Buddhahood, a practitioner of the Mahayana lineage[9] should not enter the Hinayana path and pursue the status of an *arhat*. Rather, he should listen to the Mahayana dharma and establish a propensity for that teaching in his mindstream. Even if he should later develop a wrong view toward the Mahayana and have to be reborn in the hells, he will still achieve ultimate enlightenment sooner than a Hinayana *arhat*. Therefore, he is better off following such a course.

Once, the Listener *arhat* Kashyapa was preparing to teach Hinayana dharma to a group of sixty *bhikshus*. Realizing that this would cause the monks to become *arhats*, Mañjushri intervened and taught them Mahayana dharma. However, since the monks could not properly comprehend this dharma, they developed wrong view toward it [290b] and ended up being reborn in the hells. When Kashyapa informed the Buddha of this, the Master replied that Mañjushri had exercised skillful means and that the teaching he had given was quite proper.

Those Listener and Solitary Realizer *arhats* who have entered the mental absorption known as the extreme of peace[10] are eventually awakened from that state by the Buddha and urged to enter the Mahayana path. However, because they have become so habituated to the peaceful bliss of their former state of absorption, they do not want to make the effort to develop enlightenment mind and practice the Mahayana path. Even when they do make some effort, they find it difficult to develop compassion and other virtuous minds since they have completely eliminated their own suffering.

[8]The eighteen qualities of leisure and fortune are described in Part Two, Day Nine, pp. 72–96.

[9]S: *gotram*, T: *rigs*. The subject of spiritual lineages is at the center of a Mahayana controversy concerning whether the Buddha taught three distinct vehicles that lead to three separate goals, or he taught only one true vehicle, the Mahayana, with the other two vehicles representing a temporary means of practice that must eventually be abandoned in favor of the Mahayana. This area of doctrine also involves another topic known popularly as "Buddha nature" (S: *tathāgatagarbhaḥ*, T: *de bzhin gshegs pa'i snying po*), according to which all sentient beings have the capacity to become a fully enlightened Buddha.

[10]T: *zhi ba'i mtha'*. Buddhism is often described as the "middle way" between two extremes. In Mahayana doctrine, this concept of two extremes is explained in different ways depending on the context. Here the extreme of peace refers to Hinayana nirvana. It represents an extreme in that one who abides in it ignores the welfare of other sentient beings. In this context, the other extreme is samsaric existence. Similarly, the Buddha's ultimate enlightenment is referred to as the state of nonabiding nirvana (S: *apratiṣṭitanirvāṇam*, T: *mi gnas pa'i mya ngan las 'das pa*) because it does not abide in either of these extremes.

For instance, when the Supreme Pair[11] were taught about the Mahayana path and its result by the Master, they responded that the Mahayana teaching was indeed marvelous, but that they could not bring themselves to practice it as they had become like charred tree trunks. In fact, this statement did not truly apply to Shariputra, since he was really a Bodhisattva who had emanated himself as a Listener *arhat*. Nevertheless, he made the statement with the understanding that it applied to those other disciples who were genuine Listener *arhats*. Thus, the condition represents a great obstacle to the attainment of supreme enlightenment.

Once we have achieved an experiential realization[12] of renunciation, it is essential that we enter the Mahayana path. In fact, the reason for practicing the path that is held in common with persons of moderate capacity is to develop the attitude of renunciation. But it is not intended that we should actually enter that path. The main element of the Lamrim path is to train ourselves in enlightenment mind, a practice meant for persons of great capacity. Thus, the teachings that relate to persons of lesser and moderate capacities represent the preparatory stage of this path. Similarly, the general discussion on how to train oneself in the Bodhisattva practices[13] represents the concluding stage.

In keeping with the instructions found in *Mañjughosha's Oral Instruction*,[14] there is a tradition that holds that the benefits of developing enlightenment mind should be presented before the actual explanations of how to train oneself in the path for persons of great capacity. This is done so that we will generate enthusiasm for carrying out those practices [291a]. Therefore, I shall explain these ten points: (1) generating enlightenment mind is the sole means of entering the Mahayana path; (2) we will be called a

[11]T: *mchog zung*. Epithet that refers to Shariputra and Maudgalyayana, two of Buddha Shakyamuni's foremost disciples.

[12]T: *myong ba thon pa*. See Part Two, Appendix F for a discussion of how analytic meditation serves as the method for eliciting experiential realizations of the Lamrim topics.

[13]T: *spyod pa spyi bslab*. In the Lamrim teachings as taught by Je Tsongkapa, a "general discussion" of the six perfections and the four principles of attracting a following (S: *catur saṃgrahavastūni*, T: *bsdu ba'i dngos po bzhi*) is made after the instructions for generating enlightenment mind. This is followed by extensive instructions on quiescence and insight. The six perfections are covered in Day Twenty and the four principles for attracting a following are described briefly in Day Twenty-three, pp. 304–305.

[14]This work of the Fifth Dalai Lama only briefly mentions the benefits of generating enlightenment mind. In other works, however, Kyabje Pabongka Rinpoche states that this tradition was established by his own lama and that its scriptural source is the *Ornament of Losang's View: An Instructional Treatise on Training One's Mind in the Mahayana Practices* (T: *Theg pa chen po'i blo sbyong gi khrid yig blo bzang dgongs rgyan*). The ten points that make up the tradition are covered extensively in this work (pp. 294–332). In Bibliography, see listing under (*Tse mchog gling Yongs 'dzin*) *Ye shes rgyal mtsan*.

"Conqueror's son"; (3) we will surpass the Listeners and Solitary Realizers by virtue of our spiritual lineage; (4) we will become the supreme field to which offerings should be made; (5) we will easily accumulate extensive merit; (6) we will quickly purify ourselves of bad karma and mental obscurations; (7) we will achieve whatever goals we seek; (8) we will become invulnerable to harms and obstacles; (9) we will quickly complete all the paths and levels; and (10) we will become a field that produces every form of well-being and happiness for sentient beings.

1) Generating enlightenment mind is the sole means of entering the Mahayana path

Our entry into the ranks of Mahayana practitioners is solely determined by whether or not we have generated enlightenment mind. As Je Lama[15] declared:

> It is not enough that the dharma [we are interested in] should be the Mahayana; the person [who is interested in it] must be one who has entered the ranks of the Mahayana. And what makes someone a Mahayanist depends solely on whether or not he has achieved enlightenment mind. If a person has nothing more than a conceptual understanding of this attitude, that is the extent to which he can be called a Mahayanist.[16]

If we lack enlightenment mind, then it doesn't matter that we might be practicing the generation and completion stages of the king of all tantra systems, the supreme Guhya Samaja. Not only will our efforts fail to bring ultimate enlightenment, we will not even succeed in entering the Mahayana accumulation path. In fact, our efforts will not be any kind of Mahayana dharma practice at all. But if we develop this mind, even reciting the *Mani* mantra one time becomes Mahayana dharma practice and therefore serves as a cause for achieving ultimate enlightenment. As the *Jewel Garland* declares:

> If you and the rest of the world
> Wish to gain ultimate enlightenment,

[15] An epithet of Je Tsongkapa.

[16] *Great Stages of the Path* (T: *Lam rim chen mo*), p.402 (f. 185b).

Its roots are an enlightenment mind [291b]
As firm as the supreme lord of mountains . . .[17]

If we lack enlightenment mind, our efforts to meditate on the generation stage practices of the secret Mantrayana system will be like a person who stands gazing at a temple ineffectually. Similarly, attempting to do completion stage practices—such as the yoga of psychic winds referred to in the line "Inhalation, retention, and exhalation"[18]—will have no more meaning than blowing air through a bellows.

The swiftness of the secret Mantrayana path stems from the way it enhances this mind. Changkya Rölbey Dorje[19] praised his teacher with these words:

> I heard the dharma from Purchok Ngawang Jampa.[20] Even when Lama Jampa was giving a great initiation, he would only teach Lamrim instructions as he explained the initiation ritual. To another observer it might have seemed that he wasn't explaining secret Mantrayana teachings at all. But this was the speech of one who had realized the path's key elements.

Astonished at hearing that a certain Hevajra yogi who lacked enlightenment mind had achieved the stream enterer's fruit, the great Lord[21] remarked, "This happened because he did not have my enlightenment mind. Some Hevajra practitioners even end up in the hells."

This particular practitioner was actually quite fortunate. Many others who haven't achieved enlightenment mind but constantly recite the mantra of a wrathful deity and try to propitiate the deity do not fare as well. They meet with such results as being reborn as a harmful spirit or in a hell. (Kyabje

[17]S:*Ratnāvalī*, ch. 2, vv. 73–74. These lines are not among the available Sanskrit fragments of the text. In Bibliography, see listing for the Tibetan translation under *Nāgārjuna*.

[18]T: *rngub dang dgang dang gzhil ba dang*. This passage refers to meditation practices for developing psychic heat (T: *gtum mo*).

[19]T: *lCang skya rol pa'i rdo rje*, 1717–1786. Third in the lineage of Changkya Lamas; his ordination name was Losang Tenbey Drönme (T: *Blo bzang bstan pa'i sgron me*). He was an important Gelukpa lama who served as spiritual preceptor to the Chinese Emperor Chien-lung, 5th in the line of the Ching dynasty.

[20]T: *Phur bu lcog Ngag dbang byams pa*, 1682–1762. See *Lives of the Lamrim Teachers* (T: *Lam rim bla ma brgyud pa'i rnam thar*), vol. 2, pp. 469–544.

[21]T: *Jo bo chen po*. An epithet of Atisha.

Rinpoche then told us how a local spirit of Chushur[22] had been a tantric practitioner who completed a great retreat in his former life. Nevertheless, he was reborn as the local spirit of this region.)

If only he had been able to gain enlightenment mind, that Hevajra yogi who achieved the stream enterer's fruit might have achieved ultimate enlightenment during his lifetime. However, the reason he achieved one of the Hinayana path's results instead of Buddhahood was because he lacked enlightenment mind [292a]. This kind of incident illustrates why the dharma is said to be so profound.

Earlier, I mentioned several stories that also explain this point. For instance, I told you about the Brahmin youth Chanakya. Another incident was the Indian Yamantaka practitioner who was reborn as a demon. When he came to Tibet, Atisha drove him away after giving him a torma offering. There was also the Vajra Bhairava yogi from Penbo who was reborn as a hungry ghost whose outer form resembled the tutelary deity. This hungry ghost appeared before some practitioners whom he had known in his previous life when they made a burnt offering to him.[23]

Most of us today are greatly impressed by such things as experiencing a vision of our tutelary deity or achieving supernormal wisdom and miraculous powers. But even persons who have achieved these qualities fall into the lower states if they lack enlightenment mind. So no matter what kind of supernormal wisdom or miraculous powers we may achieve, these cannot help us. But if we possess enlightenment mind, even though we might not strive after any other goal, we will have achieved the foundation of Mahayana dharma. It makes no difference whether you are talking about the Sutrayana or the Mantrayana teachings, the person who achieves this mind is truly practicing Mahayana dharma. If supported by this mind, every virtuous act a practitioner does—even something as small as giving a morsel of food to an animal—will serve as a cause for him to achieve supreme enlightenment. Acts that are indeterminate[24] in nature can also be turned into causes for achieving supreme enlightenment. Great Bodhisattvas can even transform what would otherwise be nonvirtuous acts into virtuous ones if they are done under the influence of this mind.[25]

[22]T: *Chu shur*. A district lying southwest of Lhasa where the Kyichu and Yarlung Rivers meet. A "local spirit" or *shi-dak* (T: *gzhi bdag*) is a type of demon who lays claim to a particular area and is propitiated by local inhabitants.

[23]A reference to these same three incidents can be found in Part Two, Day Thirteen, pp. 229–230.

[24]Deeds that are morally neutral. See also Day Fifteen, note 84.

[25]See Part One, Day Four, p. 139, where the story is told of one of the Buddha's past lives in which he was a ship's captain.

Depending on the spiritual qualities that accompany it, the wisdom that perceives emptiness can serve as a cause for achieving any of the three vehicles' different levels of enlightenment. Therefore, this wisdom is like a mother. But since enlightenment mind serves as a cause that leads exclusively to a Buddha's supreme enlightenment, it is like a father.[26] This distinction also explains why the former knowledge is also called the Mother.[27]

In short, unless we have no interest in achieving Buddhahood [292b], all of us should make enlightenment mind our most fundamental practice. If we analyze the virtuous qualities that are contained in the three vehicles, we will discover that they all derive from enlightenment mind. Now if someone were to ask us what our most important practice is, we would probably say "Hayagriva," or "Vajrapani," or "Vajra Bhairava." Yet the way most of us actually conduct ourselves suggests that we have adopted the three poisons[28] as our most important practice.

Even the great Lord Atisha did not feel satisfied with having mastered all aspects of the dharma. At the cost of great hardship to himself, he traveled across the ocean in a ship for thirteen months in pursuit of this precious enlightenment mind. After meeting Suvarnadvipa Guru, the great Lord received from him a complete set of instructions on enlightenment mind. Atisha then made this instruction his most fundamental practice and revered the guru who had taught it to him above all his other teachers. He did this even though Suvarnadvipa Guru adhered to the philosophical view of the Chittamatra or Mind Only School, a "lower" view than Atisha's.[29] Therefore, we should regard enlightenment mind as the one knowledge we must try hardest to develop within ourselves. There is no better physical basis for generating this mind than the one we currently have. And there is no better dharma instruction for training oneself in enlightenment mind than this one, called the stages of the path to enlightenment. Since we have had the good

[26]The enlightenment of both the Listeners' and Solitary Realizers' vehicles is Hinayana nirvana; the enlightenment of the Mahayana is the omniscience of a Buddha. According to the Madhyamaka Prasangika School, the realization of emptiness is necessary for achieving all three forms of enlightenment. This analogy comparing wisdom to a mother and enlightenment mind to a father appears in Je Tsongkapa's *Great Stages of the Path* (T: *Lam rim chen mo*, pp. 402–403 [ff. 185b–186a]). This instruction derives from a passage in the *Higher Science of the Mahayana* (S: *Mahāyānottaratantraśāstram*, ch.1, v.33); see below p. 122.

[27]Transcendent wisdom (S: *prajñāpāramitā*, T: *shes rab kyi pha rol tu phyin pa*) is also referred to as the Mother (T: *yum*), because it produces the "children"—that is, the *aryas*—who practice both the Hinayana and Mahayana paths, and who ultimately achieve the results of those paths.

[28]Desire, hatred, and ignorance—that is, all the mental afflictions.

[29]Atisha was a follower of the Madhyamaka Prasangika School. See Day Twenty-two, p. 270, where he is quoted as saying that Chandrakirti taught the instruction that is required to realize ultimate truth.

fortune to meet with this teaching, it would be a very great pity if we did not try to develop enlightenment mind.

We can see many examples of people who vainly think of themselves as the highest of dharma practitioners, simply because they have spent a lifetime sustaining themselves through the ascetic exercise known as mineral *chülen*.[30] But by disregarding enlightenment mind, these practitioners [293a] have strayed from the very path that leads to ultimate enlightenment. The best result would be for us to develop the uncontrived form of enlightenment mind. If we can't do that, we should try to gain a contrived experiential realization of it. Failing even that, we must at least become proficient in understanding how the instructions should be practiced.[31]

(Kyabje Rinpoche concluded with this point: The practitioner who does nothing but meditate on a tutelary deity and recite mantras without ever trying to cultivate enlightenment mind for even one meditation period is laboring in vain. It would be most regrettable to lose such an opportunity.)

2) We will be called a Conqueror's son

> The instant enlightenment mind is developed,
> A wretched being enchained in samsara's prison
> Is called a son or daughter of the Sugatas.[32]

Several other lines also state:

> Today I am born into the Buddhas' family.
> Now I have become a child of the Buddhas.[33]

As these words indicate, it is enlightenment mind that determines whether or not someone becomes a Conqueror's son. Although an individual may have achieved supernormal wisdom and miraculous powers, or become

[30]Chülen (S: *rasāyanaḥ*, T: *bcud len*) generally means a life-prolonging medicine or elixir. Here it refers to a regimen in which a practitioner sustains himself solely by ingesting various minerals in powder form—hence "mineral *chülen*" (T: *rde'u bcud len*). A similar exercise, in which different types of flowering plants are eaten, is called "flower *chülen*" (T: *me tog bcud len*). See also Part Two, Day Ten, p.110 and accompanying note 45.

[31]This paragraph makes reference to the three stages of analytic meditation (T: *dpyad sgom*): (1) becoming proficient in the instructions, (2) generating contrived experiential realizations, and (3) achieving uncontrived experiential realizations. Part Two, Appendix F describes how to practice analytic meditation with regard to the topics that are held in common with a practitioner of lesser capacity. The three stages of analytic meditation, in particular, are described in Part Two, Appendix F, p. 330.

[32]*Engaging in Bodhisattva Activities* (S: *Bodhicaryāvatāraḥ*), ch. 1, v. 9.

[33]Ibid, ch. 3, v. 25.

well-versed in the five sciences[34] or even achieved a direct realization of emptiness and completely abandoned all the mental afflictions, he is not a Bodhisattva or a Conqueror's son if he has not developed enlightenment mind. Nor can he claim to have entered the ranks of Mahayana practitioners.

On the other hand, a being that succeeds in generating this mind does enter the ranks of Mahayanists, even though he may be a dog, a pig, or some other animal. This is true though he may be as stupid as a donkey and lacking any other kind of knowledge. Whenever anyone generates enlightenment mind, various auspicious signs occur. For instance, the earth trembles and all the thrones on which the Buddhas sit are caused to shake. The earth trembles because it is formed through the common karma of sentient beings. When someone generates enlightenment mind, [293b] this means that many sentient beings will be led to liberation. This is so disruptive to samsara that it causes the earth to tremble.

Whenever someone gains this mind, that person is regarded by all the Bodhisattvas as their spiritual brother or sister. All the Buddhas of the ten directions also become as deeply pleased as a wheel-wielding monarch would at the birth of a new son. This is why such a person is called a Conqueror's son.

On the other hand, if someone were to lose this mind he would no longer dwell among the ranks of Mahayanists. We have gained supernormal wisdom and miraculous powers many times in the past, but these did not bring us any far-reaching benefit. Instead of those powers, it would have been far better if we had gained an understanding of this teaching on the stages of the path to enlightenment.

(Kyabje Rinpoche concluded by saying that supernormal wisdom and miraculous powers are neither rare nor especially valuable. For instance, each time that we pass away from one life and reach the intermediate state, we acquire some degree of these powers.[35])

[34]S: *pañcavidyā*, T: *rig gnas lnga*. According to tradition, the five major sciences are: (1) crafts (S: *śilpavidyā*, T: *bzo rig pa*)—such as carpentry, architecture, making jewelry, metalworking; (2) medicine (S: *cikitsāvidyā*, T: *gso ba rig pa*); (3) grammar (S: *śabdavidyā*, T: *sgra rig pa*); (4) logic (S: *hetuvidyā*, T: *gtan tsigs rig pa*); and (5) religion/philosophy (S: *adhyātmavidyā*, T: *nang don rig pa*). There are also five minor sciences: (1) poetry (S: *kāvyam*, T: *snyan ngag*); (2) word meaning and usage (S: *abhidhānam*, T: *mngon brjod*); (3) prosody (S: *chandas*, T: *sdeb sbyor*); (4) performing arts (S: *nāṭakam*, T: *zlos gar*); and (5) astronomy/astrology (S: *jyotis*, T: *dkar rtzis*).

[35]An intermediate-state being gains certain miraculous powers just by reaching that form of existence. For instance, that being is able to pass unimpeded through physical objects and can reach a particular place merely by thinking of it. The point is that even though all of us acquire these powers when we reach this state, they don't help us to accomplish anything of lasting value.

3) We surpass the Listeners and Solitary Realizers by virtue of our spiritual lineage

The *Stalks in Array Sutra* declares that a person who develops enlightenment mind is spiritually superior to all the Listener and Solitary Realizer disciples, just as a jewel in the ocean is more magnificent than all the quartz crystals in this Jambudvipa.[36] The chapter from this sutra entitled the "Liberating Deeds of Maitreya" also mentions a number of other similes that describe how the novice Bodhisattva who has just developed enlightenment mind is superior to all the Listener and Solitary Realizer disciples. For instance, the novice Bodhisattva is like a young prince who is more exalted than all the king's elderly ministers. He is also like a *garuda*[37] chick that is more magnificent than all other birds. This superiority is due to the Bodhisattva's extraordinary intention.[38]

The same sutra also describes how even a broken diamond [294a] is still called a diamond and is more splendid than ornaments made of gold. It can also dispel poverty everywhere. Similarly, a person who has generated enlightenment mind but has not yet developed the ability to practice the Bodhisattva activities is still called a Conqueror's son by virtue of his having generated that mind. The enlightenment mind he possesses is a more valuable "jewel" than all other virtuous qualities and is more magnificent than all the gold-like virtues of the Listener disciples and Solitary Realizer disciples. Enlightenment mind is also what dispels all the poverty of samsara.

Nothing, then, is more worthy of being identified as the essence of all the eighty-four thousand heaps of dharma[39] than this mind. The supreme lord

[36]T: *'Dzam bu gling*. According to Buddhist cosmology, this is one of the world's four continents. Located in the southern region, it is where Buddha Shakyamuni took birth. See also Part Two, Day Nine, p. 81, note 76. The exact wording of the simile states: "O son of good family, just as a priceless jewel in the hand of a merchant who is in a boat on the high seas surpasses in beauty and value hundreds of thousands of quartz crystals that are located in a town, the great priceless jewel of the enlightenment mind that is dedicated to the attainment of omniscience surpasses all the quartz crystals of Listener disciples and Solitary Realizer disciples who have already entered the city of individual liberation—even though it is situated in the boat of prayers of aspiration on the great ocean of samsara, and even though it is present in the mind of a novice Bodhisattva who has only generated the extraordinary determination but not yet reached the city of omniscience" (S: *Gaṇḍavyūhasūtram*, p. 400).

[37]T: *mkha' lding*. An eagle-like bird, regarded as the king of the feathered species.

[38]S: *adhyāśayaḥ*, T: *lhag pa'i bsam pa*. "Extraordinary intention" refers to the Bodhisattva's determination to personally save all sentient beings. See Day Seventeen, p. 146.

[39]The entire teaching of a Buddha is said to be encompassed in eighty-four thousand "heaps." According to Mahayana doctrine, one dharma heap is represented by the number of scriptures that could be written with all the ink that the great elephant Airavana (the mount that the deity Shakra rides) can carry on his back in a single load.

Atisha taught almost exclusively about these two subjects: renouncing attachment to this life and meditating on loving-kindness, compassion, and enlightenment mind.

4) We will become the supreme object to which offerings should be made

When we develop enlightenment mind, we will become the supreme object to which offerings should be made. This is described in the line that states such persons "deserve veneration by the world of gods and men."[40]

Enlightenment mind is not something that can be developed after training oneself for only a short period of time. The great Atisha practiced it for twelve years. When we observe that some practitioners exert themselves for many years just to meditate on a tutelary deity and recite its mantras, it is only proper that we should be willing to practice arduously in order to develop this mind. The former Kadampa masters had a saying: "Everyone has a tutelary deity's form to meditate on and a mantra to recite. This is because no one has a dharma teaching to contemplate." Therefore, it's very important that we at least establish an impression of it in our mind [294b].[41] For instance, long ago there were five hundred geese who were reborn as gods merely by having heard the sound of the Buddha's voice. Later, they were able to achieve a realization of Truth.[42]

King Ajatashatru also previously had established a very strong impression in his mind about the meaning of emptiness. Then, at a noon meal for the sangha, he tried to present a cloak worth a thousand *sang* of gold to Mañjushri as a gift. But when the one to whom he wished to make the offering disappeared from view and could not be found, the king decided he would wear the cloak himself. Then he too vanished from view, and soon after gained a realization of emptiness. This story illustrates how the dormant power of an impression that was previously planted in a person's mind can be awakened.[43]

[40] *Engaging in Bodhisattva Activities* (S: *Bodhicaryāvatāraḥ*), ch. 1, v. 9.

[41] T: *bag chags 'jog pa*. As this phrase is being used here, it refers to the smallest benefit that a person can derive from listening to a dharma teaching. The impression or imprint (S: *vāsanā*, T: *bag chags*) that becomes fixed in a listener's mind when he hears a teaching will help him to develop deeper knowledge at some future occasion when he has the opportunity to hear such a subject again.

[42] A brief account appears in the *Sutra of the Wise and the Foolish* (T: *mDzangs blun zhes bya ba'i mdo*), ch. 49.

[43] This incident is described in the sutra entitled *The Dispelling of Ajatashatru's Remorse* (T: *Ma skyes dgra'i 'gyod pa bsal ba*).

When a person succeeds in developing enlightenment mind, gods such as Brahma and Shakra come and venerate him. They cause his body to take on a radiance and help him to achieve all his aims.

The scriptures declare that even the Buddhas pay homage to Bodhisattvas, because a completely enlightened Buddha comes from a Bodhisattva and a Bodhisattva, in turn, comes from enlightenment mind. As a sutra declares:

> Just as people pay homage to a new moon over a full moon, those who have deep reverence for me should pay homage to Bodhisattvas rather than to the Tathagatas.[44]

(Kyabje Rinpoche made reference to several other scriptural accounts. For instance, he described how a Buddha would fasten a cart-pulling rope to his own head if there was no one else to pull a cart in which a Bodhisattva was seated, even though that Bodhisattva might be taking pleasure in the five sense objects.[45] But even though the Arya Shariputra might abide in the realm of peace for many kalpas, the Tathagata would not honor him. Kyabje Rinpoche also told us about an incident in which the Buddha's alms bowl [295a] sank deep into the earth because he did not offer the choice part of his food to Mañjushri.[46])

[44] *Kashyapa Chapter* (T: *Kāśyapaparivartaḥ*), p. 129.

[45] This point is made in a passage cited in Nagarjuna's *Sutra Anthology* (T: *mDo kun las btus pa*), f. 158a. The source is identified as *Jewel Heap Sutra* (T: *Rin po che'i phung po*); however, this is not the sutra of the same name found in the *dKon brtzegs* section of Kg.

[46] This is also from *The Dispelling of Ajatashatru's Remorse* (T: *Ma skyes dgra'i 'gyod pa bsal ba*). A magically emanated householder once offered the Blessed One an alms bowl filled with food. Mañjushri then said that it would be an expression of ingratitude if the Blessed One did not offer the choice part of this food to him. When the rest of the assembly wondered what benefit Mañjushri might have performed on behalf of the Blessed One, the Buddha's alms bowl sank down beneath the earth and reached a distance of countless world systems away. The Blessed One directed his two supreme disciples, Shariputra and Maudgalyayana, to retrieve the bowl but they were unable to do so. Then, without leaving his seat, Mañjushri stretched his arm downward and, seizing the bowl, presented it to the Buddha. The benefit that Mañjushri had previously extended to the Buddha was this: During the time of the Tathagata Durjayadvaja (T: *Mi thub rgyal mtsan)*, Mañjushri had been a monk named Jñanaraja. One day, as Jñanaraja was walking along the road with an alms bowl filled with food, a young boy named Vimalabala (T: *Dri med dpung*) approached him and asked for something to eat. This boy was none other than the person who later became Buddha Shakyamuni. Not only did Jñanaraja give the boy food, he also introduced him to the Tathagata Durjayadvaja, which enabled the boy to take refuge in the Triple Gem and also to generate enlightenment mind.

5) We easily accumulate extensive merit

Enlightenment mind enables us to accumulate extensive merit easily. For instance, Nyukrumba[47] said:

> If we can develop this one knowledge—enlightenment mind—from the outset, it alone will collect merit for us, it alone will purify us of our obscurations, and it alone will remove our obstacles.

Je Lama also wrote:

> It is like an alchemic elixir for all forms of the two
> accumulations;
> It's a treasure of merit that gathers myriad collections
> of virtue.[48]

As the following lines also indicate, nothing surpasses enlightenment mind for enabling us to accumulate immense quantities of merit:

> Hold this enlightenment mind very firmly.
> It is the unsurpassed alchemic elixir
> That changes this impure body we've taken
> Into the priceless jewel of a Conqueror's body.[49]

Another verse from the same work also declares:

> All other forms of virtue, like the plantain,
> Simply perish after yielding their fruit.
> But the tree of enlightenment mind thrives;
> It bears fruit always and does not die.[50]

Even though we might fill a billion worlds with jewels and offer them to a hundred thousand beings for many hundreds of thousands of kalpas, if this

[47]T *sNyug rum pa*, fl. Early 12th century. A main disciple of the Kadampa teacher Chenngawa Tsultrim Bar. His name, which means "person from Nyukrum," stems from the monastery of the same name that he founded. See *Lives of the Lamrim Teachers* (T: *Lam rim bla ma brgyud pa'i rnam thar*), vol. 1, pp. 589–590.

[48]*Brief Stages of the Path* (T: *Lam rim bsdus don*), v. 21.

[49]*Engaging in Bodhisattva Activities* (S: *Bodhicaryāvatāraḥ*) ch. 1, v. 10.

[50]Ibid., ch. 1, v. 12.

deed was not motivated by enlightenment mind, it would eventually cease producing beneficial results. It would not be the act of a Conqueror's son, and would not serve as a cause that helps to bring us Buddhahood. But even the simple act of giving a morsel of food to an animal—if motivated by enlightenment mind—yields endless beneficial results. This would be the act of a Conqueror's son, and it would serve as a cause that helps to bring Buddhahood [295b].

If someone is motivated by this mind and offers a single stick of incense, it is said that he will gain the same benefit as if he had offered as many sticks of incense as there are sentient beings in the universe. Therefore, if we recite the *Mani* mantra only once while motivated by this mind, we will gain benefits that are equal in number to all sentient beings in the universe.

The scriptures also describe how, during the time that the Buddha was still living, a pauper who was motivated by enlightenment mind made an offering of a small oil lamp. When Ananda was unable to extinguish the lamp, the Tathagata declared that it could not be extinguished even by the great winds that destroy the world at the end of a kalpa. This was because enlightenment mind so greatly increased the merit of the act.

As the following verses from *Engaging in Bodhisattva Activities* state, from the moment that we adopt the Bodhisattva vows associated with the active form of enlightenment mind,[51] we will generate virtue continuously, even when we are sleeping or in an inattentive state of mind:

> From the moment one adopts
> The mind that seeks to liberate
> An endless sphere of sentient beings
> With unswerving determination—
>
> From then on, even while sleeping
> Or in an unmindful state, one will generate
> Many continuous streams of merit
> That are as vast as space.[52]

[51]There are two basic types of enlightenment mind: conventional and ultimate (for a description, see Part One, Day Five, note 37). Conventional enlightenment mind is further distinguished between a wishing form (S: *praṇidhicittotpādaḥ*, T: *smon pa sems bskyed*) and an active form (S: *pravṛtticittotpādaḥ*, T: *'jug pa sems bskyed*). With wishing enlightenment mind, the practitioner has the desire to attain the ultimate enlightenment of a Buddha in order to benefit all sentient beings, but does not directly engage in the practices of generosity and so forth that will lead him to the attainment of that goal. With active enlightenment mind, he not only desires to attain enlightenment, but also adopts the Bodhisattva vows and engages in the Bodhisattva practices that lead to that goal (see also Part One, Day Two, note 37).

[52]Ibid., ch.1, vv. 18–19.

If we derive great benefit just by generating the desire to ease a single person's headache, why wouldn't we also derive great merit by generating the wish to liberate all sentient beings from the incomprehensibly great disease of samsara's suffering? This point is made in the following verses from *Engaging in Bodhisattva Activities*:

> A person who contemplates removing
> The severe headaches of several beings
> Has developed a wholesome state of mind
> That is endowed with limitless merit.
>
> Would this not be all the more true
> For someone who wishes to remove
> The endless pain [296a] of every sentient being
> And bring measureless virtue to each one?[53]

Several more verses from this work also state:

> The world honors as a doer of good
> Someone who offers a meal to a few persons,
> Though it is a momentary gift of mere food,
> Done with contempt, and satisfying for half a day.
>
> What, then, of those who bestow endlessly
> Upon limitless numbers of beings
> The unsurpassed bliss of the Sugatas,
> Which fully satisfies one's every wish?[54]

(Kyabje Rinpoche summed up this point by saying that any virtuous act motivated by enlightenment mind will bring benefits that are equal in number to all the sentient beings in the universe.)

6) We quickly purify ourselves of bad karma and mental obscurations

Nothing surpasses enlightenment mind for its ability to remove our bad karma. If we develop this mind, we can terminate even those extremely grave bad deeds and mental obscurations that no other method of purification can remove. This is stated in the following verse from *Engaging in Bodhisattva Activities*:

[53] Ibid., ch. 1, vv. 21–22.
[54] Ibid., ch. 1, vv. 32–33.

The power of evil is great and so terrifying.
Indeed, if there were no enlightenment mind,
What other virtue could overcome it?[55]

(Kyabje Rinpoche then described how Arya Asanga was able to purify himself of bad karma and mental obscurations much more effectively through a single act of genuine compassion than with all the virtue he had accumulated over twelve years of spiritual practice.)

Another verse from *Engaging in Bodhisattva Activities* also declares:

How could ignorant beings fail to rely upon
That which instantly frees even one who commits
The most terrible of misdeeds, just as reliance
On a hero allows one to escape great dangers [296b]?[56]

A person who has enlightenment mind can avoid the perils associated with bad deeds, mental obscurations, and their consequences, just as someone traveling over a treacherous mountain path can ensure his safety if he is accompanied by a great hero. Several more lines also state:

It destroys great misdeeds in an instant,
Like the fire at the end of an eon.[57]

Enlightenment mind can clear away a mountain of our misdeeds no matter how great it may be. It burns up our bad karma like the fire at the end of a kalpa would burn kindling. Therefore, meditating on enlightenment mind for a single meditation period is a much better way of destroying our misdeeds than practicing strenuously for a hundred years any other method of purification that lacks the special qualities of this mind.

7) We will achieve whatever goals we seek

Anyone who develops enlightenment mind will achieve all temporary and ultimate goals effortlessly. In fact, enlightenment mind accomplishes the highest of all goals: it eliminates the suffering that all sentient beings do not want and brings them the happiness that they do want. Therefore, a verse from

[55] Ibid., ch. 1, v. 6.
[56] Ibid., ch. 1, v. 13.
[57] Ibid., ch. 1, v. 14.

Engaging in Bodhisattva Activities declares that "it raises countless multitudes of beings/ With great ease to the highest form of happiness."[58]

Moreover, enlightenment mind also enables us to gain all the powers that the tantric scriptures say can be achieved through reciting mantras and performing rituals, even though most practitioners who strive after these goals are unable to achieve them. Indeed, the main reason we fail to achieve the various powers described in sutras, tantras, and other manuals—such as the ability to make rain, protect crops from hail, and the like—is that we do not have enlightenment mind. Therefore, if we wish to develop great spiritual powers and have the ability to remove such obstacles as illness—both our own and others'—we must develop this enlightenment mind [297a]. It's wrong to think that the reason we don't achieve these powers is because the instructions that explain how to gain them are flawed.

Nor is it necessary to recite mantras that include syllables like *Hung Hung* and *Pet Pet*, or to rely on charms and other ritual objects, in order to achieve these powers. We can achieve them simply through invoking the power of truth. For instance, the Bodhisattva Sadaprarudita was able to restore his injured body by reciting such words of truth.[59]

Another example was when words of truth had the power to turn back the waters of the Tsang River. The river had begun to overflow its banks and was threatening the city of Lhasa. Just as it appeared that no one could stop the flood, Je Mönlam Pel carved these words on a stone: "If Mönlam Pel is a Bodhisattva, by the power of this truth may the waters turn back quickly!" As soon as the stone was placed by the riverbank, the waters receded. Therefore, enlightenment mind has the power to bring us everything from such lesser spiritual powers up to the ultimate goal of omniscience.

8) We become invulnerable to harms and obstacles

A wheel-wielding monarch is protected even when he is sleeping, by such deities as Vajrapani, Brahma, Shakra, and the four Maharajikas. Similarly, a Bodhisattva is guarded by twice as many protectors as these throughout the

[58]Ch. 1, v. 7. The complete verse states: "The Lords of Sages reflected for many kalpas/ And saw that this alone is most beneficial,/ Because it raises countless multitudes of beings/ With great ease to the highest form of happiness."

[59]See Chapter 30 of the *Perfection of Wisdom Sutra in Eight Thousand Lines* (S: *Aṣṭasāhasrikāprajñāpāramitā*). Sadaprarudita (T: *rTag tu rngu*) wanted to sell his body so that he could buy an offering for the teacher Dharmodgata. To test Sadaprarudita's resolve, the deity Shakra appeared in the guise of a young man and offered to buy his heart, blood, and bone marrow. Sadaprarudita then gladly cut his own flesh and was preparing to break his bones. After a merchant's daughter interceded and offered to help him buy whatever he needed, Sadaprarudita restored his body by invoking an oath in which he attested to the fact that he had been prophesied by the Buddhas as irreversibly destined to achieve complete enlightenment.

day and night. Because of this, a Bodhisattva doesn't meet with any kind of harm, including those caused by malicious spirits and demons. On the other hand, a person who lacks enlightenment mind may perform rituals of propitiation in which drums are beaten and musical instruments are played in an effort to invite protector deities. But such a practitioner can never be sure whether the protector deity will actually appear or not. And yet, if we succeed in generating this mind, Vaishravana and all the four Maharajika deities will protect us as if they were our servants, even though we do not formally ask them to do so.

The *Stalks in Array Sutra* mentions several kinds of medicine including a remedy known as "Unforsaken," which, if applied to the body, renders one invulnerable to illnesses and other unfavorable circumstances [297b]. Another is the king of herbs called "Maghi," which has the power to drive away snakes. Yet a third is the king of medicines called "Indomitable," which renders one incapable of being overcome by one's enemies. Enlightenment mind is compared to these medicines in that it protects one from such things as the illnesses of the mental afflictions.[60]

(Kyabje Rinpoche concluded this point by relating a number of incidents, including these:

Geshe Khamlungpa[61] had been staying in the uplands of Yungwa, a section in Penbo, where he was meditating on enlightenment mind. At that time, some spirits decided to do him harm. But then a certain demon said, "We can't harm him because he has become like Sadaprarudita; he is more concerned about us than he is about himself."

The compassionate Master also overcame the Evil One's host through the power of his loving-kindness.[62]

A group of five *yaksha* spirits were unable to steal the life force of herdsmen in King Maitribala's kingdom.[63]

[60]These medicines appear in the list of similes found in the chapter entitled "Liberating Deeds of Maitreya." See above p. 109.

[61]T: *Khams pa lung pa*, 1023–1115. An early Kadampa teacher; his actual name was Shakya Yönten (T: *Shākya yon tan*). See *Lives of the Lamrim Teachers* (T: *Lam rim bla ma brgyud pa'i rnam thar*), vol. 1, pp. 435–438.

[62]This is a reference to Buddha Shakyamuni's defeat of the Evil One and his army of demons while seated under the Bodhi tree, just before he attained supreme enlightenment. See the sutra entitled *Extensive Cosmic Sport* (S: *Lalitavistaraḥ*), ch. 21.

[63]The Maitribala birth story appears in the *Principal Subjects of Discipline* (T: *'Dul ba lung gzhi*), in *'Dul ba* section of Kg., vol. 4 (*nga*), ff. 175a–177a (in section 93). See also the *Garland of Birth Stories* (S: *Jātakamālā*), ch. 8.

Kyabje Rinpoche also told us how Pehar[64] was able to offer an iron pen both to Butön[65] and to Lama Dampa,[66] but not to Ngulchu Gyel-se Tokme Sangpo. And once, when Butön was ill, he summoned Gyel-se Rinpoche. The latter succeeded in alleviating Butön's pain by meditating on enlightenment mind.

After describing these incidents, Kyabje Rinpoche remarked that there are endless such examples illustrating the benefit that we will become invulnerable to harms and obstacles. Then he made this final comment: Suffice it to say that our own experience will reveal to us how meditating on enlightenment mind makes us invulnerable to the harm of malevolent spirits.)

9) We will quickly complete all the paths and their levels

The realization of emptiness by itself—that is, without the benefit of enlightenment mind—only enables us to complete the wisdom accumulation; it does not help us to complete the merit accumulation. However, the ultimate goal of completing the two accumulations and abandoning the two types of obscurations along with their traces is mainly [298a] accomplished through the power of conventional enlightenment mind.[67] Developing this mind is also what makes it possible for us to achieve supreme enlightenment within a single lifetime through practicing the Mantrayana path. On the other hand, if we fail to develop enlightenment mind, the tantric practices will not even bring us to the lowest level of the Mahayana accumulation path.

In short, enlightenment mind is the root of all virtuous qualities. If we have it, we can transform all our virtuous acts—from giving a single morsel of food to a crow on up—into causes that bring us closer to the attainment of Buddhahood. This is why it enables us to complete all the paths and their levels quickly.

[64]T: *Pe har*. Initially a Tibetan spirit, Pehar was subdued by the 7th-century Indian tantric *mahasiddha* Padma Sambhava, who directed him to become a protector of Buddhism. By offering Butön Rinpoche and Lama Dampa an iron pen, Pehar was encouraging them to compose treatises on the dharma. However, this work limited the opportunity that the two great scholars had to devote to their meditation practice. Because Gyel-se Tokme Sangpo (see Day Fifteen, note 55) was a great Bodhisattva, Pehar could not influence him as he had the other two.

[65]T: *Bu ston Rin chen grub*, 1290–1364. An influential scholar whose extensive collection of writings covers all subjects of both sutra and tantra. He is recognized as having established the current structure of the Tengyur collection of Buddhist treatises by Indian scholars. Je Tsongkapa received tantric instructions from teachers in the lineage preserved by his disciples.

[66]T: *Bla ma dam pa bSod nams rgyal mtsan*, 1312–1375.

[67]See note 51 above.

10) We will become a field that produces every form of well-being and happiness for sentient beings

A verse from the *Introduction to the Middle Way* contains these lines:

> Listeners and Intermediate Buddhas[68] arise from the
> Lords of Sages;
> The Supreme Buddhas, for their part, come from
> Bodhisattvas.[69]

Happiness and well-being in this world, achieving the status of a Listener or a Solitary Realizer *arhat*, or that of a wheel-wielding monarch, and so on, are all produced through the power of the Buddhas. The Supreme Buddhas, however, originate from Bodhisattvas. And Bodhisattvas, in turn, come into being by developing enlightenment mind. Therefore, enlightenment mind is the sole root of all sentient beings' happiness and well-being.

Furthermore, this mind is the essence of all the dharma heaps. It is the main practice of all the pure sons of the Conquerors. And it is also through the power of this mind that we are able to gain the extraordinary qualities of the Mantrayana path.

(Kyabje Rinpoche then told us how Geshe Tönba once inquired about the "Three Brothers."[70] After being told what each of them was doing, he replied, "Wonderful! That's one topic." Then he asked about Khamlungpa and was told that this practitioner was living near the edge of a ravine, sometimes sitting with eyes half-closed while at other times just crying [298b]. Upon hearing this, Drom Rinpoche joined his palms together reverently and praised him by saying, "He is truly practicing dharma!")

This enlightenment mind is the quintessence of all the dharma. As a verse from *Engaging in Bodhisattva Activities* states in part:

[68]This is a reference to Solitary Realizer *arhats*. Chandrakirti's autocommentary explains that the term Buddha ("Enlightened One") applies equally to Listeners, Solitary Realizers, and Supreme Buddhas, because it refers to any individual who has realized the emptiness that is the ultimate nature of reality. Furthermore, a Solitary Realizer *arhat* is called an Intermediate Buddha because his merit and wisdom are superior to those of a Listener *arhat*, but not as great as those of a Supreme Buddha.

[69]T: *dBu ma la 'jug pa*, ch. 1, v. 1.

[70]T: *sKu mched gsum*. Three early Kadampa teachers: Potowa Rinchen Sel (T: *Po to ba Rin chen gsal*, 1027–1105), Chen-nga Tsultrim Bar (T: *sPyan snga Tsul khrims 'bar*, 1038–1103), and Puchungwa Shönu Gyeltsen (T: *Phu chung ba gZhon nu rgyal mtsan*, 1031–1107).

By churning the milk of holy dharma,
It is the fresh butter that rises to the top.[71]

Thus, I urge all of you to strive with every effort possible to generate this enlightenment mind. Since enlightenment mind is the one factor that determines whether or not your efforts qualify as Mahayana practice, for the time being you should put aside pursuing those other instructions that are considered exceedingly profound and apply yourselves to this practice. Many dharma practitioners, regardless of the tradition they follow—Sakya, Geluk, Kagyu, or Nyingma—fail to understand the importance of this point. While having in common the desire to achieve Buddhahood, they meditate on the two stages of the secret Mantrayana instructions without thinking it necessary to cultivate enlightenment mind. But anyone who hopes to traverse the path swiftly in this manner can be described with the saying of ordinary householders: "I want my neck, but not this goiter."[72] Not one of the Buddhas of the three times has ever or will ever achieve Buddhahood without generating enlightenment mind. If ever there should appear such a Buddha who did not have to cultivate enlightenment mind, he won't be like any Buddha we've ever heard of. Therefore, anyone who wishes to achieve Buddhahood cannot possibly do so without developing enlightenment mind. Put another way, by losing this mind, we lose the hope of ever achieving Buddhahood. So I urge you to devote yourselves earnestly to this practice.

A certain Rego Acharya once said to Je Drupkangba:[73] "My body becomes filled with a great feeling of lightness when you visit me and we discuss enlightenment mind. These days there is no one else I can converse with on this subject [299a]." Some of us are guilty of dismissing enlightenment mind by regarding it as too lofty a goal. We say it is so difficult to practice that we could not possibly generate it. Others dismiss enlightenment mind by treating it in a disparaging manner. They refer to it as a common element of all Mahayana traditions and suggest that we should meditate on other more profound topics instead, such as the two stages of

[71] S: *Bodhicaryāvatāraḥ*, ch. 3, v. 31.

[72] T: *ske 'dod la sba ba mi 'dod*. As it is being used here, the saying means that the goiter can't be removed without harming a vital part of one's body; therefore, the two are inseparable. Similarly, a practitioner cannot hope to pursue the secret Mantrayana path without also making a special effort to develop enlightenment mind.

[73] T: *rJe sGrub khang pa dGe legs rgya mtso*, 1641–1712. See *Lives of the Lamrim Teachers* (T: *Lam rim bla ma brgyud pa'i rnam thar*), vol. 2, pp. 433–462. Rego Acharya was his teacher. This incident is described in the *Transcript from Teachings on the Shorter Stages of the Path to Enlightenment* (T: *Byang chub lam gyi rim pa chung ngu'i zin bris*, p. 768). In Bibliography, see listing under (*Ke'u tsang*) *Blo bzang 'jam dbyangs smon lam*.

Anuttarayoga Tantra.[74] As a result, there are very few who actually practice the instructions for developing enlightenment mind. This is like searching for a wishing jewel in a puddle of water the size of a cow's hoof print instead of in the great ocean.

Je Lama also praised this very enlightenment mind as the one object we should consider as the foremost element of our practice:

> Having realized this, those heroes—the sons of
> the Conquerors—
> Hold the supreme mind-jewel as their most
> fundamental practice.[75]

Nowadays, some say that we should regard a tutelary deity as our most fundamental practice. Others ascribe the highest value to such practices as the *Chinese Ritual for Overcoming Obstacles*[76] and the *Dharani Spell That Settles Legal Disputes*.[77] But a person who finds no opportunity to meditate on enlightenment mind will never be able to achieve Buddhahood.

Lord Atisha regarded his Suvarnadvipa Guru as the most precious of all his teachers. Once, when there was something wrong with his arm, Atisha said to Dromtönba: "You have achieved the benevolent mind. Bless my arm." This remark by Lord Atisha showed his great esteem for enlightenment mind.

Although the Guru Dharmarakshita[78] initially held the philosophical view of the Vaibhashika School, eventually he became a follower of the Madhyamaka School through the spiritual power of his enlightenment mind.

Lord Atisha was able to do such extensive spiritual activities in both India and Tibet because of the way he served his spiritual teachers and by the power of his enlightenment mind. An early Kadampa teacher said that even though you achieve one-pointed concentration of such firmness that you

[74]The Anuttarayoga Tantra path is divided into two stages: the generation stage (S: *utpattikramaḥ*, T: *bskyed rim*) and the completion stage (S: *saṃpannakramaḥ*, T: *rdzogs rim*). See also Part Two, Day Seven, note 5.

[75]*Brief Stages of the Path* (T: *Lam rim bsdus don*), v. 22.

[76]T: *rGya nag skag bzlog*. A scripture based on astrology that was introduced from China and purports to remove obstacles associated with inauspicious astrological periods. These times can be identified with a particular year, month, or even day.

[77]T: *Kha mchu nag po zhi bar byed pa i gzungs*.

[78]One of three Indian teachers from whom Lord Atisha received extensive teachings on enlightenment mind. The other two were Suvarnadvipa Guru and Maitri Yogi (T: *Byams pa'i rNal 'byor pa*). The latter was also known as Kusali the Younger.

would not hear a giant drum if it were beaten next to your ear [299b], without this mind you will make no spiritual progress whatsoever.[79]

The Guru Rahulagupta also told Atisha that it is no great accomplishment to have a vision of one's tutelary deity, achieve supernormal wisdom and magical powers, or possess one-pointed concentration as firm as a mountain. He then urged him to meditate on loving-kindness and compassion.[80]

In the sutras, enlightenment mind is compared to such things as the precious wheel by which a universal monarch wields power, as well as a person's hands and even his very life force.[81] The *Higher Science of the Mahayana* declares:

> Aspiration for the supreme vehicle is the seed; wisdom is
> the mother
> Who gives birth to the good qualities of a Buddha.[82]

A father is the unique cause that determines the race of the child. A mother is the general or non-determining cause. Similarly, precious enlightenment mind is the unique cause of a Buddha, while the wisdom that realizes emptiness is the general cause for all three types of enlightenment. Thus, the wisdom that realizes emptiness serves as a cause for reaching the enlightenment of whatever Hinayana or Mahayana path one is practicing. Even a person who has only a conceptual understanding of enlightenment mind will reach Buddhahood more quickly than those who, without developing enlightenment mind, attempt to practice the two stages of Anuttarayoga Tantra, or the teachings of the Mahamudra and Dzokchen traditions, even though they may have achieved visions of many tutelary deities together with their divine assemblies. The great Lord Atisha understood and achieved realizations of all the holy Buddhist teachings. And his most precious

[79] This is very similar to a remark made by Dromtönba to Neljorba Chenpo, which is quoted in Je Tsongkapa's *Great Treatise* (T: *Lam rim chen mo*), p. 445 (f. 207a).

[80] See Part One, Day Two, p. 38.

[81] The *Great Stages of the Path* (T: *Lam rim chen mo*), pp. 414–415 (ff. 191b–192a) cites a passage from the sutra entitled *Hymn in Praise of the Dharma* (T: *Chos yang dag par sdud pa*), which mentions two of these similes: "For example, Blessed One, wherever the precious wheel of a wheel-wielding monarch is, all his military forces are there as well. Similarly, Blessed One, wherever a Bodhisattva's great compassion is, all the qualities of a Buddha are there as well. . . . For example, Blessed One, wherever there is life force, there will also be all the other faculties. Similarly, Blessed One, wherever there is great compassion, there will also be all the other qualities of a Bodhisattva." Two of these similes are also used to describe enlightenment mind in the *Stalks in Array Sutra* (S: *Gaṇḍavyūhasūtram*): "It is like a hand, in that it protects the body that possesses transcendent virtues. . . . It is like the life force, in that it sustains the great compassion of all Bodhisattvas."

[82] S: *Mahāyānottaratantraśāstram*, ch. 1, v. 34.

saying was this: "Meditate on loving-kindness, compassion, and enlightenment mind." Therefore, we must direct our efforts toward trying to develop these attitudes, rather than only being interested in meditating on a tutelary deity or reciting mantras. These attitudes I just mentioned are the very heart of the dharma; so we must strive greatly to develop them in our minds. Not only is it proper for us to exert ourselves in this way [300a], it is also true that if we meditate on these attitudes we definitely can develop them, because composed entities do not remain in one unalterable state.[83]

Before the great Lord Atisha came to Tibet, some persons thought that enlightenment mind could be developed simply by taking part in the offering ritual for generating enlightenment mind[84] and reciting the words "I wish to achieve Buddhahood for the sake of all mother sentient beings," which occur at the beginning of the ceremony. But genuine enlightenment mind can only be generated by engaging in a process of mental training. Without such mental training, we couldn't possibly generate enlightenment mind simply by participating in a formal ritual like the one that is performed when the Pratimoksha vows are given. Indeed, merely participating in a ceremony won't even help us understand what the nature of enlightenment mind is. Lord Atisha once expressed his disapproval of Tibetan practitioners when he said, "Only you Tibetans are able to regard someone who has no understanding of loving-kindness and compassion as a Bodhisattva." When asked what was needed to be able to practice properly, he replied that a person must train himself gradually.[85]

(Kyabje Rinpoche concluded by saying that what Lord Atisha meant was this: Enlightenment mind cannot be generated without first developing an experiential awareness of great compassion. Therefore, we must train our mind step by step.)

ii. How to generate enlightenment mind

The topic of how to generate enlightenment mind has two parts: (1) the actual stages for training oneself in enlightenment mind, and (2) the ritual method of adopting enlightenment mind.

[83]See Part One, Day Five, p.169 for a similar statement by Geshe Dölba.

[84]T: *sems bskyed mchod pa'i cho ga*. This ritual is performed for the purpose of generating enlightenment mind. However, the point is that you participate in the ritual only after having cultivated a set of instructions that will enable you to effectively generate enlightenment mind during the ritual. According to tradition, it is usually performed on the last day of a Lamrim teaching. The ritual is first discussed at the end of Day Twenty-three and then the actual ceremony is described on Day Twenty-four.

[85]This exchange appears in Je Tsongkapa's *Great Treatise* (T: *Lam rim chen mo*) pp. 444–445 (ff. 206b–207a).

1) The actual stages for training oneself in enlightenment mind

This section is also comprised of two parts: (1) training one's mind with the Sevenfold Instruction of Cause and Effect and (2) training one's mind with the instruction called Equality and Exchange of Self and Others.

a) Training one's mind with the Sevenfold Instruction of Cause and Effect

The main focus of the Sevenfold Instruction of Cause and Effect is to develop an attitude that regards all sentient beings as dear. This method was used by such great teachers as Chandrakirti, Chandragomi, and Shantarakshita [300b]. The system of mind training called Equality and Exchange of Self and Others was taught by Shantideva. These two traditions, which originated with the Master, Buddha Shakyamuni, were handed down by Maitreya and Mañjugosha in separate teaching lineages. Although a practitioner can develop enlightenment mind by cultivating either of them, the instructions that Lord Atisha set forth in such works as his *Lamp of the Path to Enlightenment* are the ones he received from Suvarnadvipa Guru, a teacher who possessed the instructions contained in both lineages.

During the time of the Early Kadampas,[86] the Sevenfold Instruction of Cause and Effect was disseminated widely. The body of teachings known as the Equality and Exchange of Self and Others, however, was considered an esoteric teaching and was only revealed in private to a limited number of disciples. Nevertheless, Je Rinpoche received all the instructions from these two lineages and taught a system for training the mind that incorporates elements from both teachings. The instructions that I shall give here follow this unique system and are the method that you should practice. The instructions from the two lineages must be combined together when a practitioner is meditating on them to actually develop enlightenment mind. When taught, however, they must be presented separately.

The method of training the mind according to the Sevenfold Instruction of Cause and Effect is made up of eight sections: (1) immeasurable equanimity, (2) recognizing all sentient beings as our mothers, (3) recalling the kindness of all mother sentient beings, (4) developing the intention to repay their kindness, (5) the loving-kindness that regards all sentient beings as dear, (6) compassion, (7) the extraordinary intention, and (8) enlightenment mind. Of these eight, the six from recognizing all beings as our mothers up

[86]This should be taken to mean the Kadampa lineage from the time of Atisha up to Je Tsongkapa. The followers of Je Tsongkapa, who are more commonly known as Gelukpas, are also referred to as New Kadampas (T: *bKa' gdams gsar ma*).

to the extraordinary intention represent causes, and the act of generating enlightenment mind represents the result.

The cause and effect relationship that exists between these points is as follows: Before we can generate the enlightenment mind that desires to achieve Buddhahood in order to benefit all sentient beings, we must develop the extraordinary intention that takes personal responsibility for the well-being of others. But this feeling of personal responsibility cannot be developed if we lack the compassion that cannot bear the way in which all sentient beings are tormented by suffering. In order to develop this compassion [301a], we must first gain the loving-kindness that regards all sentient beings with the same tenderness and affection that a mother feels for her own dearly cherished child.

Right now, we can develop that kind of attitude toward family and friends, but not toward our enemies. Therefore, before we can develop the kind of loving-kindness that I just described, we must come to regard all sentient beings in the same way as we view our family. And since the closest relative of all is one's own mother, we must begin by establishing that all sentient beings have been our mothers. After that, if we recall the kindness of our mothers and develop the attitude that wishes to repay their kindness, we will also be able to gain the loving-kindness that feels tenderness and affection toward all sentient beings.

Thus, the phrase "cause and effect" as it is being used here means that each succeeding step in the instruction can only be gained after developing the one that precedes it. Moreover, we must not let ourselves doubt whether we are able to do this practice, thinking it is too long a road for us to travel. By training ourselves gradually, we can definitely gain the final result.

Speaking generally, the instructions preserved in the Kadampa tradition are most profound. However, the teaching of the great Jamgön[87] Tsongkapa is especially profound, much more so than those preserved in all other traditions. It is complete and free of any impurity concerning both the Sutrayana and the Tantrayana traditions; indeed, it is still imbued with the warmth of the exalted Mañjughosha's very own breath. My own guru, my precious savior and lord, said this about it:

> All the early Tibetan teachings were a preparation for Je Lama's teaching, which is like refined gold.

[87]T: *'Jam mgon*. An epithet of Je Tsongkapa, which means literally Gentle Lord. See also Part Two, Day Eight, note 122.

Taktsang Lotsawa[88] wrote:

> I praise you for the great treasure of your unprecedented
> and eloquent writings
> Covering all the sutra and mantra teachings—especially
> the Vajrayana;
> All the categories of tantra—especially the meaning of
> Anuttarayoga;
> As well as everything about the two stages[89]—especially
> the illusory body.[90]

The Dzokchen teacher Pelgey also wrote a verse containing the line [301b] "Tsongkapa, the source of eloquent writings on the sutra and mantra teachings." Anyone who can maintain an impartial attitude will realize that these words of praise are truly accurate.

Certain vaunted teachings are said to give you "Buddhahood in the grasp of your hand";[91] yet they cannot place within our grasp even the lowest level of the accumulation path.[92] But if we rely on this very Lamrim teaching, Buddhahood truly is placed directly in our hands. We cannot achieve the results of this Lamrim teaching, however, unless we cultivate the instructions systematically and in the proper order. Therefore, as relates to the present topic,[93] we must begin by training ourselves in the first point: recognizing all sentient beings as our mothers.

Anyone who fails to cultivate these instructions diligently is like those who, though desiring happiness, act in a manner completely contrary to that end by engaging in nonvirtuous deeds. A person who claims that he wants to achieve Buddhahood but makes no effort to develop enlightenment mind is practicing in a misguided way. Even though someone might be trying to practice the swift path of the Secret Mantra teachings, he may, in fact, be like the man who wanted to go to Tsang. After getting on his horse and

[88]T: *sTag tsang lo tzā ba*. The Translator from Taktsang was a noted Sakya scholar of his time. His ordination name was Sherab Rinchen Gyeltsen (T: *Shes rab rin chen rgyal mtsan*, fl. early 15th century). See also Part Two, Day Nine, p. 78.

[89]That is, the two stages of the Anuttarayoga Tantra path. See above, note 74.

[90]*Sun of Praise that Develops the Lotus of Faith* (T: *Dad pa'i padma rgyas par byed pa'i bstod tsig gi nyi ma*), p. 223. In Bibliography, see listing under *sTag tsang lo tzā ba*.

[91]T: *sangs rgyas sbar bcang*.

[92]T: *tsogs lam chung ngu*. The accumulation path, which itself contains three levels called small, medium, and great, represents the first of five major divisions in the path to liberation. See also Part One, Day Three, note 90; and Part Two, Day Seven, note 14.

[93]That is, the instructions for developing enlightenment mind.

riding for a very long time, he thought that he must have reached Tsang. But instead, he had actually reached Kongpo Rong.[94] So, we must apply ourselves diligently to the methods for cultivating enlightenment mind.

i) Equanimity

In order to develop the recognition that all sentient beings have been our mothers, we must first generate immeasurable equanimity. For example, an artist can't paint a mural properly until he has prepared the wall by making it smooth and even. Similarly, unless we first cultivate an attitude of evenmindedness toward all sentient beings, we will not be able to develop an unbiased form of loving-kindness, compassion, and so on, when we meditate on the topics of this instruction.

It should be understood that while the system for training one's mind according to the Sevenfold Instruction of Cause and Effect doesn't contain all the elements of the instruction known as Equality and Exchange of Self and Others, the system based on the Equality and Exchange of Self and Others does include all the elements of the Sevenfold Instruction of Cause and Effect. You should also be aware that the equanimity that forms the first meditation topic in the Sevenfold Instruction of Cause and Effect [302a] is immeasurable equanimity.[95] This is an awareness in which we seek to generate in *our* mind an attitude of evenmindedness toward all sentient beings.[96]

At present, our lack of evenmindedness is shown by the fact that we generate animosity toward some and attachment toward others. As relates to the

[94]Tsang (T: *gTzang*) is one of the main geographical regions of Tibet, occupying the area west and southwest of Lhasa. Kongpo, on the other hand, lies in the opposite direction, about 100 miles due east of Lhasa, in the area surrounding the upper reaches of the Nyang River (T: *Nyang chu*).

[95]The term equanimity (S: *upekṣā*, T: *btang snyoms*) can refer to three different mental states. To distinguish them, they are called (1) immeasurable equanimity (S: *apramāṇopekṣā*, T: *tsad med btang snyoms*), (2) equanimity of feeling (S: *vedanopekṣā*, T: *tsor ba btang snyoms*), and (3) the compositional factor of equanimity (S: *saṃskāropeksā*, T: *'du byed btang snyoms*). Immeasurable equanimity is the one explained here. Equanimity of feeling refers to neutral feelings; that is, feelings that are neither painful nor pleasurable. The compositional factor of equanimity is so called because it is a mental state that forms part of the fourth of the five heaps (S: *skandhaḥ*, T: *phung po*); that is, the heap of compositional factors (S: *saṃskāraskandhaḥ*, T: *'du byed kyi phung po*). Its significance is discussed in connection with the instructions on cultivating quiescence (S: *śamathaḥ*, T: *zhi gnas*; see Day Twenty-one, p. 254 and accompanying note 65).

[96]Note that the immeasurable equanimity to be cultivated here differs from the practice of the same name that is done during the recitation of the six preliminary practices (See Part One, Day Five, p. 162). There, the aspiration is to establish others (that is, all sentient beings) in the state of equanimity that is free of attachment and hatred. Here, the practitioner's aim is to develop this same equanimity within himself (that is, he seeks to overcome any tendency within his own mind to manifest feelings of attachment or hatred toward others).

meditation object, there are two different approaches we can use in our efforts to overcome this tendency. In the first method, we train ourselves by meditating on three types of objects separately and in a sequential manner. That is, the practitioner begins by focusing on a neutral person, then shifts to a friend, and finally directs his attention to an enemy. In the second method, we focus on all three types of object—neutral person, friend, and enemy—at the same time.

Since the second method is more comprehensive, you should meditate on all three types of objects at once. When you fix your attention simultaneously on a friend, an enemy, and a neutral person, you will experience three different reactions: toward the first object you will feel attachment, toward the second you will feel anger, and toward the third you will have the kind of indifference that allows you to forgo any concern for him.

At this point, we should analyze the dislike we feel toward the enemy and consider why it is that we generate anger toward him. What we will find is that this reaction stems from our having gone over in our mind how this individual harmed us in the past. In spite of this past harm, we should stop our anger by meditating on the uncertain nature of relationships with other people and by reflecting how this enemy has also been a close family relative many times in our past lives. This point was explained earlier during the section on contemplating the general suffering in samsara.[97]

If we examine the reasons why we feel such a strong liking for the person whom we currently regard as a friend, we will find that it stems from some recent incident—perhaps a minor and temporary benefit such as giving us food, clothing, or the like. Then we should stop our attachment toward this person by reflecting that he has also been an enemy to us countless times in our past lives.

We should do a similar exercise with regard to the neutral object—that is, a person who is neither an enemy nor a friend [302b], and for whom we feel no particular concern. We should reflect that this person has been both our enemy and our friend in the past.

If all three of these individuals are similar in having been both our enemy and our friend at different times, then each of them is alike in having been variously an enemy, a friend, or a neutral person. Who, then, should be an object of our attachment? Who should be an object of our hatred? Thus, reflect that it is improper to feel attachment for a current friend, because he has been our enemy many times in the past. And reflect that it is improper to feel hatred toward a current enemy, because he has also been a close relative many times in the past.

[97]See the topic entitled "The defect of being uncertain" in Day Fourteen, pp. 8–10.

Moreover, those whom we have known briefly in this life merely appear to us as an enemy or a friend at this moment in time. There is no individual anywhere who remains our enemy or our friend forever. From our own standpoint, then, we have no justification for generating feelings of attachment toward some and hatred toward others.

In addition, from the standpoint of the sentient beings toward whom we develop such feelings, they should all be regarded the same. They are all alike in that they are subject to the same desperate conditions of samsara. They are also alike in their desire to find happiness and escape from suffering. Therefore, not only from our own perspectives but from the perspective of those about whom we form judgments as well, all sentient beings are alike in that no one should be looked upon in a one-sided or biased manner.

Now, you might think to yourself, "Not everyone is the same. What makes these persons different is that they either helped or harmed me *in this life*." But this is a mistaken view. One individual who helped you in a past life and another who helped you in this life are identical in their having helped you. Likewise, someone who harmed you in a past life and someone who harmed you in this life are identical in their having done you harm. For instance, a person who hit you in the head with a club last year and another person who hits you in the head with a club this year are alike in that they both harmed you in the same way. Similarly, someone who gave you a brick of tea last year and another who gives you one this year are alike in that they both gave you a gift [303a].

Here is another analogy. If ten beggars approach you asking for alms, these individuals are alike from their standpoint, in the sense that they all suffer from hunger and thirst. They are also alike in their act of begging. They are the same from your standpoint as well, since none of them has done you any harm or helped you in any way.

If, after contemplating these points, you succeed in developing evenmindedness toward these three objects of enemy, friend, and neutral person, then you should shift your focus to include all sentient beings. With them as your meditation object, once again try to develop the same feeling of evenmindedness. After gaining evenmindedness toward all sentient beings, you will no longer discriminate between friends and enemies. This will completely stop you from engaging in the inferior worldly activity of trying to defeat enemies and promote the well-being of friends. All those who fail to develop such evenmindedness face this consequence: no one who singles out and excludes certain individuals from the general category of all sentient beings and then refuses to feel any concern for them will ever succeed in generating true enlightenment mind.

This topic of equanimity alone must be practiced with great effort for many months or possibly even years. And we will not make any spiritual progress at all by hoping to firmly establish the root of ultimate enlightenment after practicing for only a few meditation periods. This topic of enlightenment mind is not like deity yoga, mantra recitation, meditating on the mind's essence, and the like. We can devote our whole lives to those practices and gain very little.[98] On the other hand, striving to practice the instruction on enlightenment mind is definitely an effort worth making and a subject worth meditating on.

(Kyabje Rinpoche then concluded the discourse by reviewing all the topics he had taught throughout the day.)

[98]The point is that ordinary practitioners who have not mastered the Lamrim instruction gain little by trying to meditate on other more esoteric instructions that they are not yet ready to practice.

DAY SEVENTEEN: THE SEVENFOLD INSTRUCTION OF CAUSE AND EFFECT, AND THE SEVEN-POINT MIND TRAINING INSTRUCTION

(Kyabje Rinpoche began the discourse by describing several benefits of enlightenment mind. One is that a person who possesses enlightenment mind will lead to a state of permanent happiness even those who have abused him verbally or created some other negative relationship with him. The great son of the Conquerors, Shantideva, described this quality in the following verse:

> I bow down to the bodies of those in whom
> The ultimate jewel-mind has arisen [303b];
> I take refuge in those mines of goodness
> Who bring happiness even to those who harm them.[1]

In short, everything we do when we are motivated by this mind represents true dharma. This is because enlightenment mind turns all such actions into Mahayana dharma, and that is the cause that enables us to achieve Buddhahood.

Kyabje Rinpoche then explained that we should not allow our spiritual efforts to consist only of trying to practice deity yoga and recite mantras. We must make this teaching on the stages of the path to enlightenment the foundation of our spiritual practice, and within this body of teachings we must focus our efforts especially on trying to develop enlightenment mind. Even though we might spend our entire lives on some isolated mountaintop trying to meditate on any other subject, we will not come the slightest bit closer to our goal of Buddhahood. Therefore, we must adopt this very topic of enlightenment mind as our most fundamental spiritual practice.

Among several other points, Kyabje Rinpoche also reminded us that in order to develop enlightenment mind we must rely on a body of instructions that teaches us a method for training the mind. After briefly describing how to correct our motivation, he enumerated the sections of the outline that had already been covered. Then he reviewed the benefits of developing enlightenment mind and the method of meditating on equanimity.)

i) Recognizing all sentient beings as our mothers

Recognizing all sentient beings as our mothers is the first topic in the Sevenfold Cause and Effect Instruction for training oneself in enlightenment mind. It is also extremely difficult to generate a proper realization of this

[1] *Engaging in Bodhisattva Activities* (S: *Bodhicaryāvatāraḥ*), ch 1, v. 36.

topic. However, if we don't, we also won't be able to generate a realization of any of the subsequent cause-and-effect elements of this instruction, such as recalling how kind our mothers have been to us [304a]. Therefore, we must strive especially hard to practice this first topic.

"Recognizing all sentient beings as our mothers," the first causal link in this instruction, means to realize that each of us is connected to all sentient beings by the most intimate of family relationships—that of having been our mother. If we fail to develop a realization of this topic, we will lose whatever opportunity we have for generating enlightenment mind.

Other topics, such as profound emptiness, are not as difficult to realize precisely because they can be contemplated using many different logical reasons. And a sure and deeply felt understanding of the present topic is especially difficult to achieve if we try to contemplate it by means of scriptural citation alone.[2] Therefore, those persons of sharp faculties who are self-reliant in pursuing the dharma[3] must prove this point to themselves on the basis of reasoning. However, it is still quite difficult to achieve a realization of this point, since there is only one argument that can be used—namely, the one contained in these lines from the *Extensive Treatise on Knowledge*:

> Whenever a being takes birth, his breath,
> Faculties, and mind do not arise solely
> From the physical body, independent of
> Other entities that are of the same kind.[4]

Here is the first part of this argument, which seeks to prove that a person's mind continuum has no beginning: Today's mind is a continuation of yesterday's mind, and yesterday's mind is a continuation of the mind from the day before yesterday. This chain can be traced all the way back to the

[2]As a scriptural citation, the *Great Stages of the Path* (T: *Lam rim chen mo*), p. 422 (f. 195b) quotes the following brief passage that appears in Asanga's *Essential Nature of the Levels* (S: *Bhūmivastu*, T: *Sa'i dngos gzhi;* Skt. ed., p. 198): "The Blessed One declared: 'When looking into the distant past, it is difficult for me to see [i.e., I cannot see] that place where you have not taken birth, lived, and died. When looking into the distant past, it is difficult for me to see that person who has not been your father, mother, brother, sister, instructor, preceptor, spiritual master, or teacher.'" (For Skt. edition in Bibliography, see listing for *Yogācārabhūmiḥ*, sections 1–5.)

[3]S: *dharmānusarī*, T: *chos kyi rje 'brang*. They are contrasted with persons of duller faculties who must rely on their faith in pursuing the dharma (S: *śraddhānusarī*, T: *dad pa'i rjes 'brang*). See Vasubandhu's *Commentary to the Treasury of Higher Knowledge* (S: *Abhidharmakośa-bhāṣyam*), in explanation of ch. 6, v. 29 of the root text.

[4]S: *Pramāṇivarttikam*, ch. 2, v. 36. This verse appears in the chapter entitled "Establishing the Nature of Knowledge" (S: *pramāṇasiddiḥ*, T: *tsad ma grub pa*). In Tibetan editions, this chapter is listed as the second chapter; however, Sanskrit editions place it first.

mind that existed at the moment of a person's conception in his mother's womb. But the mind at the moment of conception must be the continuation of a mind that existed just prior to the moment of conception, because the mind that becomes established in the womb at conception is part of a mind continuum that existed before the moment of conception in the womb. And since samsara has no beginning, there is no event we can point to and say: "This is when my mind first came into being."

Because the mind has no beginning, it can be established that our births have no beginning. This allows us to establish that each of us has taken birth countless times and that our former lives are without limit.

Just as we had a mother in this life [304b], we also had a mother in each of those previous lives that was either a womb birth or birth from an egg.[5] And just as we had one mother for each of those lives, we had a hundred mothers when we took birth that way a hundred times, and a thousand mothers when we took birth that way a thousand times. Therefore, since we have had an infinite number of such mothers, it is impossible that all sentient beings have not been our mothers.

Now, you might find yourself thinking this: "I agree that I must have had many different mothers. But it can't be true that all sentient beings have been my mother, because the number of sentient beings is infinite."

However, it isn't just in a general sense that our rebirths represent such a large number. We have taken birth as each of the countless species of sentient beings that there are—including all the wild animals such as deer and mountain goats, as well as all the various kinds of worms, insects, and the like. In addition, we have taken birth countless times as each of these countless species. Therefore, the number of births we have taken is much greater than the number of sentient beings that there are. And since we must have had the same number of mothers as we did births, not only have all sentient beings been our mothers, we would not have been able to find enough mothers unless each of them had been our mothers a great many times.

Here we should recall the lines from the *Letter to a Friend* that state in part:

> If we tried to count our maternal lineage with pellets
> of soil
> The size of juniper berries . . .[6]

[5]As distinct from those births in which we did not have a mother—that is, those that were birth from warmth and moisture, and those that were spontaneous or miraculous births. See Day Fourteen, note 9.

[6]T: *bShes pa'i spring yig,* v. 68. See also Day Fourteen, p. 14.

These lines refer explicitly to the lineage of your mother's mother, the mother of her mother, and so on. However, according to the oral instruction of the lineage gurus, we should modify this idea and take it to mean the lineage of your mother in this life, your mother in the life just before this one, your mother in the life before that, and so on. Thus, if we made pellets of earth the size of juniper berries to represent each of these mothers, we would use up all the earth's soil before we had counted one one-hundredth or even one one-thousandth of all our mothers. Therefore, unless each and every sentient being has been our mother, there would not be enough sentient beings to account for all these mothers.

Moreover, since all sentient beings [305a] are certain to achieve Buddhahood, the time will come when there are no longer any unenlightened beings. But our own individual samsaras go back an infinite length of time into the past. So it must be true that the number of times we have taken birth in samsara is much greater than the number of sentient beings there are in the universe. Therefore, unless each and every sentient being has been our mother countless times, there would not be enough sentient beings to account for all our mothers. We should conclude, then, that not only have all sentient beings been our mothers, but that every sentient being has been our mother many times.

We should also reflect how there is no form of sentient being in which we have not taken birth, and how we have taken birth in each of these forms numberless times. For example, consider the way in which we have taken birth as a human being. There is no place on this continent where we can claim not to have been born as a human being. And we have been born in all of these places countless times. Similarly, we have been born as human beings countless times in all the worlds that lie in the east, south, west, north, and all the corners of the universe. After reflecting in this way, we should reach the following conclusion: "Since I have taken birth so many more times than there are sentient beings, not only have all sentient beings been my mother, there isn't a single one who has not been my mother for a human birth. Thus, it is certain that all sentient beings are my mothers."

If after such reflection you are unable to develop the understanding that all sentient beings are your mothers, then you should pursue the opposite line of thought. Think to yourself, "Is it possible that I've never had a mother?" To this you will react, "No, because I have direct knowledge of my mother in this life." Then you can infer that you must also have had a mother in the life before this one, and so on. Eventually, you can return to the arguments mentioned before.

Both the *Easy Path* and the *Quick Path* only briefly mention how to meditate on recognizing all sentient beings as our mothers. The points I have explained here are the fruit of my own efforts to learn the subject directly from my guru. Since I have added considerably more detail to this topic of instruction, those of you who are dedicated practitioners, as well as those of you who must take responsibility for preserving the teachings, should strive to keep this method of explanation intact. If you do, it will be very effective in helping others to bring forth realizations of the various topics in this teaching on the stages of the path to enlightenment [305b].

When you meditate on this topic, begin by reflecting how your mother in this life has also been your mother many times in past lives. After that, reflect in the same way with regard to your father and other family members. Then do the same with a neutral person. When you have developed an experiential awareness toward each of these examples, focus your attention on an enemy. Reflect how that person, too, has been your mother. Finally, train yourself by focusing on all sentient beings.

During this practice, you might find yourself thinking: "If someone is my mother, I must be able to recognize that person as my mother. Therefore, if I don't recognize someone as my mother, that person *isn't* my mother." But the Buddha himself was unable to perceive a single sentient being who has not been our mother. Therefore, even though we may not be able to recognize other beings as having been our mothers, they truly are our mothers. For example, our mother of this life may have been reborn as a dog that lives nearby, without our being able to recognize her any longer. There are also cases where someone may not realize that a particular person is in fact his mother of that very same life. This kind of uncertainty is illustrated in the story of Bhikshuni Utpalavarna and that of the householder referred to in the verse that states: "Eating his father's flesh, a son beats his mother."[7] Therefore, the inability to recognize someone as your mother isn't a valid reason to establish that that person isn't your mother.

Nor is it true that a person ceases to be your mother because she has passed away. If that were so, one could argue that the person who was your mother in the early part of your life is no longer your mother in the latter part of your life, because the person who existed in the early part of your life is no longer alive. One could also argue that the person who was your mother yesterday is no longer your mother today, because she is no longer alive.

This argument is based on the principle of subtle impermanence. Therefore, those of you who have not studied Buddhist philosophical works will find it difficult to understand. Nevertheless, consider the following example: A monk's shawl such as this one did not have any stains last year when it was new. Nor did it have any holes. But the part of that continuum that represents the shawl as it exists now does have stains and is torn in a few

[7] See Day Fourteen, p. 9, where the entire verse is cited, together with the story with which it is associated.

places. Therefore, last year's shawl and today's shawl are, in a certain sense, distinct objects.

Nevertheless, we must reflect that there is no difference between two beings who were our mothers in two different lives [306a]. For instance, if someone saved your life last year, you must still recognize that kindness a year later.

After training yourself in this topic for an extended period of time, you will develop an attitude that is a sign you have achieved a true realization of how all sentient beings are your mothers. Whenever you see even an ant or small bug, you will react spontaneously and intensely with this thought: "When I was the child of this sentient being, I had to rely on her completely for all my happiness and well-being."

(Kyabje Rinpoche concluded this topic by noting that we must achieve the same level of realization as Lord Atisha did about how all sentient beings have been our mothers.)

iii) Recalling the kindness of all mother sentient beings

After recognizing that all sentient beings are alike in having been our mothers, we must contemplate how incredibly kind they were to us when they were our mothers. For instance, if we consider our mother in this life, we should recall the great kindness that she showed us in all three stages of our relationship with her—that is, in the beginning, middle, and end.

In the beginning, she carried us inside her body for nine months and ten days. During that time, she nurtured us lovingly. For instance, out of concern for our safety, she was very careful in all her behavior—such as sitting, walking, eating, drinking, and so on. If our mother had not nurtured us with such skill, we would not now be enjoying this opportunity of meeting with and practicing the holy dharma. This did not come about because of our great cleverness; rather, it is a result of our mother's kindness.

In the middle period of our relationship—that is, right after we were born—we didn't know anything and were little more than worm-like lumps of flesh. Yet our mother lifted us up so joyfully with the tips of her ten fingers, as if she had discovered some great treasure. She held us close to her own warm body, laid us down on a soft bed, and greeted us with loving smiles. Although she could have wiped the snot from our nose with her hands, she wiped it away with her tongue fearing her hand might be too rough. Similarly, she could have wiped our behinds clean with a stick or some other object [306b]; but she wiped us with her hand instead, fearing a stick might hurt us.

If she had left us alone for a day or even just an hour, there is little chance we would have survived. We might have been killed and eaten by a dog, pecked to death by birds of prey, fallen to our death from some high place, or died in some other way. Each day, she saved our life hundreds of times.

Our mother would have gladly chosen to suffer for us herself rather than see us suffer. She could not relax even while sleeping, as she once had, because she continued to think only about us, her child. Gradually, she taught us everything, including how to walk and talk and even the proper way to eat food. It is only because of her efforts that we now know how to do effortlessly such basic things as walking, sitting, talking, and the like.

During the final period of reliance on our mother, she gave us everything we needed. Our mother committed bad deeds, endured a bad reputation, and ignored physical suffering just for the sake of a few coins. She considered the wealth that she accumulated in this way more precious than her own flesh. Not daring to spend this money on herself, she gave it all to us. She set up a household for her sons, arranged marriages for her daughters, and supported her children so they could renounce the householder's state and become monks and nuns. Our mother showed us such great kindness by looking after us as best she could. In short, she strove to the very limits of her knowledge and ability in trying to provide us with every possible form of benefit and happiness. She also showed us immeasurable kindness by protecting us from harm and suffering.

After reflecting on this life's mother in this way, we should then reflect how this life's father, and all other sentient beings as well, have been equally kind to us.

All sentient beings have been our mother countless times even just in human births. As our human mothers, they have taken care of us with the same kindness as our mother in this life [307a]. In addition, all sentient beings have nurtured us lovingly when they were our mothers in other types of birth. For instance, when they were our mother in births as deer or other wild animals, they did everything for us, even down to licking us with their tongue.

They were also our mother when we were born as birds, and kept us warm with their feathers for up to a month. If humans threatened us with clubs and other weapons, they could have escaped themselves by flying away. But because of their affection for their offspring, they risked their own life to protect us. Later, even if they only managed to find a single worm or insect, they gave it to us so that we could be nourished. Moreover, it isn't only once or twice that sentient beings have cared for us in this way; they have shown us great kindness every time they have been our mother, and they have done so countless times.

There was once a bandit from Golok who stabbed a horse with his knife and cut open its belly. When a foal dropped out onto the ground, the mare licked it just before she died. Upon seeing this act of motherly love, the bandit was so deeply moved that he gave up robbing people. How can any of us know for sure that we were not this foal, and that the mare was not our mother of this life? This is how we must contemplate that all sentient beings have cared for us with the same great kindness that our mother in this life has.

iv) Repaying the kindness of all mother sentient beings

A verse that appears in the *Compendium of Training* declares:

> Driven mad by the mental afflictions, blinded
> by ignorance,
> And stumbling with each and every step
> Down a path beset with many steep cliffs,
> I and others are always in a lamentable state.
> All beings share in this universal plight.[8]

Suppose that your mother of this life [307b] was blind and had no one to guide her. Suppose also that she was not of sound mind and was standing at the edge of a cliff about to leap off. Now, what if you, her very own son, happened to be standing nearby. Who else might this mother turn to for help if not her own child? And who might that son consider saving if not his own mother?

In fact, all sentient beings lack the eyes that distinguish between the true dharma they ought to practice and the evil they ought to avoid. Moment by moment, they stumble along committing misdeeds under the influence of desire and misguided spiritual practice. Like blind persons with no one to guide them, they have no spiritual teacher who could show them what they should and should not do. Disturbed by the demons of the three poisons—the mental afflictions—they have lost control of their mind and gone mad. Having flung themselves into the great abyss of the three lower realms, they have dwelt there for many kalpas in regions where their body cannot be distinguished from the fire that consumes it.

We, on the other hand, have met a spiritual teacher, found the Mahayana dharma, and gained some understanding of what we should and should not do. Therefore, we must contemplate that since our own circumstances are so much better than those of other sentient beings, it is our responsibility to find a way of saving them from their misery.

[8]S: *Śikṣāsamuccayaḥ*, p. 195.

The *Letter to a Disciple* also states:

> While they are not recognized through the passing of birth
> and death,
> We can see that they are like beings who have fallen into
> a whirlpool;
> Hence nothing could be more ungrateful than to abandon
> all those relatives,
> Who remain trapped in the ocean of samsara, and pursue
> liberation alone.[9]

We should develop the desire to repay all the kindness that sentient beings have shown us by meditating in the following way: "Since I currently have the means of rescuing all mother sentient beings that have fallen into samsara's vast whirlpool, it would be mean and contemptible of me not to do so. It is my duty to rescue these mother sentient beings [308a]."

The proper way to repay the kindness of sentient beings is described in these verses from the *Essence of the Middle Way*:

> Further, having been overcome by the demons
> Of the mental afflictions in the past,
> I tormented beings already afflicted with suffering,
> Like one who puts salt on another's wounds.
>
> What other form of benefit could I undertake
> To repay those who in other rebirths
> Befriended, served, and assisted me,
> Than to lead them to liberation?[10]

By giving others food, clothing, and the like, we only relieve them of temporary hardships, such as hunger and thirst. This does not benefit them in any ultimate sense. On the other hand, if we could enable them to gain every happiness and become free of every suffering, we would be providing a great and lasting benefit. And, in fact, by leading beings to Buddhahood, we would be enabling them to achieve a state that possesses every happiness and is free of every suffering. Therefore, we must make this determination: "I shall establish all sentient beings in the state of Buddhahood."

[9] *Śiṣyalekhaḥ*, v. 95. In Bibliography, see listing under *Candragomī*.

[10] *dBu ma'i snying po'i tsig le'ur byas pa*, ch. 1, vv. 14–15. In Bibliography, see listing under *Bhavya*.

(Kyabje Rinpoche concluded this section with the following example: If your mother went crazy and came toward you, her own son, with a knife intending to kill you, you would not become angry with her. Instead, you would try to find a way of curing her insanity. In just such a way, we must develop the desire to repay the kindness of others and we must develop this attitude even toward our enemies.)

v) The loving-kindness that regards all sentient beings as dear

The type of attitude we must develop when meditating on loving-kindness is one in which sentient beings appear to us as beloved, precious, and dear to our heart. Geshe Potowa described it to an old mother with these words: "The loving-kindness that regards beings as dear is just like the love that you have for your son Tölekor [308b]." Thus, the attitude that sees all sentient beings like a beloved child is called "the loving-kindness that views all sentient beings as dear."

This meditation topic does not require any separate points on which to reflect. If you succeed in generating the experiential realizations associated with the three earlier topics of recognizing all sentient beings as your mothers, recalling their kindness, and developing the desire to repay their kindness, loving-kindness will arise naturally.

All sentient beings have not even been able to gain impure forms of happiness, let alone happiness that is free of the mental afflictions.[11] At present, the experiences they mistakenly take for happiness are in truth only various forms of suffering. Therefore, you should reflect as follows: "If only all sentient beings would come to find every form of happiness. I pray that they do find it. I personally vow to make sure that they find such happiness."

The benefits of meditating on loving-kindness are truly vast. The following verses from the *Jewel Garland*, for instance, state that loving-kindness will bring the practitioner eight specific benefits:

> Giving three hundred dishes of food
> Three times each day does not equal
> A portion of the merit contained
> In a brief moment of loving-kindness.

[11] Literally, "happiness that is free of the outflows" (S: *anāsravasukham*, T: *zag pa med pa'i bde ba*). "Outflow" is a synonym for the mental afflictions (see Day Fourteen, note 5). This kind of untainted happiness is achieved when one reaches the path of seeing. It is pure in the sense that it does not cause the mental afflictions to become stronger. Because ordinary happiness can cause the mental afflictions to become stronger, it is impure, or more technically, "happiness that is related to the outflows" (S: *sāsravasukham*, T: *zag bcas kyi bde ba*).

Though you don't achieve liberation, you will
Gain the eight benefits of loving-kindness:
(1) Gods and men will befriend you and
(2) They will also protect you.

You will find (3) joy and (4) much happiness;
(5) Poisons and (6) weapons will not harm you;
(7) You will achieve your aims effortlessly; and
(8) You will be reborn in Brahma's realm.[12]

The magnitude of the object held in the mind when meditating on loving-kindness directly affects the result of the practice. For example, we will be reborn as a wheel-wielding monarch with authority over the same number of continents that we held in our mind when we practiced this meditation. We will be reborn as Brahma if we can hold the entire cosmic system of one billion worlds in our mind [309a]. This is one reason the practice is referred to as a "divine state."[13] According to another explanation, if we can direct the mind toward all the sentient beings that exist within the limitless reaches of space, our practice will serve as a cause for attaining the great divine state of "nonabiding" nirvana.[14]

vi) Great compassion

Great compassion is the unique and potent cause that brings us closer to achieving Buddhahood. When Je Rinpoche was formulating the portion of the outline for his *Great Stages of the Path* that deals with the instructions for developing enlightenment mind, he stressed the importance of great compassion by referring to it as the "root of the Mahayana path" and by explaining how all the other elements of the instruction are linked to it through being either one of its causes or one of its results. In describing how great compassion is the determining factor that enables us to attain all the qualities of the Mahayana path as well as its result, one sutra[15] compares it to the wheel by which a wheel-wielding monarch reigns and also to a person's life force.

[12]S: *Ratnāvalī*, ch. 3, vv. 76–78.

[13]S: *brahmavihāraḥ*, T: *tsangs pa'i gnas*. See Part Two, Appendix E, p. 299, for a description of the four divine states.

[14]S: *apratiṣṭhitanirvāṇam*, T: *mi gnas pa'i mya ngan las 'das pa*. A synonym for Buddhahood, the state in which a Buddha does not abide in either of the two extremes—samsara or Hinayana nirvana.

[15]This is a reference to the sutra entitled *Hymn in Praise of the Dharma* (T: *Chos yang dag par sdud pa*). See Day Sixteen, note 81.

In one of the opening verses from his *Introduction to the Middle Way*, the glorious Chandrakirti also wrote:

> Compassion alone is known as the seed of the Conquerors'
> excellent harvest,
> The water that makes it grow, and the means of its
> fruition—
> Ensuring that it will be enjoyed and remain in existence
> for a long time.
> For these reasons, I praise compassion at the beginning.[16]

Compassion is important at the beginning of our spiritual practice because it determines that a teaching belongs to the Mahayana tradition. Like a seed, it is the foundation for the act in which we resolve to achieve enlightenment.

It is also important in the middle part of our practice, when it can be compared to water and fertilizer. During that period, compassion enables us to generate the armor-like effort that keeps us from becoming discouraged as we engage in Bodhisattva activities. Finally, compassion is important in the last part of our practice, which is like the stage of enjoying crops that have ripened. That is, once we reach the goal of ultimate enlightenment, compassion serves as the means by which a Buddha's activities on behalf of others continue uninterruptedly [309b].

The strength of our enlightenment mind is wholly determined by our compassion. The reason some Bodhisattvas proceed along the levels of the path more quickly than others is also because the compassion that forms the root of their practice is deeper. Those Bodhisattvas who enter the Mantrayana path seeking a swifter path, and who do proceed extremely quickly by means of that path, meet with success because of the power of their compassion.

For instance, if a child were to fall into a fire pit, his mother and father would immediately do whatever was necessary to get him out. Other family members or friends, however, would not act as quickly. The reason for this is that parents have stronger compassion for their own child than others do.

When you are ready to begin meditating on compassion, the following technique will enable you to develop it more easily. First, visualize the image of a sheep that is in the process of being slaughtered by a butcher. Imagine that the animal has been forced onto its back, as if the sky and earth had suddenly changed places. Picture that the sheep's legs are bound with a cord, and that it is struggling in vain to free itself. It realizes clearly that it is about to lose its life. There is no way it could possibly escape by running away.

[16]T: *dBu ma la 'jug pa*, ch. 1, v. 2.

Lacking anyone who might protect or rescue it, its eyes well up with tears and it stares helplessly at the butcher's face. Having been driven to this terrible state of fear and anguish, imagine how finally the sheep is put to death by the various cruel methods used in slaughtering animals.

If you should actually witness the killing of a sheep in this way, you might think to yourself, "I doubt that this sheep understands what is happening." But then consider the story of a butcher who once was slaughtering many sheep. After having killed a few, he was tying up the next one to get it ready for slaughtering. Meanwhile, he had left his knife lying next to another sheep. While the butcher was occupied a short distance away, this sheep tried to hide the knife by pawing dirt over it with its hoof. So there is no question that these animals experience unbearably great fear and suffering [310a].

Now turn your attention to sheep that haven't gone to the slaughterhouse yet and that are still grazing in a mountain pasture. Consider how the only difference between them and the ones that already met with the horrible fate just described is that their time has not yet come. But when it does, they too will surely meet with the same end. After reflecting in this way, generate compassion toward these animals by recalling how they have been your very own mother in past lives.

When you have developed genuine compassion toward these sentient beings, the next step is to reflect how they have had to experience suffering in the lower states in the past, and how they continue to experience it now. This is done in just the same way that you contemplated the suffering of the lower states earlier in relation to yourself.[17] Continue developing compassion as you meditate, for instance, on how some of these mothers must live in the hells, where they are roasted on a ground of red-hot iron or boiled in molten iron. Reflect also how others are born as hungry ghosts, and must suffer the torment of hunger and thirst.

When you succeed in generating compassion in this way, next turn your attention to those human beings of this world who are quick to do evil deeds. Contemplate how, just as there is very little difference between a sheep that is actually being slaughtered and those that are still grazing on a mountain, human beings that commit evil are no different from those sentient beings who are already dwelling in the lower states, since they themselves are certain to fall into the lower states as well.

After that, meditate on your mother in this life. Generate compassion toward her by contemplating how she performs the causes that will bring her suffering in the future. Then reflect how your other family members, your friends, and others devote themselves exclusively to bad deeds and moral

[17]See Part Two, Day Eleven.

transgressions in the course of pursuing their livelihoods. Reflect how even as they endure the three kinds of suffering here in this level of the higher states, they are actively pursuing the causes that in the future will force them to experience the much greater sufferings of the lower states.

After that, contemplate how all sentient beings are continually experiencing suffering [310b] and engaging in the causes that will bring more suffering. In this way, generate the great compassion in which you reflect to yourself, "If only all these mother sentient beings could become free of their suffering and the causes of their suffering. I vow personally to make sure that they become free of them." You should take special care to meditate in this way on those beings toward whom it is particularly difficult to develop compassion. For instance, if you have difficulty generating compassion toward Brahma and other such beings, the way to develop it is by reflecting on the points that were explained during the topics for persons of moderate capacity.[18]

There is a measure or sign by which we can recognize that we have truly developed great compassion. It is reached when our desire to free all sentient beings from suffering, even while we are eating food or having something to drink, is as strong as the feeling a mother has toward her dear child when he is suffering from a grave illness.

One form of compassion is an attitude in which a person merely wishes that beings should become free of suffering. This type of compassion is also practiced by followers of the Listeners' and Solitary Realizers' vehicles. However, we must develop the compassion that is unique to the Mahayana tradition. This is an attitude in which a person feels that he must be the one who saves beings from their suffering. And difficult though it may be, we must strive with great effort to achieve it.

If we see someone who is suffering from an illness that we ourselves have experienced in the past, our experience serves as the basis for generating compassion toward that person. Similarly, those practitioners who meditate earnestly on the topics for persons of lesser and moderate capacity will have reflected on the suffering of lower states and samsara as it relates to themselves. This will make it much easier for them to develop compassion toward others.

Both the loving-kindness that cherishes sentient beings and regards them as precious and dear, and the loving-kindness that wants sentient beings to meet with happiness are forms of loving-kindness. However, there is a slight difference between the two in that the former is a particular kind of loving-

[18]The suffering of the gods in general is covered in Day Fourteen, pp. 34–38. The suffering of deities in the form and formless realms in particular is discussed on pp. 36–38. Brahma is the chief deity in the first of the four levels that make up the form realm.

kindness while the latter possesses the general characteristic that is common to all forms of loving-kindness.

The loving-kindness that regards sentient beings as dear is developed by practicing the three topics of (1) recognizing all sentient beings as our mothers, (2) recalling their kindness, and (3) developing the wish to repay their kindness [311a]. It is also the attitude that enables us to generate great compassion. Therefore, we must meditate on that special form of loving-kindness before we attempt to develop great compassion. On the other hand, the general form of loving-kindness—namely, the attitude that wants sentient beings to meet with happiness—is not a necessary cause for developing compassion in its general form,[19] and does not have to be cultivated before it.

(Kyabje Rinpoche concluded this section by making the following points. The *Great Stages of the Path* states that the place to meditate on the loving-kindness that wants sentient beings to meet with happiness is right after practicing the topic of wishing to repay the kindness of one's mothers. Because of this, some teachers hold that it is proper to meditate on this form of loving-kindness prior to cultivating compassion. But the position expressed in oral instructions[20] on how to meditate on these topics is that the loving-kindness that wants sentient beings to meet with happiness[21] should be meditated on *after* we have meditated on compassion. Following that,[22] we should undertake to develop the extraordinary intention. According to oral instruction, then, the main place to cultivate the general loving-kindness that wants sentient beings to meet with happiness is right here. Oral instruction further holds that, in keeping with the outline of the *Great Stages of the Path*, we should also meditate for a short while on the loving-kindness that regards sentient beings as dear before we meditate on compassion.)

[19]That is, the wish that sentient beings become free of suffering. See text above where general compassion is distinguished from great compassion.

[20]This is a reference to the oral instruction in which the two systems for generating enlightenment mind are combined. See Day Nineteen, pp. 181–182, where a list of eleven topics is discussed. This particular oral instruction also holds that the "taking" portion of the Giving and Taking practice (T: *gtong len*) should be carried out before the "giving" portion. See Day Eighteen, p. 169.

[21]That is, loving-kindness in its general form as opposed to the loving-kindness that regards sentient beings as dear. This loving-kindness also refers to the "giving" portion of the Giving and Taking practice.

[22]That is, after we have meditated on loving-kindness in its general form. This loving-kindness is step nine in the eleven-part instruction that combines the two methods of generating enlightenment mind.

vi) Extraordinary intention

Extraordinary intention is like the duty that a son has to look after his mother. It is the mental act that takes personal responsibility for removing the suffering of all sentient beings and for providing them with every form of happiness. Furthermore, this attitude culminates in the determination that you yourself will establish all sentient beings in the state of Buddhahood. It is extraordinary in the sense that it surpasses the aim of both those who follow the Listeners' vehicle and those who follow the Solitary Realizers' vehicle. For example, if you are moved by the sight of someone falling into an abyss to think, "If only this person could be saved," this resembles the attitudes of loving-kindness and compassion. The practitioner who develops the extraordinary intention, however, would not stop with such a thought; he would resolve to save the person himself. Thus, while followers of both the Listeners' and Solitary Realizers' vehicles can develop the general forms of loving-kindness and compassion, neither of them develops the extraordinary intention [311b]. (Kyabje Rinpoche concluded by saying, "My precious guru used the following example to distinguish between the sense of responsibility developed in the topic of wishing to repay the kindness of our mothers and the one developed here in the topic of the extraordinary intention. The former attitude is like that of a merchant when he is first considering what kind of goods he might like to carry in his business. The latter attitude is like that of a merchant when he has made up his mind about what he is going to sell.")

vii) Generating enlightenment mind

Once we have taken on the kind of personal responsibility just described, we must consider whether we have the ability to fulfill our intention. When we do, we will realize that we don't have the ability to bring about the ultimate well-being of even one sentient being. Then we must try to discover if anyone else has such an ability, and whether it is possible for us to achieve that ability ourselves.

Now, the most powerful gods in this world, such as Brahma and Shakra, cannot bring about the ultimate well-being of sentient beings even to a partial degree. Nor can the Listener *arhats* and Solitary Realizer *arhats* help beings, except in a limited way, since they have not yet abandoned all the fetters. On the other hand, a Bodhisattva who has reached the first of the ten levels does have the ability to benefit sentient beings in a very far-reaching manner. However, he cannot accomplish even a portion of the beneficial acts that are done for others by a Bodhisattva who will be reborn only one more time before achieving enlightenment. Yet this Bodhisattva cannot benefit sentient beings over his entire lifetime the way that a Bodhisattva who is in his final existence and is seated beneath the Bodhi tree can in a single day. Finally, the way that a Bodhisattva seated beneath the Bodhi tree benefits beings cannot begin to compare with the abilities of a fully enlightened Buddha. Their difference is as great as the size of a person's palm when compared to the limitless reaches of space.

Thus, the abilities of a fully enlightened Buddha are unparalleled. No one but he can accomplish the welfare of all sentient beings effortlessly, spontaneously, and in a manner that is appropriate to their character, wishes, and level of understanding.

At this point, you should reflect on the various qualities that are gained upon achieving Buddhahood [312a], by reviewing the explanations that were given earlier in the topic of taking refuge.[23] This is done so that you will develop the conviction that it is absolutely necessary for you to achieve omniscience in order to benefit others in an ultimate way. After this, you should generate the wish to achieve perfect enlightenment for the benefit of all sentient beings.

Of the topics we have just covered, the foundation for developing the desire to benefit all sentient beings is established by cultivating equanimity, recognizing all sentient beings as our mothers, recalling their kindness, and the wish to repay their kindness. Loving-kindness, compassion, and the extraordinary intention represent the actual method for generating this desire to benefit others. Furthermore, when we develop the wish to achieve perfect enlightenment, there are several essential elements that must be present in this attitude, as suggested in the lines that declare:

> Development of the mind is the desire to achieve
> Perfect enlightenment for the sake of others.[24]

In order for the act of generating enlightenment mind to have all the necessary elements, our desire to achieve Buddhahood cannot derive only from the recognition that it is needed to accomplish the interests of others. Our desire to achieve enlightenment must also be based on the recognition that unless we achieve the Buddhahood that includes the attainment of ultimate knowledge and the complete abandonment of all the mental obscurations we will not be able to gain the fulfillment of our own interests. But still, the desire to achieve perfect enlightenment should not be generated merely to accomplish our own selfish interests. This attitude must also be motivated

[23]See Part Two, Day Twelve, pp. 186–201, and Appendix E.

[24]*Ornament of Realizations* (S: *Abhisamayālamkāraḥ*), ch. 1, v. 19. "Mind" here refers to a Bodhisattva's enlightenment mind. In Bibliography, see listing under *Maitreya Nātha*.

by the desire to accomplish the interests of others, which is developed by cultivating loving-kindness, compassion, and the extraordinary intention in the manner that was described earlier.

Now, you might wonder, "I can meditate on all these points, but is it really possible for me to develop true enlightenment mind?" In spite of that, you should realize that you definitely can. There is no better time for us than now to generate enlightenment mind. The physical basis we now have is one that enables us to pursue Buddhahood. Our dharma is the teachings of the Buddha. And among those teachings, we have found the Mahayana dharma. [312b] But most important, we have met with the secret Mantrayana teaching, which enables us to achieve enlightenment within a single lifetime.

These points apply to all Tibetan Buddhist traditions. However, we have also met with the Oral Transmission teaching of the great Je Tsongkapa, a tradition that has the capacity to bestow enlightenment within a mere twelve human years. In fact, this teaching can even bring enlightenment much sooner than that. The biographies of many former practitioners—such as those of the Father,[25] his spiritual sons, and other disciples—detail how they were able to attain the state of Ultimate Union[26] within the short period of three years and three months.

Although the present era is called a "degenerate age," we have never encountered a more fortunate time than the one we now enjoy. Neither Lord Milarepa nor the great Ensaba possessed a better physical form than the one we currently have. Therefore, we must exert ourselves strenuously on this occasion, when we are like the lame man from the Drugu clan who found himself riding on the back of a wild ass.[27]

We regard having to actually meditate on the Lamrim teachings as almost more terrifying than death itself. Most of us would rather spend our lives reading scriptures, studying Buddhist philosophy, or reciting prayers. But this attitude stems from a lack of understanding about the most crucial elements of the dharma. We cannot be sure that in the future we will find another physical form like the one we now have. And even if we did find one, it would be extremely difficult for us to meet with the Buddha's teaching

[25]Je Tsongkapa himself.

[26]S: *yuganaddaḥ*, T: *zung 'jug*. A tantric term for the ultimate state of Buddhahood.

[27]There was once a lame man from the northern Drugu clan (T: *Gru gu*), who accidentally fell onto the back of a wild ass. He was so pleased by this unusual occurrence that he began to sing. When asked why he was singing, he replied, "If a lame person doesn't sing when he's had the chance to ride a wild ass, when should he sing?" We too, then, should take advantage of this rare opportunity we currently have for practicing the dharma. If we don't practice now, when should we? See the *Hundred Thousand Explanations to the Jewel Heap of Edifying Similes* (T: *dPe chos rin chen spungs pa'i 'bum 'grel*), p. 62, in the explanation of a simile called "the man riding a wild ass" (T: *rkyang la zhon*).

again, especially a complete and unerring teaching like that of this second Buddha.[28] Therefore, we must think hard about whether or not we can generate, within this lifetime, the enlightenment mind that is a necessary cause for achieving perfect enlightenment.

If we do succeed in generating enlightenment mind, we will achieve both our own interests and those of all sentient beings. This can be illustrated by the following story: Once, long ago, there was a famine in a certain land, and all the members of a particular family, both parents and children, were on the verge of starving to death. Then one day they found a piece of meat. First the father thought, "We could divide this meat equally and eat it [313a], but everyone would get such a small piece that our hunger would not be satisfied and we would only be kept alive for a very short time." Then he thought, "If I eat all the food myself, I will gain enough strength to go out in search of food so that I can nourish everyone else." So the father ate all the meat. He then went out to search for food and was able to sustain the whole family. Therefore, whether we are practicing tantra or just reciting one round of the *Mani* mantra on our prayer beads, or if we are simply humble monks walking to a monastery assembly or to the debate ground, we must be sure that our actions are motivated by this enlightenment mind.

If you are able to develop a contrived experiential realization[29] of the desire to achieve Buddhahood for the sake of all sentient beings, then you have generated the enlightenment mind that is like the taste of the skin of sugar cane. If you go beyond this, to the point where you gain an uncontrived experiential realization of this mind—that is, if the mere sight of a sentient being is enough to bring forth the desire to achieve perfect enlightenment for the sake of all sentient beings—then you have succeeded in generating a realization of the genuine enlightenment mind. By accomplishing this, you enter the Mahayana accumulation path[30] and begin the process of accumulating merit for three periods that each last a "countless" number of great kalpas.[31] When you gain this experiential realization, you become a Bodhisattva and achieve limitless good qualities, such as becoming worthy of being called a spiritual child of the Conquerors. And if you add the practices of the Mantrayana path to this realization, you will surely attain Buddhahood very quickly.

[28] A reference to Je Tsongkapa, whose appearance was as if Buddha Shakyamuni himself had returned a second time.

[29] T: *rtzol bcas kyi myong ba*. See Part Two, Appendix F, p. 330, where a contrived experiential realization is described as "a spiritual awareness that arises after continuous reflection on many scriptural citations and reasonings, but that fails to arise without such reflection."

[30] S: *sambhāramārgaḥ*, T: *tsogs lam*. See Part One, Day Three, note 90.

[31] See Part Two, Day Twelve, pp. 203–204, along with the accompanying note 78.

(Kyabje Rinpoche concluded by saying that it is important for us to learn all the topics that are taught in connection with the subject of enlightenment mind. For instance, enlightenment mind is classified into two basic types: (1) wishing enlightenment mind, and (2) active enlightenment mind.[32] It is classified into four types according to the level of practice that has been reached, such as the enlightenment mind in which practice is founded on conceptual determination.[33] It is differentiated according to the three ways it can be generated [313b], as in the manner of a king and so on.[34] Enlightenment mind is also described with twenty-two similes.[35] This concludes the

[32]See Part One, Day Two, note 37.

[33]S: *adhimokṣikaḥ*, T: *mos pas spyod pa*. During the accumulation and preparation paths, enlightenment mind is described as an attitude that is founded on conceptual determination, because the practitioner has only a conceptual understanding of emptiness. See also Part Two, Day Twelve, p. 203. The other three are as follows: (1) On the first seven Bodhisattva levels, enlightenment mind is referred to as one in which the extraordinary intention has become pure (S: *śuddhādhyāśayikaḥ*, T: *lhag bsam dag pa*), because on these levels the seeds for all conceptualized forms of belief in real entities (S: *parikalpitasatyagrāhaḥ*, T: *bden 'dzin kun btags*)—that is, those which arise from incorrect reasoning—have been irreversibly destroyed. (2) On the last three of the ten Bodhisattva levels, enlightenment mind is described as completely mature (S: *vaipākikaḥ*, T: *rnam par smin pa*), because on those levels a Bodhisattva's nonconceptualizing wisdom is almost completely spontaneous, allowing him to practice generosity and the other perfections virtually without effort. (3) A Buddha's enlightenment mind is described as free of obscurations (S: *anāvaraṇikaḥ*, T: *sgrib pa spangs pa*), because a Buddha has completely abandoned the obscurations of the mental afflictions and the obscurations to omniscience.

[34]T: *rgyal po lta bu'i sems bskyed*. In this method, a person vows to attain enlightenment himself first, and then lead all others to it. With the enlightenment mind that is generated in the manner of a herder (T: *rdzi'u*), a person vows to establish all other sentient beings in enlightenment before achieving it himself. With the enlightenment mind that is generated in the manner of a ship's captain (T: *mnyan pa*), a person vows to lead others to enlightenment along with him, so that everyone achieves it together.

[35]The twenty-two similes, enumerated in Maitreya Natha's *Ornament of Realizations* (S: *Abhisamayālaṃkāraḥ*), ch. 1, vv. 20–21, serve to illustrate twenty-two levels of enlightenment mind that are described in several of the longer versions of the *Perfection of Wisdom* sutras. For a Tibetan text that identifies specific sutra passages for each of the twenty-two enlightenment minds, see Haribhadra's arrangement of the *Perfection of Wisdom Sutra in Twenty-five Thousand Lines*, vol. 1, ff. 25b–46a. For an English version, see Edward Conze's translation entitled the *Large Sutra on Perfect Wisdom*, pp. 46–55. The following explanation of the twenty-two similes is from Haribhadra's commentary, the *Illuminator of the Ornament of Realizations* (S: *Abhisamayālaṃkārālokaḥ*, pp. 284–285): (1) The Bodhisattvas' first enlightenment mind is one that is accompanied by aspiration (S: *chandaḥ*, T: *'dun pa*), and it is like the earth, because it is the foundation of the merit that produces the complete realization of all dharmas in all their aspects. (2) The second enlightenment mind, accompanied by a noble intention (S: *āśayaḥ*, T: *bsam pa*), is like brilliant gold, because the noble intention that is governed by the six perfections and seeks to benefit others by bringing them happiness both in this and future lives does not waver throughout the entire period that culminates in perfect enlightenment. (3) The third enlightenment mind, accompanied by an extraordinary intention, is like a waxing new moon, because all pure and virtuous dharmas are developing continually.

These three enlightenment minds in lesser, moderate, and great degrees are largely associated with a beginning practitioner and are included within the accumulation path. (4) The fourth enlightenment mind—one that is accompanied by superior practice—is likened to a blazing fire, in that the practices associated with the three knowledges are becoming progressively stronger, just as a fire becomes stronger as more fuel is burned. This enlightenment mind is also associated with the preparation path that takes one to the first Bodhisattva level; thus it corresponds to the level where practice is founded on conceptual determination (S: *adhimukticāryabhūmi*, T: *mos pas spyod pa'i sa*). (5) The fifth enlightenment mind, associated with the perfection of giving, is like a great treasure in that it never becomes exhausted even though it satisfies immeasurable numbers of sentient beings with material wealth of every kind. (6) The sixth enlightenment mind, associated with the perfection of ethics, is like a jewel mine, in that it is the basis upon which all the jewels of good qualities depend, and from which they originate. (7) The seventh enlightenment mind, associated with the perfection of patience, is like a great ocean, because it remains undisturbed by all the troubles that befall it. (8) The eighth enlightenment mind, associated with the perfection of effort, is like a vajra in that it cannot be broken, due to the firmness of one's convictions. (9) The ninth enlightenment mind, associated with the perfection of one-pointed concentration, is like a great mountain, in that it cannot be shaken from its object by any form of distraction. (10) The tenth enlightenment mind, associated with the perfection of wisdom, is like an extraordinary medicine, in that it cures all the diseases of the mental afflictions and the obscurations to omniscience. (11) The eleventh enlightenment mind, associated with the perfection of skillful means, is like a spiritual teacher, in that it never abandons the interests of sentient beings in any circumstance. (12) The twelfth enlightenment mind, associated with the perfection of prayer (S: *praṇidhānam*, T: *smon lam*), is like the wish-granting gem, in that it provides results in accord with one's hopeful prayers. (13) The thirteenth enlightenment mind, associated with the perfection of strength, is like the sun, in that it ripens the crops of beings that are to be tamed by the dharma. (14) The fourteenth enlightenment mind, associated with the perfection of wisdom, is like the sound of a pleasing chant, in that it teaches the dharma in a way that is attractive to followers. These last ten enlightenment minds are mainly associated with the ten Bodhisattva levels of Joy and the rest, and thus operate on the paths of seeing and meditation. (15) The fifteenth enlightenment mind, associated with supernormal wisdoms (S: *abhijñā*, T: *mngon par shes pa*), is like a great king in that it carries out the interests of others with unobstructed power. (16) The sixteenth enlightenment mind, associated with the collections of wisdom and merit, is like a storehouse in that it is a treasury containing great quantities of the collections of wisdom and merit. (17) The seventeenth enlightenment mind, associated with the aids to enlightenment (S: *bodhipakṣadharmaḥ*, T: *byang chub kyi phyogs kyi chos*; see Part Two, Appendix E, pp. 296–299), is like a great highway in that it is the path traveled by all the *aryas* (see Part Two, Day Eight, note 66). (18) The eighteenth enlightenment mind, associated with quiescence and insight, is like a conveyance in that it allows one to proceed easily and without falling into either samsara or nirvana, through the joint application of these two practices. (19) The nineteenth enlightenment mind, associated with the powers of retention (S: *dharaṇī*, T: *gzungs*; see Part Two, Appendix E, note 30) and with self-assured knowledge (S: *pratibhāna*, T: *spobs pa*)—the last of the four informative knowledges (S: *pratisamvit*, T: *so sor yang dag par rig pa*; see Part Two, Appendix E, pp. 305–306)—is like a spring, in that it retains whatever dharma has been either heard or unheard and it also expounds the dharma inexhaustibly, just as a spring both holds water and gives it forth inexhaustibly. These five enlightenment minds occur on the "extraordinary" Bodhisattva levels (that is, the final three levels). (20) The twentieth enlightenment mind, associated with the feast of dharma, is like a joyous sound in that it joyously proclaims the dharma to those followers who are desirous of attaining liberation. This enlightenment mind is still within the Bodhisattva levels, although it represents a stage of the path that directly causes the practitioner to reach Buddhahood. (21) The twenty-first enlightenment mind, associated with the singular path, is like a river's current, because it is able to apply great compassion, wisdom, and skillful explanations for how to generate enlightenment mind according to the Sevenfold Instruction of Cause and Effect.)

b) Training one's mind with the instruction called Equality and Exchange of Self and Others

Now I shall explain the method of training the mind called Equality and Exchange of Self and Others that was taught by the great Conquerors' son Shantideva. Although we can definitely generate enlightenment mind by practicing the seven-part instruction that I just finished explaining, we should also cultivate the form of mental training known as Equality and Exchange of Self and Others, because it is a very powerful system of practice.

In earlier times, this latter instruction was a restricted teaching. It, along with the practice called "Giving and Taking," make up the main elements in a class of teachings known as Mind Training.[36] The teaching on Equality and Exchange of Self and Others is such that those who are unfit to hear it will not be able to comprehend it properly. This is alluded to in a verse from *Engaging in Bodhisattva Activities* that declares:

> The one who desires to save
> Both himself and others quickly
> Should practice the ultimate secret
> Of exchanging self and others.[37]

Thus, from the time of the great Lord Atisha until Chekawa[38] it was considered an esoteric teaching and was only revealed in private to a limited number of disciples. While there are many different Mind Training instructions, such as the *Peacock that Overcomes Poison*,[39] the only one that contains

means in order to accomplish the interests of others continuously, through having realized the ultimate sameness of both mind and its objects. This enlightenment mind is possessed by a Buddha and represents the attainment of the ultimate state of enlightenment. (22) The twenty-second enlightenment mind, associated with the dharma body, is like a great cloud in that all the acts carried out by emanation bodies in order to accomplish the interests of sentient beings, beginning with taking up residence in Tushita and so on, depend upon it. This enlightenment mind is also possessed by a Buddha. It represents the attainment of a post-meditative state, a pure "mundane" wisdom that is comprehensible to followers and that has the ability to manifest emanation bodies through the agency of a Buddha's nonconceptualizing wisdom.

[36]T: *blo sbyong.*

[37]S: *Bodhicāryāvatāraḥ*, ch. 8, v. 120.

[38]T: *mChad ka wa Ye shes rdo rje*, 1101–1175. See *Lives of the Lamrim Teachers* (T: *Lam rim bla ma brgyud pa'i rnam thar*), vol. 1, pp. 541–552.

[39]*T: rMa bya dug 'joms.* A verse text by the Indian yogi Dharmarakshita, one of Atisha's teachers. The colophon of the edition contained in the *Hundred Mind Training Works* (T: *Blo*

the complete body of Mind Training instructions is the *Seven-Point Instruction on Mind Training*. Of all the Mind Training instructions, this one will also benefit your practice the most. That is why I decided to teach the *Seven-Point Instruction* here. It will be based on an early edition of the root text.[40]

The Seven-Point Instruction on Mind Training

There are many teaching lineages for this body of instructions. However, the one I am going to follow here is that of Ngulchu Dharmabhadra[41] and his spiritual sons. According to this tradition, the first topic is to explain the greatness of the teaching's originator [314a].

The greatness of the teaching's originator

The lineage for this instruction begins with the Lord of Sages and continues down to the great Atisha, who taught it to Drom Rinpoche and also admonished him to preserve its secrecy.

While Dromtönba taught the general Lamrim teachings publicly, he kept this particular Mind Training instruction secret and taught it only to Potowa and several other disciples. Potowa taught it to two of his disciples, Langri Tangba and Sharawa. Sharawa, in turn, revealed it to his disciple Geshe Chekawa, who became the lineage holder for Sharawa's teachings on enlightenment mind. From Chekawa's time on, the *Seven-Point Instruction on Mind Training* was taught more openly to large audiences.

Geshe Chekawa was born into a family who were descendants of a great Nyingma practitioner. Although he had become very learned in the five sciences,[42] he was not satisfied. Having been introduced to Langri Tangba's *Eight Verses on Mind Training*—which includes the admonition to give all your gain and success to others, while taking from them their loss and failures—he came to Central Tibet seeking to gain a better understanding of this teaching's meaning. As Langri Tangba had already passed away, he

sbyong brgya rtza) describes the title as the *Peacock that Wanders in the Forest of Powerful Poison* (T: *bTzan dug nags su rma bya rgyu ba*).

[40] There are various editions of the root text for this instruction. Some time after this teaching, Kyabje Pabongka Rinpoche compiled an edition of what he considered the most authoritative version, which is included in his collected works. A translation of that version is found in Appendix H.

[41] T: *dNgul chu Dharma bhadra*, 1772–1851. See Bibliography for a transcript of oral instruction (T: *zin bris*) by this teacher on the *Seven-Point Instruction*, which is entitled *Innermost Treasure of the Conquerors' Sons* (T: *rGyal sras snying nor*).

[42] See Day Sixteen, note 34.

sought out Sharawa and requested from him the instructions on Mind Training. After meditating on them, Chekawa was able to generate enlightenment mind.

Later, Chekawa taught these instructions to many people afflicted with leprosy. Because they were cured by meditating on them, the body of teachings also came to be known as the Leprosy Teaching. He taught it publicly because he thought that many people would not have the opportunity to receive its benefits if it were to remain a secret. These very teachings were arranged into seven sections and then written down to create the text we know as the *Seven-Point Instruction on Mind Training.*

The opening line of the text, which states: "This instruction, which is the Essence of the Nectar of Immortality," refers to Mind Training, that highest of instructions which enables us to achieve the state of immortality represented by Buddhahood.

The greatness of the dharma teaching

How this teaching is like a diamond [314b] can be understood from the explanations that I gave earlier on the benefits of enlightenment mind.[43] And, just as even a portion of the sun's light dispels outer darkness, this teaching removes the inner darkness of the self-cherishing attitude.[44] Similarly, this teaching can cure the illness of cherishing oneself just as the smallest portion of the great Medicinal Tree can cure ordinary illnesses.

Another quality of this Mind Training teaching is its effectiveness in times like these, when the five degeneracies[45] have become strong and we have difficulty putting the dharma into practice. This refers specifically to its helpfulness in preventing unfavorable circumstances from disrupting our practice.

[43]See Day Sixteen, p. 109.

[44]T: *bdag gces 'dzin* or *rang gces 'dzin*. See below p. 161, where this attitude is defined more precisely.

[45]S: *kaṣāyaḥ*, T: *snyigs ma*. The predominance of these five factors is what cause an age to be considered degenerate. They are: (1) degeneracy of life span, (2) degeneracy of era, (3) degeneracy with regard to mental afflictions, (4) degeneracy of views, and (5) degeneracy of beings. The first two factors diminish the power of such things as food and medicine to sustain the life force of sentient beings. The next two diminish the cause of virtue in that they promote the pursuit of worldly pleasures and foster a feeling of weariness. Alternatively, the degeneracy with regard to mental afflictions is seen as having a corrupting influence on laypersons in particular and the degeneracy of views as corrupting the clergy. The last factor diminishes beings both physically and mentally by causing the size, shape, health, and strength of their bodies to be reduced and by causing a decline in the mental qualities of intelligence, memory, effort, and firmness. See the *Commentary to the Treasury of Higher Learning* (S: *Abhidharmakośabhāṣyam*) in explanation of ch. 3, v. 94 of the root text.

These are only a few of the many qualities of greatness possessed by this body of instructions.

The opening salutation "I prostrate to great compassion" should not be understood as referring to Arya Avalokiteshvara. Rather, it is an affirmation of reverence toward the mental state of great compassion, just as Acharya Chandrakirti expressed in the opening verses of his treatise *Introduction to the Middle Way*.

Now we turn to the actual instructions on Mind Training, which are presented in seven sections.

Section one: a presentation of the preliminary teachings that form the foundation of the instructions

The teachings in this section address how to train ourselves in the practices that are held in common with persons of lesser capacity and persons of moderate capacity. They do not need to be taught again here, as they are no different from the explanations taught in the Lamrim tradition.

Section two: training oneself in the two forms of enlightenment mind

This section consists of two parts: (1) ultimate enlightenment mind, and (2) conventional enlightenment mind.[46]

Ultimate enlightenment mind

(At this point, Kyabje Pabongka Rinpoche explained that the early instruction manuals for this teaching were directed especially toward Mahayana practitioners of sharp faculties. Therefore, the explanations begin with instructions for training oneself in ultimate enlightenment mind. However, if the instructions on how to practice ultimate enlightenment mind are taught before the instructions that constitute the "means"[47] aspect of the Mahayana path, it is possible that we would experience the same result as described in the story of the great spiritual adept Mantangipa.[48] Therefore, here I shall

[46]For definitions of these two forms of enlightenment mind, see Part One, Day Five, note 37. The two types of conventional enlightenment mind are referred to earlier on p. 150; they are also described in Part One, Day Two, note 37.

[47]S: *upāyaḥ*, T: *thabs*. The two principal elements of the Mahayana path are: (1) enlightenment mind along with the extensive Bodhisattva activities, and (2) the wisdom that realizes voidness, along with the practice of one-pointed concentration. The former is also referred to as the aspect of the path that represents means.

[48]T: *Glang po'i ko ba pa*. A disciple of Nagarjuna; see lineage of Guhyasamaja tantra, Part One, Appendix B, p. 239. Although we were not able to find a description of this story, Ngulchu

follow the tradition of Tsechok Ling Yongzin[49] [315a], in which the instructions on training oneself in ultimate enlightenment mind are not taught first. Rather, the explanations that relate to ultimate enlightenment mind will be given later, when I present the instructions on the perfection of wisdom.[50]

Conventional enlightenment mind

Among the various stories identified as sources for this instruction is the story of Maitrakanyaka.[51] Another is the account of how our compassionate Master, during the time that he was still training himself on the path, once generated enlightenment mind when he was born in the hells as a worker pulling a wagon.[52]

This portion of the instructions is contained in five parts: (1) meditating on the way oneself and others are the same, (2) reflecting in many ways on the faults of cherishing oneself, (3) reflecting in many ways on the benefits of cherishing others, (4) cultivating the main practice of exchanging oneself

Dharmabhadra's commentary on the *Seven-Point Instruction Mind Training* (T: *Blo sbyong don bdun ma'i zin bris rgyal sras snying nor*, pp. 290–291) makes the following related point: "The teaching on the Stages of the Path to Enlightenment and the commentary (to the *Seven-Point Instruction on Mind Training*) by Yongzin Pandita (i.e., Yongzin Yeshe Gyeltsen) teach conventional enlightenment mind before ultimate enlightenment mind. This approach is intended for followers who possess relatively dull faculties. If those who possess duller faculties are taught emptiness before they have gained a firm understanding of the entities that comprise conventional truth, various errors might occur. For instance, they might become frightened and turn away from the path. On the other hand, followers who possess especially sharp faculties can learn emptiness first and then, after gaining a realization of the correct view, generate compassion toward those beings who have not yet realized emptiness. After that, they generate the conventional enlightenment mind in which they seek to achieve Buddhahood for the purpose of liberating beings from their suffering. This latter approach represents the viewpoint of Acharya Shantarakshita. Based on this distinction, it should be understood that the two approaches are not contradictory."

[49]T: *mTse mchog gling yongs 'dzin Ye shes rgyal mtsan*, 1713–1793. Tutor of the Eighth Dalai Lama, he composed two major works on the *Seven-Point Instruction on Mind Training*. One is entitled the *Essence of Nectar: An Instructional Treatise on Training One's Mind in the Mahayana Practices* (T: *Theg chen blo sbyong gi khrid yig rdud rtzi'i snying po*) and focuses on how to meditate on the instruction. The other work, entitled the *Ornament of Losang's View: An Instructional Treatise on Training One's Mind in the Mahayana Practices* (T: *Theg pa chen po'i blo sbyong gi khrid yig Blo bzang dgongs rgyan*), is much lengthier and an excellent source of scriptural passages that relate to the instructions of the Mind Training tradition.

[50]See Day Twenty-two.

[51]T: *mDza bo'i bu mo*. For a Sanskrit version, see the "Maitrakanyaka Narrative" in *Divine Narratives* (S: *Divyāvadanam*), ch. 38. For a Tibetan version, see Yongzin Yeshe Gyeltsen's *Ornament of Losang's View* (T: *Blo bzang dgongs rgyan*), pp. 373–379.

[52]*Sutra on the Skillful Means of Repaying Kindness* (T: *Thabs la mkhas pa drin lan bsab pa'i mdo*), ch. 4, "Generating enlightenment mind."

and others, and (5) meditating on Giving and Taking, once we have completed the earlier points.

1. Meditating on the sameness of oneself and others

First, meditate on the topics ranging from equanimity to the loving-kindness that views sentient beings as dear, as they were explained earlier. Then you must reflect on instructions such as those referred to in the verse from the *Guru Worship* ritual that states "no one ever wants the slightest suffering."[53]

In our present state, we cherish ourselves and hold ourselves very dear. However, we don't feel that way at all toward others. This is because we fail to perceive the way that we and others are the same. So we should reflect in this way: "It isn't right for me to make such a great distinction between myself and others. In fact, we are exactly alike in the sense that we both want to find happiness and avoid suffering." That is all that really needs to be said about this first point. There aren't many different arguments to consider.[54]

Five of the topics from the earlier teaching on the Sevenfold Instruction of Cause and Effect are practiced in the same way here in these instructions on Mind Training. Three of the five topics are: recognizing all sentient beings as our mothers, recalling their kindness, and developing the wish to repay their kindness. The other two are the final ones of the extraordinary intention and enlightenment mind [315b]. However, the instructions for the other two topics—the loving-kindness that views beings as dear and compassion—are taught in a more powerful form in this teaching. The reason these two topics are practiced differently in this tradition has to do with another topic, recalling the kindness of our mothers. In the earlier teaching, the instructions only describe the kindness of sentient beings when they are actually our mothers. In this teaching, the instructions add explanations for how we should recall the kindness of sentient beings even when they are not our mothers.[55]

[53]T.: *Bla ma mchod pa'i cho ga*. The complete verse states: "Bless me to rejoice at others' happiness/ By reflecting on this sameness of oneself and others:/ No one ever wants the slightest suffering/ Or feels that the happiness he finds is enough." In Bibliography, see listing under (*Paṇ chen*) *Blo bzang chos kyi rgyal mtsan*.

[54]The classic source for the teaching on the Equality and Exchange of Oneself and Others is the last half of the eighth chapter from Shantideva's *Engaging in Bodhisattva Activities*. The section that deals with the sameness between self and others is contained in verses 89–112.

[55]This is called the extraordinary method of recalling our mothers' kindness (T: *drin dran khyad par can*). See below, p. 165.

Before we can carry out the practice of exchanging ourselves with others, we must first meditate on the main obstacle—cherishing oneself—by reflecting on its faults, and on the main supporting attitude of cherishing others, by reflecting on its benefits.

2. Reflecting in many ways on the faults of cherishing oneself

The self-cherishing mind bears the ultimate responsibility for all the unfavorable things that happen to us. This includes the harm done to us by other humans with weapons or poison, for example, as well as that which is done to us by worldly gods, *nagas*, and other nonhuman beings. It is even responsible for our having to be reborn in the hells, as hungry ghosts, or as animals, and so on, since those consequences are brought about by the perverse belief that killing or mistreating other sentient beings, being stingy, and other similar behavior is a way of gaining happiness for ourselves.

This point is made in a verse from the *Guru Worship* that states in part:

> Bless me to recognize that the chronic illness
> Of cherishing oneself is the source of unwanted suffering . . .[56]

It is also expressed in these lines from *Engaging in Bodhisattva Activities*:

> All the suffering there is in the world
> Comes from desiring happiness for oneself.[57]

Elsewhere, the same work states:

> Whatever adversity there is in the world,
> However much suffering and fear there is as well—
> Are all produced by self-cherishing mind.
> What good can this great demon do for me?[58]

[56]T: *Bla ma mchod pa*. The full verse states: "Bless me to recognize that the chronic illness/ Of cherishing oneself is the source of unwanted suffering;/ And enable me to destroy the great demon/ Of cherishing oneself, by blaming it and being hostile to it."

[57]S: *Bodhicaryāvatāraḥ*, ch. 8, v. 129.

[58]Ibid., ch. 8, v. 134.

The root text of this teaching also states:

> All blame rests with one.[59]

Self-cherishing mind alone is to blame for all the various sicknesses we experience, such as an imbalance in the humors of wind, bile, or phlegm. It is responsible for all the different fears that we face, such as that of being harmed by an enemy [316a], suffering a loss, becoming the object of a lawsuit, or being punished by a judge. Our self-cherishing mind is responsible for all these difficulties because it leads us to engage in such unwholesome behavior as not regulating the amount of food we eat; it prevents us from giving up our attachment to the three worldly concerns of food, clothing, and reputation; and it also makes us unwilling to tolerate any unfavorable circumstance we may encounter.

The self-cherishing mind is responsible for the problems that occur between persons in high positions, such as kings and ministers, and it even foments disputes between separate countries. It also causes problems at a lower level—including disagreements among the ordinary people of a country, between members of the same family, or even among simple monks. But none of the difficulties I have mentioned would occur if we overcame our self-cherishing attitude and said to our potential adversaries, "It doesn't matter to me. Do whatever you like."

All the suffering we feel at having been victimized by thieves and robbers is brought on by our self-cherishing mind. This is true even for something as insignificant as a mouse nibbling a hole in our *tsamba* bag. If we should die from poison or through having eaten some sort of disagreeable food, it wouldn't be the poison that killed us. The real cause would be the self-cherishing mind that encouraged us to eat all kinds of improper food. Thus, it would be our own self-cherishing mind that killed us. If we should find ourselves being wrongly accused of stealing something, this too is a result brought about by our having harmed someone else in the past at the urging of our self-cherishing mind.

The self-cherishing mind is also described with a variety of similes such as these: It is like a butcher who destroys the life force of our ability to achieve the higher realms and liberation. It is like a thief who, carrying the sack of the three poisons, steals the crops of our virtue. It is like a farmer who grows the crops of samsara by planting the seeds of bad deeds in the field of ignorance [316b]. It is like a greedy person who hopes to gain something by jumping into a battle being fought with arrows, spears, and swords. It is like a wicked and shameless person who, to avoid experiencing some

[59] That is, with the self-cherishing mind.

loss himself, would even resort to blaming his guru, spiritual preceptor, father, and mother.

Self-cherishing mind is also like a naked, empty-handed person who since beginningless time has failed to gain even the slightest virtuous quality. It is like a person who hopes to gain something in places where there is nothing to be gained and who fears being harmed in places where there is nothing to fear. It is jealous of those who are superior, competitive with those who are equal, and contemptuous of those who are inferior. It becomes arrogant if praised and angry if denounced. It brings on every kind of bad thing known in the world and is the source of all nonvirtuous deeds.

Self-cherishing mind is also described as a ruinous, owl-headed fiend who has caused us to suffer throughout beginningless time. Therefore, the object toward whom we should direct destructive curses is the self-cherishing mind that dwells in the center of our very own heart. Anyone who wants to urge dharma protectors to subdue their enemies or destroy them with magic spells should direct such efforts toward this object. When a *tor-gyak*[60] ritual is performed, many of us direct the *torma* to one of our mother sentient beings as the "mother of all my enemies." But this is a mistaken understanding of the practice.

These descriptions illustrate why the self-cherishing mind is called the "little blue-headed bird of bad luck."[61] They also illustrate why these instructions are known as the "teaching that banishes evil spirits."[62]

My precious guru used to tell us how long ago a certain *chö* practitioner[63] was living in a place that he had seized from a fierce demon. One day a violent argument broke out between two of the *chö* practitioner's benefactors. So he decided to go and settle their dispute. But when the *chö* practitioner met with the two benefactors, one of them hurled a knife that

[60]T: *gtor rgyag*. A ritual in which mantras and *tormas* are used to bring an end to the harmful activities of evil persons.

[61]T: *ltas ngan bye'u mgo sngon*. In his *Explanation of Terms in the Mahayana Treatise on Mind Training that is Like the Rays of the Sun* (T: *Theg pa chen po'i blo sbyong nyi ma'i 'od zer gyi brda don*, p. 128) Akya Yongzin Yangchen Gawey Lodrö (T: *dByangs can dga' ba'i blo gros*, fl. 19th century) explains this phrase: "Among the small birds that nowadays commonly fly around in the vicinity of a town, we never see any with a blue coloring on its head. Therefore, everyone would consider it an inauspicious sign if such a bird appeared."

[62]T: *'gong po 'gong rdzong gi chos*.

[63]T: *gcod pa*. There are various lineages of the *chö* (T: *gcod*) or "ego-cutting" practice. Typically, *chö* practitioners are wandering yogis who can be seen carrying a drum and a thighbone trumpet, ritual instruments that are used in the practice. They meditate in cemeteries and recite special chants in an effort to "cut" or overcome their belief in an independently real self. One element of the practice involves inviting evil spirits to appear before them and then presenting their own body to them as an offering. This is done as an exercise to help these practitioners recognize the manner in which they cling to the false notion of a real self.

accidentally struck the yogi and killed him. The root cause and main reason why this person was killed by a knife lies exclusively with self-cherishing mind [317a]. As a verse from *Engaging in Bodhisattva Activities* states, this self-cherishing mind is the sole entity that has forced us to experience suffering throughout beginningless samsara:

> Over the course of numberless kalpas
> You have sought to achieve your own aims.
> But, despite having made this great exertion,
> You have gained nothing but suffering.[64]

Although self-cherishing mind and the mind that believes in an independently real self are actually distinct entities, the Mind Training teachings describe them as if they were one and the same. This is because they are similar in kind. In essence, these two states of mind are the root of everything bad. One perceives the self as a truly existent entity. The other cannot let go of the self and continually holds it dear.

(Kyabje Rinpoche concluded with these observations: In short, all harm comes from harboring the notion "I need to find happiness for myself" in the deepest part of our mind. But unless we overcome this self-cherishing attitude, we will never really be happy. The reason we have not been able to subdue it before now is that we have failed to investigate where the true blame for our suffering lies. Now that we know where this blame lies, we must regard the self-cherishing mind as our true enemy and make every effort to destroy it.)

3. Reflecting in many ways on the benefits of cherishing others

Shantideva declared that:

> All the well-being there is in the world
> Comes from desiring happiness for others.[65]

[64] S: *Bodhicaryāvatāraḥ*, ch. 8, v. 155.
[65] Ibid., ch. 8, v. 129.

Several lines in the *Guru Worship* ritual also state:

> Bless me to see that the mind which cherishes all mothers
> and wishes
> To make them happy is the door that brings unlimited good
> qualities . . .[66]

Similarly, a line from this Mind Training instruction urges:

> Meditate on the great kindness of all beings [317b].

These passages are alike in affirming that all good qualities—such as being reborn in the higher states, acquiring material wealth, and an excellent following—derive from cherishing others. For instance, if we avoid killing other beings because we cherish all life, we will experience the results of the virtuous deed of abandoning killing. These results include being reborn in the higher states and having a long life. Similarly, when the attitude of cherishing others moves us to practice virtues such as generosity and refraining from stealing, these acts will bring us great wealth and other favorable results in the future.[67]

This point is summarized in the following verse:

> Why go on at great length?
> Simply consider this difference:
> The foolish pursue their own interests;
> The Sage acts in the interest of others.[68]

A verse from the *Guru Worship* also states:

> In sum, bless me to accomplish the equality and exchange
> of self and others,
> Based on the mind that achieves a realization of
> the difference

[66]T: T: *Bla ma mchod pa*. The full verse states: "Bless me to see that the mind that cherishes all mothers and wishes/ To make them happy is the door that brings unlimited good qualities;/ And enable me to cherish beings more dearly than I do my own life,/ Even if they should all rise against me as enemies."

[67]For a discussion of the ten black and ten white karmic paths, as well as their results, see Part Two, Day Thirteen, pp. 242–259.

[68]S: *Bodhicaryāvatāraḥ*, ch. 8, v. 130.

Between the disadvantages of the foolish, who pursue
only their own interests,
And the virtues of the Lord of Sages, who acts solely
on behalf of others.[69]

Initially, the Master and we were alike in that all of us were wandering about helplessly in samsara together. But long ago, the Supreme Sage removed all his faults and gained all the realizations by developing the mind that cherishes others. In this way, he succeeded in fulfilling the two interests.[70] We, on the other hand, have clung to our self-cherishing attitude and striven continuously throughout beginningless samsara spurred by this one thought: "I must find happiness for myself." But we have failed to achieve even the smallest portion of our own interests. Not only have we failed to achieve even the means that would keep us from having to be reborn in the lower states, we still find ourselves in this agonizing condition of having to endure nothing but suffering.

However, had we done the opposite—that is, had we long ago acted as our compassionate Master did—there is no doubt that by this time we would have rid ourselves of all suffering and achieved both our own ultimate happiness [318a] and the perfection of others' interests. So the reason we now find ourselves in these wretched circumstances is that our actions were not motivated by the right attitude.

A certain *geshe* from Dakpo[71] established the custom at his monastery that a series of verses from the Mind Training treatise called the *Wheel of Sharp Weapons*[72] should be recited whenever rituals such as those for invoking and propitiating dharma protectors were performed. The verses, which are an exhortation to destroy the self-cherishing mind, begin with the line "Because of this, O enemy, I have caught you now!" They also include the line "Oh my! It is this self-grasping mind without a doubt." During the recitation of these verses, an atmosphere of great turbulence would fill the room. This was caused by the fact that the true enemy had been recognized.

(Kyabje Rinpoche then recounted a series of stories. For instance, he told us how long ago a practitioner of black magic had cast a spell that caused the death of many thieves. Then Gyelwa Döndrup,[73] who was a son of Ma Chik

[69]T: *Bla ma mchod pa.*

[70]See Day Sixteen, note 4.

[71]T: *Dvags po.* A region in the southeastern part of Tibet.

[72]The full title of the work is the *Wheel of Sharp Weapons That Strikes at the Enemy's Vital Points* (T: *dGra bo gnad la dbab pa blo sbyong tson cha'i 'khor lo*). In Bibliography, see listing under *Dharmarakṣita.*

[73]T: *rGyal ba don grub.*

Labdrön,[74] prayed that all the power of the magician's curse should fall directly upon his self-cherishing mind. But as Gyelwa Döndrup did not possess any self-cherishing mind, the magician's curse was unable to harm him.

Rinpoche also told us how once Drukpa Kunlek[75] was performing a ritual to overcome certain adversities being experienced by his younger brother Chögyel. Usually, at the appropriate place in the ritual, a *torsor*[76] offering is taken outside and thrown symbolically onto the source of one's troubles. But Drukpa Kunlek decided to direct the offering against Chögyel's self-cherishing mind instead; so he threw it onto his brother's lap.

Kyabje Rinpoche also recounted in great detail a number of our compassionate Master's birth stories in which he displayed the attitude of cherishing others when he was still a Bodhisattva. For instance, Rinpoche described how, when the Buddha had taken birth as King Padmaka, he decided to take birth as a *rohita* fish in order to stop the spread of a contagious disease. By doing so, he cured many sick persons when he allowed them to eat his flesh.[77]

Another time he was born as a sea turtle and saved five hundred shipwrecked merchants who had fallen into the ocean by carrying them safely to shore. In this same birth he also gave his body to eighty thousand worms.[78] As King Shrisena, he gave away half of his body. As Chudamani [318b], he cut a crown jewel from his body and gave it away. When he took birth as a courageous Bodhisattva youth, he gave his body to a starving tigress that was about to eat her own cubs. And as Chandraprabha, he gave away his head.)

These stories describe how our compassionate Master acted on behalf of others. Since we are motivated exclusively by concern for our own welfare, it is not likely that we could emulate these deeds. But we should at least train ourselves by praying that someday we might gain the ability to do so.

[74]T: *Ma cig Lab kyi sgron ma*, 1062–1129.

[75]T: *'Brug pa kun legs*, fl. first half of 16th century. A yogi of the Drukpa Kagyu (T: *'Brug pa bka' brgyud*) school, which was founded by followers of the great yogi Lingrepa Padma Dorje (T: *Gling ras pa Padma rDo rje*, 1128–1188) and Tsangpa Gyare Yeshe Dorje (T: *gTzang pa rGya ras Ye shes rDo rje*, 1161–1211). While he is recognized as a great yogi, few details of Drukpa Kunlek's life are certain. He is well-known, however, as the source of a great many humorous yet instructive sayings. For example, he is reported to have said: "I lost my self-cherishing mind many years ago. I had been looking for it everywhere but was unable to find it. Now I have found it living in a great monastery. They have changed its name from 'self-cherishing mind' to 'loyalty to one's faction' (T: *las la rgya*)."

[76]T: *gtor zor*.

[77]See the "Padmaka Narrative," number 99 in the *Wish-Granting Vine of Bodhisattva Narratives* (S: *Avadānakalpalatā*). In Bibliography, see listing under *Kṣemendra*.

[78]See *'Dul ba lung gzhi*, in *'Dul ba* section of Kg., vol. 4 (*nga*), ff. 173b–175a (in section 93).

Another line of thought for us to contemplate is the following: It is proper for us to develop the mind that cherishes others, because sentient beings are like a field that produces excellent crops. They are also like a wishing jewel, in that it is through them that we acquire food, clothing, and other temporary necessities. Moreover, sentient beings don't only nurture us with great kindness on those occasions when they are our mothers. We are also nurtured by their kindness when they are not our actual mothers. In order to produce a bagful of *tsamba*, many people must first do an immense amount of work. For example, someone must plow the field. Another must water the field. And yet another must drive cattle over the harvested crops in order to separate the grain from the stalks, and so on.

Even this building was produced through the kindness of sentient beings. It was constructed by many humans and animals, who did such work as hauling loads of earth, building the walls, laboring as carpenters, and carrying water.

To make this shawl I am wearing, first the wool of many sheep had to be shorn. Then someone had to weave it into cloth and someone else had to sew it before it became a garment ready to be worn.

Likewise, it is through the kindness of sentient beings that we obtain the temporary goal of finding a human form possessing leisure and fortune, as well as the ultimate goals of generating enlightenment mind [319a], training ourselves in the Bodhisattva activities, and finally, achieving Buddhahood. All these results are gained through the kindness of sentient beings, because they represent the object toward whom we generate compassion and they are the object on whose behalf we generate enlightenment mind. Sentient beings are also the object toward whom we practice generosity, the basis for practicing ethics, the object toward whom we practice patience, and so on.

(Kyabje Rinpoche then summarized by saying that Buddhahood is achieved in part through the kindness of our gurus and in part through the kindness of sentient beings. As a verse from *Engaging in Bodhisattva Activities* declares:

> When a Buddha's qualities are equally gained
> Through sentient beings and the Conquerors,
> What kind of manner is it not to revere beings
> In the same way as we do the Conquerors?[79]

[79]S: *Bodhicaryāvatāraḥ*, ch. 6, 113.

He also noted how Langri Tangba taught that, in our pursuit of the temporary and ultimate goals, sentient beings are more valuable to us than a precious wishing gem. A verse by this great scholar states:

> May I always cherish all beings
> As more precious than a wishing jewel
> By seeing how they enable me
> To achieve the supreme goal.[80]

Therefore, as these points reveal, it is entirely proper for us to develop the mind that cherishes others.)

[80] *Eight Verses on Mind Training* (T: *Blo sbyong tsig brgyad ma*), v. 1. In Bibliography, see listing under (*Glang ri thang pa*) *rDo rje Seng ge*.

DAY EIGHTEEN: THE SEVEN-POINT INSTRUCTION ON MIND TRAINING, CONTINUED

(Kyabje Rinpoche opened the discourse by quoting a pair of verses by the great king of dharma Je Tsongkapa that begin with the line "Swept along by the current of four powerful rivers . . .[1] Then he briefly described the preliminary exercise of correcting one's motivation and listed the sections of the outline that he had already taught. He also made several general points about how we should train ourselves in enlightenment mind and reviewed the Sevenfold Cause and Effect Instruction. After that, he reminded us that we had reached the second section of the *Seven-Point Instruction on Mind Training*, which is the main practice of training ourselves in enlightenment mind [319b]. He further noted that this section consists of five parts: (1) meditating on the way oneself and others are the same, (2) reflecting in many ways on the faults of cherishing oneself, (3) reflecting in many ways on the benefits of cherishing others, (4) cultivating the main practice of exchanging oneself and others, and (5) meditating on Giving and Taking once we have completed the earlier points. Finally, he reviewed the instructions he had already taught on the first three of these topics.

4. Cultivating the main practice of exchanging oneself and others

After completing the analysis that consists of reflecting on the various disadvantages and benefits described earlier, we should perform the act of exchanging oneself and others, which is described in the four verses that begin with the lines:

> Bless me to recognize that the chronic illness
> Of cherishing oneself is the source of unwanted suffering . . .[2]

[1] *Three Principal Elements of the Path* (T: *Lam gyi gtzo bo rnam gsum*), vv. 7–8. The complete verses state: "Swept along by the current of four powerful rivers,/ Tightly bound with karmic bonds so hard to overcome,/ Deeply ensnared in the iron trap of ego-grasping,/ Completely enveloped in the deep darkness of ignorance,/ Reborn endlessly in samsara and constantly tortured/ In these births by the three kinds of suffering—contemplate these qualities/ That describe the condition of all mother beings and generate supreme enlightenment mind."

[2] T: *bLa ma mchod pa*. The first two of these verses were mentioned in Day Seventeen; see notes 56 and 66. The third verse also appears in the body of that day's text on pp. 162–163. The fourth verse states: "Bless me to make the act of exchanging oneself and others/ The essence of my practice, through having realized/ That cherishing oneself is the source of all ruin/ And cherishing mother beings is the basis of all good qualities."

The practice of exchanging oneself and others is based on the recognition of the disadvantages associated with the self-cherishing mind and the benefits associated with the mind that cherishes others. The act itself consists of exchanging the objects toward whom these two attitudes are directed. This does *not* mean that you should come to regard others as yourself and yourself as others. Rather, it means that while you formerly cherished yourself and felt no deep concern for others, you should now reverse the focus of these attitudes. Therefore, exchanging oneself and others means to transfer the focus of your self-cherishing attitude by directing it to others. The way to train your mind in this practice is to cultivate the following attitudes: "Just as I previously had no concern for others, now I will abandon concern for myself. And just as I previously cherished myself, now I will cherish others."

(Kyabje Rinpoche then declared: "You definitely can accomplish such an exchange between yourself and others by cultivating this practice. The possibility of switching your mental perspective is illustrated by this analogy. For example, you always regard the place you happen to be sitting as 'here,' and the area that lies some distance away as 'there.' But if you move to that other spot, your perspective will be reversed. Now the place that you used to view as 'there' becomes 'here.')

5. Meditating on Giving and Taking once we have practiced the earlier points

This section consists of training oneself in the two meditations called "giving" and "taking." Taking is cultivated by reflecting intently on the objects toward whom we generate compassion and giving is cultivated by doing the same for the objects toward whom we generate loving-kindness.

The root text declares:

> Cultivate alternately the two of Giving and Taking [320a].

This practice is one that strengthens the very attitude that was just explained.[3]

[3] That is, exchanging oneself and others.

The practice of taking, which is done by reflecting intently on the objects toward whom we generate compassion

Although many instruction manuals explain "giving" before "taking," in our actual practice we should do taking first. It is even acceptable to forego the practice of giving entirely and only practice taking.

If you don't begin by taking or removing the suffering of beings, it won't benefit them greatly for you to give them your happiness. So you should initially devote special attention to the objects toward whom compassion is generated. Start developing compassion by thinking to yourself, "I shall relieve mother beings of their suffering." Then imagine that you actually do remove their suffering by visualizing that it separates from them the way a razor shaves hair from a person's head or beard. Finally, visualize that this suffering—which appears in the form of black light—dissolves into the self-cherishing mind that remains in your own heart.

When doing the practice in a more extensive form, first visualize that all the suffering experienced by beings in the hot hells, together with the actual fires that exist there, dissolve with all their intensity into the demon of the self-cherishing mind that resides in your heart. Then do similar visualizations for the various forms of suffering that sentient beings experience in the cold hells, as well as the suffering of hungry ghosts, animals, demigods, humans, gods, and so on, up to the subtle obstacles of Bodhisattvas of the tenth level. After taking upon yourself all the suffering, bad deeds, mental obscurations, and other negative qualities of these beings, then reflect that all their suffering has been removed and that they have been purified of all their bad deeds and mental obscurations. You should also pray: "May all these bad qualities ripen upon me." There are, however, two objects toward whom the Taking meditation should not be directed: your gurus and the Buddhas.

Among practitioners, there are many levels of ability. Some beginning practitioners are unable to meditate on Giving and Taking right away. It is for this type of person that the root text declares:

> The order for taking should start with yourself.

This means that, if we are meditating in the morning, we should start by taking upon ourselves whatever suffering we may experience during the latter part of that same day [320b]. Then we should extend the practice by taking upon ourselves today all the suffering we will experience tomorrow. We can gradually increase the visualization to include the suffering that we will experience next month, next year, throughout the remainder of this life, in our next life, and then in all our future lives. Eventually, we can develop our practice further by focusing on the suffering of our father and mother, relatives, people toward whom we are neutral, enemies, and so on, until we are able to include all sentient beings. It is important to cultivate this practice by following just such an order. We should not meditate on the next object in this series of visualizations until we have perfected the visualization for the one before it. In this way, we will gradually be able to take on more and more suffering, bad deeds, and mental obscurations. We will not succeed, however, if we try from the very beginning to take the bad deeds and suffering of such beings as our enemies and the like.

Later, you can also practice different sets of visualizations. Sometimes begin by meditating on your own suffering, and gradually extend your object to include the suffering of others. On other occasions, start with the suffering of hell beings and continue until you reach tenth stage Bodhisattvas. Or you can begin by meditating on beings that live in the interior, mountainous parts of a region and gradually move down into the valley. Similarly, you can begin with beings that live in the lower part of a valley and gradually move up to the higher ground of the interior.

The suffering that you take from beings should include suffering in all its forms, even down to the skin diseases that dogs experience. Also, you should not imagine that the suffering you take simply disappears or that you can discard it on the ground beside you. Visualize that you take it into the center of your heart. If you experience fear when doing so, that is a good sign.

(Kyabje Rinpoche explained that when we reflect in this way, we will accumulate vast amounts of merit even though we may not actually be able to remove any of the suffering that beings experience. He also said that a sufficiently accomplished practitioner actually *can* remove the suffering of others. Then he told us the story of Maitri Yogi.[4])

[4]T: *Byams pa'i rnal 'byor pa.* One of Lord Atisha's Indian teachers, he was also known as Kusali the Younger. See *Lives of the Lamrim Teachers* (T: *Lam rim bla ma brgyud pa'i rnam thar*), vol. 1, pp. 223–229. The following incident is described there: "Once as this guru was teaching dharma, someone standing nearby hit a dog with a club. The guru cried out and fell to the ground. This caused some of the others to think: 'The dog was not injured at all; this teacher is a great charlatan.' Understanding their thoughts, the guru showed them his back, which was badly swollen in the very area where the dog had been struck. Upon seeing this, everyone believed in him."

The practice of giving, which is done by reflecting intently on the objects toward whom we generate loving-kindness

The practice of giving is done by mentally giving away such things as one's body and wealth. It is described in the following lines:

> Let your body provide whatever is wished for,
> In order to accomplish the welfare of beings.[5]

It is also described in the *Stalks in Array* and the *Adamantine Banner* sutras [321a]. One form of the practice is to mentally transform your body into whatever objects sentient beings need and then give them to those beings. Another aspect of giving your body is to visualize that you can remove all the samsaric defects from the environment in which beings live and transform it into a pure Buddha realm.

For instance, start by emanating your body in the form of a rain that falls on the beings who inhabit the hot hells and reflect that it removes their suffering. Then transform your body into a physical form endowed with the qualities of leisure and fortune and reflect that the hell beings are able to acquire such a body.

Next, transform your body into a beautiful mansion. Then reflect that you give this mansion to the hell beings and that they are able to enjoy it. Transform your body as well into excellent food and drink. Then imagine that you give these to the hell beings and that it fully satisfies them. Transform your body into clothing and dress these beings with it. Finally, reflect that your body transforms into spiritual teachers who teach them dharma and bring them to the point of attaining enlightenment.

After that, emanate your body in the form of sunlight and clothing, which you give to beings in the cold hells. Likewise emanate and give food, drink, and so on to hungry ghosts; the wisdom that discerns the nature of things to animals; armor to the demigods; and the objects that bring pleasure to the five senses to the gods. Because humans are filled with such great desire, transform yourself into whatever objects they might wish for and then give these things to them.

A similar practice of giving should be done with your wealth and your virtue. You may also emanate your body as an offering cloud and present it to your gurus and the Buddhas. Imagine that by doing this you are able to extend your guru's life span and increase the extent of his spiritual activities.

[5] *Engaging in Bodhisattva Activities* (S: *Bodhicaryāvatāraḥ*), ch. 5, v. 70.

In giving your virtue, you can do so with the virtue related to all the three times. With your body and your wealth, however, you can only give those that are related to the present and future; you cannot give those of the past.

When you practice giving, the main focus is on generating loving-kindness by reflecting on all the various forms of happiness that sentient beings lack, as I have described. You must make these very visualizations the most important element of your Mind Training practice [321b].

To urge us to remember these points, the root text declares:

> To remind yourself of the practice
> Recite it aloud during all your activities.[6]

To remind ourselves about the practice, we should continually recite words or passages that describe Giving and Taking. While several groups of verses from the *Golden Light Sutra*[7] are particularly suitable for this exercise, those who are not familiar with them may also recite the verse that begins: "Bless me, then, O holy and compassionate gurus . . ."[8] There are even stories of former gurus who made a practice of repeating this verse over and over, keeping count of the number of times they recited it.

We must also transform all our activities into a means of strengthening our enlightenment mind. To learn how to do this, we should study the *Buddha Ornament Sutra*[9] and the sutra called *Purifying the Field of Activities*.[10] In fact, those of you who wish to make enlightenment mind the most important element of your practice should emulate the spiritual activities of the great Jamgön Lama Tsongkapa by reading and contemplating the *Buddha Ornament Sutra* again and again.

Once we achieve some proficiency with the Giving and Taking practice, we should perform the giving visualizations in conjunction with each exhalation

[6]This version of the root text is the one that appears in Ngulchu Dharmabhadra's commentary. As found in other texts, Kyabje Pabongka Rinpoche's own edition (see Appendix H, p. 340) adds the line "An abbreviated instruction for the period after meditation/ Is . . ." before the two that are quoted here.

[7]S: *Suvarṇaprabhāsottamasūtram*, ch. 4. The *Compendium of Training* (S: *Śikṣāsamuccayaḥ*, ch. 12, pp. 119–120) also quotes several groups of verses from this chapter (vv. 5–12, 75–83, 87–89, and 91–92). See also Part Two, Day Thirteen, p. 274, where some of the same verses are recommended in connection with the practice of confession.

[8]T: *Bla ma mchod pa*. The complete verse states: "Bless me, then, O holy and compassionate gurus,/ So that all the suffering, evil, and obscurations of/ Mother beings may ripen upon me right now,/ And I may bring happiness to all beings/ Through giving them my happiness and virtue."

[9]T: *Sangs rgyas phal po che*.

[10]T: *sPyod yul yongs su dag pa'i mdo*. This is actually chapter eleven of the *Buddha Ornament Sutra*.

of the breath and the taking visualizations in conjunction with each inhalation. As the root text declares:

> Let these two practices ride on your breath.

You will not be able to combine these meditations with your breath right away. Nevertheless, after practicing the visualizations repeatedly, you will gain the ability to let your thoughts ride on your breath. And since mind and the inner winds operate jointly, this exercise becomes a powerful device for generating enlightenment mind with relative ease, according to the instruction known as the Equality and Exchange of Self and Others. There are some parallels between this practice and the tantric one called Adamantine Recitation,[11] as Kedrup Je suggests in the following lines from his poem in praise of Je Lama:

> O Lord, when even the very breath from your mouth [322a]
> Serves as a healing medicine for all sentient beings . . .[12]

(Kyabje Rinpoche noted that while there are more instructions that could be taught in connection with this portion of the teachings, it would be improper to explain them to those who will not practice them regularly and continuously.)

Section three: Transforming unfavorable conditions into elements of the path to enlightenment

This instruction is especially beneficial during degenerate times such as the ones we now live in. When there are many obstacles to our dharma practice and we are unable to overcome such adversity, we must gain the ability to transform unfavorable conditions into favorable ones. Otherwise, we will lose our dharma practice whenever we encounter any unusual situation, regardless of whether it is good or bad.

[11]S: *vajrajapaḥ*, T: *rdo rje'i bzlas pa*.

[12]This is from a poem of supplication to Je Tsongkapa known popularly as the *Glorious Three Realms* (T: *dPal ldan sa gsum ma*), in *Collected Works*, vol. 9, p. 479. The full verse states: "O Lord, when even the very breath from your mouth/ Is a means of benefiting all sentient beings,/ What then of your other deeds that constitute the two accumulations!/ I supplicate the true friend of the three realms' beings." The description at the end of the poem states: *Verses of Supplication Describing in Brief the Spiritual Life of the Glorious and Holy Guru, the Great and Venerable Tsongkapa* (T: *dPal ldan bla ma dam pa rJe brtzun Tzong kha pa chen po nyid kyi rnam par thar pa mdo tzam zhig brjod pa'i sgo nas gsol ba 'debs pa'i tsigs su bcad pa*). In Bibliography, see listing under *mKhas grub rje* (*dGe legs dpal bzang*).

For instance, some practitioners lose the dharma by becoming conceited when they acquire a position of status, and the like. Others lose the dharma when they gain some wealth and become preoccupied with managing their financial affairs. Still others lose the dharma by becoming discouraged when they encounter some problem or difficulty. If we react to all these circumstances in this way, it will become very difficult for us to practice dharma successfully. Since it would be disgraceful to give up even the meager attempt at dharma practice that we do make, rather than letting the difficulties we encounter harm our practice, we must gain the ability to transform them into elements of the path.

This topic consists of two parts: (1) transforming unfavorable circumstances with our mind, and (2) transforming unfavorable circumstances with our actions.

The first section is further divided into two parts: (1) transforming unfavorable circumstances through conduct, and (2) transforming unfavorable circumstances through our views.

Transforming unfavorable circumstances through conduct

This point is described in a verse from the *Guru Worship* ritual that states in part: ". . . although the world and its inhabitants are filled with the results of evil deeds . . ."[13]

The root text of this teaching on Mind Training also states:

> When the world and its inhabitants have become filled
> with evil,
> Transform unfavorable circumstances into the path to
> enlightenment.

What we typically do when we experience anything unpleasant—such as an illness or hostility from enemies and evil spirits—is to blame it on someone or something else [322b]. Failing to realize that all sicknesses are created by our own karma, we say that they were caused by food, demons, and so on. But if we investigate what the root causes of these experiences are and where the ultimate blame for them lies, we will discover that all the unwanted events we experience are produced by our own karma. This is a point that I explained earlier during the discourse on karma and its results, as part of the teachings for a person of lesser capacity. Karma is something that we

[13]T: *Bla ma mchod pa'i cho ga*. The full verse states: "Bless me to turn adversity into an element of the path/ By seeing that although the world and its inhabitants are filled/ With the results of evil deeds and unwanted suffering falls like rain,/ This condition represents the exhaustion of bad deeds' results."

create under the influence of our self-cherishing mind. Therefore, the root cause of all of our misfortune is self-cherishing mind.

Even if someone robs us, we shouldn't blame the thief. The real fault lies with our own bad karma and the self-cherishing mind that caused it. Therefore, whenever we experience anything unfavorable such as an illness or some other suffering, we must think about it in such a way that will help us in our pursuit of enlightenment.

For instance, we should feel extremely happy when something bad happens, by thinking: "Some of my former bad karma and mental obscurations have ripened in this life. This has removed some 'definite' karma that otherwise would have forced me to be reborn in the lower states." This attitude is described in a poem that states, "Illness is a broom that sweeps away evil and mental obscurations."[14]

You should also rejoice with this thought: "Earlier, through the practice of Giving and Taking, I mentally took upon myself all the bad karma and suffering of sentient beings. Now I have actually achieved my aim." Then pray that the remainder of their suffering ripens on you as well, and meditate: "May this hardship take the place of all future suffering that sentient beings might otherwise have to experience." Finally, think: "Now I have actually succeeded in taking on myself the suffering of sentient beings. What an accomplishment!"

If you are totally sincere in doing such a practice of Giving and Taking, you can even transform an illness into something that increases your virtuous activities rather than having it become an obstacle. This point is illustrated by the story of a certain disciple of the great ascetic Drakpa Gyeltsen who contracted leprosy [323a] and was later cured at Kyimo Dzatreng.[15]

There is a line that states: "Adversity is a goad urging you to do virtue." Therefore, we must regard suffering as a message that says, "If you wish to avoid suffering, abandon bad deeds!" and strive to accumulate merit and remove our obscurations. If we never experienced any hardship, we would be so content that we would never think of practicing dharma. But by experiencing such difficulties as being accused of some wrong or contracting an illness, we will develop renunciation, overcome idleness, and devote ourselves to virtuous activities.

[14] *A Teaching That Brings Spiritual Self-Discipline to Those Who Live in an Outlying Region* (T: *Mtha' 'khob 'dul ba'i chos*), in *A Hundred Mind Training Teachings* (T: *Blo sbyong brgya rtza*; listed in Bibliography under title), p. 137. The work cited here is a Mind Training teaching composed by Lord Atisha's teacher Suvarnadvipa Guru.

[15] The details of this incident and how they relate to the instruction were not identified.

Several lines of verse declare:

> Demons and spirits are the Conquerors' magical power;
> Suffering is the turbulent expression of ultimate reality.[16]

Thus, whenever a demon, fiend, devil, or some other evil spirit tries to harm us, we should meditate on this thought: "In the past, I let myself get caught up in worldly activities and didn't think about practicing dharma. But now this spirit has done me a great kindness by urging me to pursue dharma." If we learn how to develop the right mental attitudes, it is even possible for suffering to be a positive factor that helps us achieve a realization of ultimate reality.

Illnesses and other difficulties are caused by our self-cherishing mind. Therefore, we should look upon an illness or an evil spirit in the following way: "This being is most kind. He is helping me to subdue the enemy of self-cherishing mind that I haven't been able to defeat on my own."

(Kyabje Rinpoche noted that the way we typically react when we experience some difficulty is simply to abandon our dharma practice. But this is not the right thing to do. Instead, we should be like a traveler who treads cautiously when he comes to a treacherous path cut into the side of a steep mountain. We should be especially careful not to put off our dharma practice when we become ill or experience some other misfortune. At those times, it is very important that we make a special effort to do practices such as Giving and Taking.)

A verse from *Engaging in Bodhisattva Activities* declares [323b]:

> And suffering's other benefits
> Are loss of pride through discontent,
> Compassion for samsara's beings,
> Dread of evil, and love of good.[17]

By dampening our spirits, suffering drives away pride. Reflecting on our own suffering helps us to develop compassion toward others. It also makes us want to abandon its causes.

Normally, we consider it better to be comfortable and happy than to experience suffering. But this isn't always the right attitude to have, as the following lines describe:

[16] *A Teaching That Brings Spiritual Self-Discipline to Those Who Live in an Outlying Region* (T: *Mtha' 'khob 'dul ba'i chos*), in *A Hundred Mind Training Works* (T: *Blo sbyong brgya rtza*), p. 137.

[17] S: *Bodhicaryāvatāraḥ*, ch. 6, v. 21.

> Don't rejoice in happiness; rejoice instead in suffering.
> Happiness uses up the merit you gained in the past;
> Suffering removes bad deeds and mental obscurations.[18]

If we receive a position of high standing, it is like being isolated in a comfortable prison. For instance, high lamas and important government officials do not enjoy the freedom to go wherever they like. The supreme adept Losang Namgyel[19] also described a high position as a comfortable prison.

There is a saying that "a low position is the seat of the Conquerors." This means that all the former pandits and spiritual adepts reached the status of a Conqueror by remaining humble. We should also be like the precious Dromtönba who made prostration to Shang Trangka Berchung, and who maintained such a low position that nothing but water moved below him.[20] This attitude will also help us maintain good relations with everyone that we associate with.

Consider the lines that say:

> Don't rejoice in praise; rejoice in scorn instead.
> When scorned, our faults are exposed.[21]

When others praise us, our pride increases. But this harms us both in this and in future lives. It also prevents us from seeing our faults [324a]. Scorn, on the other hand, may be unpleasant in the short term but it will cause us to examine our actions in the future. As a result, we will become more careful in our behavior. For instance, scorn is described in the following line as being like a magical power bestowed by the gods:

> Criticism is a blessing from the gods.[22]

[18] These lines were composed by Yang-gönba Gyeltsen Pel (T: *Yang dgon pa rGyal mtsan dpal*, 1213–1258), a teacher of the Drukpa Kagyu lineage.

[19] T: *Blo bzang rnam rgyal*, 1670–1741. See *Lives of the Lamrim Teachers* (T: *Lam rim bla ma brgyud pa'i rnam thar*), vol. 2, pp. 345–409.

[20] See *Blue Annals* pp. 252–253 for the description of a meeting between Drom Rinpoche and Shang Trangka Berchung in which Drom Rinpoche willingly pays homage to Trangka Berchung when asked to, and then defeats him in a religious debate. The story is repeated verbatim in *Lives of the Lamrim Teachers* (T: *Lam rim bla ma brgyud pa'i rnam thar*), vol. 1, pp. 388–389. Because Drom Rinpoche placed all other sentient beings above himself in importance, the only thing lower than him that moved was water.

[21] We were unable to identify the source of these lines.

[22] We were unable to identify the source of this line.

This is how we should learn to think in times like these, when the world is so embroiled in criticism and other adversities.

(Finally, Kyabje Rinpoche noted that when we feel happy and comfortable, we should think to ourselves, "I am experiencing the result of some virtuous deed." We should also generate an especially strong enthusiasm for meditating on enlightenment mind.)

Transforming adversity through our views

The portion of the root text that relates to this topic consists of the lines, "[The unsurpassed form of protection is the voidness]/ In which erroneous appearances are viewed as the four bodies." However, the instruction contained in these lines represents the view of teachers from an earlier era. If we examine it carefully, there are certain elements of it that will make us feel uncomfortable.[23] The instruction teaches that when we experience any form of suffering, we should focus on its essence and view it as a Buddha's dharma body, since it did not arise from any self-existent source. Then we should regard other aspects of the experience as a Buddha's other three bodies.

(Kyabje Rinpoche remarked that he did not consider this an especially crucial practice. He explained that no matter what kind of experience we encounter—good or bad, favorable or unfavorable—it is sufficient for us to examine its essence and think as follows:

> This direct experience is one that I have undeniably had. Yet it is pleasant or unpleasant and favorable or unfavorable only in a nominally ascribed sense. It has arisen in dependence upon and through the convergence of various causes and conditions. In an ultimate sense, it is void of any self-existent essence.

We should also stop ourselves from feeling unhappy about or developing attachment toward anything or anyone by examining the way in which the concepts of "self" and "other" are not truly existent.

Practitioners who have not gained a firm understanding of emptiness should reflect in this way:

> In the future when I am about to die, all the pleasant and unpleasant experiences I have had will be nothing more than memories. They will be like the objects that appear in my

[23]Many instruction manuals on this *Seven-Point Instruction on Mind Training* include these lines. Out of concern over certain philosophical implications, Kyabje Rinpoche left them out of the edition he compiled.

dreams [324b]. Therefore, it is wrong for me to feel attachment or aversion toward them during this short life.)

DAY NINETEEN: THE SEVEN-POINT INSTRUCTION ON MIND TRAINING, CONCLUDED

(Kyabje Rinpoche opened the discourse by quoting a verse from *Maitreya's Prayer*, which includes the lines:

> [I prostrate to the enlightenment mind]
> That reverses the path to the lower states . . .[1]

Then, after briefly describing the preliminary exercise of correcting one's motivation, he cited the sections of the teaching that had been completed. Following that, he reviewed the topic of Exchanging Oneself and Others, along with the method of meditating on the practice of Giving and Taking that is based on that exchange.

Kyabje Rinpoche also reviewed the first two sections of the *Seven-Point Instruction*. In connection with this, he again described how we should turn the focus of our self-cherishing attitude away from ourselves so that we come to cherish others, and likewise shift our lack of concern away from others so that we ignore our own selfish concerns. He also noted how, after completing this exchange of self and others, we should strengthen it by practicing Giving and Taking. As he explained earlier, "taking" consists of focusing intently on the objects toward whom compassion is generated. Similarly, "giving" consists of focusing intently on the objects toward whom loving-kindness is generated, and giving our body, wealth, and virtue.

When we become proficient at Giving and Taking, we should do the practice in conjunction with the movement of our breath. Finally, he reiterated that, to ensure that we do not lose our sense of concern for others, we should recite passages that will remind us of this practice during all our daily activities.[2])

There are several explanations of how to integrate the two sets of instructions for training oneself in enlightenment mind and meditating on them in combination with each other. They vary somewhat in regard to the order, number, and classifications of the topics to be practiced. Nevertheless, [325a] here is a brief explanation of how to combine the two instructions by practicing the following eleven meditation topics.

[1]T: *Byams pa'i smon lam*. The full verse states: "I prostrate to the enlightenment mind/ That reverses the path to the lower states,/ Reveals the path to the higher states,/ And leads to the state beyond aging and death." The prayer can be found in many modern Tibetan prayer books. It is actually an extract from the *Sutra of Questions Posed by Maitreya* (T: [*'Phags pa*] *Byams pas zhus pa'i le'u zhe bya ba'i theg pa chen po'i mdo*). See listing in Bibliography.

[2]See Day Eighteen, p. 172.

Begin by practicing the topics of (1) equanimity, (2) recognizing all sentient beings as our mothers, (3) the ordinary and extraordinary methods of recalling their kindness,[3] and (4) repaying their kindness. After that, meditate on (5) the equality of oneself and others, and reflect in many ways on (6) the faults of cherishing oneself and (7) the benefits of cherishing others. Then, in combination with the main practice of exchanging oneself and others, first practice (8) the taking meditation as you focus intently on the objects toward whom compassion is generated. Then practice (9) the giving meditation as you focus intently on the objects toward whom loving-kindness is generated. Of the two types of loving-kindness, the one cultivated here is the general form that wants sentient beings to gain happiness.[4]

After completing those meditations, examine whether the Giving and Taking practice that you did brought about any real change in the condition of sentient beings. You will recognize that these were merely visualizations that you formed in your imagination; you did not actually provide beings with the happiness and benefit that you contemplated during the meditation. Then reflect to yourself, "Now I must actually cause sentient beings to gain the benefits and happiness that I visualized," and generate (10) the extraordinary intention in which you take personal responsibility for the welfare of all sentient beings. Finally, generate (11) the actual mind that wishes to achieve perfect enlightenment in order to accomplish that goal.

These eleven topics, practiced in this order, represent the method of combining the two sets of teachings on enlightenment mind—that is, the Sevenfold Instruction of Cause and Effect and the instruction known as the Equality and Exchange of Self and Others.

When you have finished meditating on these eleven topics, think to yourself, "Now all sentient beings have obtained complete happiness," and again generate enlightenment mind by doing the visualization called "taking the result as the path."[5] This is a practice that will allow you to accumulate a great amount of merit. It is similar to the tantric practice called the Victory

[3]The ordinary method is to recall the kindness that sentient beings extended to us when they were actually our mothers. This is described in Day Seventeen, pp. 136–138. The extraordinary method is to recall the kindness that is extended by sentient beings even when they are not our mothers. This is briefly described in Day Seventeen, p. 165.

[4]T: *bde ba dang ldan 'dod kyi byams pa*. This type is distinguished from the loving-kindness that is taught in the Sevenfold Instruction of Cause and Effect (see Day Seventeen, pp. 140–141). The main element in cultivating "general" loving-kindness is to consider the way in which beings lack happiness and then generate the wish that they gain it. The other type, called the "loving-kindness that holds all sentient beings as dear" (T: *yid 'ong gi byams pa*), is cultivated in connection with the three topics of recognizing all beings as your mother, recalling their kindness, and wanting to repay their kindness.

[5]T: *'bras bu lam byed kyi dmigs pa*. A similar visualization is done during the six preliminary practices; see Part One, Day Four, p. 161.

Mandala,[6] and will serve as an auspicious karmic factor [325b]. It is also similar to the prayers of King Aranemi and the brahmin Samudraraja regarding what they wanted to accomplish in the future.[7]

You do this meditation by visualizing that you achieve enlightenment in the form of Buddha Munindra.[8] After that, light that emanates from your body removes the suffering of all sentient beings, causing them also to achieve enlightenment in the form of Buddha Munindra. Then rejoice at the thought that you have accomplished your ultimate aim.

A line from the root text states:

> There are three objects, three poisons, and three
> virtue-roots.

This aphorism refers to a practice that should be done whenever we encounter the three types of objects that cause us to develop desire, hatred, and ignorance. The three are attractive objects, unattractive objects, and objects about which we feel neutral. Upon perceiving any of these objects, first we should take upon ourselves all the mental afflictions of desire, hatred, and ignorance that other sentient beings generate toward such objects. Then we should take upon ourselves the rebirths in the lower states that other beings would have to experience by having generated those three mental afflictions. Finally, because we have taken all the samsaric suffering, along with its causes, that other beings would otherwise have had to experience, we should think: "Now I have caused all sentient beings to obtain the virtue-roots of nonattachment, nonhatred, and freedom from ignorance."

Once we recognize that the blame for all difficulties such as arguing, fighting, and illness lies with the self-cherishing mind, we will be able to view these experiences as opportunities for exhausting our bad karma and bringing their results to an end. And, we will always be able to remain in a happy state of mind by recognizing these hardships as the ripening of the suffering of other beings that we took upon ourselves [326a]. Therefore, the one who meditates on these Mind Training instructions is able to perceive adversity as an aid to his practice. Because this also allows him to avoid feeling unhappy when he experiences any difficulty, the Mind Training teachings are also referred to as "the source of a city's happiness."[9]

[6]S: *vijayamandalam*, T: *dkyil 'khor rgyal mchog*. This term is taken from the Guhya Samaja teaching system.

[7]See the *White Lotus of Compassion Sutra* (S: *Kāruṇāpuṇḍarīkasūtram*).

[8]S: *munīndraḥ*, T: *thub pa'i dbang po*. Literally, "Lord of Sages," this is an epithet of Buddha Shakyamuni. For a description of how to visualize this form, see Part One, Appendix C, p. 245.

[9]T: *grong khyer skyid pa'i 'byung gnas*.

We must overcome our inability to bear even the slightest form of hardship. We must become like those merchants who can see some advantage in the difficulties that they experience when traveling. For instance, they view rain as deterring bandits and snow as helping to keep the pack animals' hooves from being damaged when they are carrying goods on their backs.

A verse from *Engaging in Bodhisattva Activities* states:

> If indeed there is a remedy,
> What good is it to be unhappy?
> But even if there is no remedy,
> What good is it to be unhappy?[10]

When we experience suffering, we don't gain anything at all by becoming unhappy. Therefore, we must learn how to view such experiences in a way that will help us in our practice. For instance, we all have seen how some people naturally develop a sense of their impermanence when an illness or some other tragedy strikes them and brings them close to death. They react this way even though they may never have heard teachings like this one on the stages of the path to enlightenment.

(Kyabje Rinpoche then described how there is no practice more spiritually beneficial than to reflect in the following way whenever we experience some difficulty: "No matter what happens to me, may the great misfortunes of all sentient beings fall on me." He concluded by reviewing the topic of transforming adversity with our mind, which forms part of the larger section entitled "Transforming unfavorable circumstances into elements of the path to enlightenment.")

Transforming adversity with our actions

This topic consists of four types of action: (1) accumulating merit, (2) purifying ourselves of obscurations, (3) making *torma* offerings to spirits, and (4) urging the dharma protectors to act [326b].

When a person who has mastered the Mind Training instructions experiences an illness or some other hardship, he can urge the dharma protectors with these words:

> This illness has come about because the suffering of all sentient beings has ripened upon me. Therefore, I have accomplished the aim of the Giving and Taking practice. Now you must bring down on me something even worse.

[10] S: *Bodhicaryāvatāraḥ*, ch. 6, v. 10.

When making *torma* offerings to spirits, he should also direct these thoughts to them:

> The harms that you have inflicted on me were acts of great kindness. They enabled me to accumulate merit, purify myself of bad karma and mental obscurations, and greatly improve my spiritual practice. Therefore, now you must do even greater harm to me, and do it more often than before.

Someone who is frightened by these practices because he has not gained enough proficiency should urge the dharma protectors and spirits to act in a more conventional way. That is, he should urge them to help him avoid having to experience illnesses and other misfortunes.

Whenever we experience suffering, we should recognize that the way to avoid having to experience it in the future is by determining its root cause. For instance, if the area where we live becomes flooded with water, the way to turn back the water is by determining its source. Similarly, the way to turn back suffering is by avoiding the bad karma that is its cause and by pursuing the causes of happiness—that is, by practicing virtue and accumulating merit.

If we perform a Hundred Torma Offering[11] and then practice confession by reciting the *Confession of Transgressions Sutra*,[12] we will be doing an extensive practice of all four of the activities described here. A similar practice would be to do a Hundred Torma Offering and a recitation of a prayer related to the Mind Training teachings.

A line from the root text declares:

> Immediately apply your practice to whatever you
> encounter.

(Kyabje Rinpoche explained that this line means we must learn how to immediately incorporate into our Mind Training practice any good or bad situation that we may happen to encounter.)

[11]T: *gTor ma brgya rtza*. This is the name of a particular *torma* ritual.

[12]The longer descriptive title is *Confession of a Bodhisattva's Transgressions* (T: *Byang chub sems dpa'i ltung ba bshags pa*); see Part One, Day Six, pp. 208–210 for an explanation of the practice.

Section four: A summary of what to do as one's lifelong practice

This section presents a combination of instructions that should be practiced throughout our life. The practices, which are known as the five strengths, are (1) the strength of the white seed, (2) the strength of repeated practice, (3) the strength of intention, (4) the strength that removes obstacles, and (5) the strength of prayer.

The strength of intention

Among these five [327a], the strength of intention is particularly crucial. As soon as we get up in the morning, we must make a firm resolution by developing the following attitude:

> In general, I must not allow this life to go by without accomplishing anything of real value. More specifically, I must not allow this year to go by without accomplishing anything of value. And I must especially not allow today to go by without accomplishing anything of value. Therefore, I will bring meaning to my life by defeating my enemy, the self-cherishing mind.

Our motivations are what generate all our activities and behavior. They are what cause us to do all our virtuous and nonvirtuous deeds. They also determine whether our spiritual practice belongs to the Hinayana or to the Mahayana paths. All our actions, even trivial ones such as killing a louse or preparing lunch, are done only after we form the intention to do them. From the moment we get up in the morning and tie a sash around our waist,[13] most of us begin to decide how we will go about obtaining the pleasures that relate to this life—such as food, clothing, a good reputation, and so on. To avoid this, we might even attach a note to our sash, so that as we tie it around our waist we will remind ourselves to generate the resolve that I just described, and fix it deeply in our mind.

The strength of the white seed

The strength of the white seed is to accumulate merit and purify ourselves of obscurations in order to further develop our enlightenment mind. This can be accomplished through a variety of activities, such as the

[13]The traditional form of dress for Tibetans, whether ordained or layperson, involves tying a sash around the waist.

preliminary practices.[14] Almost all the virtuous acts that most of us do are associated with this life's aims. It is extremely important that we strive to overcome this tendency.

The strength of repeated practice

This means to strive to develop the two forms of enlightenment mind at all times and during all four activities of walking, standing, sitting, and reclining. In other words, we should be engaging in our spiritual practice continuously.

At present, the practices that the great Bodhisattvas do are beyond our comprehension. Nevertheless, we should realize that their ability to do such difficult acts as giving their head and arms to others is developed through a process of repeated mental practice [327b]. For example, in the very beginning, an unskilled worker does not know how to do the tasks involved in metalworking and carpentry. But later, after he has learned the trade, he no longer finds them difficult. Similarly, in the future after an extended period of mental practice, we, too, will be able to do such activities as giving up our body and life as easily as if we were giving away vegetables. This is alluded to in the following lines of verse:

> There is nothing at all that remains difficult
> For someone who engages in repeated practice.[15]

It is said that certain great spiritual beings of the past could even complete a reflective meditation[16] on all the topics of the Lamrim teaching between the time that they put a foot in the first stirrup and the time that they finished mounting a horse's back and put the other foot in the second stirrup. They are able to accomplish this, as well, through continuous mental practice.

The terms "repeated mental practice"[17] and "meditation"[18] are virtually identical in meaning. Even such small acts as drinking tea from a cup would not be easy to do if we had not become used to them through repeated practice.

[14]This is a reference to the Six Preliminary Practices (T: *sbyor ba'i chos drug*). Part One, Days Four through Six are a commentary on this ritual.

[15]*Engaging in Bodhisattva Activities* (S: *Bodhicaryāvatāraḥ*), ch. 6, v. 14.

[16]T: *bshar sgom*. See description in Part One, Day Six, note 92. Part Two, Appendix F, pp. 327–331 distinguishes between reflective meditation and analytic meditation (T: *dpyad sgom*).

[17]S: *abhyāsaḥ*, T: *goms pa*.

[18]S: *bhāvanā*, T: *bsgom pa*.

The strength that removes obstacles

The strength that removes obstacles eliminates the self-cherishing attitude from our mind. This strength stops the self-cherishing attitude as soon as it starts to develop in the mind and then overcomes it forcefully, just as stray dogs are driven away when they try to steal something to eat from a home.

The strength of prayer

The strength of prayer consists of dedicating whatever virtue we perform each day to the goal of increasing the two types of enlightenment mind. This should be done at night just before we go to sleep.

These are the five strengths that we should practice throughout our life. There is another set of five strengths that we should practice when we are about to die. These are referred to as the "transference"[19] practice of the Mind Training tradition. The root text alludes to them with the following words:

> The Mahayana instruction for transference is to practice
> These very five strengths and take special care with
> your body position.

The instruction on transference that is taught in the Mind Training tradition doesn't include exclamations like *Hik*! and *Pet*! And yet this practice is more profound than all the other teachings on transference. The terms that are used to describe this instruction are the same as the ones that were just mentioned.

The strength of intention

We should resolve not to give up enlightenment mind either at the moment of our death or while we are in the intermediate state [328a].

The strength of the white seed

The strength of the white seed is to give away to a superior "field"[20] all of our material possessions, especially those things that we have strong attachment for. This can be done either in the form of offerings to high spiritual

[19] S: *cyāvanam*, T: *'pho ba*. This practice is more commonly associated with a tantric meditation that aims at ensuring that a person who is about to die will be reborn in a favorable place.

[20] See Part One, Day Five, note 101 for a description of different types of "fields."

beings or acts of generosity to ordinary persons. Alternatively, we may designate how our possessions should be divided and to whom they should be given after we die. It is much more beneficial for us to overcome our attachment for these objects before we die than for others to perform virtuous acts with them after we are gone.

If we fail to indicate how our possessions are to be distributed, we risk becoming like the *bhikshu* who died feeling attachment toward his begging bowl.[21] When he was reborn as a snake, Buddha drove him into the forest. The snake became so angered that the fire of his hatred caused both the forest and himself to be consumed by the flames of an actual fire. The snake was then reborn in one of the hells. As a result, each of the *bhikshu*'s bodies from three consecutive births was engulfed in its own separate fire.

There is also the story of a man who had buried gold under the ground and died feeling great attachment toward it. He was reborn as a snake that persuaded Buddha to offer gold on his behalf.[22]

It is also possible for a person to die feeling great attachment toward his or her own body and then be reborn as an insect living inside the corpse of that former life's body. For instance, long ago the dead body of a woman was found along the ocean shore. A snake-like worm was also observed there with the corpse, crawling back and forth through its mouth, eye-sockets, nostrils, and ears. The body was that of a woman who had been greatly attached to her body and constantly looked at herself in a mirror. When she died, she was reborn as this worm that crawled all over her previous life's body.[23]

Therefore, it is very important when death approaches that we accumulate merit and pray fervently that our enlightenment mind grow stronger and stronger. It is also especially important that we not become attached to our own body. (Kyabje Rinpoche then told us how there was once a simple monk who was greatly attached to some money. When he died, he was reborn as a frog [328b] that clutched the same money with its two front feet.)

There are also cases in which a person is near death but cannot pass away because of attachment. Once an old monk from Amdo couldn't pass away because of his attachment to the butter that was mixed with his tea. Gungtang Jampel Yang then showed skillful means by telling the monk: "Turn your aspirations to Tushita heaven. There is much better food to be had up

[21]T: *'Dul ba lung gzhi*, in *'Dul ba* section of Kg., vol. 3 (*ga*), ff. 155a–155b (in section 65). In Bibliography, see listing for Tibetan translation of *Vinayavastu*.

[22]*Sutra of the Wise and the Foolish* (T: *mDzangs blun zhes bya ba'i mdo*), ch. 28. This story is about one of the Buddha'a previous lives at a time before he had attained enlightenment. The gold was offered to the sangha.

[23]This story is described in the *Sutra of the Wise and the Foolish* (T: *mDzangs blun zhes bya ba'i mdo*), ch. 16.

there than the butter at our Rikdra ceremony."[24] As soon as he heard this, the monk was able to release his final breath. Because we, too, run the risk of becoming like this monk, it is important that we let go of our attachments.

The strength that removes obstacles

The strength that removes obstacles at the time of death is to make strong acts of confession for our past misdeeds and resolve not to do them again. If you are a tantric practitioner, you should restore your Bodhisattva and tantric vows either by performing a self-initiation ritual or requesting that you be given the initiation of your tutelary deity once again. Even if you don't do this, you should still confess your misdeeds as purely as you know how and resolve not to do them again.

This is an important point that you should generally practice at all times. However, it is especially important to do so when you are about to die. Not doing so can become an obstruction for you. For example, even though you might be ready to be reborn in a pure Buddha field or some other favorable rebirth, you can fail to reach there by not practicing this point.

The strength of prayer

In this instance, the strength of prayer does not mean we should pray for such aims as being reborn in a pure Buddha field. Rather, it means we should pray that the suffering, bad deeds, and mental obscurations of all sentient beings ripen upon us and we should pray to be successful in generating enlightenment mind.

The strength of repeated practice

The strength of repeated practice means to prepare ourselves to be able to pass away while meditating on enlightenment mind. This is accomplished by meditating regularly and continuously on enlightenment mind during our life, so that the strength of this habit will enable us to generate enlightenment mind when we are about to die. There is no greater spiritual practice that we can do when this moment comes.

[24]T: *rigs grva*. A religious festival held at the main Gelukpa monasteries. *Rigs* is short for *rigs lam* or logic; *grva* is an abbreviation for *grva pa* or monk. At Sera, monks from both the Mey and Je colleges gathered in the main assembly hall twice a day. Part of the activities involved a debate between the best scholars from each college. *Tsamba*, fried bread, and tea were provided to all the monks by the Tibetan government. Apparently, the butter served with this tea is noted for its quality and abundance.

Body position

The body position that we should take when dying is to follow the example of our compassionate Master at the time that he entered nirvana [329a]. That is, we should lie down on our right side and pass away in the position known as the "lion's repose." This very position can greatly increase the possibility of our reaching a pure Buddha field.

Generally, a practitioner who is cultivating the instructions for a person of lesser capacity should pass away while taking refuge. Similarly, a practitioner who is training himself in the instructions for a person of great capacity should do so while meditating on enlightenment mind. You may have some doubt about whether this practice can enable us to reach a pure Buddha field; but it definitely can. Just before Chekawa died, he said to his attendant:

> Arrange offerings for me. Though I have been praying to reach the hell of Unrelenting Torment in order to help all sentient beings, I shall not be going there since I keep having visions of a pure Buddha field.

(Kyabje Rinpoche also described how Geshe Potowa passed away in a similar manner.)

Once, long ago, a mother and daughter were being swept away by a river. Because they each generated a loving attitude toward one another, both were reborn in Tushita heaven.

A similar incident took place at Jasa in the Hloka region.[25] A boat made of animal hides had been loaded with too many passengers and goods, and was about to sink. A messenger who was in the boat generated an altruistic attitude and decided to leap into the river. But he did not die, and a rainbow appeared in the place where he crossed. These examples illustrate how we should never doubt that by generating an attitude filled with great caring for others—including a contrived form of enlightenment mind—we can be reborn in an auspicious place.

Most of us place great importance on those *powa* or transference instructions that include such utterances as *Hik*! and *Pet*! We also hold in high regard anyone who achieves physical signs that he has successfully completed the preparatory exercises of this practice. However, any practitioner who performs the *Hik* recitation repeatedly can achieve the physical signs on the crown of his head, even though he doesn't meditate on more

[25]Jasa (T: *Bya sa*) is a place name and the site of a monastery that lies along a riverbank. Hloka (T: *lHo kha*) is a major region of southern Tibet between the Yarlung River (T: *gYar klung*) and the Himalayas.

substantive teachings of any sort. Because the physical signs are achieved simply through manipulation of psychic wind, there is no reason to view them as especially remarkable. On the other hand, the transference instruction that is practiced in the Mind Training tradition is the most profound of all transference teachings, even though it does not include the utterances *Hik* and *Pet* [329b].

(Kyabje Rinpoche concluded by saying that although we might practice any of the other transference instructions, we can never be sure that when we are about to die we will be able to close the door that leads to rebirth in the lower states. But if we pass away while practicing the five strengths that were just taught here, we can definitely avoid falling into a lower birth state.)

Section Five: The standard for determining proficiency in the Mind Training practices

The root text states:

> All dharma is based on one underlying thought.

All the dharma heaps that the Blessed One taught come down to this: they are meant to serve as an antidote for the self-cherishing mind. The line that divides dharma from nondharma is said to be whether or not a teaching or practice counteracts the mental afflictions. The best sign of a practitioner's having achieved spiritual attainments is that his mental afflictions have decreased. As for the commonly recognized signs, they are not sure indications of spiritual attainment. For example, vultures can also fly in the air, mice can also go below the earth's surface, and fish can travel under water.

This Mind Training teaching is called the scale that weighs whether something represents dharma or nondharma. Therefore, a good dharma practice should have the effect of reducing our self-cherishing mind. This is also a sign that we have attained some proficiency in the Mind Training practice.

The root text states:

> Heed the more important of the two witnesses.

The two kinds of witness are oneself and others. Even though someone may not keep an exemplary dharma practice, by pretending to be virtuous he can fool others into thinking he is kind-hearted and following a pure moral practice. Of the four kinds of mango fruit that can appear either ripe or unripe on the outside while actually being ripe or unripe on the inside, this type of person is like a mango that appears ripe on the outside but is unripe on the inside.[26] He is also sly and cunning, like a cat. Those who lack much knowledge of the dharma may consider such a person to be good [330a], but we should not conduct ourselves in this way.

We should also avoid appearing unripe from the outside even though we are ripe on the inside. The proper way is both to have pure outer behavior and actually be pure on the inside. A subdued outer manner keeps us from having to feel ashamed in front of others. By remaining subdued inwardly, we can develop a mind that is rich in spiritual practice.

(Kyabje Rinpoche noted that Bodhisattvas are careful to abandon the kind of outer behavior that would bring them dishonor, as indicated in the line that says "not avoiding a bad reputation."[27] Therefore, an important principle to follow is that we have no reason to be ashamed of our own practice.)

The root text states:

> Always maintain a happy mind.

If we happen to acquire some wealth, we should not make ourselves miserable by continually thinking about how to safeguard and increase it. Similarly, we should not let poverty and the need to seek money keep us in a state of mental distress. Instead, we should contemplate the disadvantages of having wealth and learn how to remain happy and contented by turning any circumstance we encounter—favorable or unfavorable—into the spiritual path.

(Kyabje Rinpoche then told us that we should be indifferent to the eight worldly dharmas of praise, scorn, and the rest.[28] He also noted that if we investigate the reasons why we become happy or unhappy in different circumstances, we can eventually reach a stage where nothing can upset us.)

The root text states:

> Mastery is when you can practice even if distracted.

[26]Nagarjuna's *Letter to a Friend* (T: *bShes pa'i spring yig*, v. 20) contains the following verse: "Understand that people are like mango fruit:/ There are unripe ones that seem ripe and ripe ones/ That seem unripe. Some that are unripe also/ Appear unripe and some ripe ones appear ripe."

[27]This line from Chandragomi's *Twenty Verses on the Bodhisattva Vows* (T: *Byang chub sems dpa'i sdom pa nyi shu pa*) refers to one of the forty-six secondary transgressions (S: *duś-caritam*, T: *nyes byas*) that a person who has taken the Bodhisattva vows must avoid. See also *Six-Session Guru Yoga*, Appendix B, p. 173, listed in Bibliography under Sermey Khensur Lobsang Tharchin.

[28]See Part One, Prologue, p. 1, note 5 and Part Two, Day Ten, p. 105.

A horseman who is not particularly skilled can avoid being thrown as long as he remains alert. But the horse may throw him off if he becomes distracted. A skilled rider, however, will not be thrown even though he isn't paying close attention to what the horse is doing.

A person who has practiced the Mind Training instructions but has not mastered them is like someone who can ride a horse but doesn't have great skill. If such a practitioner is distracted, he may become angry when someone says something unpleasant to him. Later, after regaining his composure, he can stop his anger [330b]. But a person who is proficient in the instruction will not become angry even though someone might beat him or speak harshly to him while he is in a distracted state of mind. This is one standard for determining whether or not we have mastered the instructions on Mind Training.

The root text states:

> The measure of mastery is for self-cherishing mind
> to have been overcome.

The sign of mastery for the topic of impermanence in the form of death is to have overcome all thoughts related to this life. In the case of renunciation, it is to have overcome any longing for the well-being and prosperity that occur in samsara. In the present context of the Mind Training instructions, the sign of mastery is to have overcome the self-cherishing mind.

The root text also declares:

> The signs of mastery are the five greatnesses.

(Kyabje Rinpoche explained that a person who has meditated successfully on these Mind Training instructions gains these five traits: He becomes (1) a great ascetic who can endure any form of suffering or harm without becoming disturbed by mental afflictions; (2) a great being who cherishes others more than himself; (3) a great spiritual practitioner whose conduct never strays from the ten dharma activities;[29] (4) a great Vinaya-holder who abides in a state of tranquility and self-discipline, untainted by even the slightest form of nonvirtuous deed; and (5) a great yogi who unites himself with the true practice of the Mahayana path.)

[29] S: *daśadharmacaryāḥ*, T: *chos spyod bcu*. They are: (1) to copy scriptures, (2) to present offerings, (3) to practice charity, (4) to hear dharma, (5) to memorize dharma, (6) to read dharma, (7) to teach dharma, (8) to recite dharma, (9) to reflect on the dharma's meaning, and (10) to meditate on the dharma's meaning.

Section Six: The pledges that a practitioner of the Mind Training instruction should observe

There are eighteen pledges that a practitioner should observe. The first three are indicated in the following line from the root text:

> Always train yourself in the three general principles.

(1) The first of the three principles is not to let your Mind Training practice conflict with other precepts. This means that we should not use our Mind Training practice to justify disregarding lower forms of vows, such as those taught in the Hinayana Vinaya system.

(2) The second principle is not to let your Mind Training practice become tainted with reckless behavior. This means that we should not use our Mind Training practice to justify doing actions that might disturb human beings or spirits, in an attempt to give the impression that we have overcome our self-cherishing mind. An example of such reckless behavior would be to cut down a tree inhabited by a powerful spirit [331a].

(3) The third principle is not to let your Mind Training practice be biased. This means that we should avoid the partiality of being patient with our friends but not with our enemies, or being patient with human beings but not with spirits. These are the three general principles.

> (4) Change your aspirations but remain natural.

This means we should not allow our mind to remain as coarse as it was in the past. We should try to correct our mind by steadily improving it. The best aspiration would be to think that we could generate a proper attitude within one day. A middling one would be to think that we could do so within a month. The lowest aspiration would be to think that we could generate it within a year. If we fail even to develop this last way of thinking, our mind will still be in the same condition as it was before we became a monk or nun, even though we may be a lot older than we were when we left the householder's state.

Therefore, we must change our aspirations and avoid being like "the boulder behind the family home."[30] What method should we use to change our aspirations? We must change them with enlightenment mind, renunciation, reflecting on impermanence, and so on. At the same time, our outer conduct should remain natural. It isn't proper, for instance, to raise our eyebrows as

[30]T: *khang ltag gi brag gong bzhin*. This Tibetan saying means we should avoid being as unchangeable as a rock.

a sign that we are devout practitioners or to make other outer gestures of piety when we haven't actually gained a *kar-nga*'s[31] worth of inner spiritual knowledge. Whatever religious experiences or improvement in our spiritual knowledge we may have should only be manifest in our mind.

(Kyabje Rinpoche told us we must be like the Bodhisattva Shantideva and Arya Pantaka.[32] They were very advanced in their practice, yet no one knew that they had abandoned many of the path's obstacles and reached a high state of spiritual realization. Rinpoche also told us a story about the glorious Chandrakirti. Although he was not highly esteemed and was thought to be just an ordinary pandit, inwardly he had reached such a high level of attainment that he could draw real milk from the picture of a cow.)

None of these great beings displayed any outer sign of their spirituality. Moreover, the lamas of this Kadampa tradition [331b] deliberately avoided becoming widely known as great practitioners and gaining fame through displaying signs of their spiritual attainment. We must also attempt to conduct ourselves in a similar manner. Otherwise, if we make our spiritual knowledge too widely known—like a person who shows off a wishing jewel to others—it can bring us many obstacles.

(Kyabje Rinpoche then said that some of us have a practice that is motivated by this life's aims, making us no different from ordinary worldly people. Others may do a genuine dharma practice, but then behave as if they are waving a banner on some high place. These are not proper attitudes. In this Kadampa tradition established by Lord Atisha's followers, we must keep our spiritual knowledge hidden, like a lamp inside a pot.)

(5) Do not mention others' flaws.

This simply means that we should avoid talking about the faults of others.

(6) Never think negatively about others.

This means that we should completely give up searching for faults in others. Instead, we should examine our own faults. If we scrutinize others—including our dharma friends or the monks of our college or house—for the sole purpose of finding their faults, the natural result is that we will come to see faults even in the Buddha. This will only increase our tendency to

[31] T: *skar lnga*. Literally five "stars" (T: *skar ma*), this is a Tibetan coin of modest value, roughly equivalent to a dime.

[32] For the story of Arya Pantaka, see Part One, Day Four, pp. 118–123.

engage in such misdeeds as disregarding and defaming the Buddha and his teaching. Therefore, we should avoid criticizing others.

(7) First strive to remove your worst mental affliction.

We should first try to remove from our mind whichever of our mental afflictions is strongest. For instance, a person in whom desire is predominant should try to overcome this mental affliction by practicing its antidote—for example, by meditating on the body's ugliness.[33]

(8) Give up all expectation of reward.

We should not do any virtuous action with the hope that it will bring us something favorable in return or that it will bring us a favorable karmic maturation.

The remaining pledges are described in a series of brief aphorisms:

(9) Avoid poisonous food.

This means we should not eat food—that is, virtuous activities—that has been tainted with the poison of a self-cherishing mind [332a].

(10) Don't be steadfast.[34]

This means that when we develop any of the mental afflictions we should not allow them to continue unchecked because we failed to apply the appropriate antidote.

(11) Don't engage in bitter quarreling.

We are not religious ascetics unless we possess the four essential qualities of an ascetic, since we agreed in the presence of our preceptor and

[33] See Day Fifteen, pp. 49–50.

[34] T: *gzhung bzang po*. This term generally means the quality of being loyal to one's friends (T: *phyi thag ring ba*). Here it is being used, presumably with deliberate irony, in a different sense. The principal explanation of the aphorism, which is repeated in numerous commentaries, is that we should not cling steadfastly to the resentment that stems from being harmed by others. Ngulchu Dharmabhadra and Yongzin Yeshe Gyeltsen add that "steadfastness" also refers to the strong and enduring habituation we have toward our mental afflictions. According to this interpretation, the aphorism means that we should abandon such "loyalty" to our mental afflictions by overcoming them as soon as they appear. Kyabje Pabongka Rinpoche is following this second explanation here.

instructor to adhere to these principles.[35] Therefore, if someone calls us an old dog, we should not call him a thief in return. And if someone strikes us once, we should not hit him back twice.

(12) Don't wait along a back road.

Sometimes a person will wait along an isolated back road in order to get revenge on someone who harmed him earlier. We should not wait for such an opportunity to harm another.

This is the kind of deceit in which a person has a smile on his face while his heart is black. Foolish worldly people view this as a good quality. This also shows why the spiritual and worldly spheres are in direct opposition to one another.

(13) Don't strike a vulnerable point.

If we learn that someone has a serious fault, we should not denounce or criticize him for it in public. This aphorism also means that we should not recite harmful mantras to overcome spirits and other sentient beings.

(14) Don't place a *dzo*'s[36] load onto an ox.

We should avoid using deceit to lay the responsibility for some action on another person. We should also avoid trying to shift the blame for something from ourselves onto another person.

(15) Don't practice perversely as if doing worldly rituals.

The main purpose of this Mind Training teaching is to overcome our self-cherishing mind. If we meditate on the instructions for a different reason—such as to avoid being harmed by spirits or to gain wealth, honor, and fame—our practice will only serve to increase our self-cherishing mind.

[35]The four essential qualities of a religious ascetic (S: *catvāraḥ śramaṇakārakadharmāḥ*, T: *dge sbyong du byed pa'i chos bzhi*) are: (1) not to respond to abusive speech with abusive speech, (2) not to respond to anger with anger, (3) not to respond to criticism with criticism, and (4) not to respond to physical blows with physical blows. Monks and nuns accept these four principles when they take ordination. The preceptor (S: *upadhyāyaḥ*, T: *mkhan po*) and instructor (S: *ācāryaḥ*, T: *slob dpon*) are the two major functionaries who preside at the ordination ceremony.

[36]T: *mdzo*. A cross between a yak and a cow, or a bull and a *dri* (T: *'bri*, i.e., female of the yak species).

Therefore, we should avoid this sort of false dharma practice, which is like the *tochö*[37] rituals that are done for worldly reasons [332b].

(16) Don't try to be the fastest.

We should not try to gain sole possession, as quickly as possible, of property that is jointly owned. Nor should we attempt to obtain the best portion of anything before others.

(17) Don't turn a god into a demon.

We should not let our Mind Training practice strengthen our self-cherishing mind instead of serving as its antidote.

(18) Don't seek misery as a means to happiness.

If we hope that our enemies meet with misfortune or that they die so we may gain some form of comfort or happiness, then we are violating this pledge.

This completes the eighteen pledges.

Section Seven: A presentation of the precepts that practitioners of the Mind Training instructions must observe

The twenty-two precepts are taught with the following aphorisms:

(1) Do all yoga practice with one thought.

The person who is practicing this teaching does not need to cultivate many different types of virtuous activities. He should do everything in connection with the attitude that exchanges self and others. For instance, since we have given ourselves to all sentient beings, when eating we should reflect as follows: "I am nurturing this body so that I can benefit all sentient beings." This same principle should be applied to all our activities. We should also be motivated by this attitude when we do all tantric activities, such as reciting mantras and urging dharma protectors to do various deeds on our behalf.

[37]T: *lto bcos*. A type of ritual that is performed to remove obstacles or avert misfortune.

(2) Respond with one thought when overwhelmed by obstacles.

If a physician cannot cure a patient with medicine, he will resort to a more radical treatment such as *tarsek*.[38] Similarly, this single mental practice of exchanging self and others can effectively cure all the hundreds of diseases of the mental afflictions.

(3) Two actions are for the beginning and the end.

There are two important exercises we should do: (1) at the beginning of all our spiritual practices we should correct our motivation, and (2) at the end, we should dedicate whatever virtue we accumulated. We should also examine the activities we do throughout the day to determine whether they are consistent with the resolve that we made when we got up in the morning.[39]

(4) Be patient, no matter which of the two you encounter.

We must make sure that whenever we encounter either good fortune or bad we do not lose our Mind Training practice. Some persons lose their dharma practice when they experience good fortune, such as gaining a high position or wealth. Others lose their dharma practice when they encounter an enemy who causes them to experience misery [333a].

(5) Protect the two even at the cost of your life.

We must observe both the general pledges that relate to dharma and the pledges of this Mind Training teaching with even greater concern than we have for our very lives.

(6) Train yourself in the three that are difficult.

We must exert ourselves intensely in three difficult exercises, first by learning what they are and then by training ourselves to practice them. The three are: the difficult practice of recognizing the mental afflictions, the difficult practice of applying their antidotes, and the difficult practice of preventing their recurrence.

[38]T: *gtar sreg*. This refers to a treatment used in traditional Tibetan medicine that includes bloodletting and applying lighted cotton tapers or hot needles.

[39]See the section called "The strength of intention" above, p. 186.

(7) Take up the three principal causes.

We should pray that we and others are able to acquire the three principal causes for practicing dharma: to meet with an excellent guru, to have a mind that is well-disposed to practice, and to gain the material necessities—such as food, clothing, and so forth—that facilitate spiritual practice.

(8) Meditate on the three in an undiminished form.

We should cultivate the following three attitudes in such a way that we do not let them become weakened: reverence and respect for our guru, devotion to the Mind Training teachings, and a commitment to observing the Mind Training precepts through practicing recollection and vigilance.[40]

(9) Maintain the three you should never be without.

We should never let ourselves become lax about continually practicing virtuous activities of body, speech, and mind. Moreover, virtuous activities of the body doesn't only mean doing prostrations and circumambulations. Even sitting up straight can be a physical virtue.[41]

(10) Train yourself impartially toward all objects.

We must practice the Mind Training teachings impartially toward both sentient beings and inanimate objects. Thus, we must avoid distinguishing between those we consider enemies and those we consider friends, or feeling a dislike for any geographical region or climate.

(11) Cherish everything with a practice that is heartfelt and all-encompassing.

We also must practice Mind Training from the bottom of our heart and in a way that encompasses every object, just as Chekawa did.

[40]Recollection (S: *smṛtiḥ*, T: *dran pa*) and vigilance (S: *saṃprajanyam*, T: *shes bzhin*) are discussed in relation to ordinary activities in Part Two, Day Nine, pp. 69–71. They also form the fifth and sixth of eight "remedial factors" in the instruction for achieving quiescence (see Day Twenty-one, pp. 244–249).

[41]For example, when listening to a dharma teaching.

(12) Train yourself constantly toward special objects.

We should meditate with particular intensity in relation to certain special objects, including those with whom we live. Other special objects include our enemies, toward whom we have great difficulty generating patience and similar virtuous attitudes, and our gurus and parents, because the actions we do in relation to them are very powerful karma.

(13) Don't let your practice depend on conditions.

We should meditate on the Mind Training instructions regardless of whether or not the circumstances are favorable, or we have material necessities such as food and clothing. We should not be like the individual described in these lines:

> Though pious with a full stomach and a sun that warms,
> He turns ordinary whenever misfortune descends [333b].

(14) This time, practice what is most important.

Although the practices we are doing at this time—such as meditating on enlightenment mind—are difficult, they hold great meaning for us. We must also practice them with the aim of bringing ultimate benefit both to ourselves and others, not merely to gain something that will benefit us in this life.

(Kyabje Rinpoche further remarked that we must consider future lives to be more important than this life, the dharma to be more important than worldly concerns, and meditation on this Mind Training instruction to be more important than any other dharma teaching or practice.)

The remaining precepts are presented in a series of brief aphorisms:

(15) Don't do mistaken activities.

The instructions describe six mistaken activities. Mistaken patience is being able to endure the hardships of worldly activities, but not those of practicing dharma with great effort.

Mistaken enjoyments are engaging in or thinking about such activities as worldly conversation, business affairs, wars, and the like. The proper enjoyment is to practice the three dharma activities of listening, reflection, and meditation.

Mistaken compassion is to pity someone who endures hardships for the sake of the dharma, instead of pitying those who engage in nonvirtuous deeds.

Mistaken aspiration is wanting to achieve worldly happiness, wealth, and power, instead of wanting to practice a genuine dharma.

Mistaken counsel is to teach others skills that might bring them great harm in future lives—such as how to sell things or how to engage in litigation. Proper counsel would be to convince those who trust us to do what will benefit them in future lives—that is, we should try to persuade them to practice dharma.

Mistaken rejoicing is to rejoice when someone does nonvirtuous deeds or when an enemy experiences suffering. Proper rejoicing is to rejoice at our own and others' virtuous deeds, and when others experience happiness.

(Kyabje Rinpoche made this further point about mistaken rejoicing: Long ago, a certain monk became pleased when he learned that a rival had committed an expulsory transgression.[42] When Geshe Potowa heard this, he declared that rejoicing at the rival's defeat was a greater misdeed than the expulsory transgression [334a].)

(16) Don't practice sporadically.

When we listen to dharma from a guru, we sometimes generate a shallow form of renunciation that causes us to become extremely earnest about doing all kinds of virtuous activities for a few days.[43] After a short while, though, we tire of this and give up doing virtuous activities. We should avoid this sort of sporadic behavior.

Gomba Rinchen Lama had a saying: "Train your eyes far ahead, keep a strong mind, and remain inwardly free."[44] This means, in part, that we should take a long-term view toward the dharma, and maintain an evenmindedness in which we are neither too strained nor too lax about our practice.

(Kyabje Rinpoche then made this point: We should begin by establishing a basic understanding of what our entire practice is, from the waking meditation up through the end. Later, we can learn the practices in greater detail.

[42]S: *parājikaḥ*, T: *phas pham pa*. Any of four offenses that require a monk or nun to be expelled. See also Day Fifteen, note 159.

[43]See Day Fifteen, p. 43 and accompanying note 4 for another reference to this attitude, which is called "goose-bump renunciation."

[44]This saying is also quoted and explained in Part Two, Day Ten, p. 102.

He illustrated the effectiveness of this approach using the story of the louse and the flea.[45])

The next precept states:

(17) Train in a way that cuts through indecision.

This precept is sometimes explained as meaning that we should devote ourselves completely to the Mind Training practice. However, a more vivid description is the following: When a physician is letting blood from a patient, he cuts through the flesh and various small blood vessels, deeply and all at once. Similarly, when we practice the Mind Training instructions, we must apply them to our mind with a firmness that is like rock meeting bone.[46]

(18) Free yourself using deliberation and reflection.

Furthermore, we must practice analytic meditation by applying deliberation[47] and reflection[48] to the Mind Training instructions, so that we can remove any uncertainty we may have about them. We should also practice the antidote to whichever one of our mental afflictions is the strongest.

(19) Don't be conceited.

It is only proper that we exert ourselves on behalf of all sentient beings. Indeed, we have pledged ourselves to the pursuit of this goal. Therefore, we should never boast to anyone about how we have devoted ourselves to such activities.

(20) Don't be resentful.

If someone belittles us when we are in the company of others, we should not become angry and so forth.

[45]A Tibetan version of the fable of the tortoise and the hare.

[46]T: *rdo rus thug pa bzhin*. This saying is also quoted in Part Two, Day Ten, p. 101.

[47]S: *vitarkaḥ*, T: *rtog pa*. One of the mental states discussed in Buddhist Abhidharma literature. It is defined as a kind of discursive thought in which the faculties of volition (S: *cetanā*, T: *sems pa*) and wisdom (S: *prajñā*, T: *shes rab*) are used to examine an object in a relatively coarse manner.

[48]S: *vicāraḥ*, T: *dpyod pa*. This mental state is similar to deliberation, except that it examines its object in a more subtle or careful manner.

(21) Don't be fickle.

We should avoid becoming quickly pleased or upset at the slightest provocation, like the sky in springtime.

(22) Don't yearn to be thanked.

Whenever we help someone, we must not long to be thanked or receive some other expression of gratitude.

This completes the explanation of the precepts.

If we can practice all these instructions [334b], we will be able to transform unfavorable conditions into elements of the path to enlightenment, even during times when the five degeneracies—that is, the degeneracy of life spans and the rest—have become strong.[49]

These instructions have been transmitted through a lineage that comes down to us from Suvarnadvipa Guru. Chekawa himself gained such contentment through practicing them that he declared he could face death with no regrets.

With the above explanations, I have taught everything except the instructions that relate to the correct view. While many of the commentaries to this teaching describe the instructions on correct view according to the opinions of early Kadampa teachers, those explanations are not completely reliable.

The commentary entitled the *Mind Training Like the Rays of the Sun* explains the instructions on correct view according to the Madhyamaka Prasangika School. Therefore, we must contemplate that portion of the root text in a way that is consistent with the Prasangika viewpoint. Suvarnadvipa Guru originally held the view of the Chittamatra or Mind Only School. It is said that later he became a follower of the Madhyamaka School.

(Kyabje Rinpoche made this final comment at the end of the discourse: When a practical instruction[50] on the stages of the path to enlightenment is being taught, the custom of explaining and then reviewing all the major points three or four times is only followed up through the topic of generating enlightenment mind. For the remaining topics, this practice does not need to be followed.)

[49] See Day Seventeen, note 45 for a description of these five factors.

[50] T: *nyams khrid*. See Part One, Day One, p. 25 for a description of various types of instruction, including a practical instruction.

DAY TWENTY:
A GENERAL DISCUSSION OF THE SIX PERFECTIONS

(Kyabje Rinpoche opened the discourse by quoting a verse from the *Collection of Jewel-like Qualities*, which includes the lines:

> The past and future Conquerors and those who now
> abide
> In all the ten directions followed this path of the perfections
> and no other.[1]

He explained how the path traversed by all the Buddhas of the three times is the one that encompasses the activities of the six perfections. There is no sutra or tantra scripture anywhere that describes a path different from this one. He further explained how this very path is the one taught in all the Lamrim treatises.

Then he described briefly the preliminary exercise of correcting one's motivation and listed the topics of the outline that had already been completed [335a]. Next he reviewed all the instructions of the *Seven-Point Instruction on Mind Training* from the third and fourth sections, entitled "Transforming unfavorable conditions into elements of the path to enlightenment" and "A practice for one's entire lifetime" respectively, to the end.

After declaring that the instructions on how to generate the aspiration to achieve supreme enlightenment were now completed, he said that although the next topic in the outline is the one entitled "The ritual method of adopting enlightenment mind," he would put it off until later.[2]

He went on to say that anyone who fails to generate enlightenment mind but still hopes to achieve Buddhahood by meditating on instructions such as Mahamudra,[3] Dzokchen,[4] the philosophical tenets of the Madhyamaka School, or the generation and completion stages of Anuttarayoga Tantra will fail even to pass through the door to the Mahayana path, much less come the slightest bit closer to the goal of supreme enlightenment. Therefore, all of us must make enlightenment mind the most important of all our

[1]S: *Ratnaguṇasaṃcayagāthā*, ch. 22, v. 3. The entire verse states: "The past and future Conquerors and those who now abide/ In all the ten directions followed this path of the perfections and no other./ These perfections were revealed as an illumination, a torch, a resplendent light/ And a teacher to those who have set out for supreme enlightenment."

[2]See Days Twenty-three and Twenty-four.

[3]S: *Mahāmudrā*, T: *Phyag rgya chen po*.

[4]T: *rDzogs pa chen po*.

spiritual practices. Although the Buddhas might search for many kalpas with their omniscient wisdom, they would not discover any spiritual method of practice nor any point of entry for the path that is superior to this enlightenment mind.)

iii. How to train oneself in Bodhisattva activities once enlightenment mind has been generated

It is not enough for us simply to generate enlightenment mind. Once we have done so, we must undertake to train ourselves in the Bodhisattva activities. For instance, a person who wishes to go to India cannot reach there unless he actually sets out for his destination. Similarly, in order to achieve a Conqueror's two bodies—the dharma body and the form body—we must accumulate the two accumulations of merit and wisdom, and train ourselves in a practice that includes both wisdom and means.

The activities of the Conquerors' sons are included in the two categories of means and wisdom [335b]. Of these, means is represented by the first five perfections and wisdom by the last perfection—also known as the practice of insight.[5]

This section of the teaching is made up of two parts: (1) how to ripen one's own mind by training oneself in the six perfections, and (2) how to ripen others' minds by training oneself in the four methods of attracting a following.

1) How to ripen one's own mind by training oneself in the six perfections

The first of these includes three divisions: (1) a general discussion of how to train oneself in all of the perfections, (2) a specific discussion of how to train oneself in the last two perfections, and (3) how to train oneself in the Vajrayana path.

a) A general discussion of how to train oneself in all of the perfections

This section of the outline includes the six topics of how to train oneself in: (1) generosity, (2) ethics, (3) patience, (4) effort, (5) concentration, and (6) wisdom.

[5]S: *vipaśyanā*, T: *hlag mthong*. This topic is taught in Day Twenty-two.

i) How to train oneself in generosity

The essence of generosity is the mental act of wanting to give one's body, material possessions, and virtue-roots. It is classified into three types: (1) giving material objects, (2) giving dharma, and (3) giving freedom from fear.

Giving material objects

The material things can range anywhere from such extraordinary objects as one's body or life to minor ones like a spoonful of *tsamba*. If we feel unable to part with something, we should reflect in the following way:

> We have possessed immense wealth in the past, for instance, when we were born as the gods Brahma and Shakra or as a wheel-wielding monarch. However, we did not gain anything of real value in those lives largely because we failed to practice generosity. This is also why we find ourselves in such undistinguished circumstances now.

Then we must be willing to give away the object without expecting to receive something in return and without hoping that this act will bring a positive karmic ripening. If we are motivated by enlightenment mind, everything from giving just a morsel of food or a small amount of fresh *tsamba* to the poor or even ants and other insects represents the perfection of giving and is one of the activities done by the Conquerors' sons.

(Kyabje Rinpoche further explained that whenever we practice generosity, we must do so in a way that does not diminish its effectiveness. For instance, we should make sure that whatever we give someone actually brings them satisfaction. He mentioned that sometimes when we make a large offering to the Triple Gem [336a], we become filled with pride and think, "What a tremendous act of generosity!" But this is an impure form of giving. Similarly, it is improper to regret one's generosity, for instance, by thinking, "I gave too much," or "I gave it to the wrong person."

He went on to say that we must correct our motivation carefully when practicing generosity—both at the beginning and the end—so that our intention is to benefit all sentient beings. We should also pray fervently that this aim comes to pass. Finally, no matter how great or small our generosity, we must avoid any selfish thoughts, such as hoping that the act will bring us some form of material gain or honor.)

Giving dharma

Giving dharma includes all acts of teaching—even those of interpreting four lines of verse—with a good motivation, to someone who wishes to hear them, and explaining the meaning of scriptures to one's students. It doesn't have to be a formal discourse delivered from a dharma throne by someone who is recognized as a lama. Compared to all other types of giving, giving dharma is the highest form of generosity.

When we are memorizing and reciting scriptures aloud, we should imagine that virtuous gods and all sentient beings are seated around us listening. By doing this, our memorizing exercises will become a form of giving dharma. If even bugs and worms have seeds planted in their minds by hearing the sound of dharma, the same will also certainly be true for higher beings. Visualizing oneself surrounded by sentient beings should also be done in other situations, for instance when we have been invited to recite scriptures in the home of a benefactor.

We monks must be especially careful when we go to laypersons' homes to perform rituals. We must not take the tantric teachings that were taught by our compassionate Master as the means of gaining Buddhahood within a single lifetime and turn them into a means of acquiring material gain and honor. Anyone who does this is selling the dharma for money. This is like forcing a king to come down from his throne and sweep garbage [336b]. Therefore, when we go to laypersons' homes to perform rituals, we must make sure that we have a pure motivation.

In general, when someone teaches dharma, this is obviously giving dharma. However, we can also give dharma during ordinary conversation, by directly or indirectly leading others to the dharma.

The primary form of generosity for monks and nuns is the giving of dharma. However, they should also give material objects, if they can acquire them effortlessly. Nevertheless, the Kadampa Geshe Sharawa said to those practitioners who had left the householder's state, "I have not described to you the benefits of giving; I have explained the disadvantages of stinginess."[6]

Giving freedom from fear

This form of generosity includes acts such as gaining the freedom of those who are suffering in prisons, rescuing those who are in danger of

[6]Quoted in the *Great Stages of the Path* (T: *Lam rim chen mo*), p. 515 (f. 242a). This disapproval of material giving for monks and nuns is based on the view that prolonged and strenuous efforts to acquire and retain property could damage their ethical practice.

drowning, and saving insects and other creatures during the summer or winter when they are endangered by heat or cold.

We do not need to search far and wide for opportunities to free beings from fear. This kind of giving can be practiced even toward the lice we find on our body. It is also very easy to free insects that are in danger of drowning; all we have to do is reach down with our hands.

The visualizations for the giving meditation in the Mind Training instructions[7] also represent the practice of generosity. The main element in practicing the perfection of generosity is described in this verse from *Engaging in Bodhisattva Activities*:

> If the perfection of giving meant
> To remove the world's poverty,
> How did previous Saviors perfect this,
> Since there is still poverty in the world?[8]

Thus, the perfection of generosity does not mean a practice that eliminates sentient beings' poverty. Nor is it just the overcoming of stinginess, since that is accomplished by *arhats* of both the Listeners' and Solitary Realizers' vehicles. Rather, it is described in another verse from *Engaging in Bodhisattva Activities*:

> The perfection of generosity is described
> As the willingness to give all beings
> Everything one has, together with its fruit.
> Therefore, [337a] it is in fact a mental state.[9]

The perfection of generosity can be explained as the practice of cultivating, to the fullest extent, the desire to give others our body, our wealth, and our merit. This attitude is developed through contemplating the advantages of practicing generosity and the disadvantages of failing to do so. Furthermore, the desire to be generous should be completely free of stinginess, it should be generated with a heartfelt sincerity, and it should not be practiced with the anticipation of receiving a favorable karmic result. The most important element in this practice, then, is the aim of increasing our desire to be generous.

If a poor person were to ask us to give even such things as our three monk's garments, we must immediately and sincerely generate the thought

[7]See Day Eighteen, pp. 171–172.

[8]S: *Bodhicaryāvatāraḥ*, ch. 5, v. 9.

[9]Ibid., ch. 5, v. 10.

that we are willing to give the object. Since this attitude can only be developed through practice, we must cultivate it gradually, beginning with small objects. We must continue expanding the desire to be generous until we reach the point where we could even give away our very body.

One technique for increasing this attitude is to reflect on our impermanence. For instance, there is not a single part of our wealth and property that we can take with us when we die; we must leave it all behind without having been able to use it. On the other hand, if we dedicate all our wealth to others from the bottom of our heart, we will lessen the degree to which we commit such moral transgressions as using material objects with a selfish attitude.[10] This dedication will also constitute one form of practicing generosity.

It is not enough, however, that we simply do such mental exercises as these. We must also be as generous as we can by actually giving things to others, including alms when a beggar asks for them. It is also not proper to acquire objects through wrong livelihood so that we can practice giving.

Generally speaking, the first three perfections[11] are the main forms of practice for householders. As a scripture declares:

> For householders, the Sugatas mainly praised
> The three practices of giving and the rest.[12]

There are many circumstances and factors that make it improper to give something. For instance, we should not actually give away our body until we have mastered the practice of generosity. For the time being, we should only try to increase the willingness to do so [337b]. As *Engaging in Bodhisattva Activities* describes,[13] at some point in the future it will be no more difficult for us to give up our body than it would be to give away vegetables. When we reach that level, we can actually give up our body.

Here are a number of other examples that illustrate situations in which it is improper to give something because of the unsuitability of the recipient, the time, or the object. Monks and nuns should not give away such things as their three religious garments. Food should not be given to monks or nuns after midday. Foul-smelling food should not be given to anyone. Things

[10]T: *bdag 'brel gyi ltung ba*. See *Great Stages of the Path* (T: *Lam rim chen mo*), pp. 511–512 (ff. 240a-240b). This point is based on a passage from the *Compendium of Training* (S: *Śikṣāsamauccayaḥ*, ch. 6, p. 79).

[11]Generosity, morality, and patience.

[12]*Introduction to the Middle Way* (T: *dBu ma la 'jug pa*), ch. 3, v. 12.

[13]Ch. 7, v. 25.

that are considered impure, such as onions and garlic, should not be given to Brahmans and others who follow dietary restrictions against them.

We should not give a scripture book to a contentious person seeking to find fault with the dharma. Nor should we give poison or a weapon to someone who wishes to die.

It is improper to teach secret instructions to those who are not spiritually mature. We should also avoid helping anyone overcome legal difficulties if they are evil and certain to do harm to the teaching or other sentient beings.

In addition, we should train ourselves so that we are not tainted by any of the following faults: We should avoid the wrong view that believes generosity does not produce beneficial results. Our generosity should not be made insignificant by helping only one individual while ignoring the interests of many. We should never perform animal sacrifices, which are acts motivated by wrong view. Our generosity should be done without showing any scorn toward the recipient and it should not be done as a way of showing up rivals. We should also practice a generosity that is free of arrogance, the desire for fame, despondency, regret, and bias.

(Kyabje Rinpoche concluded by explaining how we should also train ourselves according to three groups of four activities that are taught in the *Compendium of Training*.[14] The first group of activities is: (1) to strengthen the desire to give our body; (2) to protect our body from unfavorable human and nonhuman conditions until we are ready to give it away; (3) to keep our body pure by not allowing ourselves to become tainted by nonvirtuous deeds; and (4) to develop or improve our body by using this life's body to do the virtuous activities that in the future will bring a human form having the eight maturation qualities.[15]

The second group of activities is: (1) to actually give our wealth [338a] as well as to strengthen our desire to give it; (2) to protect our wealth until it is given to an extraordinary field;[16] (3) to keep our wealth pure by not allowing ourselves to become tainted by wrong livelihood and bad deeds;

[14]Shantideva's *Compendium of Training* (S: *Śikṣāsamuccayaḥ*) includes twenty-seven "root verses" composed by him as an outline to his collection of passages from Mahayana sutras. Verse 4, in particular, states that a Bodhisattva's entire training can be classified into four activities that should be cultivated in relation to three objects. They are: "To give to all beings/ One's body, wealth, and virtue/ Done in the three times;/ As well as to protect, purify, and develop them." This classification is being applied here in relation to the perfection of generosity.

[15]Eight qualities that permit a Bodhisattva to effectively pursue both his own welfare and that of others. See Part Two, Day Thirteen, pp. 266–270.

[16]That is, one's guru and the Triple Gem. See also Part One, Day Five, note 101 for a description of different kinds of fields.

and (4) to develop our wealth by practicing generosity so that we will be able to gain additional wealth in the future.

The third group of activities is: (1) to sincerely give all our virtue to sentient beings; (2) to protect our virtue by not allowing anger to destroy it; (3) to keep our virtue pure by not allowing it to become tainted by such impure and selfish motives as seeking this life's happiness and seeking only to avoid being reborn in the lower states in our future lives; and (4) to increase our virtue by rejoicing in it.)

ii) How to train oneself in ethics

Engaging in Bodhisattva Activities states:

> The perfection of ethics is understood as
> Gaining the desire to avoid doing harm.[17]

Ethics is defined as the mind that avoids harming others by turning away from even the motivation to do such acts. The perfection of ethics is achieved by practicing this attitude until it is developed to the fullest extent.

There are three types of ethics: (1) the ethics of restraining oneself from doing misdeeds, (2) the ethics of collecting virtue, and (3) the ethics of benefiting sentient beings.

The ethics of restraining oneself from doing misdeeds

This form of ethics is illustrated by keeping any of the three classes of vows.[18]

A verse from the *Lamp of the Path* states:

> Only when a person continually holds
> Any of the seven types
> Of Pratimoksha vows is he fit for
> The Bodhisattva vows; not otherwise.[19]

The explicit wording of this verse seems to indicate that possessing a form of the Pratimoksha vows is a prerequisite for taking the Bodhisattva

[17]S: *Bodhicaryāvatāraḥ*, ch. 5, v. 11.

[18]The Pratimoksha, Bodhisattva, and Tantrayana vows. See Part One, Day Four, note 26.

[19]S: *Bodhipathapradīpaḥ*, v. 20.

vows.[20] However, this assertion is not being made in an absolute sense. Its intent is that we should regard a *bhikshu* as the ideal form in which to cultivate the Bodhisattva trainings, just as a *bhikshu* is said to represent the ideal form for practicing the tantric teachings [338b]. In fact, there are also gods and *nagas* who cultivate the Bodhisattva trainings.[21]

How, then, should we understand the ethics of restraint? For a practitioner of the Bodhisattva trainings who also holds a form of the Pratimoksha vows, it is the commitment to avoid doing harm that is shared by his Bodhisattva and Pratimoksha vows. For a practitioner who does not hold any of the Pratimoksha vows, it is the commitment to avoid doing harm that is inherent in the practice of abandoning the ten nonvirtuous deeds. Furthermore, the Bodhisattva vow itself is said to be distinct from both a Bodhisattva's ethical practice of abandoning the ten nonvirtuous deeds and his Pratimoksha vows.[22]

The ethics of collecting virtue

All virtuous activities that a practitioner of the Bodhisattva trainings undertakes through any of the three doors of body, speech, or mind constitute the ethics of collecting virtue. These include making prostrations and presenting offerings to, as well as revering and honoring, an extraordinary field; engaging in the three activities of hearing, contemplating, and meditating on the dharma; and listening to or teaching the dharma. In short, it includes any activities related to the six perfections that help to spiritually ripen our own mind and the minds of others.

In fact, all the Bodhisattva activities can be subsumed within the three types of Mahayana ethics. Broadly speaking, it can also be said that all the

[20]The Pratimoksha system recognizes eight types of vows. One of them—the *upavasa* (T: *bsynen gnas*) vow—is only observed for a twenty-four-hour period (see Part Two, Day Thirteen, note 76). Therefore, the reference to seven types of vows here is to those that are maintained for the duration of one's life. They are: two monks' vows—the novice *shramanera* (T: *dge tsul*) and the fully ordained *bhikshu* (T: *dge slong*); three nuns' vows—the novice *shramanerika* (T: *dge tsul ma*), an intermediate level *shikshamana* (T: *dge slob ma*), and the fully ordained *bhikshuni* (T: *dge slong ma*); the layman or *upasaka* vow (T: *dge bsnyen*), and the laywoman or *upasika* vow (T: *dge bsnyen ma*).

[21]Since only humans can take the Pratimoksha vows, this comment is meant to show that the Pratimoksha vows are not a prerequisite for receiving the Bodhisattva vows and practicing Mahayana ethics.

[22]Je Tsongkapa addresses this relationship between the Pratimoksha vows and the Mahayana ethics of restraint in his *Highway to Enlightenment: A Commentary on Bodhisattva Ethics* (T: *Byang chub sems dpa'i tsul khrims kyi rnam bshad byang chub gzhung lam*), pp. 528–536 (ff. 8b–12b). See listing in Bibliography.

stages of the path to enlightenment serve to strengthen these same three types of ethics.

The ethics of benefiting sentient beings

The ethics of benefiting sentient beings is represented by such activities as practicing the four principles for attracting a following.[23] The ways to benefit others are classified into eleven types: (1) helping others with their work and helping those who are suffering; (2) helping those who do not know what is proper; (3) helping those who have helped us; (4) helping those who are facing some danger; (5) helping those who are overcome with grief; (6) helping the needy; (7) helping those who wish to establish themselves in the dharma [339a]; (8) helping others by complying with their wishes; (9) helping those who are following the right path; (10) helping those who are following a wrong path; and (11) helping others by displaying miraculous powers.

Except for displaying miraculous powers, we can definitely practice the other ten ways of benefiting sentient beings. In short, this form of ethics includes all activities of the three doors that are motivated by the wish to benefit others.

Therefore, the way to train ourselves in the three types of Mahayana ethics can be summarized as follows: (1) We should train ourselves in the ethics of avoiding any of the ten nonvirtuous deeds, even if we haven't taken any form of Pratimoksha vows; (2) we should train ourselves in the six perfections in order to ripen our own mind spiritually; and (3) we should train ourselves to do whatever activities benefit others.

iii) How to train oneself in patience

The essence of patience is a mind that does not become disturbed by suffering or harm inflicted by others. As the following verse from *Engaging in Bodhisattva Activities* states, this means we must overcome our anger:

> How could I slay all wicked beings
> Who are as limitless as space?
> Yet if I slay this angry mind,
> My enemies will all be slain.[24]

[23]S: *catur saṃgrahavastūni*, T: *bsdu ba'i dngos po bzhi*. They are: (1) generosity, (2) pleasant speech, (3) beneficial conduct, and (4) sameness of purpose. These four practices are described in Day Twenty-three, pp. 304–305.

[24]S: *Bodhicaryāvatāraḥ*, ch. 5, v. 12.

If we fail to overcome our anger and allow ourselves to express it, we commit an extremely grave misdeed. As several more lines from the same work state:

> There is no evil like hatred,
> And no austerity like patience.[25]

There are three types of patience: (1) the patience of enduring harm from another person; (2) the patience of accepting suffering; and (3) the patience gained through a firm conviction regarding the dharma.

The patience of enduring harm from another person

The patience of enduring harm from another person means to cultivate patience toward and not become angry with our enemies and others when they harm us. In order to do this, we must learn the disadvantages of anger.

Anger is the worst kind of nonvirtuous mind. It is said that each moment we allow our anger to continue [339b] destroys an amount of virtue that would take us a thousand kalpas to accumulate.[26] Therefore, we must recognize what a terrible fault anger is and strive to practice patience continually.

We can never be sure who among us may be a Bodhisattva. And as the *Introduction to the Middle Way*[27] describes, a Bodhisattva of lesser spiritual development will destroy the virtue that he accumulated over a hundred kalpas if he should become angry with a Bodhisattva of greater spiritual development. *Engaging in Bodhisattva Activities*[28] also describes how someone who is not a Bodhisattva will destroy virtue accumulated over a thousand kalpas by developing anger toward a Bodhisattva. Therefore, one reason we must practice patience is that the negative consequences of anger are so enormous. This also indicates one of the ways to cultivate patience: whether it is before or after we have become angry, we should recall the disadvantages

[25]Ibid., ch. 6, v. 2.

[26]Kalpa is the term by which cosmic time is measured. A "great kalpa," which is made up of eighty "intermediate kalpas," represents the vast period in which a physical world comes into being, is populated by sentient beings, undergoes destruction, and finally disappears, leaving behind empty space. See Part Two, Day Nine, p. 92, as well as note 103 on the same page.

[27]T: *dBu ma la 'jug pa*, ch. 3, v. 6. In his commentary on this verse, Je Tsongkapa presents a detailed explanation of anger's negative consequences; see *Elucidation of the Underlying Intent: An Extensive Commentary on the Introduction to the Middle Way* (T: *dBu ma la 'jug pa'i rgya cher bshad pa dgongs pa rab gsal*), pp. 107–116 (ff. 53a–57b). In fact, Je Rinpoche explains the verse as describing a higher Bodhisattva becoming angry with a Bodhisattva of lesser spiritual development.

[28]S: *Bodhicaryāvatāraḥ*, ch. 6, v. 1

of anger and generate the willingness to tolerate whatever difficulty we are experiencing.

If we fail to develop patience, anger will bring unhappiness both to ourselves and to others. Anger can even make us take our own life, not to mention the lives of others. It can also cause us to have many enemies.

Now, some of you might think: "What you say is true, but I still can't develop patience because there are so many people that make me angry." However, as a verse from *Engaging in Bodhisattva Activities* says:

> How could there be enough leather
> To cover the entire world?
> Yet with just the leather of your shoes,
> You can cause the earth to be covered.[29]

Do you think you can get rid of all your enemies by defeating them? As long as there are sentient beings, you will never run out of enemies and you will never be able to defeat them all. And yet if you defeat your own anger, you will never encounter a single enemy again and it will be as if you had defeated all the ones you had.

If we remain completely filled with anger even after studying exhaustively such topics as the essence of patience, its classifications, the disadvantages of anger, and so on [340a], our efforts will have amounted to nothing. There was once a disciple who was beating a thief. His lama tried to intervene but couldn't stop him. When all else failed, the lama poked the disciple on the nose with his finger and cried, "Patience! Patience!" Finally, the disciple was able to gain patience. What good does it do to wait until an entire episode of anger is over before we make some pretense of trying to show patience? Although it is difficult at first, after we have trained ourselves and cultivated patience for some time, it becomes easier to develop.

Here is a series of points that explains why we shouldn't become angry with those who try to harm us. Suppose someone hits you on the head with a club. Instead of becoming angry with the attacker, you should think: "If I want to direct my anger toward the actual cause of my pain, I should be angry with the club."

Such a suggestion might lead to this thought: "It isn't right to be angry with the club, because it has no control over the way it is used." But the person who hit you has no control over himself, either. He is compelled to act by his mental afflictions. Therefore, your anger should be directed toward them and not the person who hit you.[30]

[29]Ibid., ch. 5, v. 13.

[30]See *Engaging in Bodhisattva Activities* (S: *Bodhicaryāvatāraḥ*), ch. 6, v. 41.

Here is another approach. The direct cause for being struck by a club is some sort of ill-considered behavior on our part. But the root cause is the bad karma of hurting others that we accumulated in the past. This is where the ultimate blame lies. Why, then, should we become angry at the ripening of our own past deeds?[31]

The *Four Hundred Verses* also states:

> The Muni[32] regarded the mental afflictions as the foe,
> Not the person affected by the mental afflictions.[33]

For instance, if a sick person becomes crazy and strikes his doctor or a son becomes crazy and strikes his father, neither the doctor nor the father is angered by his attacker. Instead, they both try to cure the insanity of the afflicted person. We, too, [340b] should not become angry with anyone who harms us, because they are persons who have been driven insane by their mental afflictions and who have no control over their actions. In fact, we must try to cure such persons of their mental afflictions.

Here is another point. If we burn our hand in a fire, it isn't appropriate to become angry with the fire; rather, it's our own fault for having touched the fire. In the same way, we shouldn't become angry with someone for harming us, because we are responsible, in a sense, for having provoked him. Just as it is fire's nature to be hot and to burn objects, some persons naturally seek to harm others. Since we don't become angry with a fire when it burns us, neither is it reasonable to become angry with a person who is harmful by nature.[34]

We might find ourselves having this thought: "Perhaps it isn't right to be angry with someone if it's his nature to be harmful. But I am angry with this person because it was a chance occurrence."[35] In that case, it would be right to become angry with the sky when it sends down hail. Just as there is no reason to become angry with the sky when unusual events occur, we should not become angry with a person even though he is not by nature harmful.[36]

[31]Ibid., ch. 6, v. 42.

[32]T: *thub pa*. Literally "sage" or "ascetic"; the term is also an epithet of the Buddha, who was known as the Sage of the Shakya clan (S: *Śākyamuniḥ*).

[33]T: *bZhi brgya pa*, ch. 5, v. 9. In Bibliography, see listing under *Āryadeva*.

[34]See *Engaging in Bodhisattva Activities* (S: *Bodhicaryāvatāraḥ*), ch. 6, v. 39.

[35]S: *āgantuḥ*, T: *lo bur ba*. That is, it was not part of his inherent nature and therefore he was free to commit it or not.

[36]*Engaging in Bodhisattva Activities* (S: *Bodhicaryāvatāraḥ*), ch. 6, v. 40.

Thus, whenever anyone beats us or speaks badly about us and brings us physical or mental suffering, we must resist trying to do harm in return, as this will only cause us to be reborn in the lower states. What we should do instead is cultivate one of the antidotes to anger and practice patience. As a verse from *Engaging in Bodhisattva Activities* declares:

> If I am not able to endure now
> Even this small suffering,
> Why don't I turn back the anger
> That causes torment in the hells?[37]

The patience of enduring harm from another person can only be cultivated toward someone who actually does us harm; it cannot be cultivated toward someone who benefits us. A practitioner who is harmed by many will have many opportunities to cultivate patience; therefore, he should view those who harm him as giving him the opportunity to increase his patience.

For example, a certain King Asanga had an ill-natured spiritual advisor who was always in the monarch's presence. When others urged the king not to rely on such a person [341a], he replied, "It is because of him that I have been able to perfect the virtue of patience."

(Kyabje Rinpoche summarized this section by advising us to reflect in the following manner: "Disciples of the Listeners' vehicle strive to achieve only their own personal aims. Yet even they don't allow themselves to become angry with persons who harm them. How, then, could it be proper for someone like me to get angry, since I have dedicated myself to the goals of the Mahayana path?" Finally, Kyabje Rinpoche told us the story of Kshantivadin[38] and urged us to train ourselves as he did.)

The patience of accepting suffering

Not only must we avoid becoming attached to pleasures, we must also come to regard suffering as something that has positive value[39] and receive it as if it were medicine. For instance, as I described earlier during the teachings on Mind Training,[40] we should transform all forms of suffering that we experience, such as hardships endured for the sake of dharma,

[37]Ibid., ch. 6, v. 73.

[38]See *Garland of Birth Stories* (S: *Jātakamālā*), ch. 28. In Bibliography, see listing under *Āryaśūra*.

[39]Literally, "we must regard suffering as an ornament"; that is, as something to be appreciated for its beneficial qualities and not just as something to be avoided.

[40]See Day Eighteen pp. 173–179, and Day Nineteen pp. 184–185.

illnesses, unwelcome enemies, and even the pain felt in a dream, into elements that enhance our dharma practice. We should strengthen our patience by contemplating how experiencing suffering exhausts our bad karma, how reflecting on our own suffering helps us develop compassion toward others, and how such experiences exemplify samsara's flaws.

As we experience suffering, we should rejoice in the thought that our pain can take the place of what we would otherwise have to experience by being born in the lower states in a future life. This is like the joy a condemned man would feel if, instead of being executed, he was set free after only having his hand cut off.

In order to cure the greater suffering of an illness, we are willing to undergo the pain involved in treatments such as *tarsek*.[41] In the same way, we should regard the hardships that we endure for the sake of the dharma as worthwhile, because they allow us to avoid the many sufferings we would otherwise have to experience by being born in the lower states.

We should also recall the benefits that can come from experiencing suffering. These are described in the following verse from *Engaging in Bodhisattva Activities*:

> And suffering's other benefits [341b]
> Are loss of pride through discontent,
> Compassion for samsara's beings,
> Dread of evil, and love of good.[42]

Not only that, those of us who have left the householder's state and become monks or nuns should cultivate the virtues of having few wants and being satisfied with what we have. We should also willingly accept the asceticism and material hardship that form part of a spiritual way of life. Even though we live in modest dwellings and our food and clothing are of poor quality, and so forth, we should contemplate how fortunate we are to have the opportunity of training ourselves in the four attributes of the Arya lineage, which include being satisfied with dharma robes of poor quality, alms food of poor quality, and a bed and seat of poor quality.[43]

If we fail to cultivate these attitudes, we will develop a desire for material things, such as excellent food and abundant wealth. This desire will lead us to spend all our time looking for ways to increase our wealth and material

[41] See Day Nineteen, note 38.

[42] S: *Bodhicaryāvatāraḥ*, ch. 6, v. 21.

[43] S: *caturāryavamsāḥ*, T: *'phags pa'i rigs bzhi*. Only the first three attributes are mentioned here. The fourth one is to delight in abandoning the mental afflictions and practicing meditation.

possessions. As a result, we won't devote any time to contemplating dharma and our entire life will be wasted in meaningless pursuits.

Once, when the Master came upon a treasure, a woodcutter overheard him remark, "This is a poison that quickly spreads everywhere; this is a powerful poison."[44] After the Master left, the woodcutter went to see what was there and discovered a quantity of gold.

When the king asked the woodcutter how he had come by his riches, the woodcutter lied. After discovering that he had been misled, the king ordered that the woodcutter be put to death.

Just as he was about to be executed, the woodcutter repeated the phrases, "This is a poison that quickly spreads everywhere; this is a powerful poison." When asked what they meant, the woodcutter described everything that had happened and was eventually allowed to live.

As this story reveals, wealth is like poison. But if we simple monks cultivate the virtues of having few wants and being satisfied with what we have, we will definitely be able to acquire the basic necessities. For example, Je Rinpoche only possessed eight *sho*[45] when he went into retreat with eight of his disciples. Still, the teacher and his disciples all practiced the virtues of having few wants and being satisfied with what they had. They also remained happy with whatever clothing they could find, even though it was of poor quality [342a]. On the other hand, if we do find ample food and clothing through our good karma, we can make use of them as long as they do not harm our spiritual practice.

We must practice patience when someone attacks us verbally or when we acquire a bad reputation, and so forth.[46]

We must accept the suffering associated with physical activities, such as the discomfort that can come from having to sit up straight.

We must accept whatever suffering is experienced in pursuit of the dharma, such as when we make offerings to the Triple Gem.

We must accept whatever suffering stems from our means of subsistence. This means, for instance, that since we have turned away from the pleasures of the senses and abandoned all interest in good clothing, an attractive

[44]This story appears in *Expounding the Discipline* (T: *'Dul ba rnam par byed pa*), in the *'Dul ba* section of Kg., Vol. 7 (*ja*), ff. 342a–346b.

[45]T: *zho*. A Tibetan unit of money roughly equivalent to a dollar.

[46]This refers to a category made up of nine forms of suffering that derive from worldly conditions: (1) loss; (2) scorn; (3) bad reputation; (4) pain; (5) the disintegration of things that are subject to disintegration; (6) the exhaustion of things that are subject to exhaustion; (7) the aging of things that are subject to aging; (8) the illnesses experienced by things that are subject to illness; and (9) the death of things that are subject to death. See Asanga's *Bodhisattva Levels* (S: *Bodhisattvabhūmiḥ*), p. 133.

physical appearance, and so on, we must accept the hardships associated with being physically unattractive[47] and wearing unattractive clothing.

We must accept the suffering of fatigue brought on by striving to practice the dharma.

We must accept the suffering that comes from benefiting others. For example, we must be willing to endure the suffering that we know we will have to experience when we try to save sentient beings who are in danger of being killed.

We must accept the suffering that comes from our regular duties. This means, for example, that we must also endure the hardship brought about by having abandoned such activities as selling goods, cultivating fields, and the like, as a means of acquiring wealth.[48]

These points illustrate the wide-ranging manner in which the patience of accepting suffering can be practiced.

The patience gained through having a firm conviction about dharma

This type of patience is described extensively in the *Quick Path*.[49] It consists of developing a firm conviction with regard to a range of dharma topics. This conviction can be gained by meditating on the key points concerning how to practice virtuous activities; by memorizing and reciting scriptures in order to help determine what practices to take up and what activities to abandon; by contemplating such topics as the virtuous qualities of the Triple Gem, the ultimate goal of enlightenment, the path that leads to this goal, and the insubstantiality of the self; and by reflecting on the meaning of the profound and wide-ranging collections of the scriptures [342b].

In the present context, a firm conviction about the dharma can be achieved through developing a sure understanding of the words and meanings of this very teaching on the stages of the path to enlightenment. It can

[47]This is a reference to the fact that monks and nuns shave their heads as a sign of having abandoned the worldly life of a householder.

[48]Asanga distinguishes between the regular duties (S: *itikaraṇīyaḥ*, T *'phral gyi bya ba*) of householders and those of ordained persons. Kyabje Pabongka Rinpoche's comment here refers specifically to the duties of ordained persons in the following sense: Earlier he noted that monks and nuns must give up any attachment to having an attractive physical appearance. That theme of abandonment is again being alluded to here by saying that the ordained must also give up any worldly means of acquiring wealth. Therefore, the suffering that they experience from their everyday activities stems from having to rely on the generosity of others in order to find the robes and food that provide their means of subsistence. For householders, the suffering of regular duties means whatever difficulties must be endured while pursuing one's particular means of livelihood.

[49]T: *Myur lam*, f. 73b.

also refer to the sort of reflection that monk-scholars engage in when they debate about the meaning of religious and philosophical subjects.

Of the three types of patience, the first one can only be gained when we are being subjected to some form of harm, but the other two can be practiced anytime. For instance, when a dharma teaching is being given, we should be patient if it goes on for a long period of time. We should also listen with one-pointed concentration and contemplate the meanings that are being explained. When we gather in the main assembly hall or attend class on the debate ground, we should be mindful of our physical conduct and endure whatever feelings of hunger and thirst we may experience. When we are memorizing and reciting scriptures, we should concentrate one-pointedly on these activities. Moreover, we even have the opportunity to practice the latter two types of patience when we go to laypersons' homes to perform rituals.

iv) How to train oneself in effort

The essence of effort[50] is to exert oneself in doing activities of a virtuous nature. This is described in the line of verse that states:

> What is effort? Exertion directed toward virtue.[51]

This practice is the highest method for bringing virtues to completion. As the *Ornament of the Mahayana Sutras* declares, effort is the supreme of all the virtuous qualities and is the source of all good qualities up to and including Buddhahood:

> Effort is the highest among the collection of virtues,
> Because all others are gained by relying on it.
> Through effort, one abides instantly in a state of great ease.
> One also achieves the worldly and transcendent attainments.
>
> Through effort, the desired enjoyments of the world are achieved.
> Through effort, one gains a purity that has great power.
> Effort brings liberation through transcending the perishable assemblage.
> Through effort, one awakens to supreme enlightenment [343a].[52]

[50]S: *vīryam*, T: *brtzon 'grus*.

[51]*Engaging in Bodhisattva Activities* (S: *Bodhicaryāvatāraḥ*), ch. 7, v. 2.

[52]S: *Mahāyānasūtrālaṃkāraḥ*, ch. 16, vv. 65–66.

The *Introduction to the Middle Way* also declares:

> All good qualities without exception follow effort . . .[53]

Thus, when doing our daily recitations and other such activities, we shouldn't behave like a tired donkey that has to be driven up a hill. Instead, we must practice virtuous activities with energy and enthusiasm. We should start developing such an attitude on a small scale and for short periods of time, and then gradually make our effort stronger and stronger.

The obstacles to effort are three types of laziness: (1) the laziness of being idle, (2) the laziness of attachment to improper activities, and (3) the laziness of feeling discouraged.

The laziness of being idle

Idleness is the state in which a person falls victim to procrastination and spends all his time doing meaningless activities. Because of this, we become unwilling to do virtuous activities promptly. The antidote for this is to meditate on the topics of impermanence in the form of death, the great value of a human life possessing leisure and fortune, and the difficulty of acquiring such a life.

The laziness of being attached to improper activities

Attachment to improper activities means having an attachment that never tires of pursuing such nonvirtuous activities as seeking gain and honor or indulging in excessive social interaction and idle chatter. It also includes having a similar attitude toward such worldly endeavors as farming, selling goods, sewing clothes, spinning wool, and the like. This sort of exertion does not represent spiritual effort; it is merely hard work. The antidote to this type of laziness is described in *Engaging in Bodhisattva Activities*:

> How can you forsake the supreme delight
> Of dharma—the cause of endless joy—
> And take pleasure in such causes of suffering
> As excitement and merriment?[54]

[53]T: *dBu ma la 'jug pa*, ch. 4, v. 1.

[54]S: *Bodhicaryāvatāraḥ*, ch. 7, v. 15.

Thus, we must overcome this type of laziness by contemplating the meaninglessness of samsaric activities and the fact that they are a source of continued suffering.

The laziness of feeling discouraged

The laziness of feeling discouraged is the lack of confidence characterized by such thoughts as: "How can someone like me achieve Buddhahood?" "How can someone like me benefit all sentient beings?" And, "How can someone like me give away my head, or my arms and legs [343b]?"

Each and every one of the Buddha's teachings is an antidote to this type of laziness. For instance, we should think, "If I have to, I will even spend my whole life just meditating on any of the various points in the topic entitled "The difficulty of acquiring leisure and fortune."[55] We should also reflect in this way: "Even the merchants of this world and others like them work very hard in pursuit of meaningless goals and endure great hardships to gain only a small monetary profit. If I exert myself with the same amount of effort in pursuit of enlightenment, I will definitely be able to achieve my goal."

Engaging in Bodhisattva Activities declares:

> Don't feel despondent, thinking to yourself,
> "How could I ever gain enlightenment?"
> Because the one who speaks the truth—
> the Tathagata—has declared this truth:
>
> Even they[56]—having once been stinging gnats,
> Mosquitoes, bees and even crawling worms—
> By means of effort reached enlightenment,
> That supreme state so difficult to gain.
>
> Why should I—born a human
> Who knows right from wrong—
> Not reach Buddhahood, if I don't forsake
> The system of practice that brings omniscience?[57]

[55] See Part Two, Day Nine, pp. 85–96.

[56] That is, even the Buddhas were once the lowest of sentient beings; however, through effort they achieved the ultimate goal.

[57] S: *Bodhicaryāvatāraḥ*, ch. 7, vv. 17–19.

Thus, we should think to ourselves, "Our Master, who spoke the truth, declared that even gnats can achieve Buddhahood. Why, then, should someone like me, who was born a human being that can speak and reason, not be able to achieve enlightenment? Of course I can!"

We might have this fear: "Though it is possible to achieve that goal, I couldn't do such difficult acts as giving away my head, or my arms and legs." This feeling is addressed in the following lines from *Engaging in Bodhisattva Activities*:

> And yet I am afraid to give up
> Such things as my hands and feet.
> This ignorance of what has true value
> Is due to a lack of reflection.[58]

Again, several verses later:

> The Savior also directed us to give
> Vegetables and the like at first [344a].
>
> When, regarding your body, you develop
> An attitude like you have toward vegetables,
> Why, then, would it be difficult
> To give such things as your flesh?[59]

Therefore, we should encourage ourselves by thinking: "If I begin practicing generosity with small items, eventually I can feel the same way about giving away my head or my limbs as I do now about giving away vegetables. When I reach that point, it won't be difficult for me to give them away."

We may also be concerned that since the qualities of a Buddha are unlimited, it will be very difficult for us to achieve them. In that case, we should think: "The path that leads to those qualities is also immeasurably vast and profound. Therefore, if I practice it, I can definitely achieve them."

Then again, some might wonder: "What about the difficult acts that we must do in order to benefit sentient beings, such as having to take birth in the lower states?" This worry is answered in several verses from *Engaging in Bodhisattva Activities*, which begin with these lines:

[58]Ibid., ch. 7, v. 20

[59]Ibid., ch. 7, vv. 25–26.

Through renouncing misdeeds, you do not feel pain.
Through learning, your mind is untroubled.[60]

Therefore, we should reflect: "When a practitioner abandons wrongful deeds, he does not feel any suffering or discomfort. Even if he should decide to go to the hell called Unrelenting Torment in order to help sentient beings, he could stay there without having to experience any pain, as if he were entering a Buddha's paradise. This is explained by the principle that one cannot meet with a karma that one did not perform.[61]

There are three types of effort: (1) the effort of donning armor, (2) the effort of collecting virtue, and (3) the effort of benefiting sentient beings.

The effort of donning armor

The effort of donning armor is described in a verse from the *Guru Worship* that states in part: "[Even though I might have to dwell for oceans of kalpas]/ In Unrelenting Torment's fires for each and every sentient being."[62] Thus, we should cultivate the willingness to stay in the hells for a hundred thousand kalpas for each and every sentient being [344b]. In the context of the tantric path, our attitude should be that although we are ready to endure such an extremely difficult task, sentient beings would then have to experience suffering for too long a period of time. Therefore, we must try to free beings from their suffering as soon as possible, just as a mother would want to do for a beloved child that was being swept away by a river.

Some of you may think that the attitude in the effort of donning armor contradicts what was taught during the practices for persons of moderate capacity. That is, here we should be willing to stay in the hell of Unrelenting Torment in order to help all sentient beings, but earlier we generated a desire to free ourselves from samsara.

In fact, these two practices are not contradictory. A Bodhisattva also fears having to be reborn in the lower states through the power of karma and the mental afflictions; if that were to happen, he could not even achieve his own aims, let alone those of others. But after a Bodhisattva has trained extensively in enlightenment mind, he gains a sense of self-assurance that does not fear being reborn in the lower states, and he does so happily

[60]Ibid., ch. 7, v. 27.

[61]See Part Two, Day Thirteen, pp. 238–239.

[62]The complete verse states: "Bless me to keep courage through compassion and to complete/ The perfection of effort that would keep striving for enlightenment,/ Even though I might have to dwell for oceans of kalpas/ In Unrelenting Torment's fires for each and every sentient being."

through the power of his compassion and his prayers. Because of this, he doesn't experience the slightest physical pain or mental suffering.

(Kyabje Rinpoche concluded with this remark: The time for practicing the effort of donning armor is when we feel it is too difficult for us to act on behalf of others or when we view our own dharma practice as too weak.)

The effort of collecting virtue

The effort of collecting virtue is the exertion that we put forth to accumulate merit, purify ourselves of bad karma and mental obscurations, make offerings, practice the six perfections, and so on.

The effort of benefiting sentient beings

The effort of benefiting sentient beings is the exertion that we put forth to do such practices as the four principles for attracting a following. This practice is also similar to the ethics of benefiting sentient beings.

(Kyabje Rinpoche then made the following point: Some of you may think the latter two types of effort, ethics, and patience are indistinguishable from one another.[63] While all three practices in each of the two focus on the same objects, they can be differentiated on the basis of the willingness to exert oneself [345a], the desire to pursue one's spiritual practice, and the desire to abandon obstacles to one's practice.[64]

Thus, even when we practice the generation stage of Anuttarayoga Tantra for only one meditation period, we are engaging in all six of the perfections as long as our practice is imbued with enlightenment mind.

[63]That is, the ethics of collecting virtue, the patience of collecting virtue, and the effort of collecting virtue are indistinguishable from one another. Likewise, the ethics of benefiting sentient beings, the patience of benefiting sentient beings, and the effort of benefiting sentient beings are indistinguishable from one another.

[64]Thus, the ethics, patience, and effort of collecting virtue are all practiced with regard to the same kinds of activities. Likewise, the ethics, patience, and effort of benefiting sentient beings are all practiced in relation to the same eleven categories that were mentioned in the description of the ethics of benefiting sentient beings (see p. 216). Nonetheless, the willingness to exert oneself while doing virtuous activities is the effort of collecting virtue; the willingness to endure any hardships while doing virtuous activities is the patience of collecting virtue; and the desire to abandon the obstacles that prevent one from doing virtuous activities represents the ethics of collecting virtue. Similarly, the willingness to exert oneself in helping others with their work is the first of the eleven categories in the effort of benefiting sentient beings. The desire to endure whatever difficulty occurs when helping others in their work is the first of the eleven categories in the patience of benefiting sentient beings. And the desire to abandon the obstacles that prevent one from helping others with their work is the first of the eleven categories in the ethics of benefiting sentient beings.

Following this, Kyabje Rinpoche ended the discourse with a brief description of the final two perfections—that is, the perfection of one-pointed concentration and of wisdom. He also said that he would give a more detailed explanation of them in the coming days.)

DAY TWENTY-ONE:
HOW TO DEVELOP QUIESCENCE

(Kyabje Rinpoche began the discourse by quoting the following lines taught by the future Buddha, Lord Maitreya:

> Proper attention, on the basis of learning, develops here first.
> Through proper attention comes the wisdom that has reality
> as its object.[1]

After a brief discussion of the preliminary exercises, he listed the topics of the outline that had already been taught. Then, as part of the general discussion on how to train oneself in the Bodhisattva activities, he gave a short review of the first four perfections of generosity and so on.)

b) A specific discussion of how to train oneself in the last two perfections

This topic of the outline is comprised of two parts: (1) how to train oneself in quiescence, which is the essence of one-pointed meditation, and (2) how to train oneself in insight, which is the essence of wisdom.

i) How to train oneself in quiescence, which is the essence of one-pointed meditation

This part is further made up of six sections: (1) cultivating the requisites for achieving quiescence; (2) the actual method of achieving quiescence; (3) how to attain the nine levels of mental stability on the basis of the instruction; (4) how the nine levels are attained by means of the six powers; (5) the four kinds of attention that are applied in cultivating quiescence; and (6) how the actual state of quiescence arises on the basis of this practice [345b].

The reason I did not explain the trainings of one-pointed concentration and wisdom during the instructions for persons of moderate capacity is that I intended to explain them here as part of the instructions on the final two perfections.[2]

[1] *Ornament of the Mahayana Sutras* (S: *Mahāyānasūtrālaṃkāraḥ*), ch. 1, v. 16.

[2] See Day Fifteen, p. 86.

The practice of quiescence is one that is held in common with non-Buddhist traditions. For non-Buddhists, it is considered the lowest type of practice among the various states of meditative composure associated with the form and formless realms. We Buddhists, however, hold that spiritual practices motivated by renunciation serve as a cause for attaining liberation and those that are motivated by the act of taking refuge are genuine dharma.[3] We also maintain that, without quiescence, practitioners would not be able to generate any of the great realizations that are gained by meditation—such as the realization of emptiness that is taught in the Sutrayana tradition or the realizations of the generation and completion stages that are taught in the Tantrayana tradition. In short, no matter what Sutrayana or Tantrayana qualities of one-pointed concentration we may wish to develop, we could not achieve them without quiescence. It is as indispensable as a pitcher is to someone who wants to pour water. Therefore, it is important from the very outset that we seek to achieve a firm state of quiescence.

Even just to accomplish the goal of cutting samsara's roots and achieving our own liberation, it is necessary to develop the insight that realizes emptiness. But to develop such insight, we must first gain a firm state of quiescence. This is because a firm and stable mind is needed to clearly perceive the nature of ultimate reality. For instance, to remove the darkness that prevents us from viewing a wall painting at night, we need a lamp with a flame that is both bright and steady.

Moreover, if we achieve quiescence, it will become very easy to greatly improve spiritual realizations of such topics as the leisure and fortune of a human rebirth, the difficulty of attaining leisure and fortune, and impermanence in the form of death. The *Lamp of the Path to Enlightenment* states that we should generate quiescence in order to achieve the supernormal wisdoms,[4] but this is merely one of the purposes. The main reason we must achieve quiescence and the reason we must pursue it first is described by Shantideva in the following verse [346a]:

[3]That is, for Buddhists, taking refuge and renunciation, not quiescence, are the most basic practices. Furthermore, far from being the lowest form of meditation, quiescence is indispensable to gaining all the higher realizations of both the Sutrayana and Tantrayana paths.

[4]S: *abhijñā*, T: *mngon par shes pa*. An eight-verse section of the text (S: *Bodhipathapradīpaḥ*, vv. 34–41) addresses the topics of supernormal wisdom and quiescence. Verse 34, in particular, states: "All the Buddhas acknowledged that/ Developing supernormal wisdom is a necessary cause/ For completing the accumulations/ Whose nature is wisdom and merit." Similarly, verse 38 states in part: "Without having gained quiescence/ One cannot develop supernormal wisdom . . ." There are six types of supernormal wisdom: (1) miraculous powers, (2) the divine ear, (3) knowledge of others' thoughts, (4) recollection of former births, (5) knowledge of death and rebirth, and (6) knowledge that the mental afflictions have been terminated. See Part Two, Appendix E, pp. 304–305 for a description of them.

Realizing that insight well yoked to quiescence
Brings destruction of the mental afflictions,
Quiescence should be pursued first
With a joyous detachment from the world.[5]

Moreover, it isn't true that we should only pursue quiescence after generating enlightenment mind. It can be pursued at any stage of our practice. If we succeed in achieving quiescence, we will make extremely great progress in whatever meditation practice of the three vehicles we happen to be doing.

In trying to achieve quiescence we must first cultivate the requisites,[6] because without them our efforts will not be successful. As the *Lamp of the Path to Enlightenment* declares:

One who lacks the requisites for quiescence
May practice meditation strenuously,
But he will not gain a one-pointed mind
Even after a thousand years.[7]

(1) Cultivating the requisites for achieving quiescence

There are six requisites that must be cultivated in order to achieve quiescence: (1) staying in a favorable place; (2) having few wants; (3) being satisfied with what one has; (4) avoiding the disturbance caused by being involved in many activities; (5) having a pure moral practice; and (6) overcoming thoughts about sense objects and other things.

[5]*Engaging in Bodhisattva Activities* (S: *Bodhicaryāvatāraḥ*), ch. 8, v. 4.

[6]S: *śamathasambhāraḥ, T: zhi gnas kyi tsogs*. This formulation of the six requisites for achieving quiescence is based on a section from the second of Kamalashila's three *Stages of Meditation* (S: *Dvitīyabhāvanākramaḥ*, pp. 236–237; in Tib. edition: ff. 46a–47a). Je Tsongkapa further urges the dedicated practitioner to cultivate the thirteen requisites for enlightenment that are extensively described in Asanga's *Listeners' Levels* (S: *Śrāvakabhūmiḥ*, pp. 36–166; see also Part Two, Day Twelve, note 72). In the *Lamp of the Path to Enlightenment* (S: *Bodhipathapradīpaḥ*, v. 40), Lord Atisha recommends a work by one of his own teachers, Bodhibhadra, that is entitled *Chapter on the Requisites for One-pointed Concentration* (T: *Ting nge 'dzin gyi tsogs kyi le'u*).

[7]S: *Bodhipathapradīpaḥ*, v. 39.

Staying in a favorable place

The place where a practitioner pursues quiescence should have the five qualities that are mentioned in this verse from the *Ornament to the Mahayana Sutras*:

> The place where a wise person practices
> Should allow material needs to be easily gained,
> Be a safe area and a wholesome location,
> Have good companions present and be conducive
> to meditation.[8]

If a practitioner cannot acquire material needs easily and do so in a way that conforms to the principles of dharma, he will have to enter the town to find a means of support. Moreover, provisions acquired in a way that conforms to the principles of dharma means that they must be acquired properly [346b]. Although a practitioner may obtain food through wrong livelihood[9] or receive food that was procured by committing evil deeds, lamas describe such food as having been wrongly acquired. Therefore, we must find a place in which provisions are acquired properly—that is, easily and without having been tainted by heavy misdeeds.

The area where we stay should "be a safe area" and, if possible, a site that was blessed by having been visited in the past by holy beings. Such a place has the power to bestow a blessing upon those who meditate there, especially if they are novice practitioners. If you cannot find such a location, you should at least be sure to avoid any place that is inhabited by persons who have abandoned their spiritual commitments. Other areas to avoid include those where an act of dissension in the sangha community was committed,[10] or where dangerous animals, robbers, or wrathful spirits live. If we disregard this instruction out of boldness and choose to stay in an inauspicious area anyway, it is very likely that we will encounter some form of external harm.

(Kyabje Rinpoche then described how a certain lama had once stayed in an unfavorable place and was eventually harmed by a powerful spirit.

[8]S: *Mahāyānasutrālaṃkāraḥ*, ch. 13, v. 7.

[9]S: *mithyājīvaḥ*, T: *log 'tso*. See Part One, Day Four, pp. 127–129 for a description of five types of wrong livelihood.

[10]See Part One, Day Four, p. 155.

If we find that a spirit lives in the place where we are meditating, it is important that we avoid trying to drive it away and instead employ some gentle method of subduing it by calming its mind.)

A "wholesome location" means a place that does not bring on either cold or feverish illnesses, and one where the earth and water elements are beneficial to our health.

Our companions should be persons who hold views and engage in conduct similar to our own. There is a line that says we should stay "with a companion who is like a second shadow." This doesn't mean that we should avoid having more than two companions or that we should remain completely alone. Rather, it means that we should have a good rapport with those who accompany us when we are trying to meditate.

Because it can be harmful for a beginning practitioner to stay alone, such a person should have at least three companions. It would be even better for a novice to stay with a larger number, provided everyone can maintain the principles of good dharma practice. Whatever the number of companions, we should rely upon individuals who will feel the weight of a disapproving glance [347a] rather than those who behave in a carefree and unrestrained manner.

The scriptures state that "sound is a thorn to meditative concentration." Therefore, we should stay in a place that is free of human sounds during the daytime and the sounds of dogs or water and the like at night.[11] My own guru declared that the quality of being "conducive to meditation" also means for the practitioner to be well acquainted with all aspects of his practice and to have eliminated all doubt about what he is going to meditate on. This is accomplished through the activities of listening and contemplation. This instruction also means that the practitioner has already received whatever initiation, instructions, clarifying examples, and so on that are needed. The main point is that he should be knowledgeable in all aspects of his practice.

Nowadays, we can see that many practitioners mainly concern themselves with arranging for their material needs. Later, when they realize that they do not know how to do the actual meditation practice well, they become anxious and feel they must ask a lama to perform a divination.[12] We should avoid this type of behavior and make sure that we are well prepared and ready to do our dharma practice.

[11] This is the classic description of a place that is "conducive to meditation."

[12] That is, they hope the divination will inform them what dharma practice to do so that they will be successful.

Having few wants

"Having few wants" means not to crave large amounts of food, clothing, and the like, and not to desire that they be of the best quality.

Being satisfied with what one has

"Being satisfied with what one has" means to be content with whatever food and clothing we find, no matter how poor they may be.

If we fail to develop the qualities of having few wants and being satisfied with what we have, we will generate attachment for sense objects and become distracted by such concerns as trying to accumulate and take care of material wealth and possessions. Because of this, we will not be able to gain one-pointed concentration.

Having a pure moral practice

Generally speaking, morality is the foundation of all virtuous qualities. More specifically, the quelling of subtle inner distractions depends on our ability to overcome rough outer distractions. If we tend to have many rough conceptual thoughts, this prevents the mind from remaining in a naturally calm state [347b]. Therefore, by stopping us from committing verbal and physical misdeeds, our moral practice enables us to quell the outer distractions that come from having many conceptual thoughts.

Avoiding the disturbance caused by being involved in many activities

If we don't avoid the disturbance and confusion caused by having many activities, we will spend all our time pursuing meaningless interests or engaging in conversation and the like. A life of few pursuits and few activities frees us from these distractions. The reason we must cultivate such a life is to promote the development of meditative concentration. Furthermore, if we have few wants and are satisfied with what we have, this will naturally cause us to have few interests and not be involved in many activities.

If we wish to dedicate ourselves wholly to our spiritual practice, even astrology, medicine, performing divinations, and going to laypersons' homes to perform rituals are distractions and must be abandoned.

(Kyabje Rinpoche told us that such pursuits can be very damaging even for great spiritual beings, let alone beginning practitioners. For instance, the spirit Pehar harmed both Butön and Lama Dampa by offering them iron pens. They used up a thousand of these pens during their lifetimes, and allowed themselves to be distracted by studying the science of grammar and language. Because of this, neither of them was able to achieve the ultimate attainment.[13])

Because the Bodhisattva Tokme Sangpo[14] continually meditated on loving-kindness and compassion, this same spirit was unable to harm him. Je Rinpoche also composed eighteen volumes of writings, but he did not follow the custom of writing the title in three versions.[15] This was not because he didn't know Sanskrit, but because he felt that it might detract from our spiritual practice.

I, too, studied Sanskrit writing and composition meticulously for about a year, during which I wore away the skin on my fingers and also wore out the surface of two or three *samṭa* boards.[16] But this proved to be nothing more than a distraction and was of no benefit to my spiritual practice.

If we devote ourselves to efforts such as these, the only kind of karmic impressions that we will plant in our mind are those that further the same kind of activities in the future [348a]. We will not succeed in creating any of the karmic impressions that will help us to attain the elevated states or the ultimate good.[17] Therefore, we should not fail to devote ourselves to those practices that have genuine spiritual value, unlike the person who becomes attached to the skin of sugarcane and misses the real taste that lies within. Also, we should ask ourselves what we hope to accomplish by devoting ourselves to such insignificant pursuits as one of the minor sciences.[18]

(Kyabje Rinpoche then told us that persons who continue to pursue sense objects even after they have reached an advanced age are deserving of pity. He also recounted the story of the pauper Surata[19] who, after finding a wish-granting gem, gave it to King Prasenajit and said, "You are the greediest

[13]See Day Sixteen, p. 118 for an earlier reference to this same point.

[14]See Day Fifteen, note 55.

[15]T: *sum phab*. This refers to the custom of writing the title of a work three times, one below the other in successive lines. The first line is written in Sanskrit in an ornamental script called Lañtsa; beneath that is the same Sanskrit title transliterated into Tibetan characters; and finally the third line contains the actual title "translated" into Tibetan.

[16]Lined wooden slates that are used to practice writing, in this instance, Sanskrit.

[17]The expression "elevated states" (S: *abhyudāyaḥ*, T: *mgnon par mtho ba*) refers to birth as a god or as a human. All the practices taught in Part Two have as their near-term aim the attainment of this goal. "Ultimate good" (S: *niḥśreyasaḥ*, T: *nges par legs pa*) refers both to Hinayana nirvana and to the complete enlightenment of Buddhahood. The paths by which these goals can be attained form the subject matter of this volume. These terms represent the two types of spiritual goals that a Buddhist practitioner strives to attain.

[18]See Day Sixteen, note 34 for a list of the traditional major and minor sciences.

[19]See the *Sutra of Questions Posed by Surata* (T: ['*Phags pa*] *Des pas bzhus pa'i mdo*).

person in this land and, therefore, the poorest." Kyabje Rinpoche also told us the story of Geshe Ben's preparations for travel.[20])

Overcoming thoughts about sense objects and other things

We must overcome thoughts about sense objects and other things by contemplating the disadvantages of having attachment for sense objects and by contemplating impermanence in the form of death.

(Kyabje Rinpoche concluded this section by saying that if we develop all of these favorable causal factors and practice diligently, we can achieve quiescence within six months.)

(2) The actual method of achieving quiescence

Several lines from *Differentiating the Middle View and the Extreme View* declare that there are five faults and eight factors we must cultivate as their antidote:

> Abandonment of the five faults occurs
> Through cultivating the eight factors.
>
> Laziness, forgetting the instruction,
> Languor and excitation, lack of application,
> And likewise application—
> These are recognized as the five faults.[21]

The unsurpassed instructions for achieving one-pointed concentration are the ones that are taught in such great philosophical treatises as the Maitreya Teachings, the Collection of Works on the Levels of the Path, and the trilogy of Madhyamaka or Middle Way School texts entitled *Stages of Meditation* [348b].[22] It is very important that we seek out instructions such as

[20]This incident is described in the following passage from Yongzin Yeshe Gyeltsen's *Lives of the Lamrim Teachers* (T: *Lam rim bla ma brgyud pa'i rnam thar*, vol. 1, pp. 447–448): "Once, a gathering of monks from many monasteries in the Tö part of Penyul was being planned. As monks from all the monasteries collected the provisions that were going to be taken along, it is said that Geshe Ben simply put on his monks' robes, took his water pot in his hand and declared, 'Now then, what preparations do I need to make besides these?' Later, when Potowa heard about this, he became extremely pleased and remarked, 'His travel preparations were the right ones. Ben Gung-gyel's travel preparations were the right ones. If we want to train ourselves as monks, this is how we must train.'"

[21]S: *Madhyāntavibhāgakārikā*, ch. 4, vv. 3–4.

[22]The Maitreya Teachings (T: *Byams chos*) are five treatises that Maitreya imparted to Asanga when the latter traveled miraculously to Tushita paradise (see Part One, Day One, note 53 for a

these in order to develop our meditation practice. What we should *not* do is look upon these great works merely as theoretical explanations and revere instead some insignificant source that contradicts them, such as explanations reputed to be some lama's oral instruction, short manuals known as *beu bum*, transcription notes from an oral teaching, or notebooks of someone's explanations. Je Lama refers to persons who act this way in a series of verses at the end of the section on quiescence in his *Great Stages of the Path*.[23] He said that it would be impossible for them to find genuine instruction, because they search for it in places where it doesn't exist and fail to search for it in places where it does exist.

Therefore, those who overlook the great Buddhist philosophical works and rely indiscriminately on the words and instructions of any lama they happen to meet can easily go wrong and fall into serious error. Many practitioners who spent their entire lives meditating on a mountain have made the mistake of taking what is actually subtle languor[24] for genuine meditation. Others have cultivated a form of quiescence in which the mind is taken as one's meditation object, and then wrongly considered this to be an element of the path known as the Great Secret.[25] No matter how diligently we pursue practices such as these, we will only be wasting our lives in meaningless effort.

Many Tibetans who were renowned as learned scholars had a mistaken understanding of the correct view or how to practice meditation. Those of you with discerning minds can discover these errors by carefully examining their writings.

Je Tsongkapa, on the other hand, relied upon and held as authoritative the writings of India's greatest pandits and realized adepts in all three areas of philosophical view, meditation practice, and ethical conduct.[26] Moreover, he resolved all his questions by communicating directly with the holy Lord Mañjugosha himself. Because he left us so many flawless works that were

list). The Collection of Works on the Levels of the Path (T: *Sa sde*) is a five-part set of writings by Asanga on the levels of practice (S: *Yogācarabhūmī*, T: *rNal 'byor spyod pa'i sa*). For a list of the five works and a description of their contents, see Butön's *History of Buddhism* (T: *Bu ston chos 'byung*, pp. 673–674; in English translation Part I, pp. 54–56). The trilogy of works entitled *Stages of Meditation* (S: *Bhāvanākramaḥ*) is a series on meditation practice composed by the 8th-century Madhyamaka scholar Kamalashila.

[23] T: *Lam rim chen mo*, pp. 760–761 (ff. 364b–365a).

[24] Subtle languor (T: *bying ba phra mo*) is mentioned repeatedly in the latter half of this discourse; it is described most explicitly on pp. 246 and 249.

[25] That is, they wrongly considered what is a legitimate form of quiescence meditation to represent a highly esoteric practice of the Buddhist tantric path.

[26] T: *lta sgom spyod gsum*.

set down in this manner, this is the kind of instruction that we must rely upon [349a].

If we value more highly some instruction that is not found in these great works or is inconsistent with what they teach, we run the risk of gaining realizations that no one has ever heard of before. Therefore, for all the meditation practices ranging from the most basic forms of one-pointed concentration up to the generation and completion stages of Anuttarayoga Tantra, it is absolutely essential to rely on the instructions for pursuing quiescence that are taught in authoritative treatises and explain how to abandon the five faults and cultivate the eight corrective factors.

The first fault: laziness

Four factors make up the antidote to laziness: the faith that arises from recognizing the benefits of one-pointed concentration; the aspiration[27] that strongly desires to achieve one-pointed concentration; the effort[28] that strives after one-pointed concentration; and the agility[29] that arises from that exertion.

The object that we are seeking to cultivate is one-pointed concentration. The fault that opposes our pursuit of that goal is laziness—both the lack of desire to begin cultivating one-pointed concentration and, once we have started, the mental state that keeps us from pursuing it continually. The direct antidote that removes laziness is agility. While we may lack [physical and mental] agility at the outset, we must begin by cultivating the faith that arises from contemplating the beneficial qualities of one-pointed concentration. This exercise also includes reflecting on the disadvantages of distraction, as described in the following verse from *Engaging in Bodhisattva Activities*:

> The Omniscient One declared as useless
> All recitation and austerities that are done
> With a distracted or dull mind,
> Even if practiced for a long time.[30]

[27]S: *chandaḥ*, T: *'dun pa*. This mental state is defined as "the desire (S: *abhilāṣaḥ*, T: *'dod pa*) for entities that have been contemplated."

[28]See Day Twenty, pp. 224–230 for a discussion of effort.

[29]S: *praśrabdhiḥ*, T: *shin tu sbyangs pa*. Agility is defined as the state of physical and mental fitness (S: *karmaṇyatā*, T: *las su rung ba nyid*) that puts an end to the impediments of body and mind. "Impediment" (S: *dauṣṭhulyam*, T: *gnas ngan len*) means a condition that hinders you from using your body or mind to do virtuous activities as you would like to. These physical and mental impediments are also identified with the seeds of the mental afflictions.

[30]S: *Bodhicaryāvatāraḥ*, ch. 5, v. 16.

We should also reflect on the beneficial qualities of achieving quiescence. For instance, when a practitioner who has achieved quiescence does some virtuous act, his mind engages its object firmly. Because of this mental firmness, he will achieve spiritual attainments quickly. Quiescence also enables him to gain the lesser forms of supernormal wisdom and miraculous powers.[31] His sleep will constitute a form of one-pointed concentration [349b] and his mental afflictions will decrease. Most important, he will quickly gain realizations of all the paths, from how to serve one's spiritual teacher up to the generation and completion stages of Anuttarayoga Tantra. By contemplating these positive qualities, we will develop the faith that recognizes the benefits of one-pointed concentration. If we gain this faith, the remaining three factors of aspiration, effort, and agility will follow, since each is a result of the factor that precedes it and a cause of the one that follows.

The second fault: forgetting the instruction

"Forgetting the instruction" means for a practitioner's recollection to lose its hold on the meditation object. This is a great obstacle when you are trying to develop one-pointed concentration. As the *Essence of the Middle Way* declares in the following lines, we must attach the elephant-like mind to the post of our meditation object:

> Fasten the wandering elephant mind
> To the firm post of a meditation object
> With the rope of recollection; then subdue it
> Gradually using the hook of wisdom.[32]

In order to cultivate quiescence, we need to have an object that we can fasten our mind to. Moreover, quiescence can be achieved by focusing on almost any object. Certain Indian non-Buddhists, for instance, use a small stone or stick as a meditation object. Bön followers focus on the letter *a*. However, the meditation object that a practitioner uses to cultivate quiescence should be a mental object, not, for example, something that is gazed at with the eyes. Some followers of other traditions do try to meditate by gazing at an external object, but this is a lower form of practice than the two

[31] See Part Two, Appendix E, pp. 304–305.

[32] T: *dBu ma snying po*, ch. 3, v. 16. In Bibliography, see listing under the Indian scholar *Bhavya.*

examples just cited.[33] Because quiescence is pursued with mind consciousness and not with the eyes, the Great Fifth[34] and many other scholars rejected the latter method.

Long ago, [350a] there was a practitioner in India who, after failing with other meditation objects, achieved mental stability using the horn of a bull. This shows that we can succeed by using any object that is familiar to us as a meditation object. Nevertheless, as taught in the system of the great Je Tsongkapa, it is better to focus on a Buddha image when we are trying to achieve quiescence. This has the added benefit of improving other practices, such as when we visualize a merit field to accumulate merit or purify ourselves of obscurations, when we do the tantric practice of deity yoga, and when we cultivate the practice of recollecting the Buddha.[35]

One method is to visualize that a thumb-sized duplicate of your root guru, who is on the crown of your head in the form of Buddha Shakyamuni, separates from him and seats himself in front of you at the same height as the point between your eyebrows or at the same height as your navel. This figure becomes the meditation object that you should focus upon. Another method is to visualize that you yourself take on the form of Buddha Shakyamuni, and focus on that as your meditation object.

Some practitioners find it easier to focus upon a meditation object that does not have physical form. Such individuals can cultivate quiescence using their own mind as a meditation object. Je Tsongkapa refers to this method in his *Shorter Stages of the Path* and Panchen Lama Losang Chökyi Gyeltsen explains it further in his text on the Mahamudra teachings of the Ganden tradition. This practice is similar to a teaching that followers of another tradition call Gazing at the Mind's Face.[36]

[33]That is, the Indian non-Buddhists who focus on a stone or stick and the Bön followers who focus on the letter *a*.

[34]The Fifth Dalai Lama, Ngawang Losang Gyatso. See *Mañjughosha's Oral Instruction* (T: *'Jam dpal zhal lung*), f. 72b. The author cites the great Tibetan translator Yeshe De (T: *Ye shes sde*) as a source for this view. In doing so, he is echoing the point expressed by Je Tsongkapa in his *Great Stages of the Path* (T: *Lam rim chen mo*), p. 682 (f. 325b).

[35]Recollecting the Buddha is one of six recollections (S: *anusmṛtiḥ*, T: *rjes su dran pa*). The instructions on taking refuge refer to this practice and the special advantages that it brings. See Part Two, Day Twelve, p. 219.

[36]T: *sems ngo blta ba*. In his commentary to the Panchen Lama's text on the Mahamudra instructions, Tsechok Ling Yongzin Yeshe Gyeltsen (T: *Tse mchog gling Yongs 'dzin Ye shes rgyal mtsan*) identifies two passages from the *Shorter Stages of the Path* (T: *Lam rim chung ngu*, pp. 273 and 302–303) as the source for this practice (see his *Lamp Illuminating the Noble Path* [T: *Lam bzang gsal ba'i sgron me*], pp. 334–336). The Mahamudra instructions are an esoteric lineage of oral teachings on realizing the mind's ultimate nature. The Panchen Lama Losang Chökyi Gyeltsen was the first scholar to put the Gelukpa instructions on that teaching into writing. The practice that Kyabje Pabongka Rinpoche is referring to here is only one of several that the Panchen Lama mentions. A key point, however, is that in this particular practice

It is also acceptable to cultivate quiescence in conjunction with generation stage practices by using a deity's image as your meditation object, or to cultivate it in conjunction with completion stage practices by visualizing the symbol that represents the strong *a* vowel in Sanskrit.[37]

According to another formulation, there are four categories of meditation objects for cultivating quiescence: (1) all-encompassing elements that pertain to meditation objects; (2) meditation objects about which one should gain skill; (3) meditation objects that purify specific types of improper behavior [350b]; and (4) meditation objects that purify the mental afflictions.[38]

Of these, the meditation object we should choose for our own practice is the one we are able to focus on most effectively. Then we must continue using this object and not change it until our meditation practice is successful. While the sutras describe the four categories of meditation objects that were just mentioned, this doesn't mean that we should meditate on all of them. Rather, we must select whatever object is most suitable for us individually and then fix our mind on that one alone. As the glorious Aryashura said:

> Fasten the mind firmly
> To only one meditation object.
> Holding many different objects
> Will only disturb and confuse the mind.[39]

Thus, we should fix our mind on a single object when we are cultivating quiescence. If we change meditation objects, our efforts will fail. This point

the object that is being meditated upon is the mind's conventional-truth nature, *not* the mind's ultimate-truth nature. As the Panchen Lama himself states: "I, Chökyi Gyeltsen, declare that this teaching/ Is a wondrous and skillful method/ For a novice to achieve mental stability/ And a means of being introduced to the mind's conventional-truth nature." While other Tibetan Buddhist traditions teach a similar form of meditation, a major difference is that they mistakenly suggest that in this practice one is meditating on the mind's ultimate-truth nature.

[37]T: *a shad.* Literally, "the vertical stroke representing an *a* vowel." Sanskrit uses this stroke to indicate a strong *a* vowel. Tibetan vowels are normally represented only in one form, not both a strong and weak form as they are in Sanskrit. To indicate long *a*, *i*, and *u* vowels in Tibetan transliteration of Sanskrit words, Tibetans write a small *'a* letter (T: *'a chung* or *'a thung*) under the consonant. Therefore, the Sanskrit convention of using a vertical stroke to indicate the presence of a strong *a* vowel is sometimes referred to in Tibetan as *ah-thung shad* or "short *a* stroke."

[38]These four categories are presented in Asanga's *Listeners' Levels* (S: *Śrāvakabhumiḥ*), pp. 192–258. Je Tsongkapa provides an overview of them in his *Great Stages of the Path* (T: *Lam rim chen mo*), pp. 668–678 (ff. 318b–323b).

[39]*Compendium of Perfections* (S: *Pāramitāsamāsam*), ch. 5, v 12.

can be illustrated with the analogy of a fire stick. If you keep changing the stick that you are rubbing, you won't be able to start a fire.

When we are cultivating quiescence, we must also practice continuously for the entire six months, year, or however long we intend to practice. The only time we can let up is when we are sleeping, eating, or going to the bathroom. At all other times we must meditate continuously, just as a fire stick must be rubbed without stopping. We cannot change to a different meditation object because we are dissatisfied with the one we had been using. Nor can we stop practicing in the middle and rest for a few days. If we do, we will not be successful.

Therefore, the term "instruction" in this context[40] means to take an appropriate object—such as a painting or statue of the Buddha—and, after forming an image of it in your mind, meditate on it. If you are using a different kind of meditation object, it means to visualize that object in your mind as your lama explained to you. In any case, when you can form a rough mental image of the object so that at least its main features appear in your mind with some definition [351a], you have "acquired" the meditation object.

The second fault—called "forgetting the instruction"—is when the meditation object slips from recollection's grasp and is no longer present in the mind. The antidote for this fault is recollection, the fifth of the eight corrective factors. Just as we hold prayer beads in our hand, we must use strong recollection to keep hold of the meditation object continuously. One of the main reasons that some people can achieve quiescence more easily than others is that they have strong recollection.

The *Compendium of Higher Learning* describes recollection in these words:

> What is recollection? It is the mind's ability to avoid being drawn away from a familiar object, and it serves the function of preventing distraction.[41]

There are three elements in this definition. The first relates to the object: Recollection can only grasp an object that the mind is familiar with. Therefore, the meditation object must be something that the practitioner has previously seen, and then accustomed himself to and become familiar with in his mind.

The second characteristic relates to the way in which recollection holds its object: Recollection prevents the mind from being drawn away from the

[40] As referred to in the phrase "forgetting the instruction."

[41] S: *Abhidharmasamuccayaḥ*, p. 6.

meditation object and keeps the object present in the mind continuously. This quality can be illustrated by the way we maintain a strong recollection of food in our mind when we are hungry.

The third characteristic relates to the function of recollection, which is that it prevents the mind from being distracted by another object.

To summarize, the meditation object should be an object like the figure of Buddha Shakyamuni that you visualize seated in front of you. You must hold this object tightly and not allow yourself to become distracted. And you must focus on it in such a way that no other object appears in your mind.

The third fault: languor and excitation

The third fault is languor and excitation. They occur during the main practice when you are using recollection to keep hold of the meditation object. Not being able to distinguish the three mental states of languor, torpor, and excitation is a great mistake. It is like not being able to know who your real enemies are. Therefore, we must learn how to recognize these mental states.

Torpor[42] [351b] is a heaviness of mind and body in which we feel as though we are starting to fall asleep. It is a mental state that can be either indeterminate and obstructive,[43] or nonvirtuous. There is no virtuous form of torpor and it serves as a cause of languor.

Languor[44] has two forms: coarse and subtle. Coarse languor occurs when recollection is able to keep the mind fixed on the meditation object but the quality of clarity is lacking. Subtle languor occurs when both stability and clarity are being maintained, but the clarity lacks intensity because the mind's

[42]S: *styānam*, T: *rmugs pa*.

[43]An indeterminate entity is one that is neither virtuous nor nonvirtuous. It is called "indeterminate" because Buddha did not specify that it would produce either a favorable or an unfavorable result (see also Part One, Day Four, note 51 and Part Two, Day Thirteen, p. 264, with accompanying note 95). Indeterminate entities are further classified as indeterminate and obstructive (S: *nivṛtāvyākṛtam*, T: *sgrib lung ma bstan*), or indeterminate and unobstructive (S: *anivṛtāvyākṛtam*, T: *ma sgrib lung ma bstan*). An unobstructive indeterminate entity is one that does not constitute a form of obscuration (T: *sgrib par ma gyur pa*). Two classic types are: (1) the ordinary physical activities of walking, sitting, standing, and reclining (S: *airyapatham*, T: *spyod lam*), along with the mental states that accompany or produce them; and (2) the activity of working at a craft (S: *śilpam*, T: *bzo*), as well as the mental states that accompany or produce that activity. An obstructive indeterminate entity is one that does constitute a form of obscuration (T: *sgrib par gyur pa*). Examples are those root and secondary mental afflictions that are *not* nonvirtuous (such as one form of torpor), and every type of the obscurations to knowledge (S: *jñeyāvaraṇam*, T: *shes bya'i sgrib pa*; see also Part One, Day One, note 29 and Part Two, Appendix E, note 6). Root or secondary mental afflictions that produce suffering in the desire realm are nonvirtuous; those that produce suffering in the form or formless realms are indeterminate and obstructive.

[44]*layam*, T: *bying ba*.

hold on the object has become weak. These are the main obstacles to our meditation practice.

To "lack intensity" means that, while the mind remains fixed on the meditation object, it becomes too relaxed and is without energy. In this situation, allowing the quality of stability to become stronger can result in subtle languor.

To say that the mind's clarity "has intensity" means that it is able to remain fixed, firmly and distinctly, on the meditation object.

The presence or absence of these three qualities—stability, clarity, and intensity—can be illustrated by the way that an object like a cup or a string of prayer beads can be grasped with greater or lesser force. Another example is the way in which the faith we feel toward a lama can vary in intensity. Most of the time we feel a general sense of faith toward him, but one that is not especially strong. Sometimes, though, this feeling can become heightened and we experience a faith that is very intense and powerful. This faith focuses on its object more forcefully than the former kind of faith. The difference between these two feelings is similar to the difference between a mind that is meditating with intensity and one that is not.

(Kyabje Rinpoche noted here that we must rely on our own experience to gain a clear understanding of these explanations. They cannot be fully appreciated simply by hearing words.)

Such terms as "clarity" or "lucidity" do not refer to the meditation object; they are being used to indicate whether or not the mind is focusing on its object with clarity and lucidity [352a]. When clarity is absent, it is as if the mind is being obscured by some sort of covering.

Because subtle languor and one-pointed concentration both possess the qualities of stability and clarity, it can be difficult to distinguish between the two. A person who is actually experiencing a state of subtle languor can even suspend his breath and remain in a stable mental state for as long as an entire day. Certain Tibetan practitioners of the past mistook this state of mind for genuine one-pointed concentration and praised it with expressions like "supreme relaxation is supreme meditation."[45] In fact, though, these individuals did not understand some of the most crucial points about how to meditate correctly.

(Kyabje Rinpoche then described several negative consequences that result from mistaking subtle languor for genuine meditation, including these: Our practice will not even bring rebirth in the form and formless realms.

[45]T: *glod rab la sgom rab*. See *Great Stages of the Path* (T: *Lam rim chen mo*), p. 691 (f. 330a).

Our clouded recollection[46] will become stronger in this life. Because this kind of meditation only serves to dim our wisdom, it makes us look as if we are deliberately seeking to be reborn as an animal.)

Excitation[47] is described in the *Compendium of Higher Learning* as follows:

> What is excitation? It is an unsettled state of mind that follows attractive images and constitutes a form of desire. It serves to obstruct the attainment of quiescence.[48]

Thus, excitation is a state in which the mind is drawn toward an attractive object—that is, one that we desire. An example of forming an "attractive image"[49] in the mind is when you watch a performance of the Hlamo folk opera during the daytime, and then find yourself recalling vivid images of those scenes later that night. Thus, it is the image that arises in the mind when you recall an attractive object that you feel desire for.

There is an important difference between excitation and mental scattering.[50] For instance, the distraction that accompanies feelings of animosity toward an unattractive object such as an enemy is mental scattering [352b]. So, too, is the distraction that occurs when we are trying to cultivate quiescence and our mind becomes diverted toward virtuous objects, such as practicing generosity or morality. Neither of these situations is an example of excitation.

You might then wonder, "If excitation and mental scattering are both obstacles to quiescence, why is only excitation mentioned?" It is because mental scattering toward a virtuous object or an object of anger occurs less frequently and does not last as long. However, mental scattering toward objects of desire is something that we do all the time. Therefore, only excitation is mentioned because it is the principal form of mental scattering in terms of its frequency and the ease with which it occurs.

So when we are trying to cultivate quiescence, we must overcome all forms of mental scattering because they prevent the mind from remaining

[46]S: *muṣitasmṛtiḥ*, T: *brjed ngas pa*. This is one of the twenty secondary mental afflictions. It is described in the *Compendium of Higher Learning* (S: *Abhidharmasamuccayaḥ*, p. 9) as follows: "What is clouded recollection? It is recollection that is simultaneously associated with the mental afflictions. It serves the function of providing a basis for the occurrence of distraction."

[47]S: *auddhatyam*, T: *rgod pa*.

[48]S: *Abhidharmasamuccayaḥ*, p. 9.

[49]S: *śubbhanimittam*, T: *sdug pa'i mtsan ma*.

[50]Mental scattering (S: *visaraḥ*, T: *'phro ba*) is a general term that can refer to any form of distraction. Excitation only occurs when the mind is drawn away by objects that we desire.

fixed on a single object. This is true whether the mental scattering occurs toward an unattractive or an attractive object, or even a virtuous object, such as when we think about practicing generosity or making prostrations.

Coarse excitation is when we lose the meditation object completely and no longer hold it in the mind at all. This type of excitation occurs, for example, when we are visualizing a deity and our meditation object totally disappears from the mind.

There is also a subtle form of excitation, which can occur while the meditation object is still being held in the mind. It appears when a thought begins to stir from a different part of the mind. This movement takes place beneath the main field of awareness and seems ready to come forth as a thought about some attractive object. This kind of excitation is like water flowing beneath a layer of ice.

Although vigilance is not the direct antidote to these obstacles, it is an important element in the process of overcoming them. Like a lookout keeping watch for the opposing army, it enables us to recognize whenever languor or excitation have appeared. Therefore, vigilance is the sixth corrective factor that we must cultivate [353a].

A number of points must be understood about vigilance. For example, if we exercise this mental state continuously, it will hinder our ability to keep the mind fixed on the meditation object. On the other hand, if we fail to apply vigilance at all, we will not become aware of any defect in our one-pointed concentration when it does occur. The latter situation is like when a person is unaware that a thief has stolen his property and gotten away.

Therefore, we should begin by being prepared to apply vigilance. This is described in the line from the *Root Text on the Mahamudra Teachings* that says "Exercise the vigilance that perceives movement."[51] Then keep watch over the mind by periodically examining whether languor or excitation have arisen. As a verse from *Engaging in Bodhisattva Activities* declares:

> In short, the definition of vigilance
> Is nothing more than this:
> To examine repeatedly
> The state of your body and mind.[52]

[51] *The Great Pathway of the Conquerors: The Root Text on the Mahamudra Teachings of the Gelukpa Lineage* (T: *dGe ldan bka' brgyud rin po che'i phyag chen rtza ba rGyal ba'i gzhung lam*), p. 84. In Bibliography, see listing under (*Paṇ chen*) *Blo bzang chos kyi rgyal mtsan.*

[52] *Bodhicaryāvatāraḥ*, ch. 5, v. 108. See also Part Two, Day Nine, pp. 69–71, where the same verse is quoted in relation to the practice called "restraining the doors of the senses."

The way to keep the meditation object in the mind during actual practice can be described using the analogy of how we hold a cupful of tea. That is, recollection is like the hands we use to hold the cup. Just as we use our hands to grip the cup tightly, we should use recollection to keep hold of the meditation object firmly. Similarly, just as we use our eyes to check whether the cup has tilted to one side or the other, we should use vigilance to examine whether languor or excitation have arisen.

The final point we should understand in this section is that vigilance is a form of wisdom.

The fourth fault: failing to apply the antidote

The fourth fault is not to apply the proper antidote whenever languor or excitation occur. The way to correct this fault is first to recognize by means of vigilance that either languor or excitation has appeared. Then, without letting the obstacle go unchecked, you must immediately apply the appropriate antidote depending on whether it is of the subtle or coarse type. Therefore, the seventh of the eight corrective factors is to generate whatever mental action is necessary to develop the antidote for any of these faults [353b]. This is similar to the situation in which a lookout first perceives that an enemy has appeared and then effort is put forth to repel them.

You might well ask, "What sort of antidote do I need to apply?" Subtle languor comes about through a form of mental listlessness. In fact, *languor* and *lassitude* are both used as translations for the same term.[53] Thus, if the qualities of stability and clarity are both present in your meditation practice, but your grasp of the object has slackened to the point that the clarity lacks sharpness, then you have developed subtle languor. But this condition doesn't require that you stop practicing and end the meditation period. It is enough simply to grasp the meditation object more firmly. On the other hand, trying to grasp the object too forcefully can bring about excitation. So you must use just the right amount of effort.

The Blessed One explained this point using the analogy of a lute's strings, pointing out how the instrument produces beautiful sound only when the strings have just the right amount of tension, not when they are too tight or too loose. So when it feels that the way we are holding the object will produce excitation, we should relax our grasp slightly. And when it feels as though we are going to develop languor, we must tighten our grasp slightly. However, it is extremely difficult to describe the right balance between these two extremes. The only way to achieve it is by putting the instruction

[53]The Sanskrit term *layam* (which literally means "lying down" and so, by extension, "mental inactivity") is sometimes translated in Tibetan as *jingwa* (T: *bying ba*) or languor and sometimes as s*humba* (T: *zhum pa*) or lassitude.

into practice and exercising vigilance skillfully to keep watch over the mind.

Acharya Chandragomi gave the appearance[54] of being frustrated when he wrote:

> If I exert effort, excitation develops.
> But when I abandon it, lassitude arises.
> With a proper balance so difficult to attain,
> What shall I do with this unsettled mind?[55]

One of the most dangerous kinds of enemy a person can have is one that is mistaken for an ally, since his inimical quality is so difficult to identify. Languor poses a similar danger in that it can easily be mistaken for one-pointed concentration [354a]. Therefore, we must be particularly diligent about keeping a firm hold on the meditation object.

Even though you try to grasp the meditation object more firmly, sometimes you will not be able to maintain a mental clarity that also has intensity. When this happens, you can completely lose the ability to focus your mind on the meditation object or your mind may take on a certain dimness. Unless you eliminate these obstacles, they will lead to coarse languor. Therefore, as the *Essence of the Middle Way* declares:

> Abandon lassitude by reflecting
> On meditation objects that are uplifting.[56]

Coarse languor is a fault that occurs when the mind is too narrowly constricted. Therefore, you must try to draw the mind out somewhat and then start to meditate again. If that fails to remove your languor, give up your meditation object altogether and try any of several techniques that will invigorate or gladden your languid mind. You can review such topics as the great value and difficulty of obtaining a human form that possesses leisure and fortune, the extraordinary qualities of the Triple Gem, and the benefits of serving a spiritual teacher. You can also think about the benefits of enlightenment mind. Other methods include bringing to mind an image of

[54]*Tsul mdzad*. This expression is meant to suggest that the great Bodhisattva feigned such a demeanor as a skillful way of teaching some point. See Part One, Day One, note 8 for a similar use of this phrase.

[55]*Verses of Confession* (T: *bShags pa'i bstod pa*), ff. 238a–238b.

[56]T: *dBu ma snying po*, ch. 3, v. 17.

brightness[57] and contemplating such objects as generosity.[58] If you are able to eliminate languor and reinvigorate your mind through any of these practices, then go back to focusing your mind on the main meditation object.

Because most of us have not meditated at length on topics such as the leisure of a human birth and the difficulty of acquiring it, we are not likely to benefit immediately from reflecting on them here. But someone who has will experience a joy that is as refreshing as splashing cold water on the face.

If none of these practices removes your languor, then you should use this forceful method. First envision your mind as a ball of white light[59] in your heart. Then say aloud the syllable *Pet*! [354b] as you visualize that your mind leaves your body through the crown of your head and rises high up into the sky. Finally, imagine that your mind merges inseparably with space. Repeat this exercise as often as necessary.

If this still doesn't overcome your languor, you should stop your meditation period and engage in any of various techniques for eliminating the torpor, drowsiness, mental cloudiness, and so on, that are causing your languor. These include such things as sitting in a cool place, going to an elevated spot with a wide view, walking back and forth, and washing your face with water. When your mental dimness clears up, go back to meditating on your main meditation object as before.

Subtle excitation is a form of distraction in which the meditation object is not completely lost. This fault appears when you try to hold the object too tightly. So if it does appear, you should try to relax your grip on the meditation object slightly. If that doesn't help and you continue to be distracted, a coarser form of excitation will develop. Because coarse excitation occurs when the mind becomes elated, you should avoid the kind of joy that is too exuberant. Excessive joy can be harmful, as when it prevented King Shuddhodana[60] from achieving the stream enterer result.

When you experience excitation, it isn't necessary to suspend your meditation period. Instead, reflect on topics that will diminish the mind's animated state somewhat and evoke a sense of renunciation and disgust for

[57]S: *ālokanimittam*, T: *snang ba'i mtsan ma*. To explain this expression, Je Tsongkapa quotes the following line from Asanga's *Listeners's Levels* (S: *Śrāvakabhūmiḥ*): "Visualize the image of brightness of either a lamp, the light of a fire, or the sun."

[58]Generosity is one of the six recollections. The other five are Buddha, dharma, sangha, deities, and morality. Asanga's *Levels of Yoga Practice* (S: *Yogācārabhūmiḥ*) describes a "dharma light" (S: *dharmālokaḥ*, T: *chos kyi snang ba*) that produces brightness in the mind when a practitioner reflects on certain dharma topics or meditates on any of the six recollections.

[59]The *Quick Path* (T: *Myur lam*, f. 78b) describes it as the size of a small bird's egg.

[60]T: *rGyal po Zas gtzang ma*. This was Buddha Shakyamuni's father.

samsara, such as impermanence in the form of death, and the suffering of the lower states and of samsara in general. This is suggested in the following lines from *Essence of the Middle Way*:

> Stop excitation by bringing to mind
> Topics such as impermanence and the like.[61]

If this does not remove your excitation, you should perform the forceful method of stopping excitation. This is the same exercise as the one recommended for those who have trouble controlling their discursive thinking. That is, you should focus your mind on your breath.

The practice is done as follows. As you complete an exhalation, think to yourself, "The breath has gone out [355a]." Similarly, as you complete an inhalation, think, "Now it has come back in." Then also reflect, "This is one breath." Initially, you will not be able to keep count mentally of more than three or four breaths. If you lose your concentration, you must go back and start counting from the beginning. When you can count twenty-one breaths or so without becoming distracted, you have reached the level of the first stage of mental development.[62]

Long ago there was a great adept from Yerba named Puntsok Gyatso. One of his relatives was an attendant of Desi Sang-gye Gyatso.[63] The story is told that this adept was having trouble controlling his mind during meditation practice after he learned about the difficulties that the Desi and his staff were experiencing. Finally, though, he regained control through the technique of counting his breaths. If you cannot overcome your excitation through this breathing exercise, you should temporarily stop your meditation practice altogether.

In the beginning, you should resolve to meditate for only a short period of time. If you let your practice go on too long, after a while you may feel discouraged or even repulsed by the mere sight of your meditation cushion. Therefore, it is important that you go away from your meditation practice with a positive attitude. This is what is meant by the expression, "Stop meditating while you still want to practice." For example, if two persons part on good terms, they will feel happy the next time they see each other.

Another expression says: "A practice that has clarity should be stopped while it has clarity; one that lacks clarity should be stopped while it lacks

[61]T: *dBu ma snying po*, ch. 3, v. 17.

[62]This is a reference to the first of the nine levels of mental stability, called "placement." See below pp. 256–257. Breathing meditation is also described in Part One, Day Four, pp. 136–137.

[63]Desi Sang-gye Gyatso was chief minister to the Fifth Dalai Lama. See Day Fourteen, p. 18 and accompanying note 60.

clarity." In other words, we should stop practicing while we still feel that it would be good to continue a little longer. This will allow us to remain enthusiastic about our practice and to begin again in the same positive frame of mind as when we stopped the time before. This is the proper way to approach our meditation practice.

Sometimes when our meditation loses clarity [355b] we are unable to correct this condition even though we try repeatedly. But stubborn persistence may only bring exhaustion, and then we will have to begin our next meditation period with the memory of that unclear state of mind that we left off with earlier. This is like the story about the great adept Losang Namgyel when he was giving an oral recitation blessing for the *Miscellaneous Sayings of the Kadampas*.[64] As he reached the passage that says: "The present degenerate age is a time for subduing one's own mind, not a time for subduing the minds of others," he began to weep and could not go on, so the recitation was stopped for the day. But because he had to continue from the point where he had stopped, he could not begin again the next day or the day after that.

We all would like our meditation practice to have the quality of stability from the very outset. But at first we can't really keep our mind fixed on the meditation object at all; the most we can do is briefly make contact with it. Therefore, we should start with short meditation sessions, and follow the instruction to divide the day into as many as eighteen periods. During these periods, we should strive to practice as skillfully as possible without falling into either languor or excitation. This technique of dividing the day into many short meditation periods will allow us to naturally develop the quality of stability over time. And as our practice does gain a measure of stability, we can gradually extend the length of the meditation periods.

The fifth fault: applying an antidote unnecessarily

The fifth fault is to exert effort at a time when languor and excitation are not present. The antidote for this is to cultivate the equanimity in which all mental effort is suspended. This is the eighth and final corrective factor.

Languor and excitation do not disappear until we reach the eighth stage of mental development. But since languor and excitation are quelled when we reach that point, it becomes a hindrance to the mind's steadiness if we continue to examine whether they have arisen and to exert ourselves in attempting to generate an antidote. Therefore, we may relax the effort needed

[64]T: *bKa' gdams gsung thor bu.* Listed in Bibliography as *bKa' gdams kyi skyes bu dam pa rnams kyi gsung bgros thor bu.*

to cultivate vigilance [356a] and apply instead the compositional factor of equanimity.[65]

Many holy teachers have declared that relaxation is a necessary element of meditation. This should be understood to mean that when the practitioner reaches the end of the eighth level of mental stability, he no longer comes under the influence of languor and excitation. Therefore, at that point he should stop exerting the effort that is needed to cultivate vigilance. It does not mean that the practitioner should stop applying vigilance at any other level prior to this, or that he should relax his recollection or the intensity with which he grasps the meditation object.

Certain early Tibetan teachers coined the expression: "Supreme relaxation is supreme meditation." However, this aphorism doesn't identify the correct point at which this relaxation should be exercised. And since it is a mistake to relax your recollection before you reach the level that I just described, you should not try to follow this principle. Although such an approach may allow you to gain the quality of stability quickly, it will also cause you to come under the influence of subtle languor and thus take you further away from one-pointed concentration.

These instructions on how to cultivate one-pointed meditation hold true for all the stages of the path except the completion stage of Anuttarayoga Tantra. In all the stages before then, the only thing that changes is the meditation object that you focus on.

Actual method of practice

Now I shall explain how to actually practice one-pointed meditation. First, make sure that you have all the requisites for pursuing quiescence, including a place that possesses the five qualities. Sit on a comfortable seat and observe the seven Vairochana attributes.[66] Then visualize that a thumb-sized duplicate of your root guru, who is seated on the crown of your head and appearing in the form of Buddha Shakyamuni, separates from him and sits in the space in front of you at the same level as your navel.

[65]S: *samskāropekṣā*, T: *'du byed btang snyoms*. See Day Sixteen, note 95 for a description of two other kinds of equanimity. The *Compendium of Higher Learning* (S: *Abhidharma-samuccayaḥ*, p. 6) gives this description of the equanimity being referred to here: "What is equanimity? It is an evenness of mind, a composure of mind, and an effortless steadiness of mind that is achieved through cultivating absence of desire, hatred, and ignorance, along with effort. It keeps the mind from becoming agitated and serves the function of helping not to give the mental afflictions any opportunity to arise." The terms "evenness," "composure," and "effortless steadiness" describe the equanimity that occurs at the beginning, middle, and end of one's efforts to achieve quiescence.

[66]S: *saptavairocanadharmāḥ*, T: *rnam snang chos bdun*. See Part One, Day Four, pp. 134–136.

At first, you will not be able to visualize this meditation object with much clarity. Nor is it necessary that you be able to do so at this time. It is enough for you to generate the image of a complete figure, gold in color, that includes all the general features of a head, arms, legs, and the like. Focus your mind continually and undistractedly on this object, using recollection to grasp it firmly and making sure that it doesn't slip away [356b]. A practice that relies on this kind of fully absorbed recollection includes all the qualities that will enable you to overcome both languor and excitation. Therefore, it is an unsurpassed instruction that all great meditation masters hold dear.

More specifically, one overcomes languor by maintaining a firm grasp on the object. One overcomes excitation by avoiding distraction. The nature of this practice is that when you gain stability, the likelihood of developing languor increases. Therefore, in that situation you should watch out for languor, maintain clarity, and grasp the meditation object more strongly. Similarly, when you gain more clarity, the likelihood of developing excitation increases. Therefore, at that time be on the lookout for excitation and try to generate greater stability.

Don't pretend to practice meditation without really knowing what kind of one-pointed concentration you should be trying to develop. The one-pointed concentration you are trying to cultivate must have two qualities: stability and clarity. Stability is basic, but clarity is the more critical of the two. Moreover, they are developed by holding the meditation object very firmly.

As I explained extensively earlier, you must use recollection to keep hold of the meditation object and not allow it to escape. Then use vigilance to watch out for coarse or subtle languor or excitation, so that you will immediately become aware whenever any of them is about to occur. Then apply the appropriate antidote to stop them. When you have overcome languor or excitation, keep your mind fixed one-pointedly on the meditation object without making any further effort to apply an antidote. In addition, make sure not only that your meditation has great clarity but that the clarity also possesses intensity.

In the instructions of the Mahamudra or Great Seal tradition, the meditation object and the mind that grasps the meditation object are one and the same. The aim of this practice is to overcome discursive thoughts[67] and focus one-pointedly on the mind's qualities of luminosity and consciousness. Moreover, this tradition explains two methods of overcoming discursive thoughts. One method resembles the way a herdsman keeps watch over his goats and sheep that have wandered up the side of a mountain and those

[67]S: *vikalpanā*, T: *rnam par rtog pa*.

that have not [357a]. That is, when a discursive thought arises in the mind, the practitioner overcomes it simply by examining its essence and then letting it disappear. In the other method, the practitioner overcomes discursive thoughts by applying specific antidotes.

(Kyabje Rinpoche concluded this section by saying that the details of this practice are given in teachings on the Mahamudra instructions as preserved in the Gelukpa tradition. Therefore, those who want to cultivate quiescence by using the mind as their meditation object should learn this method by attending such a teaching.)

(3) How to attain the nine levels of mental stability on the basis of this instruction

If you want to practice meditation, you must develop the quality of mental stability.[68] To accomplish this, you must learn about the nine levels of mental stability. They are called: (1) placement, (2) continued placement, (3) renewed placement, (4) close placement, (5) subduing, (6) pacification, (7) heightened pacification, (8) one-pointedness, and (9) equipoise.

The first level: placement

The first level of mental stability is achieved through hearing instruction from your guru about the meditation object. During this stage, however, you can only place your mind on the object very briefly; it will not remain there for any length of time. Therefore, you are unable to keep your mind fixed on the object.

Another characteristic is that you become aware of how easily your mind falls under the influence of distraction and excitation. You gain this awareness through applying the mental states called deliberation and reflection.[69] Because of this, you experience the feeling that you are generating more discursive thoughts than usual. However, you are not actually generating more discursive thoughts; you are just becoming more aware of them when they do occur.

[68]S: *cittasthitiḥ*, T: *sems gnas*. This term literally means "a state in which the mind remains stationary or fixed."

[69]Deliberation (S: *vitarkaḥ*, T: *rtog pa*) is a mental state in which the mind engages its object in a coarse form of examination. This takes the form of an inquiry that asks, "What is this object?" Reflection (S: *vicāraḥ*, T: *dpyod pa*) is a mental state in which the mind engages its object in a subtle form of examination. This takes the form of an analysis that determines, "The nature of this object is such and such." These two mental states are also mentioned in the instruction on Mind Training. See Day Nineteen, p. 204, along with accompanying notes 47 and 48.

The second level: continued placement

After practicing this way for a while, when you place your mind on the meditation object you will be able to keep it there for a brief period of time. For instance, if you meditate for the length of time it takes to recite one round of the *Mani* mantra on your prayer beads [357b], your mind will remain undistracted during that interval.

While you continue to have discursive thoughts at this stage, they do let up periodically. Because of this, it will feel as though your discursive thoughts occasionally "take a rest." This level is gained through the power of reflection.

(Kyabje Rinpoche then noted that on the first and second levels of mental stability, languor and excitation occur frequently, while the quality of stability is hardly present. Therefore, they are levels in which the first of the four forms of attention is applied—the one called forceful conveying.[70] They are also a stage at which periods of distraction last longer than periods of remaining on the object.)

The third level: renewed placement

The third level of mental stability is like putting a patch on a piece of cloth. As you begin to keep your mind fixed on the meditation object for longer intervals, you will quickly realize it when your mind becomes distracted and strays from the object; you will also become more adept at returning it to the object again. This explains why it is called renewed placement.

(Kyabje Rinpoche noted that the length of time that you remain distracted on this level is shorter than on the previous two levels. He also explained it as a stage in which you are able to develop powerful recollection.)

The fourth level: close placement

On this level, you are able to focus your mind on the meditation object by generating strong recollection. The level of concentration achieved on this level is superior to that of the previous three levels in that the meditation object no longer escapes from your mind. Nevertheless, because strong forms of languor and excitation still do occur, it is necessary to cultivate the antidotes to these two obstacles.

[70]S: *balavāhano manaskāraḥ*, T: *sgrims te 'jug pa'i yid la byed pa*. That is, considerable effort must be used to "convey" the mind to the meditation object.

(Kyabje Rinpoche noted that the third and fourth levels of mental stability are gained through the power of recollection. He also said that from this point on, recollection is full grown, like a full-grown adult—that is, its strength has been fully developed.)

The fifth level: subduing

During the fourth level, if you try too hard to draw your mind inward so that you can keep it focused, there is a greater likelihood that you will develop subtle languor when you reach the fifth level. Therefore, on this level it is necessary to generate powerful vigilance to keep watch over the mind and also [358a] to enliven it by reflecting on the benefits of one-pointed concentration. The difference between this level and the previous two is that here coarse languor and excitation no longer occur, while on the earlier two levels they did.

The sixth level: pacification

If the effort to enliven the mind on the fifth level was too forceful, this increases the likelihood of developing subtle excitation on the sixth level. When subtle excitation arises, you must overcome it by generating a powerful form of vigilance that recognizes subtle excitation when it occurs, and by regarding it as an obstacle. The difference between this level and the previous one is that here there is little danger of developing subtle languor.

(Kyabje Rinpoche noted that the fifth and sixth levels are both gained through the power of vigilance and that, from the sixth level on, the power of vigilance has become fully developed.)

The seventh level: enhanced pacification

Because one fully develops recollection and vigilance during the seventh level, languor and excitation do not occur easily. At this point, then, you must strive as hard as you can to abandon both subtle languor and subtle excitation by recognizing them as obstacles and by generating a powerful form of effort. The difference between this level and the previous two is that here you do not have to be as concerned about developing subtle languor and subtle excitation as you did on the previous two levels. Although there is less risk of developing these two obstacles on this level, you still have to generate effort to eliminate them.

(Kyabje Rinpoche noted that on the fifth and sixth levels you remain concerned that languor and excitation are strong enough to disrupt your practice. But on this seventh level, the effort you generate has the power to remove any languor and excitation that might arise. Therefore, languor and excitation no longer represent great obstacles.)

On all five levels of mental stability from the third level up to the seventh, you do begin to develop more and more one-pointed concentration. Nevertheless, because it is interrupted by languor and excitation, the type of mental attention that is exercised throughout this period is called interrupted conveying.[71]

The eighth level: one-pointedness

On the eighth level of mental stability [358b], you only need to generate a slight degree of effort to maintain the antidote of recollection. This is enough for you to continue practicing throughout the entire meditation period without developing any subtle languor or subtle excitation.

An analogy for how languor and excitation are gradually overcome during these levels is the way that an enemy gradually loses his strength as he is being defeated. For instance, in the beginning the enemy has considerable power. Later, he begins to lose some of his strength. Finally, he loses all his strength. From the eighth level on, you do not need to cultivate vigilance.

On this eighth level, only a small amount of effort is needed to keep from developing any languor or excitation throughout the entire meditation period. Therefore, the form of mental attention that is exercised during this period is called uninterrupted conveying.[72]

Both the seventh and the eighth levels of mental stability are gained through the power of effort.

The ninth level: equipoise

On the ninth level of mental stability, the mind can be fixed without the need to exert any effort. This ability to freely and easily engage the object is gained through the repeated practice that is carried out on the eighth level. Therefore, on this level you can enter a state of perfect one-pointed mental concentration without having to make the slightest exertion, just as a person who has memorized his prayers well can recite them effortlessly.

The ninth level is a state of mental one-pointedness that still forms part of the desire realm; and, though not actual quiescence, it does bear some resemblance to quiescence. You gain this level through the power of continued practice.

[71] S: *sacchidravāhano manaskāraḥ*, T: *chad cing 'jug pa'i yid la byed pa.*

[72] S: *niśchidravāhano manaskāraḥ*, T: *chad pa med par 'jug pa'i yid la byed pa.*

(Kyabje Rinpoche ended the day's discourse with the following summary about the nine levels of mental stability. On the first level you develop a feeling that stems from greater awareness of your discursive thoughts. On the second level, you gain the feeling that your discursive thoughts sometimes take a rest. On the third level, you gain the feeling that your discursive thoughts are becoming tired. Thus, the difference between the first and second levels of mental stability is the length of time that your mind remains fixed on the meditation object. And the difference between the second and third levels [359a] is the length of time that you remain distracted.

The difference between the fourth and fifth levels is that coarse languor occurs on the fourth but not on the fifth.

The difference between the fifth and sixth levels is that you must watch carefully for subtle languor on the fifth but not on the sixth. In addition, subtle excitation arises less frequently on the sixth level than it does on the fifth.

The difference between the sixth and seventh levels is that you must be especially attentive about developing subtle languor and excitation on the sixth, while you need not be on the seventh.

The difference between the seventh and eighth levels is that languor and excitation do occur on the seventh but not on the eighth.

The difference between the eighth and ninth levels is that you must exert some effort on the eighth while no effort is required on the ninth.

Moreover, when you reach the seventh level, you simply take whatever measures are necessary to stop languor or excitation as they occur. You no longer feel any great need to be concerned about falling under the influence of these obstacles. For instance, if after doing battle with an enemy you succeed in weakening him, you no longer feel the need to be especially cautious. You feel it is enough merely to block him if he tries to come toward you.)

DAY TWENTY-TWO: HOW TO DEVELOP INSIGHT

(Kyabje Rinpoche began the discourse by quoting the following verse by the glorious Chandrakirti:

> With his great white wings of the conventional and ultimate
> outstretched,
> The goose king[1] glides at the forefront of a multitude of geese
> Toward that supreme, far shore of the Victorious Ones' ocean
> of good qualities,
> Carried along by the swift wind currents of virtuous activities.[2]

Then he explained how, in order to travel to the land of the Conquerors, we must listen to explanations of the two types of enlightenment mind—that is, conventional enlightenment mind and ultimate enlightenment mind—and then also gather the two accumulations, since they are the means by which we reach that goal. In connection with these remarks [359b], he also briefly explained the preliminary exercise of correcting our motivation.

After listing the topics of the outline that he had already covered, Kyabje Rinpoche then reviewed the five or six requisites for cultivating quiescence and the actual method of achieving quiescence. For the latter subject, he went over how to cultivate the eight corrective factors that overcome the five faults, as well as how to attain the nine levels of mental stability on the basis of that instruction.

(4) How to attain the nine levels by means of the six powers

The first level of mental stability is gained through the power of listening. The second level is gained through the power of reflection. The third and fourth levels are gained through the power of recollection, the fifth and six through the power of vigilance, and the seventh and eighth through the power of effort. The ninth level is gained through the power of continued

[1] S: *haṁsarājā*, T: *ngang pa'i rgyal po*. In Indian culture, the white goose is a symbol of purity and spirituality; the term is also used to refer to a great religious ascetic. Here "goose king" means a Bodhisattva who has attained the sixth level or *bhumi*. The "multitude of geese" represents the other Bodhisattvas that accompany him on the path to enlightenment.

[2] *Introduction to the Middle Way* (T: *dBu ma la 'jug pa*), ch. 6, v. 226.

practice. I explained the details of these various powers earlier, when I taught the nine levels of mental stability.

(5) The four kinds of attention that are applied in cultivating quiescence

On the first and second levels of mental stability, the practitioner applies the type of attention called forceful conveying. On the next five levels, the method of attention is called interrupted conveying. On the eighth level, some effort is still needed to apply the method of attention called uninterrupted conveying. On the ninth level, one applies the method of attention called effortless conveying.

The different ways in which the practitioner applies these types of attention can be understood as follows. Because languor and excitation are strong on the first and second levels of mental stability, one-pointed concentration is only gained for very short periods of time. Concentration does not even last long enough to say that it is interrupted by languor and excitation. In any case, these two levels are a time during which one must strenuously apply recollection and vigilance. This is why the type of attention that occurs here is called forceful conveying.

Although the practitioner must strenuously apply recollection and vigilance during the next five levels, the length of time that he can maintain one-pointed concentration gradually increases [360a]. However, languor and excitation are continually interrupting his efforts to keep the mind fixed on its object. Therefore, the type of attention that occurs during these levels is called interrupted conveying.

When the eighth level is reached, it is possible to prevent any obstruction by languor and excitation throughout an entire meditation period simply by exerting a small degree of effort at the beginning. Therefore, the attention that is applied during this stage is referred to as uninterrupted conveying.

On the ninth level, the practitioner can fix his mind effortlessly on the meditation object. Therefore, the type of attention applied during this period is called effortless conveying.

(6) How the actual state of quiescence arises on the basis of this practice

After the ninth level of mental stability has been achieved, it is possible to maintain, effortlessly and for long periods of time, a type of one-pointed concentration that is free of any subtle languor or subtle excitation. However, while this state has certain qualities that are similar to those of quiescence, it is not actual quiescence. In order to achieve genuine quiescence, you must continue to practice one-pointed concentration until you gain the extraordinary ease and joy of physical and mental agility.[3]

Of these two types of agility, mental agility arises first. And of the two types of ease, the ease of physical agility arises first. When the wind element associated with body impediments[4] ceases to be active, a pronounced feeling of ease is experienced. In addition, a special kind of heaviness is felt inside the top of the head. This latter sensation is similar to what it feels like when you press your warm hands on your newly shaven head. Right after this, you develop a unique mental agility because you are no longer subject to the impediments that previously kept your mind in an afflicted state and prevented you from directing your mind at will to a virtuous object.

This mental agility causes your body to become filled with a type of wind element that brings great suppleness and eliminates all physical impediments. [360b] It also produces a physical agility that makes your body feel as light as cotton and allows you to apply yourself physically to any virtuous activity without hesitation. This physical agility is followed by an intense and extremely pleasurable bodily sensation that is known as the ease of physical agility.

As you continue to practice one-pointed concentration, your mental agility will cause you to develop a feeling of extreme joy and rapture; this is the ease of mental agility. When this happens, you lose all awareness of any other objects including your own body. It is as if they have all dissolved into the meditation object. The joy is so overwhelming that you feel as though you won't be able to keep your mind fixed on the meditation object.

After a short while, the extreme joy brought on by this mental agility subsides and your mental agility acquires an especially strong steadiness that enhances one-pointed concentration and keeps the mind fixed unshakably on its meditation object. The arising of this agility marks the attainment of quiescence—a state of one-pointed concentration that precedes the first *dhyana* or absorption level of the form realm and is known as the all-powerful.[5] It is called "all-powerful" because it is a path that is essential to the attainment of many worldly and supramundane realizations.

[3]See Day Twenty-one, note 29.

[4]S: *dauṣṭhulyam*, T: *gnas ngan len*. "Impediment" means a lack of physical and mental facility that is caused by the seeds of the mental afflictions. There are two types: impediments related to the body and impediments related to the mind. They are the opposite of corresponding forms of agility (S: *praśrabdhiḥ*, T: *shin tu sbyangs pa*).

[5]S: *anāgyamyam*, T: *mi lcogs pa med pa*. Kedrup Je writes in his *Lamp that Elucidates Difficult Points* (T: *rTogs dka'i snang ba*, f. 76a): "It is called the 'all-powerful' because it can remove all the desire associated with the three realms."

Although we can enter all eight absorptions of the form and formless realms after gaining each of their corresponding preliminary levels, we Buddhists don't seek to generate them, because there is little purpose in doing so. Non-Buddhists can suppress all active forms of the mental afflictions up to and including those of the third absorption level of the formless realm, which is known as the Sphere of Nothingness.[6] When they achieve the level called the Peak of Existence, they consider themselves to have attained liberation. However, as the following verse from *In Praise of the Praiseworthy* declares, this state does not deliver one from samsara:

> Even though they reach the Peak of Existence,
> Those who are blinded by ignorance
> And have turned away from your teaching [361a]
> Only create new births that give rise to misery.[7]

A sutra verse also declares:

> Whoever cultivates one-pointedness in this world
> But does not also destroy the belief in a self
> Will be disturbed by the mental afflictions once again,
> As Udraka was with his one-pointed concentration.[8]

(Kyabje Rinpoche explained that Udraka had entered the absorption called the Peak of Existence and remained in that state for many years. After arising from his meditation, he became angry when he noticed that a mouse had gnawed some of his long hair. It is said that this caused him to lose his powers of concentration and he eventually fell into the lower states.)

The attainment of quiescence brings many good qualities. For example, our mental clarity is so strong that we feel as though we could count the number of atoms in a wall or any other physical object. Whenever we perceive any of the ten mental images—that is, the five associated with the five sense objects, the three associated with the three poisons, and the two of a male or a female—we recall the disadvantages of these objects and feel an aversion for them. Similarly, we develop the mental afflictions only rarely

[6]S: *ākiṃcanyāyatanam*. T: *ci yang med pa'i skye mched*.

[7]S: *Varṇārhavarṇastotram*, ch. 9, v. 22. In Bibliography, see listing under *Mātṛceṭa*.

[8]*King of Concentrations Sutra* (S: *Samādhirājasūtram*), ch. 9, v. 36. Udraka (also written as Rudraka; T: *Lhag spyod*) was one of the teachers with whom the Bodhisattva Gautama studied after he left his palace in Kapilavastu. This teacher had achieved the fourth absorption of the formless realm. After becoming his disciple, Gautama also achieved this concentration but was not satisfied; so he left Udraka to pursue the knowledge that would bring true liberation.

and, when we do, they are weak. Because it is a kind of deep mental stability, even our sleep appears to take on the quality of one-pointed concentration.

Instead of studying the great Buddhist treatises, many foolish and arrogant practitioners nowadays try to use brief and simplistic explanations to gain an understanding of the philosophical views contained in such teachings as the Great Seal and the Great Completion. However, rarely do any of them even achieve the genuine quiescence that is taught in the great works, even though this meditative state is common to non-Buddhist traditions as well. In addition, as the *Root Text on the Mahamudra Teachings* [361b] explains, practices such as the one called Gazing at the Mind's Face are merely techniques for coming to recognize the mind's conventional-truth nature.[9] While these persons believe that they are meditating skillfully, in truth they have mistakenly strayed down a false path. Such a practice is like meditating that a copper ball is made of gold.

A meditation practice that mistakes cultivating languor for genuine meditation will not even bring rebirth in one of the two higher realms.[10] It is a practice that will cause the practitioner to be reborn as an animal. As Sakya Pandita wrote:

> A fool's meditation on the Mahamudra
> Will probably cause him to become an animal.
> If not that, he will fall into the Listeners' cessation
> Or else be reborn in the formless realm.[11]

A meditation practice that is not supported by any of the three principal elements of the path will not take you any further along the path or allow you to reach any higher spiritual level. For example, there are instructions that urge us to meditate on the mind by examining its colorless and shapeless nature, using aphorisms like: "Neither stop the flow of previous thoughts nor anticipate the arising of future ones." But these ineffectual kinds

[9]That is, such practices are not a form of meditation in which the practitioner is meditating on the mind's ultimate-truth nature of emptiness. See Day Twenty-one, p. 242 and accompanying note 36 for an earlier reference to this point.

[10]Quiescence and the absorptions are an essential element in the effort to achieve liberation from samsara. However, in the absence of the third Buddhist training in wisdom, these meditative states become a type of karma called "invariable" (S: *āniñjyakarma*, T: *mi gyo ba'i las*; see Day Fifteen, pp. 67–68) that brings rebirth in the form and formless realms. However, a form of meditation practice that mistakenly cultivates subtle languor is not even one-pointed concentration (S: *samādhiḥ*, T: *ting nge 'dzin*), much less a form of invariable karma.

[11]*Classification of the Three Vows* (T: *sDom pa gsum gyi rab tu dbye ba*), p. 309, f. 2, l. 2-3.

of meditation will only cause us to waste our life without bringing anything of real value.

On the other hand, if our meditation is supported by enlightenment mind, renunciation, correct view, and the act of taking refuge, it will be, in the same order, a Mahayana practice, a practice that leads to liberation, and a genuine form of Buddhist practice. Therefore, these are the kinds of unerring paths that we must pursue. Emptying the mind of all objective content and focusing on its luminous nature, without the support of any of the attitudes just mentioned, will do nothing to counteract the belief in the self-existence of entities. Such a practice offers nothing but the risk of bringing the same unhappy result that the non-Buddhist teacher Udraka experienced [362a].

(Kyabje Rinpoche concluded by saying that we must avoid the mistake of believing an inferior path to be superior, and we must learn how to distinguish between a genuine path and a false one.)

ii) How to train oneself in insight, which is the essence of wisdom

This part of the outline is made up of three sections: (1) establishing the insubstantiality of the self, (2) establishing the insubstantiality of entities, and (3) the method of developing insight.

(1) Establishing the insubstantiality of the self

The first section consists of two subsections: (1) how to cultivate the space-like realization during a state of mental composure, and (2) how to cultivate the realization that all conventional entities are like illusions during the period following meditation.

(a) How to cultivate the space-like realization during a state of mental composure

This topic is made up of four key points: (1) determining the object to be negated; (2) determining that, in order for the self to be truly existent, it must either be identical with the heaps or distinct from them; (3) determining that a truly existent self cannot be identical with the heaps; and (4) determining that a truly existent self cannot be distinct from the heaps.

Once we achieve a firm state of quiescence, we should not pursue the type of insight practice that merely suppresses the active form of the mental afflictions. In this worldly path,[12] each level of meditative composure is

[12]S: *lokamārgaḥ*, T: *'jig rten pa'i lam*. This type of insight practice is practiced by Buddhists and non-Buddhists alike. It is a method that gradually overcomes desire for the various levels of samsara, ranging from the desire realm up to, but not including, the fourth level of the

achieved by regarding a higher level as more tranquil and the level below it as coarse.

Because our main goal is to achieve liberation, the insight practice we should pursue is the supramundane path that cuts samsara's root by investigating the insubstantiality of both the self and entities. As the following verse from *In Praise of the Praiseworthy* declares, generating this type of insight gradually overcomes all of samsara's defects, even without developing the eight states of meditative composure associated with the two higher realms:[13]

> Yet those who follow your teaching
> Can overcome samsaric existence
> Without attaining the main absorptions,
> Even as the Evil One looks on.[14]

Nevertheless, in order to attain liberation we must establish the meaning of that most profound of subjects, emptiness [362b]. Otherwise, there is no way we can possibly achieve this goal. Moreover, without realizing emptiness, all our other Bodhisattva activities will be contaminated by the mistaken belief that entities are self-existent. Just as a bird with only one wing cannot fly, we cannot travel to the realm of Buddhahood with only one of the two essential elements of means and wisdom. Therefore, we must train ourselves in both the means of enlightenment mind and the wisdom that realizes emptiness. As Je Lama himself declared:

> Even after developing renunciation and enlightenment
> mind,
> You will not be able to cut the root of samsaric existence
> Without gaining the wisdom that realizes ultimate reality.
> So devote yourself to the method for realizing dependent
> origination.[15]

formless realm. However, this practice only overcomes desire temporarily; it cannot eradicate the seeds of the mental afflictions.

[13]There are eight states of meditative composure—the four absorptions (S: *dhyānam*, T: *bsam gtan*) of the form realm and the four states of composure (S: *samāpattiḥ*, T: *snyoms 'jug*) associated with the formless realm. Each of these eight states has a preliminary stage and a main stage. The first absorption of the form realm also has a third level called the superior stage. These levels of meditative composure form an ancillary topic of the *Ornament of Realizations* (S: *Abhisamayalaṃkāraḥ*), one of the five major Sutrayana treatises that are studied in Gelukpa monasteries.

[14]S: *Varṇārhavarṇastotram*, ch. 9, v. 23.

[15]*Three Principal Elements of the Path* (T: *Lam gyi gtzo bo rnam gsum*), v. 9.

Even the doubt that leans toward believing in emptiness[16] tears apart the erroneous belief that entities are self-existent, as if it were shredding a piece of cloth. It is also described as destroying the belief that entities are self-existent in the same way that hail destroys crops. As the *Four Hundred Verses* declares:

> A person of little virtue doesn't even
> Develop uncertainty about this subject.
> Yet merely developing this uncertainty
> Tears samsaric existence to shreds.[17]

However, to realize emptiness we must cultivate its requisites. This collection of essential conditions for gaining a realization of correct view includes: relying on a holy teacher who knows perfectly all the essential points of the Buddha's teachings; receiving from such a teacher the instructions that explain emptiness; carrying out practices that accumulate merit and remove mental obscurations; and making supplication to your guru, whom you regard as inseparable in nature from your tutelary deity. If we lack any of these requisites, we will not be able to develop a realization of the correct view [363a].

While Indian Buddhist scholars from the four major philosophical schools[18] held many divergent points concerning the nature of the correct view, the most important theory is that of the Prasangika branch of the Madhyamaka School. They explain emptiness to mean dependent origination, and dependent origination as being equivalent to emptiness.

To accommodate the different levels of understanding of his followers, our compassionate Master first taught that the self is not a distinct substance

[16]T: *don 'gyur gyi the tsom*. Tibetan epistemology describes three types of doubt: (1) doubt that tends toward erroneous belief about its object, (2) doubt that tends toward right belief about its object, and (3) doubt that is completely undecided about the nature of its object.

[17]T: *bZhi brgya pa*, ch. 8, v. 5.

[18]Tibetan scholars recognize four main Indian Buddhist philosophical schools: Vaibhashika, Sautrantika, Yogachara, and Madhyamaka. The first two are part of the Hinayana tradition. The Vaibhashika views, which developed from the early Abhidharma literature, are well represented in the root verses of Vasubandhu's *Treasury of Higher Learning* (S: *Abhidharma-kośakārikā*). The Sautrantika School developed largely in reaction to what were considered naive and mistaken beliefs of the Vaibhashikas. The two remaining schools, Yogachara and Madhyamaka, belong to the Mahayana tradition. Of the two, the Yogachara or Mind Only School, which accepts the existence of real mental entities, developed after the Madhyamakas. The Madhyamaka or Middle Way School rejects the existence of any inherently real entities, mental or physical, and was established around the 1st century by the great sage Nagarjuna. The Prasangika branch of the Madhyamaka School is mainly associated with the scholars Buddhapalita and Chandrakirti. Later figures such as Shantideva and Atisha are also regarded as Prasangikas.

that exists on its own,[19] in order to overcome attachment to the belief in a real self. To those disciples who were somewhat more developed, he taught that some entities are truly existent while others are not.[20] To others who were even more developed than this, he taught that although no entities are truly existent, they do exist inherently.[21] Finally, he taught his highest followers that all entities lack any inherent existence.[22] Of these doctrines, the last one represents the Blessed One's highest teaching and his ultimate view.

Moreover, we must try to learn this correct view by studying the works of the venerable Lord Nagarjuna, who was prophesied by our Master himself. Lord Buddha declared that he would be unsurpassed for his ability to explain the Conqueror's underlying thought—a doctrine free of the two extremes of eternalism and nihilism:

> A glorious and renowned monk shall appear
> In the southern land of Vedali.
> Known by the name Naga, he will destroy
> The views on being and nonbeing.[23]

There are many individuals who expound what are purported to be new theories. While these ideas are believed by some to be very profound, they should be regarded as correct explanations of the Buddha's ultimate view only to the extent that they are in agreement with Nagarjuna's system [363b]. Any opinions that differ from his are certain to be at variance with the Conqueror's underlying thought. Leaving aside those Tibetans of lesser intellect, even such great Indian pandits as Bhavaviveka and such learned Tibetan scholars as Jonangba were wrong about this key topic of the correct view.

[19] T: *gang zag rang rkya tub pa'i rdzas yod kyis stong pa*. This view, which holds that there is no real self apart from the five heaps, identifies the conventional self with either mind consciousness or the collection of the five heaps as a whole. It is referred to as the rough explanation of the insubstantiality of the self (T: *gang zag gi bdag med rags pa*) and is generally adhered to by all Buddhist schools except the Prasangikas. Here it is being associated specifically with the two Hinayana schools, the Vaibhashikas and the Sautrantikas.

[20] This is a reference to the Yogachara School, which holds that while form (S: *rūpaḥ*, T: *gzugs*) is not truly existent (i.e., real), mind is.

[21] This is a reference to the second branch of the Madhyamaka School, the Svatantrikas. This school holds that although no causally efficient entities are truly existent (i.e., nothing is real from the perspective of ultimate truth), they do exist inherently (T: *rang bzhin gyis grub pa*) in that they have distinct essences from the perspective of conventional truth.

[22] T: *chos thams cad rang bzhin gyis med pa*. This is a reference to the Madhyamaka Prasangika School.

[23] *Sutra on the Descent into Lanka* (S: *Laṅkāvatarasūtram*), ch. 10, v. 165.

Some who have tried to follow Nagarjuna's system did not understand it properly. Others not only didn't follow Nagarjuna, they even tried to refute him. But this is what Chandrakirti wrote about those who do not rely on the system established by Nagarjuna and his spiritual sons, and who devise theories that fall outside this great teacher's doctrine:

> There is no means of attaining Peace
> For those outside Acharya Nagarjunapada's path;
> They have strayed from conventional and ultimate truth.
> Anyone who strays from them cannot attain liberation.[24]

If there were a second doorway leading to Peace, we could enter that. But since there isn't, our only recourse is to follow Nagarjuna's system. And the great Atisha declared that Acharya Chandrakirti is the supreme among Nagarjuna's followers:

> How can emptiness be realized?
> Nagarjuna, who was prophesied by the Tathagata
> And who perceived the truth of ultimate reality,
> Had a disciple named Chandrakirti.
>
> The truth of ultimate reality can be realized
> Through instruction handed down by him.[25]

Many of the scholars and spiritual adepts from the various traditions that arose during the early period of Buddhism[26] in Tibet were followers of Chandrakirti [364a]. Indeed, many of the teachers who founded these Tibetan traditions held views that were in agreement with his Prasangika system. But these scholars developed a variety of teaching methods to fit the levels of their disciples, and over time many of these followers did not correctly understand the true philosophical views of their spiritual forebears. As a result, mistaken ideas gradually found their way into these systems.

Jamgön Tsongkapa also had a difficult time trying to find a teacher from whom he could learn the ultimate Buddhist philosophical view. As he felt there was no one in Tibet whom he could trust concerning the correct view,

[24]*Introduction to the Middle Way* (T: *dBu ma la 'jug pa*), ch. 6, v. 79.

[25]*Introduction to the Two Truths* (T: *bDen pa gnyis la 'jug pa*), vol. 30 (*a*) in *dBu ma* section of Tg., f. 72a.

[26]This period roughly spans the early seventh to the mid-ninth centuries. See also Part One, Day Two, p. 43 and accompanying note 45.

he was planning to go to the Land of Aryas[27] with the hope of meeting teachers such as Acharya Nagabodhi and the great spiritual adept Maitripada. But the Great Adept from Hlodrak strongly urged him to put off this trip.[28] With the Great Adept acting as intermediary, Je Tsongkapa was able to address various questions about the correct philosophical view to Vajrapani. A record of what this deity said is contained in the work entitled the *Garland of Supremely Healing Nectar: A Series of Divine Responses*.[29]

Even this deity's instructions—at least in the version that appears in contemporary editions—still form the basis of philosophical debate. Je Tsongkapa himself was not completely satisfied with this teaching, so he prayed to his guru whom he viewed as inseparable in nature from Mañjushri. He practiced intensely and over a long period to accumulate merit and purify himself of obstacles. He also meditated with great determination on the various topics of practice. Through the combination of these efforts, he eventually achieved a direct vision of Mañjushri.

In general, there are three ways a vision of a deity can occur. One way of perceiving a deity's presence is when psychic winds enter various channels of the practitioner's body. A second way is when the deity is experienced in a practitioner's mind consciousness during meditation. The third is when a practitioner directly perceives a deity with his sense consciousness, just as one human being perceives another [364b].

Because Je Rinpoche's visions of Mañjushri were of the last type, he was able to communicate with the deity just as disciples can with an ordinary human teacher. At one point, Je Rinpoche asked questions about various difficult points relating to the correct view. When he gave the appearance[30] of not understanding the profound answers that he received, the Exalted One said to him, "Go to Rendawa[31] to try and resolve your uncertainty." When this failed to clear up Je Rinpoche's difficulties, Mañjushri declared, "Use

[27]S: *Āryavartaḥ*, T: *'Phags pa'i yul*. An epithet of India.

[28]T: *lHo brag grub chen*, 1326–1401. His ordination name was Namka Gyeltsen (T: *Nam mkha' rgyal mtsan*). Je Tsongkapa received instructions for two of the three Kadampa Lamrim lineages from this teacher (see Part One, Appendix B, pp. 238 and 239).

[29]The teacher Namka Gyeltsen had visions of Vajrapani and was able to communicate with him directly. At this point in his spiritual career, Je Tsongkapa did not yet have this ability. This famous dialogue took place in 1396. The text of Vajrapani's instruction, entitled *Zhu lan sman mchog bdud rtzi'i 'phreng ba*, is listed in the Bibliography under (*rJe*) *Tzong kha pa*.

[30]T: *tsul bstan pa*. See Part One, Day One, p. 7 and accompanying note 8 for an explanation of the phrase to "give the appearance" of doing something. Se also Day Twenty-one, p. 250.

[31]Rendawa Shönu Lodrö (T: *Re mda' ba gZhon nu blo gros*, T: 1349–1412). A teacher from the Sakya tradition from whom Je Tsongkapa received extensive instructions in such treatises as Vasubandhu's *Treasury of Higher Learning* (S: *Abhidharmakośakārikā*) and Chandrakirti's *Elucidation of the Words* (S: *Prasannapadā*). Later, Venerable Rendawa also received instruction from Lama Tsongkapa. See also Day Fifteen, note 55.

what I have taught you as the basis of your understanding. If you exert yourself diligently, in the future you will gain an unerring realization of the profound view by relying on the scriptures of Indian pandits."

As foretold in this prophecy, following great efforts to accumulate merit, purify himself of obscurations, and the like, Je Rinpoche experienced a vision of Acharya Buddhapalita. Soon after that, he attained a genuine realization of the Madhyamaka Prasangika School's ultimate view of emptiness when he once again studied this teacher's commentary to the *Root Verses on the Middle Way*.[32]

Je Rinpoche did not give much importance to these visions he had experienced of many Indian pandits and spiritual adepts. Nevertheless, through the disciple called the Realized One,[33] Mañjushri conveyed the following message to Je Tsongkapa: "Do not ignore these visions. You will greatly benefit both yourself and others through the writings of these Indian Buddhist teachers."

After Je Tsongkapa gained his unerring realization of the Madhyamaka or Middle Way view, he developed such great faith toward our Master that he was moved to compose the *Shorter Essence of Eloquent Sayings*,[34] which praises Buddha for having taught dependent origination. Some time later, Bodong Chok-le Namgyel[35] overheard a beggar pilgrim reciting this poem out loud. At first, the great scholar thought it was one of Nagarjuna's works [365a]. Then, after listening further, he thought it might have been composed by Chandrakirti. But when the poem revealed toward the end that the author had relied on the writings of both Nagarjuna and Chandrakirti, he realized that it could not have been composed by either of them. So Bodong asked the beggar who had written this work and was told that its author was the great Je Tsongkapa.

Upon hearing this, Bodong felt an unshakably strong faith toward Je Lama and traveled to central Tibet hoping to meet him. But by this time Je Lama had gone to the pure realms in order to further the welfare of all sentient

[32]See also Part One, Day Five, p. 168 for another reference to this event.

[33]T: *rTogs ldan pa.* Jampel Gyatso (T: *'Jam dpal rgya mtso*, 1356–1428) was one of eight close disciples who accompanied Je Tsongkapa when he went into retreat. He also had the ability to communicate with Mañjushri. See *Lives of the Lamrim Teachers* (T: *Lam rim bla ma brgyud pa'i rnam thar*), vol. 1, pp. 849–865.

[34]T: *Legs bshad snying po chung ba.* The more common and informal title of this work is *In Praise of Dependent Origination* (T: *rTen 'brel bstod pa*). The full title in the colophon reads: *The Essence of Eloquent Sayings: A Praise of Lord Buddha, the Unsurpassed Teacher for the Entire World and a Great Friend even to Those with Whom He is Unacquainted, for Having Taught the Profound Doctrine of Dependent Origination.*

[35]T: *Bo dong phyogs las rnam rgyal*, 1375–1451. A great scholar and accomplished poet who was Tibet's most prolific writer; his collected works encompass more than a hundred volumes.

beings, so Bodong was unable to meet him. When he learned of Je Tsongkapa's passing, Bodong threw the gold and silver coins that he had intended to present as an offering into the sky and prayed that he might be able to meet Je Lama in the future. It is said that these coins miraculously landed at Ganden Monastery.

You should recognize that the eloquent writings of this great spiritual being Je Tsongkapa are unsurpassed for their ability to explain the Buddha's profound teaching on emptiness. Je Lama did not accept as authoritative the majority of those Indian treatises that purported to explain the correct philosophical view. However, in response to Je Lama's inquiries, Mañjushri declared that Chandrakirti was a high Bodhisattva of great wisdom and courage who knowingly came to this world from a Buddha's paradise in order to spread Lord Nagarjuna's teaching on the profound view. The deity further remarked that this scholar's writings are totally free of error. In keeping with this instruction, Je Tsongkapa regarded the writings of Chandrakirti [365b] along with the word of his guru, Mañjushri, as valid and authoritative.

When we study and contemplate Je Tsongkapa's writings on the correct philosophical view, we find that they are very difficult to comprehend and fathom. The reason we cannot understand these writings easily is that their subject is exceedingly weighty and deep. Nevertheless, if we read them carefully again and again, we will discover many explanations that both clarify important issues and express profound ideas in a unique and extraordinary way. Because of this, Je Tsongkapa's writings are particularly effective in giving us the understanding of emptiness that will gradually bring the different levels of wisdom, starting with the wisdom that derives from listening.[36]

Now I shall briefly explain the topic of insight based on the philosophical view that Je Tsongkapa taught, beginning with the topic called "Establishing the insubstantiality of the self." This is in keeping with the instruction on the proper order of practice described in the following lines from the *Four Hundred Verses*:

[36]S: *śrutamayīprajñā*, T: *thos byung gi shes rab*. This is the first of three levels of wisdom; the other two are wisdom that derives from contemplation (S: *cintamayīprajñā*, T: *bsam byung gi shes rab*) and wisdom that derives from meditation (S: *bhāvanāmayīprajñā*, T: *bsgom byung gi shes rab*). Listening wisdom is not knowledge (S: *pramāṇam*, T: *tsad ma*) in the epistemological sense; it is only correct belief. The second type of wisdom, that which derives from contemplation, is knowledge—more specifically, inferential knowledge (S: *anumānam*, T: *rjes su dpag pa*). The third type, meditation wisdom, is gained when the practitioner begins to cultivate quiescence and insight jointly, using emptiness as the object of meditation. This wisdom culminates in a form of direct yogic perception—in this case, the direct realization of emptiness.

First overcome what is nonvirtuous;
Then overcome belief in a self;
Finally overcome all belief in entities.
Wise is the person who understands this.[37]

We should begin by overcoming such mistaken views as the belief that karma and its results do not exist. These topics were presented in the teachings for persons of lesser and moderate capacities. Next we should overcome the belief that the self is truly existent. Finally, we should overcome the belief that all other entities are truly existent. While the self-existent nature or essence that is being denied in these two forms of insubstantiality is the same, the one that is denied in relation to the self is somewhat easier to comprehend. This is why the insubstantiality of the self is taught first.

Now there are many proofs that establish the existence of emptiness, including dependent origination and the seven-part reasoning [366a]. However, the one that is easiest for beginning practitioners to grasp is called the "lack of identity or distinctness."[38] Therefore, Je Rinpoche and many of his followers have explained this proof on the basis of four key points: (1) determining the object to be negated, (2) determining that a truly existent self must either be identical with the heaps or separate from them, (3) determining that a truly existent self cannot be identical with the heaps, and (4) determining that a truly existent self cannot be distinct from the heaps.

(i) The key point of determining the object to be refuted

Several lines from *Engaging in Bodhisattva Activities* declare:

Without grasping the fabricated mode of being,
Its nonexistence cannot be realized.[39]

Unless we can recognize the nature of the false mode of existence that is being denied, we will not be able to realize the simple negation[40] that is

[37]T: *bZhi brgya pa*, ch. 8, v. 15.

[38]S: *ekānekavirahitayuktiḥ*, T: *gcig du bral gyi rigs pa*.

[39]S: *Bodhicaryāvatāraḥ*, ch. 9, v. 140.

[40]The distinction between "affirmative objects" and "negative objects" is crucial to the central thesis of Madhyamaka philosophy. Specifically, the emptiness that is posited of all entities is explained as constituting a simple negation. This negation is realized through logically refuting the possibility of self-existent entities. In the present context, the object to be refuted is the self-existent essence or nature of a person. The following description of negative objects is from Kedrup Tenba Dargye's *Overview of Madhyamaka Philosophy* (T: *dBu ma spyi don*): "A negative object is an entity that can only be apprehended when the mind negates some object that is

established through its refutation. This difficulty is like not being able to hit a target with an arrow because you can't see the target, or like not being able to catch a thief because you don't know what he looks like. Therefore, it is vital for us to understand the nature of the self-existent essence that is being refuted.

A self-existent essence is the same as the true mode of existence[41] that is being denied in the phrase "entities are not truly existent." It is also the same as the intrinsic nature[42] that is being rejected in the phrase "entities do not have an intrinsic nature" and the unique identity[43] that is denied in the phrase "entities do not exist by way of their own unique identity." The *Commentary to the Four Hundred Verses* describes it in these words:

> Regarding that, the term "self" means an independent intrinsic essence or nature that entities [are wrongly believed to] possess. Selflessness is the absence of that.[44]

directly related to it. There are two types of negative objects: a simple negation and an affirming negation. A simple negation (S: *prasajyapratiṣedhaḥ*, T: *med dgag*) is the type of negative object in which no further entity is implied when the mind negates the object that is related to it. An example is the insubstantiality of the self. An affirming negation (*paryudāsa-pratiṣedhaḥ*, T: *ma yin dgag*) is the type of negative object in which another entity is *implied* or *affirmed* when the mind negates the object related to it. There are four types of affirming negations: (1) an affirming negation that implies another entity directly, (2) an affirming negation that implies another entity indirectly, (3) an affirming negation that implies another entity both directly and indirectly, and (4) an affirming negation that implies another entity based on special circumstances. An example of the first type is the proposition that the insubstantiality of the self exists. An example of the second type is the proposition that Devadatta does not eat food during the daytime. An example of the third type is the proposition that there exists a fat Devadatta who does not eat food during the daytime and yet he is not emaciated. An example of the fourth is the proposition in which someone determines that another person is a member of the Vaishya caste and not a member of the Brahmin caste, given that he knows the person in question is either a Vaishya or a Brahmin, but does not know to which of the two castes he belongs. When this individual asks a third person the caste to which the person in question belongs, this other person—intending only to indicate the caste to which he did not belong—replies that he is not a Brahmin (folio 88a)." In Bibliography, see listing under (*mKhas grub*) *bsTan pa dar rgyas*.

[41]S *satyasiddhiḥ*, T: *bden par grub pa*.

[42]S: *svabhāvaḥ*, T: *rang bzhin*.

[43]S: *svarūpaḥ*, T: *rang ngos*.

[44]This is Chandrakirti's commentary on the root text *Four Hundred Verses* by Aryadeva. It is commonly referred to as the *Commentary to the Four Hundred Verses* (T: *bZhi brgya pa'i 'grel pa*). The term self (S: *ātman*, T: *bdag*), as it is being used here, does not mean the self of personal identity. Rather it means a self-existent essence or nature that all entities are mistakenly believed to possess. This passage appears as part of the commentary to ch. 12, v. 13 of Aryadeva's root text (in *dBu ma* section of Tg., vol. 24 (*ya*), f. 187b).

As it is being used here, the term "self" refers to an intrinsic nature that exists independently of any other conditions—that is, a self-sufficient and inherent mode of being that does not rely or depend upon anything else.

While simply knowing and using verbal explanations such as these may be enough to silence an opponent in debate, we have not truly recognized the object to be refuted until we identify it within our own experience. For example, we cannot positively identify a thief on the basis of vague descriptions like: "The thief is a man who was wearing white clothes [366b]." Therefore, we must not be satisfied with the level of understanding that is gained by listening to another person's explanations. Nor should we stop with the theoretical and abstract understandings that are based on verbal descriptions. We must examine our own mind and find there, within the naked reality of our experience, the object to be negated.

If we fail to discover the object to be refuted, we run the risk of falling into the nihilism that destroys the teaching on dependent origination. This is true even though we may try to apply the many arguments that are meant to establish that entities are not truly existent. For instance, suppose you hold the concept of a pitcher in the back of your mind and then deny that the pitcher's spout is the pitcher or its base is the pitcher, and so on. After successively eliminating each and every part of the pitcher, you might conclude that not being able to identify the pitcher in this way constitutes the pitcher's emptiness and then proceed to meditate on such an understanding. But this approach fails to recognize that emptiness must be established in relation to a particular object, and that what is being denied of that object must have some clearly defined philosophical import.[45] Instead, it simply obliterates the very concept of a pitcher and identifies its emptiness as a complete nothingness. Such a fanciful interpretation is seriously flawed and will only lead you down a wrong path.

When you try to identify the object to be refuted, you must investigate how the innate mistaken view of the self[46] holds that the self is real because it possesses an inherently real essence. This involves examining both how the self *appears* to our natural, untutored mind and how it is *grasped* by

[45]In this case, the object or basis of analysis is the pitcher itself, and the philosophical import being denied is that the pitcher has any self-existent essence.

[46]There are two forms of the mistaken view of the self: innate (S: *sahajātmagrāhaḥ*, T: *ngar 'dzin lhan skyes*) and conceptual (S: *parikalpitātmagrāhaḥ*, T: *ngar 'dzin kun brtags*). The conceptual form believes the self to be inherently real on the basis of mistaken reasoning. The innate form, which all beings have possessed since beginningless time, believes spontaneously that the self is inherently real and it does so independently of any reasoning. The mistaken belief regarding the self is also known by the technical term "perishable-collection view" (see Day Fifteen, p. 54). Of its two forms, the innate mistaken view is more important, because we cannot gain a correct understanding of emptiness without clearly identifying the way in which it holds the self.

this mind. Introspection will reveal a sense of personal identity that does not regard the self as something that is merely projected by the mind onto the heaps. Instead, it perceives the self as a separate and independent "I" that exists within the collection of your five heaps. All ordinary beings—including worms and insects—hold this belief in the deepest part of their minds, even when they are dreaming. This is what we call the innate mistaken view of the self.

In general, there are three different ways of perceiving the self or person. Those individuals who have gained a realization of emptiness recognize that the self is not truly existent and therefore regard it as something that is merely ascribed by a conceptualizing mind in relation to its basis of ascription[47] [367a]. Ordinary people who have not been influenced by philosophical views can grasp the self in either of two ways. One is indefinite—that is, it neither regards the self as possessing nor as lacking an inherently real essence. A second way of perceiving the self, however, holds that it does possess an inherently real essence.

Of these three, the second one is the correct cognition that establishes the validity of the term "self." The unspecified "I" that is the object of this mind *does* exist conventionally. It is also the agent that performs deeds and the subject that experiences their results. The third way of perceiving the self is the erroneous belief that must be overcome by a proper antidote. A self that exists the way it is perceived by this mind is what must be refuted using correct reasoning.

Put differently, when we go along with the way the self appears to our innate perception and then form such thoughts as "I ate food" and the like, we believe that the self is real. However, the correct way to understand the logical relation between agent and action is to be satisfied with a self that is merely ascribed by an uncritical and unreflective mind, and regard that as the agent who performs the actions described in statements like "I am sitting," or "I am walking." This self only exists nominally and is merely ascribed on the basis of words and concepts.

Part of the way the self appears to our innate mistaken view is also present in the mind that establishes the conventionally valid existence of the self. However, when the self appears to this latter mind, it is commingled with other entities and therefore does not appear with the same clarity and distinctness that it does to the innate mistaken view of the self. It is important to recognize that the self appears to the mind in these two ways. That is, in one the self appears as a self-sufficient entity that possesses an

[47]T: *gdags gzhi*. In the case of the self, the basis of ascription is the five heaps. Most Buddhist schools identify this basis of ascription as the nominal self; however, the Madhyamaka Prasangika School asserts that the basis of ascription and the ascribed object (T: *btags chos*)—that is, the nominal self—are not one and the same.

inherently real essence and in the other it is not recognized as having any particular mode of existence.[48]

Although the innate belief in an inherently real self is continually present in our mind—even when we are dreaming—in most ordinary situations we cannot clearly observe how the self appears to this mind [367b]. However, in certain circumstances, such as when someone praises us or scorns us, something makes us very happy, or we experience some great misfortune, the way the self appears to this mistaken belief *does* become more evident.

For example, if someone accuses you of stealing or of having done some other wrong, you may think, "I have been falsely accused," and angrily declare, "I can't accept this!" When you experience this kind of uncontrollable emotional reaction, a vivid and strong awareness of your subjective self also rises from the innermost part of your heart. This "I" is the object that was accused of stealing and that voiced the response: "I can't accept this!" The way that this "I" presents itself within your mind is the best example of how the object to be negated occurs in the mind.

Similarly, you can use your reaction to any number of experiences like joy, fear, happiness, or suffering as a way of deliberately evoking a strong form of the innate mistaken view of the self. While you are experiencing that state of mind, you should examine how the self presents itself to your consciousness. An example of how to do this is when two people are walking side by side down a road. Just as each individual must keep an eye both on his companion and on the road, when you are examining how the self appears to your mind, the main part of your awareness must remain in the state that represents your innate view of the self. When you have generated a clear image of the object to be negated, you must use a different and subtler part of your awareness to examine how this object appears to your innate view of the self. However, if this examining part of your mind is too strong, it will destroy the intensity of your innate view of the self and the image of the object to be negated will either disappear completely or at least lose its clarity. So it is important to exercise skill when you examine how the self appears to this innate mistaken view of the self.

When you examine how the self appears to this innate belief, it can take on a variety of forms. For example, sometimes the self will appear to be related to the body alone, or it may appear to be related just to the mind [368a]. These are not the way that the self actually appears to the innate mistaken view.

The correct description is as follows. The basis of ascription and the ascribed object are actually distinct elements. Of these, the basis of ascription

[48]The former is the way the self appears to the innate mistaken view of the self (T: *ngar 'dzin lhan skyes*); the latter is the way it appears to the ordinary mind that establishes the conventional validity of the self (T: *tha snyad 'jog pa'i blo tsad ma*).

is the combination of the body and mind, and the ascribed object is the self that is your personal identity. When this self appears within the undifferentiated combination of the mind and body as a vivid and distinct entity that is able to exist on its own and not merely as a verbal designation that is ascribed by the mind, this is the unerring form of the object to be refuted.

If you correctly identify this object, you can refute it easily. However, because this is a very subtle point, some persons err by going too far in what they refute while others do not go far enough.[49]

When we don't try to identify the object to be negated, it is always present in the mind. But even when we do try to identify it, we cannot find it because it remains hidden within the combination of our mind and body. Therefore, consider the following example. If we are traveling along the edge of a steep cliff, we are likely to become afraid and think, "I could fall"; however, we wouldn't think, "My body could fall," or "My mind could fall." This "I" that we believe to be in danger of falling appears as a distinct, substantive entity situated within the undifferentiated combination of our mind and body. When I refer to the mind and body as an undifferentiated combination, I mean that they are perceived as inseparable, like water and milk that have been mixed together in a single container. The image of our personal self that forms in the mind in this kind of situation is the object to be negated.

In the same way, when we see an object such as a galloping horse, we do not refer to the horse's body or its mind as the horse. Nor do we regard the horse as something that is merely nominally ascribed to the collection of a mind and body. Rather, the thing we call a "horse" is perceived as a distinct, substantive entity that appears to be situated within the collection of a mind and body.

When we use terms such as "Sera" and "Drebung," we aren't thinking specifically of the assembly hall and other external buildings, nor do we mean just the monks who reside there. Rather, the image that forms in the mind is of a distinct, substantive entity called "Sera" or "Drebung" that is located within the combination of the buildings and its inhabitants and occupies the same area that they do [368b].

When we refer to someone as Kachu,[50] the mere collection of some person's body and mind serves as the basis of ascription for this title. But the

[49]Je Tsongkapa discusses this topic in great detail in his *Great Stages of the Path*. Positions that go too far in their identification of the object to be refuted (T: *dgag bya khyab ches pa'i lugs*) are criticized in pages 781–860 (ff. 375a–414b); positions that don't go far enough (T: *dgag bya khyab chungs pa'i lugs*) are examined in pages 860–870 (ff. 414b–419b).

[50]T: *dka' bcu*. A title of religious scholarship awarded at the Tashi Hlunpo Monastery in Tsang (T: *bKra bshis lhun po*, see Part Two, Day Ten, p. 98, and accompanying note 6), which means "One who has mastered ten difficult subjects."

image that forms in the mind is of a distinct, substantive entity that does not depend on anything else for its existence. As Keutsang Jamyang Mönlam explained, the ultimate object to be refuted by logical reasoning is a particular kind of image that forms in the mind whenever we think of some entity. It is what we are referring to when we call that entity by its name. The nature of this image is that it seems to exist from its own side and to occupy the same area as the qualities that serve as its basis of ascription. This is the same as what is meant by the phrase "the object that is apprehended by the belief in real essences."[51]

If we don't properly discern the way objects give the appearance of being truly existent, we will end up identifying the object to be refuted as some abstract notion of self-existence that is not a part of our actual experience. But no matter how hard we try to apply the many arguments found in Madhyamaka treatises to analyze a mere verbal understanding of such terms as "self-existent" or "truly existent," our efforts will only be operating at the level of theoretical concepts and therefore will do nothing to uproot the erroneous belief that entities are truly existent. Having failed to recognize the object to be negated as it naturally appears in the mind, we will invent some new way of perceiving the self as the object to be negated and apply logical analysis to this, which only results in a philosophical view that was created from artificial speculation.

As Losang Chökyi Gyeltsen declared:

> The way the object to be negated by reasoning appears to the mind is not any different from the way that entities usually appear to ordinary persons[52] like ourselves. This is because every mental state of an ordinary person is tainted by ignorance and, therefore, every object that appears to the mind of such a person possesses the quality of appearing to be truly existent.

Thus, all the various entities that we ordinary persons perceive—such as our individual selves, our heaps,[53] mountains, houses, and so on—[369a] present themselves in such a way that their conventionally existent nature

[51]*Den dzin gyi mikpey te so* (T: *bden 'dzin gyi dmigs pa'i gtad so*). *Den dzin* is the mind that erroneously "holds" entities to be "truly existent"—that is, to possess real essences. *Mikpey* means that this mind "apprehends" or perceives objects in a certain way. *Te so* refers to the "object" that is "believed" to be truly existent.

[52]S: *pṛthagjanaḥ*, T: *so so skye bo*. This term refers to any person who has not attained a direct realization of ultimate reality.

[53]That is, the five heaps (S: *skandaḥ*, T: *phung po*) of form, feeling, conception, compositional factors, and consciousness.

and the semblance of being truly existent are commingled. It isn't possible to isolate different elements in our perceptions so that we could say, "This portion of our perception is what gives the appearance of being truly existent and the rest does not have that quality." Every aspect of the perceived object appears truly existent. No object can appear to the mind of ordinary persons like ourselves without being mixed together with the image of the object to be negated. Therefore, the image of the object to be negated—which can also be described as the quality of appearing to be truly existent—is none other than the very way in which entities normally present themselves to our mind.

If we pay no attention to these very ordinary perceptions and try instead to discover the object to be negated somewhere else, we will commit the error that Changkya Rölbey Dorje[54] described in the following lines:

> Nowadays, some of the bright minds from our own
> tradition
> Have become attached to terms like "self-existent"
> and "truly existent."
> They take no interest in these concrete and substantive
> appearances
> And go looking for something with horns as the object
> to be refuted.
>
> It's said that in the unobscured vision of Mother's face
> None of these concrete, substantive experiences are found.
> There are many explanations that don't penetrate the most
> essential points
> And I fear old Mother has managed to elude them all.[55]

It is very important, therefore, that we combine the outer factor of a guru's instruction with the inner one of doing spiritual activities that accumulate merit and remove our karmic obscurations. With this as a foundation, we must carefully investigate the object to be refuted with a subtle and penetrating mind. If we succeed in identifying unerringly the object to be negated, each application of a logical proof such as the one based on dependent origination will reduce to dust even a belief in truly existent entities that is the size of Mt. Meru. By following such a method, we will experience

[54]See Day Sixteen, note 19.

[55]*Recognizing Mother: A Spiritual Song of the Correct View* (T: *Lta mgur A ma ngos 'dzin*), p. 10. In Bibliography, see listing under *lCang skya rol pa'i rdo rje*.

little difficulty achieving a realization of emptiness. As Changkya Rinpoche [369b] declared:

> No need to seek it, for it is the seeker himself.[56]

This line tells us that emptiness is not something we have to travel a great distance to find. It is something that we seekers of emptiness have always had with us. Finally, if it should prove necessary, we must be willing to meditate on this topic of identifying the object to be negated for a period of months and even years.

(ii) The key point of determining the range of logical possibilities

First, we must form in our mind a clear and unerring conceptual image[57] of the object to be negated. This should be done in the manner that I have just explained. Then we must determine the following: If the "I" that is apprehended by the innate belief in a real self does have a real or self-existent essence, that "I" or subjective self must either be identical with the heaps that are its basis of ascription[58] or it must be distinct from them. We must establish that no other alternative is possible besides these two.

It is a general principle that if anything exists, it must either be one or many. If this is true, it must also definitely follow that if something is truly existent, it must either be a truly existent one or a truly existent many. Therefore, if a truly existent self does exist, there are only two possibilities: either the self is identical with the heaps in a truly existent sense or it is distinct from them in a truly existent sense. Finally, we must determine with certainty that if the self is not consistent with either of these possibilities, then there is no such thing as a truly existent self. When we reach this understanding, we have gained the second key point of determining the range of logical possibilities. To achieve an understanding of this key point, we cannot meditate for just one or two days; we must continue meditating until we gain a firm realization of its full meaning.

[56]Ibid., p. 11.

[57]T: *don spyi*. In Buddhist epistemology, a conceptual thought (S: *vikalpaḥ*, T: *rtog pa*) perceives its object through an image that is formed by excluding everything that is not the object.

[58]See note 47 above.

(iii) The key point of determining that the self cannot be identical with the heaps in a truly existent sense

Begin by bringing to mind the kind of existence that is associated with the object to be negated. Then consider this point: If the self and the heaps were identical in a truly existent sense, they could not appear to the mind as distinct from one another and [370a] they would have to be a complete unity that is not distinguishable in any respect.

This point is based on the following reason. Some entities that have the same essential nature can appear to the mind as distinct objects.[59] However, this false quality of appearing one way while actually existing differently is only valid for entities that are conventionally existent. It is not valid for entities that are truly existent; the way truly existent entities appear must correspond to the way they actually are.

However, if the self and the heaps were identical in a truly existent sense, there would be no need to posit the existence of a self. Thus, the expression "heaps of the self" would be equivalent to saying "heaps of the heaps" or "self of the self." There would be no purpose in positing a self as something distinct from its heaps. As the *Root Text on Wisdom* declares:

> Once it has been established that no self
> Exists separately from the acquisitions,
> The self becomes just the acquisitions
> And so your self becomes nonexistent.[60]

Therefore, your view takes on the fault that there is no "acquirer"—that is, no self—distinct from the "acquisitions" of the five heaps.[61]

[59]For example, the impermanence of sound and its quality of being causally produced are both part of one and the same essence of sound, yet they can appear to the mind as distinct attributes.

[60]*Root Verses on the Middle Way* (S: *Mūlamadhyamakakārikā*), ch. 27, v. 5. In Bibliography, see listing under *Nāgārjuna*. The common names that Tibetans use for this text are the *Root Text on Wisdom* (T: *rTza ba shes rab*) and the *Root Text of the Middle Way School on Wisdom* (T: *dBu ma rtza ba shes rab*).

[61]The term being translated here as "acquisition" (S: *upādanam*, T: *nye bar len pa*) in some contexts refers to a category of mental afflictions. It is a participial noun formed from a root that means "to grasp." There are four types of "grasping": (1) grasping at sense objects, (2) grasping at views, (3) grasping at [inferior] conduct and ascetic practices, and (4) grasping at belief in a self. This is the sense of the term when it refers to the ninth limb in the twelve-part teaching of dependent origination (See Day Fifteen, p. 77). The term also refers to the act of "acquiring" in the sense of taking rebirth. The five heaps are what are acquired upon taking rebirth and, thus, in this verse they are being referred to as the "acquisitions," while the self is the agent or "acquirer" who takes them. See also Day Fourteen, p. 2, with accompanying notes

Furthermore, the *Introduction to the Middle Way* states:

> That acquirer and acquisitions are one is incorrect.
> In that case, agent and object would become one.[62]

These lines indicate that such a view brings the unwanted consequence that acquirer and acquisitions—as well as a body and the possessor of a body, or a part and a whole—become one and the same thing.

In criticizing the view that the self and the heaps are identical, the *Introduction to the Middle Way* also states the following:

> If the heaps were the self, as a consequence of that—
> Because they are many—it, too, would become many.[63]

That is, if the self and the heaps were identical, a number of unwanted consequences would follow, such as these: (1) Just as there are five heaps, there should be five selves; or, just as there is only one self, [370b] there could only be one heap and not five. (2) If the self were identical with the five heaps, there would be no purpose to entering a mother's womb at conception.[64] (3) If the self were identical with the body in a truly existent sense, when the corpse of a dead person is burned to ashes the self would also be reduced to ashes. (4) Just as the self is reborn at conception into a future life, the previous life's body would also take birth again at conception; or, just as the previous life's body cannot take birth again in the next life, neither could the self take birth again at conception. (5) It would not be possible for the self to be reborn in the formless realm. (6) The self would take on the nature of physical matter.

for another use of the term in the expression "afflicted grasping heaps" (S: *sāsravopādāna-skandhāḥ*, T: *zag bcas nyer len gyi phung po*).

[62]T: *dBu ma la 'jug pa*, ch. 6, v. 137. Chandrakirti gives this explanation of these lines in his autocommentary: "In this instance, the acquirer (S: *upādātṛ*, T: *nye bar len pa po*) is that which performs the act of acquiring—that is, it is the agent. The acquisitions (S: *upādanam*, T: *nye bar len pa*) are that which undergoes the act of being acquired—that is, they are objects. Here it is the self that should be understood as the acquirer, and the five heaps as the acquisitions. Regarding that, if the self were to consist merely of the collection of form, etc., then the agent and the object would become one and the same thing. But this is not held to be so, because then such things as the [four] elements [of earth, water, fire, and air] and their products [the secondary qualities of] visible form, etc., or a pot and the potter [who made it] would have to become one and the same thing."

[63]T: *dBu ma la 'jug pa*, ch. 6, v. 127.

[64]That is, if the self and the five heaps are one, there is no need of "acquiring" new heaps through the process of rebirth—since the old heaps would not be cast off by the self at death.

Similarly, if the self were one with the mind, it would wrongly follow that the self could not become cold or hungry, since the mind does not experience cold or hunger. It would also be improper for a person who was hot, cold, hungry or thirsty to say: "I am cold," or "I am hungry."

If the self were identical with both the body and the mind, it would be meaningless to regard the self as a subject that is distinct from its attributes of a body and a mind, as expressed in such phrases as "my body" and "my mind."

Moreover, if the self and the heaps were one in a self-existent sense, they would have to be identical in every respect including time and place. As the *Root Text on Wisdom* indicates:

> If the self were the heaps,
> It would arise and pass away.[65]

Thus, just as the heaps come into being and undergo destruction, the self, too, would be subject to the same kind of arising and disintegration. But this [371a] would mean that just as separate and distinct moments of the form aggregate come into being and then pass away, the self would also be an unrelated series of moments that come into being and pass away.[66]

The following is another error. If the self that exists in different lives has the same essence as the heaps that are present in those separate lives, then the self of a prior life must either be identical in a truly existent sense with the self of this life or it must be distinct from the self of this life. If the two are identical, then the suffering of stupidity that we experienced in a prior life as an animal would also have to be experienced in this life. Similarly,

[65]S: *Mūlamadhyamakakārikā*, ch. 18, v. 1.

[66]This argument is directed against the Buddhist realist view that the heaps are a series of self-existent physical and mental entities and the nominal self should be identified with some element of that series—for example, either the five heaps collectively or mind consciousness alone. Je Tsongkapa explains the error in this position as follows: "The reason for its incorrectness is that by positing the self as impermanent you fall into nihilism. That is to say, self-existent entities cannot form members of a continuous series in which each succeeding moment arises from the preceding moment, because two contiguous self-existent entities would be completely distinct from one another and therefore the succeeding moment would not be dependent in any way on the one that preceded it" (p. 467). As to how this relates to the self in particular, he notes elsewhere: "Moreover, if you regard [the self] as undergoing a separate arising and passing away with each separate moment, [each of these moments of the self] become distinct in a self-existent sense. In that case, one could not remember one's past lives [as the Buddha did when he declared] '[At that time] I was King Mandhatar,' because the self that existed at that time will have disappeared just as [that persons's] body has, and there will have arisen a self in this life that is distinct from the previous life's self in a truly existent sense" (p. 318).

the happiness that we experience in this life as a human being must also have been experienced in our past life as an animal.

On the other hand, if the selves of two lives are distinct in a truly existent sense, then those two lives would have to be as separate as two totally unrelated persons like Maitri and Upagupta. But then it would not be possible to attain the supernormal wisdom that remembers many past lives. This point is made in the following verse from the *Introduction to the Middle Way*:

> Qualities that are related to Maitri and Upagupta
> Do not form one continuum, because they are separate.
> Entities that are distinct in a self-existent sense
> Cannot properly form part of a single continuum.[67]

The *Root Text on Wisdom* also declares:

> If this [life] were different [from a previous life],
> It could exist even without that [former life].
> Similarly, while that [former] life still existed,
> One could take birth without having died there.
>
> There would be annihilation and the destruction
> Of deeds. Likewise, deeds performed by one
> Would come to be experienced by another.
> These and other consequences would follow.[68]

Another error is that a deed that someone committed could undergo destruction[69] [371b]. You might think that this error is avoided because even though a previous self has ceased to exist, the next self can experience the fruit of the prior deed. However, this position is still subject to many errors. For instance, it would follow that the result of a deed performed by one self-existent person would be experienced by a different self-existent person. This is known as "meeting with the result of a deed that you did not do."[70]

[67]T: *dBu ma la 'jug pa*, ch. 6, v. 61.

[68] S: *Mūlamadhyamakakārikā*, ch. 27, vv. 10–11.

[69]S: *kṛtavipranāśaḥ*, T: *byas pa chud za ba*. This would violate the karmic principle that a deed never loses its power to bear fruit. See Part Two, Day Thirteen, pp. 239–242.

[70]S: *akrtābhyāgamakarma*, T: *las ma byas pa dang phrad pa*. This violates the principle that we cannot meet with the result of a karma that we did not perform. See Part Two, Day Thirteen, pp. 238–239.

When contemplation of these errors enables us to reach a sure and certain understanding that the self cannot be one with the five heaps in a truly existent sense, we have gained a realization of the third key point.

(iv) The key point of determining that the self cannot be distinct from the heaps in a truly existent sense

After we have determined, in the manner just described, that a truly existent self cannot be one with the heaps, we should conclude: "Now no other possibility remains except that the self and the heaps are distinct in a truly existent sense." Then we should examine the errors that follow from this proposition.

For example, the *Root Text on Wisdom* declares:

> It is not correct that the self is distinct
> From the heaps. If it were distinct,
> It could be grasped without the acquisitions;
> Yet it cannot be grasped in that way.[71]

Suppose you had three animals: a goat, a sheep, and a cow. If two of the animals—say, the goat and the sheep—were set apart from the third, it would still be possible to point to the cow and say, "Here is the cow." Similarly, if the self were distinct from the heaps in a truly existent sense, it should be possible to successively eliminate each of the five heaps of form, feeling, conception, compositional factors, and consciousness, and then—after identifying some object that exists independently of the heaps—say, "Here is the self." However, the self cannot be identified in this way.

Several lines of another verse from the *Root Text on Wisdom* say:

> If it were distinct from the heaps
> It would lack the heaps' attributes.[72]

If the self were distinct from the heaps in a truly existent sense, a number of errors would follow that contradict conventional descriptions of the self. For example, the self would lack the attributes of arising, disintegrating, and so on that characterize the heaps as composed entities [372a].[73] It would

[71]Ibid., ch. 27, v. 7.

[72]Ibid, ch. 18, v. 1.

[73]Only entities that are causally produced or "composed" (S: *saṃskṛtadharmaḥ*, T: *'dus byas kyi chos*) have the qualities of arising and passing away, and only such entities could be considered as having substance or being self-existent. Uncomposed entities (S: *asaṃskṛtadharmaḥ*,

also follow that although the heaps are subject to birth, aging, sickness, and death, and the like, the self would not be. In addition, any benefit or harm done to the heaps would not benefit or harm the self.

There are many other unwanted consequences as well. For example, the idea of an "I" or personal self could arise in relation to objects other than the heaps. Also, as already mentioned, a person would not have to experience the result of a deed that he committed, and a person could meet with the result of a deed that he did not commit.

Therefore, when we gain the sure and certain understanding that the self cannot possibly be distinct from the five heaps in a truly existent sense, we have gained a realization of the fourth key point.

This method of analysis can be summarized as follows. We begin by generating in our mind an image of the object to be negated. Then, without letting this image escape from our mind, we examine it using the argument known as the "lack of identity and distinctness." When we determine that the self cannot exist in either of the two ways addressed in this argument, we will gain the clear and certain understanding that the "I" which is mistakenly held to be truly existent by the innate belief in a self does not exist.

The following analogy illustrates how we reach this understanding. Suppose that you have lost a cow and there are only two places it could have gone. Suppose that you also refuse to accept anyone else's word that the cow cannot be found, so you yourself go to those two places and search high, low, and in between. If after making this search the cow still doesn't turn up, you would conclude with a clear certainty that the cow you are looking for and whose image you are holding in your mind is nowhere to be found.

You should reach a similar conclusion about the object of the innate belief in an inherently real self. That is, you should clearly decide that the self-existent "I," which you previously thought was so distinct that it could be seen with the eye or touched with the hand, doesn't exist at all. When the object of this belief completely disappears and you are certain that this "I" is not real, you have gained a genuine understanding of the correct view as explained in the Buddhist Middle Way School. Those practitioners of sharp

T: *'dus ma byas kyi chos*) such as space, the truth of cessation, nirvana, and emptiness have no substance (S: *nirdravyam*, T: *rdzas su med pa*), and thus could not be self-existent. Nor could an uncomposed self be the object of the belief in a self, because the conventionally existent self is an entity that can act on other objects while uncomposed entities are not capable of such action. Chandrakirti writes in his *Elucidation of the Words* (S: *Prasannapadā*): "Regarding that, the heaps have the attributes of arising, abiding, and passing away because they are composed entities. Since the self does not have the attributes of the heaps, it lacks the qualities of arising, abiding, and passing away. Anything that has such a nature could never be designated a 'self,' either because it does not exist at all, like a sky flower, or because it is uncomposed like nirvana. [For the same reasons,] such an entity also could not be the object of the belief in a self" (p. 148).

faculties who have long familiarized themselves with this view [372b] will react as though they had found a precious treasure. However, those of duller faculties will feel a deep fear and apprehension, as though they had lost a precious treasure. Even so, there is nothing especially bad about experiencing this fear.

Once, when the great Je Rinpoche was giving a teaching on the correct view at the Chöding Hermitage near Sera Monastery, Je Sherab Seng-ge became frightened after gaining a realization of emptiness. Because of this, he reached up with his hand and touched the collar of his monk's robe. Realizing what had happened, Je Rinpoche felt pleased and declared, "The one from Nartang has placed something that is conventionally existent on his collar." There is also an account of how several of Je Ngulchuwa's disciples experienced this same fear when he was giving a teaching on the correct view.

After your mind has entered this state of utter emptiness, you may find yourself thinking: "This is emptiness," or "I have realized emptiness." However, because the object of such thoughts is either an affirming negation or an affirmative object,[74] you should not let your mind follow that train of thought. When you gain the realization that the self that you logically refuted does not exist, this understanding should have a cognitive aspect and a perceptual aspect. The cognitive aspect is the firm and certain awareness that the self does not have a truly existent essence. The perceptual aspect is the experience of complete emptiness that comes from merely rejecting the object to be refuted—that is, a truly existent essence. We must use recollection to hold this understanding in our mind and then meditate on it continually.

If our hold on this awareness weakens and it begins to lose clarity, we must first determine whether it is necessary to stop our meditation practice.[75] If we are able to continue, we should again apply the four-point analysis that was explained earlier. After regaining a clear and sharp understanding of emptiness, we should meditate on it continually and one-pointedly.

(Kyabje Rinpoche concluded by making the following two points. Because an absolute emptiness that resembles space appears in the mind when we meditate on this simple negation of a truly existent essence, [373a] this type of practice is called the "space-like realization cultivated during a period of mental composure." This rejection of a false self also causes us to

[74]See above, note 40, for a discussion of affirmative and negative objects, as well as simple negations and affirming negations.

[75]For a discussion of what to do when such difficulties arise, see the section entitled "The fourth fault: failing to apply the antidote," Day Twenty-one, pp. 249–253.

lose our perception of the conventionally existent "I." However, even though we cannot identify the conventionally existent "I" at this time, it isn't necessary to try and verify its existence out of concern that we may be falling into the nihilistic extreme.)

(b) The realization of illusoriness that is cultivated after a period of mental composure

If, after rising from the state of mental composure that was just described, we investigate what sort of entity remains in the wake of our having rejected the object to be negated, we will discover that the only thing left of the "I" is its name. This should bring us to the firm and certain conviction that this merely conventionally existent self is like a magically created illusion in the way it accumulates virtuous and nonvirtuous karma and experiences corresponding "white" and "black" maturations.

For instance, a magically created horse and bull are also perceived by the magician who conjures them. With his mind consciousness, however, he knows that they are not a real horse or a real bull and that they are false appearances. At the same time, he still sees directly and incontrovertibly that the magic horse and bull are doing such things as walking here and there.

Similarly, we must understand that the self lacks a truly existent essence and that it is a mere ascription existing in name only. And yet, despite its being unreal, we must also recognize incontrovertibly how the self accumulates karma and experiences happiness and suffering, and how the doctrine of dependent origination and the qualities of agent and object can be validated in relation to it. Thus, at the same time that we perceive the self to exist experientially, we must also maintain the understanding that it is void of any truly existent essence. Similarly, while having established that the self is void of any truly existent essence, we must continue to recognize that it exists experientially. Cultivating this kind of awareness is what it means to train ourselves in perceiving the self as like a magic illusion.

In the early stages of trying to gain an understanding of the correct view, it is difficult to establish in our mind the empty nature of the self, because we are so strongly conditioned to believing that it possesses a truly existent essence. However, when we reach this later point,[76] the difficulty lies in establishing the validity of the conventional self that is perceived experientially. However, as Nagarjuna declared:

> The incomparable Tathagata
> Taught this dependent origination

[76]That is, when we are trying to establish that the self is like a magic illusion.

With regard to entities, because all entities
Are void of any essence [373b].[77]

Thus, because emptiness serves as the very justification for the doctrine of dependent origination, we must recognize emptiness as giving validity to the entities that we perceive experientially. And since emptiness is explained on the basis of dependent origination, we must also recognize dependent origination as giving validity to emptiness.

How dependent origination serves as a proof of emptiness is critically important to this point. For instance, when we seek to prove that an entity such as a sprout lacks a truly existent essence because it is subject to dependent origination, we must refute the way that the innate belief holds the sprout to exist. More specifically, this innate belief holds that the sprout is not merely established on the strength of a name and a term, and that it possesses its own independent mode of being.

Here is how we refute this belief: If, as our innate belief holds, the sprout possessed a self-existent essence, it would be able to exist entirely on its own without relying on any other causes or conditions such as a name or term. But we know this is not true, because direct experience reveals that a sprout only appears when a number of external conditions—such as water, fertilizer, warmth, and the like—are present. And since its existence is dependent on and conditioned by factors that are distinct from it, it is subject to the principle of dependent origination.

In this way, dependent origination serves as a reason or proof for rejecting the extreme that entities possess self-existent essences and exist independently of other factors. This is what is meant by such phrases as "appearances remove the extreme of being"[78] and "perceive how dependent origination supports the meaning of emptiness."

If a sprout possessed a real essence, it could not be produced through the action of various causes and conditions. It would also be an entity whose essence could never undergo change. However, it is precisely because the sprout does *not* possess a real essence [374a] that we are able to recognize dependent origination as a doctrine in which all logical relations such as cause and effect, agent and object, and so on are valid. This quality of emptiness is what allows a sprout to gradually change into a mature plant, produce grain such as barley, and eventually be eaten by human beings and

[77] *Seventy Verses on Emptiness* (S: *Śūnyatāsaptatiḥ*), v. 68.

[78] "Appearances" (T: *snang ba*) refers to entities that are perceived experientially; "the extreme of being" means the wrong belief that entities possess self-existent essences. This phrase appears in the second of two verses from Je Tsongkapa's *Three Principal Elements of the Path* that are cited below, p. 293.

animals. This is what is meant by such phrases as "emptiness removes the extreme of nonbeing" and "perceive emptiness as dependent origination."[79]

The preceding two points are expressed in the following verse from the *Sutra of Questions Posed by the Naga King Anavatapta*:

> That which arises from conditions is unarisen;
> Its arising is without any essential nature.
> What depends on conditions is said to be void;
> He who knows emptiness has found mindfulness.[80]

A verse from the *Root Text on Wisdom* also declares:

> Because there is no entity whatever
> That does not arise dependently,
> For that very reason there is also
> No entity whatever that is not void.[81]

Similarly, a verse from the *Introduction to the Middle Way* declares:

> Because entities only arise dependently,
> It is not possible to form these conceptions.
> Hence, the dependent-origination proof
> Cuts the entire web of wrong views.[82]

Je Lama Tsongkapa also declared:

> When your understanding destroys all grasping
> at real objects—
> Not alternately, but as soon as you recognize
> The infallibility of dependent origination—
> Then your analysis of the correct view is complete.

[79]See verse from *Three Principal Elements of the Path* cited on the following page.

[80]T: *Klu'i rgyal po ma dros pas zhus pa'i mdo*. The Sanskrit version can be found in Chandrakirti's *Elucidation of the Words* (S: *Prasannapadā*), p. 214.

[81] S: *Mūlamadhyamakakārikā*, ch. 24, v. 19.

[82]T: *dBu ma la 'jug pa*, ch. 6, v. 115.

Moreover, when you realize how appearances remove
the extreme of being
And emptiness removes the extreme of nonbeing,
And how to perceive emptiness in causes [374b] and effects,
You will not be overcome by any extremist view.[83]

Thus, if we gain an understanding of how emptiness and dependent origination are not simply compatible doctrines but how each actually supports the other, we will develop a deeper realization of, and greater regard for, dependent origination as well as all the explanations of cause and effect, agent and object, and so on that are embodied in it. This will also motivate us to improve our spiritual practice as much as possible. In general terms, we will try harder to abandon misdeeds and do virtuous activities. More specifically, we will try to cultivate loving-kindness, compassion, enlightenment mind, and all the related instructions more strongly. In short, we will become practitioners who strive to carry out a spiritual practice in which the elements of means and wisdom are cultivated jointly and not in isolation.

(Kyabje Rinpoche concluded with this observation: Some people believe that cultivating a high regard for the doctrine of karma and other similar attitudes are suitable for beginning practitioners. Then they teach their own disciples a point of view that discredits the validity of karma and its results, claiming this to be an extraordinary instruction. However, such beliefs are actually no better than the ones held by followers of the Indian Lokayata School.[84])

(2) Establishing the insubstantiality of phenomena

This section is made up of two parts: (1) establishing that composed entities are not inherently existent, and (2) establishing that uncomposed entities are not inherently existent.

(a) Establishing that composed entities are not inherently existent

This part also has three divisions: (1) establishing that form is not inherently existent, (2) establishing that mental entities are not inherently existent, and (3) establishing that composed entities which are neither physical nor mental are not inherently existent.

[83] *Three Principal Elements of the Path* (T: *Lam gyi gtzo bo rnam gsum*), v. 12–13.

[84] S: *Lokāyataḥ*, T: *'Jig rten rgyang 'phen pa*. This school denied the existence of past lives and future lives, and was generally critical of all spiritual traditions. It is also referred to as the Charvaka School.

The explanation that I just gave for developing a firm realization that the self lacks any inherent essence can also be applied to other entities. This point is made in the following lines from a sutra:

> Just as you've understood the conception of a self,
> Focus your mind everywhere in the same way [374b].[85]

The *Four Hundred Verses* also declares:

> He who has seen one entity
> Is said to have seen all.
> That emptiness of one thing
> Is the emptiness of all things.[86]

(i) Establishing that form is not inherently existent

Because the minds of ordinary people like us are tainted by ignorance, objects such as form can only be perceived by us in a way that they appear to possess independent essences. And it is this very appearance of having an independent essence that we seek to logically refute. That is, we must refute that entities actually possess the independent essences that they seem to have.

In fact, all entities are subject to the principle of dependent origination. This means that the existence of each entity is dependent upon its own basis of ascription, which is different from the entity itself. The entity is merely projected upon this basis of ascription by means of names and terms. But this is not how objects appear to ordinary persons who have not gained an understanding of the correct view regarding emptiness.

Take an object like a pitcher. To the ordinary person's mind, a pitcher does not appear as merely an ascribed entity whose existence has been projected onto its basis of ascription. Rather, the basis of ascription and the entity projected onto it appear to be combined inseparably. And within this combination, the pitcher is perceived as a distinct and independently existent object. This is how the object to be negated appears to the mind.

Although this is how the object to be negated appears, we can prove that the pitcher does not exist in the way that it is perceived by the innate belief in truly existent entities. This is accomplished by proving that the pitcher is

[85] *King of Concentrations Sutra* (S: *Samadhirājasūtram*), ch. 12, v. 7.

[86] T: *bZhi brgya pa*, ch. 8, v. 16.

neither identical with, nor distinct from, its basis of ascription in a truly existent sense.

We can establish that the pitcher is not identical with its basis of ascription in a truly existent sense, because we know that the basis of ascription and the ascribed entity are distinct.[87] We can also establish that the pitcher is not distinct from its basis of ascription in a truly existent sense, for the following reasons: If we took away the pitcher's basis of ascription, no appearance would be left that we could point to and say, "This is the pitcher" [375b]. Therefore, a pitcher can only appear to a conventional cognition[88] in dependence upon a valid basis of ascription—in this case, a collection of parts that includes a body, spout, base, and so on. By confirming that a pitcher's existence is only valid as a conventional truth entity, we can establish that the pitcher is not distinct from its basis of ascription in a truly existent sense.

It is a general principle that if something exists, it is either one or many. Likewise, if an object is truly existent, it can only be a truly existent one or a truly existent many. If we can show that something is neither of these possibilities, then it is not truly existent. This is how we establish that objects such as a pitcher are not self-existent.

In short, all entities, including form—represented here by a pitcher—are not truly existent, because they are dependent on their respective basis of ascription and therefore cannot exist on their own. As the *Four Hundred Verses* declares:

> Because nothing is independent,
> Essences do not exist.[89]

Here is another explanation. Although, in general, a pitcher is a single entity, it is not a single entity in an inherently existent sense because it must rely on its parts, which are multiple. Moreover, while a pitcher is distinct from a pillar, the separateness that is posited with regard to them is merely that each is different from the other in a mutually dependent sense. They are not distinct in the sense that each is a separate, inherently existent entity. If they were, both a pillar and a pitcher would each have to have this quality of separateness in relation to itself. But this would lead to the error that

[87]They are distinct in a conventionally existent sense. That is, the pitcher is a single entity, while its parts are multiple, and so on.

[88]S: *vyavahārapramāṇam*, T: *tha snyad pa'i tsad ma*. Cognition here means a form of knowledge (S: *pramāṇam*, T: *tsad ma*) that establishes the valid existence of conventional truth entities.

[89]T: *bZhi brgya pa*, ch. 14, v. 23.

neither of them was a single entity. Therefore, while a pitcher is distinct from a pillar, it remains a single entity [376a]. And the singularity and distinctness that are both attributed to a pitcher are nothing but mental concepts that are ascribed to a pitcher; they are not qualities that exist inherently in the pitcher. This is described in the following lines from the *Root Text on Wisdom*:

> An other is an other in dependence on an other.
> An other cannot be an other without an other.[90]

Several lines from the next verse also state:

> If an other were other than an other,
> It would be so even without an other.[91]

(ii) Establishing that mind is not inherently existent

Mind[92] is described as an entity that has the properties of clarity and awareness, and it also engages objects. There are many types of mind, such as the main distinction between consciousness[93] and mental states.[94] These two are differentiated on the basis of whether they perceive an object's essence or its characteristics. The existence of mind is limited to that of an entity that is conceptually projected onto a basis of ascription. In this case, the basis of ascription is a collection of many momentary states. Mind does not possess the slightest degree of self-existent essence. However, this is not how mind appears to us. We perceive it as a self-existent entity that can engage an object independently and without having to rely on anything else. Put another way, mind appears to us as an object that, if analyzed, would reveal itself to have a genuine essence. Both of these descriptions express how the object to be negated appears to us.

[90] *Mūlamadhyamakakārikā*, ch. 14, v. 5.

[91] Ibid., ch. 14, v. 6.

[92] S: *jñānam*, T: *shes pa*. In Tibetan, *blo* (S: *buddhiḥ*) and *rig pa* (S: *vittiḥ*) are synonyms of *shes pa*.

[93] S: *cittam*, T: *sems*. The Tibetan terms *rnam par shes pa* (S: *vijñānam*) and *yid* (S: *manas*) are synonyms of *sems*. Consciousness is described as that which apprehends the essence of its object.

[94] S: *caittaḥ*, T: *sems byung*. Mental states are described as apprehending characteristics of the object.

If, as it appears to be, your mind were self-existent, then today's mind, for instance, would either have to be identical with its various moments in a self-existent sense, or it would have to be distinct from them. If today's mind were distinct from these moments, we could separate it from both the part that exists in the first half of the day and the part that exists in the second half of the day, and still be able to identify some entity about which we could say "this is today's mind." But because today's mind cannot be isolated in this way, it is not distinct in a self-existent sense from the parts of the mind that exist in the first and second halves of the day [376b].

On the other hand, if today's mind were identical in a self-existent sense with the parts that exist in the first and second halves of the day, it would follow incorrectly that—just as those two parts are multiple—today's mind itself would have to be multiple in nature. Another error would be that, just as today's mind exists in the first half of the day, the part of the mind that exists in the second half of the day would also have to exist in the first part of the day. Alternatively, it would follow that, just as the part of the mind that exists in the second part of the day doesn't exist in the first part of the day, neither would today's mind exist in the first part of the day. These and other similar absurd consequences are the methods we must use to gain the sure understanding that mind is not inherently existent because it is neither identical with, nor distinct from, its parts in a self-existent sense.

Another argument is that if the three spheres[95] in an act of perception were identical in a self-existent sense, it would follow erroneously that agent and object are one and the same. On the other hand, if the three spheres were distinct in a self-existent sense, it would have to be true that there could be a perceiving agent even without a perceived object. Or it would be valid for there to be an act of perception even without a perceiving agent. Because of these and other errors, it must be the case that the three spheres in an act of perception are not inherently existent.

Therefore, mind is merely an entity that a conventionally valid cognition projects onto a particular basis of ascription using terms such as "mind" and "awareness." In this case, the basis of ascription is a collection of various conditional factors, including a series of momentary elements that represent the components of mind. Nevertheless, all the causal relations that are described in relation to both samsara and nirvana can be correctly established on the basis of such a nominally existent mind.

[95]The three spheres are: (1) agent, (2) object, and (3) action.

(iii) Establishing that unassociated compositional factors are not inherently existent

I will explain this topic using time as an example.[96] A year is nothing more than the perception [of a particular unit of time] that is ascribed in dependence on a collection of twelve months. Nevertheless, the object to be negated is [a particular unit of time] that has the appearance of being the opposite of that.[97]

After gaining a clear understanding of how the object to be negated appears in the mind, the first thing to establish is that a year is not identical in a self-existent sense with its basis of ascription—that is, a collection of twelve months [377a]. This is done by recognizing the absurdity that if a year were identical with its basis of ascription, a year would have to be twelve in number just as its basis of ascription consists of twelve months. Alternatively, the collection of twelve months would have to be a single entity, just as a year is a single entity. Similarly, we can establish that a year is not distinct from its basis of ascription in a self-existent sense, because after eliminating each of the twelve months there would be nothing left that we could point to and say, "This is the year." This analysis should result in the determination that a year is nothing more than a name ascribed by a conventionally valid cognition in relation to the basis of ascription of

[96] Buddhist philosophy classifies all existent things into composed entities (S: *saṃskṛtaḥ*, T: *'du byas*) and uncomposed entities (S: *asaṃskṛtaḥ*, T: *'du ma byas*). Composed entities are those that are produced by causes; uncomposed are those that are uncaused. Composed entities—that is, entities that are causally produced and momentary—are further divided into the five heaps (S: *skandhaḥ*, T: *phung po*): form, feeling, conceptions, compositional factors (S: *saṃskāraḥ*, T: *'du byed*), and consciousness. The causally produced entities included in the five heaps are of three types: physical matter or form (S: *rūpam*, T: *gzugs*), mind (S: *jñānam*, T: *shes pa*) and the so-called "unassociated compositional factors" (*viprayuktasaṃskāraḥ*, T: *ldan min 'du byed*). Unassociated compositional factors are a group of nonphysical, nonmental relations that are discussed in Buddhist philosophical literature. Some refer to certain conditions of mental composure in which most mental activity has ceased. Others are more familiar as universal topics of philosophical inquiry. Asanga's *Compendium of Higher Learning* (S: *Abhidharmasamuccayaḥ*) includes this list of twenty-three: (1) attainment, (2) the state of mental composure in which there is no conception, (3) the state of mental composure in which all mental activity has ceased, (4) the condition whereby mental states are kept from functioning in the state of mental composure where there is no conception, (5) life force, (6) similarity, (7) arising, (8) aging, (9) continuation, (10) impermanence, (11) names, (12) words, (13) letters, (14) the condition of being an ordinary person, (15) continuity, (16) fixed diversity, (17) joining, (18) quickness, (19) sequential order, (20) time, (21) direction, (22) number, and (23) convergence.

[97] More specifically, the object to be negated here is a year that is not merely ascribed in dependence on a collection of twelve months and is an independent and truly existent unit of time.

twelve months. Hence, there is no such thing as a year that exists independently from its own side.

(b) Establishing that uncomposed entities are not inherently existent

Uncomposed entities include such things as the two cessations,[98] space, and emptiness. They are called "uncomposed," because they do not come into being on the basis of causes and conditional factors. I shall explain this topic using the example of space.

The existence of space is established only in a conventionally existent sense as a simple negation.[99] It is the mere absence of obstruction by or contact with a physical object. If the whole of space were identical with its parts in a self-existent sense—that is, if it were identical with the space located in the east, south, west, and north, etc.—then the two aspects of eastern space and western space would become a single entity. And if that were so, then whenever the sun rose in the sky of the eastern continent Videha, it would also rise in the sky of the western continent Godaniya.[100]

On the other hand, if the whole of space were distinct in a self-existent sense from its parts, then the whole and its parts would become completely separate and unrelated [377b]. In that case, it would have to be true that if we eliminated all the parts of space that exist in the cardinal and intermediate directions, as well as in the zenith and nadir, we would still be able to point to some entity and say, "This is space." Because neither of these possibilities is valid, space does not have a truly existent essence.

(Kyabje Rinpoche concluded this section with a discussion of the following point. Some people believe that emptiness has a truly existent essence.

[98]The two cessations are called "analytic cessation" (S: *pratisaṃkhyānirodham*, T: *so sor brtags pa'i 'gog pa*) and "nonanalytic cessation" (S: *apratisaṃkhyānirodham*, T: *so sor brtags pa ma yin pa'i 'gog pa*). The analytic cessation is the permanent condition of having removed any of the two types of mental obscurations. These are all the instances of the third of the Four Noble Truths—that is, the Noble Truth of Cessation. The nonanalytic cessation is defined as a condition in which an event is unable to occur because of the absence of the necessary causes. The *Commentary to the Treasury of Higher Learning* gives the following description: "For example, when [the organs of] the eye and mind are occupied with a particular visible form, all other existing visible forms, sounds, smells, tastes, and tangible objects, move into the past. When that occurs, the five sense consciousnesses that might have been directed toward any of those objects will not be able to arise, because they cannot engage objects that exist in the past."

[99]See note 40 above.

[100]Classical Buddhist cosmology describes the world as being comprised of four continents. The Tibetan equivalents of the eastern and western continents are Lüpakpo (T: *Lus 'phags po*) and Balangchö (T: *Ba lang spyod*), respectively. For a detailed account, see chapter 3 of Vasubandhu's *Commentary to the Treasury of Higher Learning* (S: *Abhidharmakośabhāṣyam*).

However, this view is mistaken and particularly unacceptable. The following sutra passage describes it as one that cannot be remedied:

> It would be better to have a belief in the existence of a real self as large as Mt. Meru than to believe that emptiness has a truly existent essence.

We can recognize the error of this position by realizing how even emptiness can be distinguished as having many parts through its basis of ascription. We should also understand how emptiness has many parts based on the range of objects about which it is predicated. We may further consider whether emptiness is either identical with or distinct from these parts in a self-existent sense, and whether emptiness and the objects about which it is predicated could exist independently of one another.

As it is declared in a sutra: "If form itself cannot be apprehended [as being self-existent], how much less then could the suchness of form be perceived.")

(3) The method of developing insight

Earlier I described how we can achieve quiescence through cultivating the concentrations associated with the nine levels of mental stability and how the mental quality known as agility[101] is related to quiescence. However, even if we can maintain the mental agility associated with quiescence, this alone will not allow us to achieve insight. So now I shall explain the process by which insight is achieved in relation to meditating on the insubstantiality of the self.

As I already explained, the innate mistaken view of the self holds that the "I" or subjective self is inherently existent. Using the four-point analysis, you must gain a certain understanding that the self that appears within the five heaps lacks any such inherently real essence. When you have gained a very clear understanding of this emptiness, use your recollection to keep hold of it firmly. Then cultivate a state of mental equipoise using vigilance to keep yourself from developing languor or excitation [378a].

If your hold on the meditation object shows signs of becoming weak or of losing its clarity, repeat the four-point analysis and other steps as before. When you have regained a firm understanding, again fix your mind one-pointedly on the meditation object of emptiness. Continue meditating this way with the aim of developing mental stability toward this object. When

[101]The two forms of agility (S: *praśrabdhiḥ*, T: *shin tu sbyangs pa*) that precede the attainment of quiescence are discussed above, p. 263. This mental state is also discussed in Day Twenty-one; see p. 240, note 29, in particular, for a definition.

you gain that stability, then practice analytic meditation energetically using such methods as the four-point proof to examine the meditation object. This exercise can be compared to a small fish darting around in an extremely clear pond whose waters are undisturbed by wind.

(Kyabje Rinpoche concluded the day's discourse with the following description of how to recognize when insight has been attained. After cultivating equal measures of stability and discriminating wisdom for an extended period of time in this way, you will gradually achieve the same nine levels of mental stability that were described before.[102] Finally, through the strength of your analytic meditation, you will develop an extraordinary form of agility that is much greater than what you experienced previously when you were cultivating quiescence. The point that marks the attainment of real insight practice is when your analytic meditation effortlessly changes into placement meditation.[103] In this instance, I have been discussing the insight practice that has emptiness as its object. This type of meditation is also known as the "union of quiescence and insight.")

[102]These are the same nine levels that were explained in relation to quiescence. See Day Twenty-one, pp. 256–260.

[103]Analytic meditation (T: *dpyad sgom*) is the main type of practice that is applied to all the Lamrim topics with the exception of quiescence. See also Day Sixteen, note 31, as well as Part One, Day Six, note 103 and Part Two, Appendix F. The aim of placement meditation (T: *'jog sgom*) is to focus the mind on an object steadily and one-pointedly. This type of meditation is what is practiced when one is trying to achieve quiescence.

DAY TWENTY-THREE: THE ADAMANTINE VEHICLE, THE FOUR PRINCIPLES FOR ATTRACTING A FOLLOWING, AND PREPARATIONS FOR THE RITUAL METHOD OF DEVELOPING ENLIGHTENMENT MIND

(Kyabje Rinpoche began the discourse by quoting a verse by the great dharma king Je Tsongkapa, which contains the lines "[O son, when you have realized properly in this way/] The key points relating to the three principal elements of the path . . ."[1] Then, after giving a brief explanation of how to correct one's motivation, he enumerated the sections of the outline that he had completed on the preceding days. Following this, he began the next topic of the outline.)

c) How to train oneself in the Vajrayana path

Now I shall describe how we train ourselves in the unique practices of the adamantine vehicle. First, we must develop an experiential realization of renunciation by practicing the paths associated with persons of lesser and moderate capacity [378b].[2] Then we must do the same with enlightenment mind, based on the practices of the path for practitioners of great capacity. After gaining that experiential realization, we must achieve a sure understanding of the correct view regarding emptiness. Only then should we undertake to practice the teachings of the secret Mantrayana.

If we attempt to enter the tantric path without first having gained those three knowledges, then our efforts will not serve as methods for achieving liberation and ultimate enlightenment. Like a small child mounted on the back of a wild horse, not only will we fail to gain any positive result but we will also be exposing ourselves to a very great danger. On the other hand, if we enter the Mantrayana path after having generated experiential realizations of the three principal elements of the path, then we are sure to benefit from the quality of swiftness that is inherent in the tantric path.

The secret Mantrayana teachings are said to be even more rare than a Buddha. And if we rely on the practices of the Anuttarayoga Tantra path in particular, it is possible to achieve the state of Ultimate Union that is beyond

[1] *Three Principal Elements of the Path* (T: *Lam gyi gtzo bo rnam gsum*), v. 14. The complete verse states: "O son, when you have realized properly in this way/ The key points relating to the three principal elements of the path,/ Take yourself to an isolated place and, after generating/ The power of effort, quickly achieve the ultimate goal."

[2] See Day Fifteen, pp. 43–45 for a description of genuine renunciation.

any need for further training, within a short lifetime of the current degenerate age. Therefore, it is essential that we undertake to train ourselves in this path.

Now, it is wrong for us to request the ritual[3] that grants permission to recite the mantras of such deities as Hayagriva and Vajrapani simply for the purpose of eliminating temporary obstacles. Rather, we must approach a qualified Vajra Acharya and seek to enter the mandala of Guhya Samaja, Chakra Samvara, or Vajra Bhairava, where we can receive in a pure and correct manner the four initiations that implant the seeds of a Buddha's four bodies. Then we must keep all the vows and pledges taken during such an initiation as if we were protecting our very own eyes. In addition, we must learn and put into practice the profound instructions on the two stages of the Anuttarayoga Tantra path. It is a very great accomplishment to complete all these steps, because it means that our practice encompasses all the teachings contained in the Buddhist tradition.

By learning well the methods for proceeding along this holy path [379a], we will gain a thorough understanding of all the aspects of both the sutra and tantra vehicles, from the starting point of how to serve a spiritual teacher all the way to the state of Ultimate Union that is beyond training. (Kyabje Rinpoche concluded by saying that when many of the disciples present at a Lamrim teaching have not received an Anuttarayoga Tantra initiation, it is customary only to give a brief outline of how to train oneself in the Vajrayana path and not to teach in detail any of the actual practices.)

2) How to ripen others' minds by training oneself in the four methods of attracting a following

A verse from the *Ornament of Mahayana Sutras* declares:

> Generosity is understood to be the same;
> Pleasant speech is to teach them;
> Beneficial conduct is causing them to be practiced;
> Sameness of purpose is adhering to them oneself.[4]

[3]S: *anujñā*, T: *rjes su gnang ba*. The term literally means "permission." As it is being used here, it refers to a type of blessing ritual that allows the practitioner to receive teachings on a particular deity's meditation practice and mantra recitation. It is distinguished from an empowerment or initiation (S: *abhiśekhaḥ*, T: *dbang*) that is usually associated with tutelary deities of Yoga Tantra and Anuttarayoga Tantra.

[4]S: *Mahāyānasūtrālaṃkāraḥ*, ch. 16, v. 72. The first line states that the generosity being referred to here is the same as the generosity that is the first of the six perfections (see Day Twenty, pp. 209–214). The pronoun "them" in this verse refers to the six perfections. Thus,

As this verse states, Bodhisattvas must strive to do what is beneficial for others. And the way to accomplish this is by bringing about the spiritual ripening of their minds through the four principles for attracting a following.[5]

The first principle is to practice generosity.[6] Because ordinary people can easily be won over by material things, we should initially please others and persuade them to become part of our following through giving them material goods. This is done so that we can eventually lead them to the path.

The second principle is to practice pleasant speech.[7] This means that once we have attracted a following, we should speak to them according to the norms of ordinary society. But primarily it means that we should teach them dharma in a manner that best suits their faculties and aspirations.

The third principle is to practice beneficial conduct.[8] This means that we should persuade our followers to train themselves gradually in the path of the holy dharma that we taught to them according to their faculties.

The fourth principle is to practice sameness of purpose.[9] This means that we ourselves should practice the dharma in the same manner that we have instructed others to practice it [379b].

These four principles for attracting a following are the method we must use to accomplish what is beneficial for sentient beings.

This concludes the explanation of the main practice.

2) The ritual method of adopting enlightenment mind

Earlier,[10] I mentioned that I was postponing until later the topic entitled "The ritual method of adopting enlightenment mind." This is what I am going to take up now.

The ritual method of adopting enlightenment mind consists of two parts: (1) the method for gaining the vow that has not been taken previously, and

pleasant speech means to teach the six perfections to others; beneficial conduct means to cause others to practice the six perfections; and sameness of purpose means to practice the six perfections oneself. All four are done as the means of attracting followers and aiding them in their spiritual development.

[5]S: *catur saṃgrahavastūni*, T: *bsdu ba'i dngos po bzhi.*

[6]S: *dānam*, T: *sbyin pa.*

[7]S: *priyavaditā*, T: *snyan par smra ba.*

[8]S: *arthacaryā*, T: *don spyod pa.*

[9]S: *samānārthatā*, T: *don mthun pa.*

[10]See Day Twenty, p. 207.

(2) the method for preserving the vow so that it will not degenerate once it has been taken.

a) The method for gaining the vow that has not been taken previously

The phrase "ritual method of adopting enlightenment mind" should be understood in the following sense. If you have previously gained at least the first elements of experiential realization in relation to enlightenment mind and you then adopt enlightenment mind by participating in this ritual, you will be able to generate the Bodhisattva vows. On the other hand, you will not be able to generate the Bodhisattva vows if you simply repeat the words of the ritual without ever having gained any experiential realization of enlightenment mind whatsoever. Nevertheless, if a person who has never gained any experiential realization of enlightenment mind participates in the ritual, he will still be able to implant a favorable karmic impression in his mind. Therefore, it is very important for even such a person to maintain an earnest and solemn attitude during the ceremony.

Those who have previously gained some experiential realization of enlightenment mind should perform the visualizations and other elements of the ceremony conscientiously. If you are able to receive the Bodhisattva vows in this manner, you will have generated them in relation to an extraordinary object. You will also raise your enlightenment mind to a higher level and cause it to become much firmer.

There are three ways of performing the ritual for generating enlightenment mind. In the abbreviated form, there is no preliminary stage. In the intermediate form, both the preliminary stage and the main ritual are performed on the same day. In the extensive form, the preliminary stage and the main ritual are performed on two separate days. Here we will be performing the extensive form of the ritual.

It is a custom in this tradition that a preparatory teaching must be given when the ritual for generating enlightenment mind is going to be performed after an initiation, an oral recitation blessing, or a teaching different from one such as I have given here on the stages of the path to enlightenment. On those occasions, it is necessary to give a complete and extensive teaching on the common elements of the path [380a].[11] However, because the ritual is being performed in connection with the present teaching on the stages of the path to enlightenment, it is not necessary to give any additional

[11] "Common elements of the path" (T: *thun mong ba'i lam gyi rim pa*) means those elements of the Mahayana path that are common to both the sutra and tantra traditions. This phrase should be taken as synonymous with the Lamrim teachings.

preliminary instructions beyond those that have already been taught extensively. (Kyabje Rinpoche also remarked that those teachers who perform the ritual for generating enlightenment mind in the future must take note of whether the ceremony is being held in connection with a teaching on the stages of the path or not.[12]

During the recitation of the ritual for the six preliminary practices, the extensive offering verses were recited and the mandala offering verses were repeated many times. After a second mandala offering was presented to Kyabje Rinpoche as part of the request to give teachings, he briefly explained the preliminary exercise of correcting one's motivation.)

Now, you must make the strongest effort possible—both tonight and tomorrow morning—to generate the various understandings and visualizations that I have explained during these teachings. In addition, tomorrow you must invite the gurus, Buddhas, and Bodhisattvas to witness your act of generating enlightenment mind. You must also make prostrations and present offerings to them.

We all know how inappropriate it would be to invite a wheel-wielding monarch to a beggar's home or to invite such a person to a home that is dirty and filled with dust. Therefore, at the conclusion of this assembly, you should sweep the floor of the hall thoroughly, taking care not to harm any sentient beings. Then sprinkle fragrant water and hang decorative flower garlands. The teacher's throne should also be prepared by adorning it with flowers and jewels.

As relates to offerings, the great Lord Atisha is reported to have said once that his Tibetan disciples would not be able to generate enlightenment mind successfully because the offerings they had prepared were inferior. Therefore, you should not prepare inadequate offerings. Tradition states that they should be equal in value to one sixth of all your wealth [380b]. In any case, arrange as many offerings as you can and in such a way that your friends would be astonished at the sight of them.

Tomorrow, during the actual ritual, you must do a number of activities to accumulate merit, purify yourselves of obscurations, protect yourselves from obstacles, and the like, so that you will be able to generate enlightenment mind successfully. For the morning period, it would be ideal if the entire Kangyur collection could be recited. Barring that, extensive scriptures like the *Buddha Ornament Sutra* should be recited. If even that is not possible, those who are able to recite well must carefully chant at least the *Perfection of Wisdom Sutra in Eight Thousand Lines* and the *Sutra on the*

[12]That is, they must consider whether it is necessary to give preliminary instructions or not.

Fortunate Aeon.[13] It is also said that a Water Torma[14] and a *torma* offering to spirits should be made. Therefore, we will also perform the Three-Part Torma offering[15] before beginning the main ritual.

We are all aware that householders celebrate worldly events that are related to this life. They also hold parties and get dressed up to mark the end of one year and the beginning of a new one. Why, then, shouldn't we dharma practitioners also hold a celebration to mark the occasion when we generate the pledge to achieve unsurpassed enlightenment, enter the Mahayana path, and become spiritual sons and daughters of the Conquerors? Therefore, tomorrow morning you should dress in new clothes. Those of you who are monks should wear your *namjar*[16] along with the other religious garments. Everyone should bathe and make themselves clean. As the former Buddhas did, you must also bring to the ceremony an appropriate offering to present at the time that you generate enlightenment mind.

When entering the hall, don't regard it as an ordinary building but rather as a divine, square-shaped palace with four doors. Visualize that each door is guarded by one of the four Maharajika[17] deities, along with his retinue of a hundred thousand followers and attendants [381a]. Reflect that all around the outside of the palace the benevolent gods have gathered for the purpose of generating enlightenment mind and receiving the Bodhisattva vows. Imagine also that the four walls inside the palace depict scenes from the former lives of our Master in which he engaged in Bodhisattva activities while he was still training in the path. Think of these paintings as so lifelike that the Master seems to be actually performing the activities right now. As you view these scenes, rejoice at the Buddha's former deeds and pray that some day you might be able to perform them yourselves.

After the guru has been invited to appear at the beginning of the second period of assembly, you must carefully do practices to accumulate merit

[13]This sutra is listed in the Kangyur as [*'Pags pa*] *bsKal pa bzang po zhes bya ba theg pa chen po'i mdo.* It lists the thousand Buddhas that are prophesied to appear in this kalpa and details such things as the lineage into which each one will be born, who their parents will be, what kind of retinue they will have, their life spans, how long their teachings will remain, and the manner in which they first generated enlightenment mind.

[14]*Chab gtor.*

[15]*Cha gsum gtor ma.* A *torma* offering that is made to three recipients: (1) the "higher" objects of the lamas and Three Jewels in general; (2) the guardians of the ten directions; and (3) the six realms' beings in general, along with harmful spirits in particular.

[16]S: *samghātiḥ*, T: *snam sbyar.* A cloak-like religious garment with strips of material sewn on it in a patchwork pattern; usually worn on formal religious occasions.

[17]T: *rGyal chen ris bzhi.* Dhirtarashtra (T: *Yul 'khor bsrung*) guards the eastern door, Virudhaka (T: *'Phags skye bo*) the southern door, Virupaksha (T: *sPyan mi bzang*) the western door, and Vaishravana (T: *rNam thos sras*) the northern door.

and purify yourselves of your obscurations as a way of helping to generate enlightenment mind. This is accomplished by reciting an extensive version of the ritual for the six preliminary practices. Be especially diligent in practicing the sections of the recitation that represent activities for accumulating merit and removing obscurations. Regard the guru as Lord Buddha Shakyamuni and when he explains the different visualizations, do them meticulously.

In general, the simple desire to achieve Buddhahood in order to benefit all sentient beings represents the wishing form of enlightenment mind.[18] The willingness to do Bodhisattva activities after having generated that aspiration represents the active form of enlightenment mind.[19] The former mind can be compared to making preparations to go to India and the latter to the actual setting out on the road that leads there.[20]

There are two traditions about the rituals for adopting these two types of enlightenment mind. According to *Bodhisattva Levels*, the wishing and active forms of enlightenment mind should be generated in separate rituals. According to *Engaging in Bodhisattva Activities*, the two can be generated simultaneously. It does not matter which of these systems is followed; both are considered valid [381b]. Some claim that the two systems represent the separate traditions of the Middle Way and the Mind Only Schools. However, there is no disagreement between these two schools over the ritual for generating enlightenment mind.

(Kyabje Rinpoche concluded with these comments. The position of our Gelukpa tradition is that the former system[21] is meant to provide a separate ritual for those who can only generate the wish to achieve enlightenment, but are not ready to train themselves in the Bodhisattva activities. The latter system is meant for those individuals who are able to generate both forms of enlightenment mind. Tomorrow, I shall follow the one in which both wishing enlightenment mind and active enlightenment mind are generated simultaneously.

[18]S: *praṇidhicittotpādaḥ*, T: *smon pa sems bskyed*. The two basic forms of enlightenment mind are conventional enlightenment mind and ultimate enlightenment mind (see Day Five, note 37). Conventional enlightenment mind is also distinguished between the wishing enlightenment mind and the active enlightenment mind (see also Day Two, note 37).

[19]S: *pravṛtticittotpādaḥ*, T: *'jug pa sems bskyed*.

[20]See Shantideva's description in his *Engaging in Bodhisattva Activities* (S: *Bodhicārya-avatāraḥ*, ch. 1, vv. 15–16): "In brief, enlightenment mind is known/ As being of just two types:/ The mind that aspires to enlightenment/ And the mind that sets out for enlightenment./ As the difference is understood/ Between going and wanting to go/ Just so do the wise recognize, respectively,/ The difference between these two."

[21]The one associated with Asanga's *Bodhisattva Levels*.

Following this, we presented the mandala offering that is meant to show appreciation for the teachings. After the Lamrim prayer, our precious guru led us in a recitation of several verses. We recited the Supremely Precious Enlightenment Mind verse[22] three times, and one time each the verses that contain the lines "May all sentient beings who are our fathers and mothers find happiness,"[23] and "May our glorious guru live a long life."[24] Finally, after reciting the prayer known as *All the Conquerors Without Exception*,[25] the preliminary stage of the ritual for generating enlightenment mind was concluded.)

[22]"May I generate that supremely precious enlightenment mind/ That I have not yet generated;/ And without losing that which I have generated,/ May I develop it to ever higher levels" (T: *Byang chub sems mchog rin po che/ Ma bskyed pa ni bskyed gyur ching/ Bskyed pa nyams pa med par yang/ Gong nas gong du 'phel bar shog*). Source not identified.

[23]"May all sentient beings, who are our fathers and mothers, find happiness./ May all the lower realms always remain empty./ No matter who they are or where they may be,/ May all Bodhisattvas see their prayers fulfilled" (T: *Pha ma sems can thams cad bde dang ldan gyur cig/ Ngan 'gro thams cad rtag tu stong pa dang/ Byang chub sems dpa' gang la sus bzhugs pa/ De dag kun gyi smon lam 'grub gyur cig*). Source not identified.

[24]"May our glorious guru live a long life;/ And after accumulating the merit and purifying the obstacles,/ May I and all others quickly achieve the Buddhahood/ That is the source of happiness for all beings as limitless as space" (T: *dPal ldang bla ma'i sku tse brtan pa dang/ mKha mnyam yongs la bde skyid 'byung ba'i gnas/ bDag gzhang ma lus tsogs bsags sgrib sbyangs nas/ Myur du sangs rgyas go 'phang thob par shog*). Source not identified.

[25]T: *rGyal ba ma lus ma*. This work is commonly found in modern Tibetan prayer books printed in India. In these prayer books, it is referred to by the title *Teaching of the Conqueror Losang* (T: *Blo bzang rgyal bstan ma*). See listing in Bibliography under author's name (*rJe Gung thang pa*) *dKon mchog bstan pa'i sgron me*. See also Day Fifteen, pp. 88–89 and accompanying note 133 for another reference to this work.

DAY TWENTY-FOUR: THE MAIN RITUAL FOR DEVELOPING ENLIGHTENMENT MIND

(During the first period of assembly, various activities were carried out, such as reciting sutras, presenting *torma* offerings, and the like. During the second teaching period, our precious guru was invited to take his seat on the teaching throne. Then the ritual for the six preliminary practices, together with the offering verses, was chanted in its extensive form. In addition, the mandala offering was presented to the guru as part of the request to perform the ritual for generating enlightenment mind and receiving the Bodhisattva vows. During the mandala offering, everyone held in their hands the special object that was to be offered as part of the act of generating enlightenment mind. When the mandala offering was completed, the special objects were brought before the guru and piled in a large heap in front of him.

Kyabje Rinpoche began the session by quoting the verses by the great Je Tsongkapa, dharma king of the three realms, which contain the line "Generating enlightenment mind is the mainstay of the supreme vehicle's path"[1] [382a]. Next he described the benefits of generating enlightenment mind as he had done on an earlier day.[2] Then he began the explanations for the day's topic.)

You must generate an experiential awareness of all the Lamrim topics one after the other, starting with the difficulty of finding a human form that possesses the various qualities of leisure and fortune. When you reach the point of reflecting on the object that motivates you to generate enlightenment mind, you should visualize that you are surrounded by all sentient beings, and that all the six classes of beings are appearing in a human form. Moreover, imagine that all male sentient beings are seated to your right and appear as your elderly fathers. Similarly, all female sentient beings are seated to your left and appear as your elderly mothers.

[1]*Brief Stages of the Path* (T: *Lam rim bsdus don*), v. 20–21. The complete passage states: "Generating enlightenment mind is the mainstay of the supreme vehicle's path./ It is the foundation and support for the powerful Bodhisattva activities./ It is like an alchemic elixir for all aspects of the two accumulations./ It is a treasure of merit that gathers myriad collections of virtue./ Having realized this, the heroic sons of the Conquerors/ View the jewel-like supreme enlightenment mind as their most important practice./ I, a yogi, have carried out such a practice./ You, O seeker of liberation, are urged to do the same."

[2]See Day Sixteen.

Next visualize the guru as appearing in the form of Buddha Munindra.[3] Surrounding him are countless Buddhas, including the thousand Buddhas of this fortunate eon. Also invite the lineage gurus and sons of the Conquerors to appear before you. Visualizing yourself in the presence of this assembly, assume a kneeling position with your right knee touching the ground.

(For the actual ceremony, our precious guru explained the meaning of each of the verses before leading his disciples in their actual recitation. First, he recited aloud, three times each, the *Buddha, Dharma, Assemblage* verse[4] and the verse called "Freeing all beings from the perils of samsara and quietude."[5] The purpose of these verses is to take refuge and generate wishing enlightenment mind in the form of a *mönlam* prayer. Next came the main verses for generating both the wishing and active enlightenment minds simultaneously. As Kyabje Rinpoche recited aloud three times the words to the verses for taking the vows, we disciples repeated them after him. The verses are the ones that begin with the supplication "O gurus, Conquerors and Conquerors' sons . . ."[6] Following this, we recited once each of the verses that urge us to rejoice in the holy act just completed and to carefully observe the Bodhisattva precepts [382b].[7]

Following the recitation, Kyabje Rinpoche said the following:

> Today, as we generated the pledge to achieve enlightenment, this caused countless Buddha fields in all the ten directions,

[3]See Day Nineteen, note 8.

[4]The complete verse states: "I go for refuge until enlightenment/ To the Buddha, dharma, and supreme assemblage./ Through performing generosity and the other perfections/ May I achieve Buddhahood for the sake of all sentient beings."

[5]The complete verse states: "In order to free all beings from the perils of samsara and quietude,/ May I hold fast to the mind that aspires to achieve/ Perfect enlightenment, from now until I reach Buddhahood./ May I never abandon this mind even to save my life." In his verse "quietude" (T: *zhi ba*) is a reference to Hinayana nirvana.

[6]The text of the verses is as follows: "O Gurus, Conquerors, and Conquerors' Sons,/ I beseech you to hear me now./ Just as the former Sugatas/ Generated enlightenment mind/ And established themselves step by step/ In the trainings of the Bodhisattvas,/ I, too, now generate enlightenment mind/ In order to benefit all sentient beings,/ And pledge to establish myself step by step/ In the trainings of the Bodhisattvas." Except for the opening two lines of supplication, the text of these verses is taken from *Engaging in Bodhisattva Activities* (S: *Bodhicaryāvatāraḥ*), ch. 3, vv. 22–23.

[7]These verses are also from *Engaging in Bodhisattva Activities* (S: *Bodhicaryāvatāraḥ*, ch. 3, vv. 24–25): "My life has now acquired true meaning./ This human existence has been made worthwhile./ Today, I have been born into the Buddhas' family./ Now I have become a son of the Buddhas./ Henceforth, I must undertake by every means possible/ Actions that are in keeping with this lineage./ I must conduct myself in a manner that does not pollute/ This pure and flawless lineage."

> along with the thrones found there, to shake greatly. When the followers of these Buddhas asked what had caused these tremors, they were told: "In the presence of their guru Jampa Tenzin Trinley Gyatso at the Chusang Hermitage in the snowy land of Tibet, a certain group of disciples has generated the pledge to achieve supreme enlightenment. The tremor was caused by the power of this act." After that, everyone present in those Buddha fields prayed that your enlightenment mind should never degenerate and that you should succeed in perfecting the Bodhisattva activities.

Next, Kyabje Rinpoche held an ample quantity of the special offerings in his hand. The remainder of the offerings was held up by several attendants. Then he said the following:)

> All of us have gained an immeasurably large amount of virtue-roots in connection with this teaching on the stages of the path to enlightenment. In order to avoid having all our virtue-roots of the three times go to ruin—especially those associated with the act of generating enlightenment mind that we just performed—we should make a dedication in which we entrust our virtue to the most holy and exalted Lord Maitreya. Then we should pray that this virtue may have the power to cause us to be among his first disciples when he appears in this continent as the supreme emanation body of the Conqueror Lord Maitreya. In addition, we should pray that after becoming his followers and enjoying the holy nectar of his speech, we might receive a prophecy of our own future attainment of unsurpassed enlightenment.
>
> After we have recited this prayer three times, I and the attendants will toss these special offerings into the air [383a]. At that time, you should visualize that all your own virtue-roots as well as these offerings become transformed into the shape of the eight auspicious symbols, the seven objects denoting royal authority, and so on. Then imagine that these offerings reach Tushita paradise and land all around the Exalted One. Finally, reflect that Lord Maitreya accepts our virtue-roots and offers a prayer of his own on our behalf.

(Then Kyabje Rinpoche led us in a recitation of the two verses known as "Some Day at Adamantine Seat"[8] and "On that Day May the Conqueror."[9] After we had recited them three times, the special offerings were tossed in the air.)

b) The method for preserving the vow so that it will not degenerate once it has been taken

This section of the outline has two parts: (1) the instructions that relate to wishing enlightenment mind, and (2) the instructions that relate to active enlightenment mind.

The instructions that relate to wishing enlightenment mind

This topic is comprised of two sections: (1) training ourselves in the causes that will prevent our enlightenment mind from degenerating in this life, and (2) training ourselves in the causes that will prevent us from losing our enlightenment mind in future lives.

Training ourselves in the causes that will prevent our enlightenment mind from degenerating in this life

This section is made up of four points: (1) recalling the benefits of generating enlightenment mind; (2) generating enlightenment mind three times each day and each night, in order to further develop it and to keep ourselves from abandoning it; (3) stopping ourselves from developing the base thought of abandoning all concern for any sentient being who may have acted improperly toward us; and (4) accumulating merit as a means of further developing our enlightenment mind.

[8]T: *Nam shik rdor gden ma*. "Some day when that sun-like Savior, Lord Maitreya,/ Shines forth above the mountaintop at Adamantine Seat,/ May the lotus blossom of my mind be opened/ So that I may satisfy the bee colony of fortunate practitioners." Adamantine Seat (T: *rDo rje gdan*) is the name of the holy site where Buddha Shakyamuni achieved enlightenment (the present-day Bodhgaya) and where all the future Buddhas of this fortunate eon will do so as well.

[9]T: *De tse rgyal ba ma*. "On that day, may the Conqueror Maitreya be greatly pleased with me/ And, after placing his right hand atop my head/ And predicting that I shall attain unsurpassed supreme enlightenment,/ May I quickly achieve Buddhahood for the sake of all beings."

Training ourselves in the causes that will prevent us from losing our enlightenment mind in future lives

This section is made up of two sets of four points. The first set consists of four "black" deeds that must be abandoned. They are: (1) deceiving such persons as our guru, preceptor, or teacher by lying to him, (2) causing another person to regret having performed virtuous deeds, (3) speaking in an unpleasant manner to a Bodhisattva from a motivation of hatred, and (4) deceiving others by being dishonest.

The second set consists of the four "white" deeds that must be cultivated. They are: (1) abandoning lying through maintaining vigilance [383b], (2) maintaining an honest attitude that avoids deceiving others, (3) developing the view toward each and every Bodhisattva that they are the Master, Buddha Shakyamuni, and praising them in a manner that reflects their true qualities, and (4) causing those beings whose spiritual ripening is our responsibility to dedicate themselves to the goal of complete enlightenment.

The instructions that relate to active enlightenment mind

(Next Kyabje Rinpoche explained in detail how we must train ourselves in observing the Bodhisattva vows by not allowing ourselves to become tainted by any of the eighteen root downfalls and forty-six secondary offenses.[10] Following this he gave the following summary remarks.)

You should make every effort to put into practice all the instructions that I have taught over the past several weeks. Do not allow them to remain as nothing more than outer explanatory teachings [that are never internalized]. This is the point being expressed in these lines:

> Realize that I can only instruct you in the means
>   to liberation;
> The actual attainment of liberation is up to you.[11]

For instance, merchants and the like place loads on horses, mules, and other animals according to the abilities of these animals to carry them. In the same way, those of you with lesser, intermediate, and superior intellect should practice dharma in accord with your abilities, at least to some minimal

[10]See *Six-Session Guru Yoga*, pp. 85–102 for an explanation of the eighteen Bodhisattva root downfalls and pp. 155–203 for an explanation of the forty-six secondary offenses. In Bibliography, see listing under Sermey Khensur Lobsang Tharchin.

[11]Source not identified.

degree. You should regard enlightenment mind as the most crucial element of your practice, and learn how to meditate on all the other Lamrim topics in such a way that they support that main practice.

The way to accomplish this is as follows. First, by serving a spiritual teacher properly, you should generate the desire to practice the instruction received from him so that you can derive value from a human form endowed with leisure and fortune. You should also realize that this human form will not last long and [384a] that you have no control over where you will be reborn after you die. If you do not begin to derive value from your life right now, you are likely to be reborn in the lower states, where you will have to experience unbearable suffering. Therefore, you must seek a source of refuge that can save you from that suffering and a method of practice that will liberate you from it.

Then you should continue reflecting carefully as follows. Even if you should escape having to be reborn in the lower states through strenuously practicing these methods, life in the higher states is not free of suffering. Nor have you permanently escaped the possibility of being reborn in the lower states again. These points will enable you to develop the desire to liberate yourself from all of samsara.

You should not, however, be satisfied just with being able to achieve your own liberation. All sentient beings without exception are our mothers and fathers who have shown us great kindness. Only a person of low character could ignore sentient beings and leave them behind. Moreover, even from the standpoint of our own interests, it is not enough that we only gain liberation from samsara. Because there is no question that we must at some point enter the Mahayana path, it would be best if we did so right now. And since the sole entrance to this path is the act of generating enlightenment mind, we must exert ourselves strenuously in practicing the methods for generating this mind.

Once we have evoked the kind of experiential realization in which we are able to generate enlightenment mind effortlessly, we must be willing to endure undertaking the necessary and difficult spiritual activities for a very long period of time in order to benefit all sentient beings. But when we consider the suffering that our elderly mothers will have to experience over that time, we should find that prospect to be completely unbearable. This concern should move us to develop the extraordinary enlightenment mind that seeks to enter the most supreme of all vehicles, the secret Mantrayana path.

The reason for wanting to enter the tantric path is so that we can achieve the state of Ultimate Union in which no more learning is required, within one short lifetime of a degenerate age. The steps for reaching this goal are to find a qualified Vajra Acharya from whom we can receive the four empowerments that will spiritually ripen us [384b]. Then we must practice the direct causes that bring about the Ultimate Union in which the mind of clear light and the illusory body become inseparably joined. In order to ripen ourselves so that we can practice these direct causes, we must also do the meditation practices of the generation stage.

Therefore, before we can achieve the state of Ultimate Union, we must first gain its direct causes, the mind of clear light and both the "pure" and "impure" forms of the illusory body. Similarly, these causes cannot be achieved until we have ripened our mind by completing at least the rough form of the generation stage. But we cannot practice the generation stage until we have received, in a pure form, the four empowerments that firmly plant in us the seeds of a Buddha's four bodies. Moreover, the path that turns us into special vessels that are fit to receive the empowerments is the common Mahayana path in which we purify our mind by cultivating enlightenment mind.

The main cause for developing enlightenment mind is the compassion that cannot bear to see how all sentient beings are tormented by suffering. The foundation of this compassion, in turn, is to cultivate the renunciation that cannot bear the general and specific kinds of suffering that we ourselves must experience in samsara. But before we can gain this attitude, we must first elicit a sense of terror and dread toward the suffering of the lower states. This fear, however, will not be genuine unless we first contemplate the instructions on karma and its results, as well as the uncertainty of the time of death. Therefore, we must also generate the spiritual attitudes that are related to these two topics.

The sole cause that will instill in us the desire to undertake these practices is to reflect on the nature of our leisure and fortune, their great value, and the difficulty of obtaining them. Moreover, all of the above-mentioned spiritual realizations can only be achieved by serving a spiritual teacher properly, through action as well as thought.

So at the very outset, we should not try to undertake too high a level of practice. We should begin with the method of serving a spiritual teacher and gradually train our mind in all the various topics until we become proficient in them [385a]. To become "proficient"[12] in a topic means to gain the confidence that allows you to think to yourself, "If I meditate on this topic at some point in the future, I will definitely be able to generate the proper spiritual realization."

After that, start by meditating on the first Lamrim topic of serving a spiritual teacher until you gain the appropriate contrived experiential

[12]T: *nyams 'og tu tsud pa*. See also Part Two, Appendix F, p. 330.

realization.[13] Then continue practicing in the same way with all the topics that follow. Once you generate the appropriate experiential realization toward a particular topic, you only need to review it by practicing reflective meditation.[14] But for those topics toward which you have not yet generated experiential realizations, train yourself intently and with great diligence.

While we are practicing these topics, it would be a very great loss if we failed to at least establish a karmic propensity for the secret Mantrayana path, since this is a time when we have been able to meet with such a pure teaching system[15] that contains in a complete and unerring form all the elements of both the sutra and tantra traditions. Therefore, we must also gain the ability at least to do reflective meditation for both the generation and completion stage practices of the path associated with any one of the three tutelary deities of Guhya Samaja, Chakra Samvara, or Vajra Bhairava. A person who does this is performing reflective meditation on the path in its totality and is therefore putting into practice the entire path within a single sitting.

Once you have gained contrived experiential realizations for all of the meditation topics up to and including enlightenment mind, go back to the beginning and practice each of them again, in order to generate uncontrived experiential realizations.[16] This method of practice is like the one and only road that leads to a particular destination.

If after achieving an experiential realization of enlightenment mind we practice diligently and properly the two stages of the secret Mantrayana path [385b], we will be able to generate the extraordinary spiritual realizations that are described both in the tantric scriptures and in the treatises composed by the great realized adepts. And before long, we will be able to achieve the same Vajradhara's state of Ultimate Union within one short lifetime of a degenerate age that Gyelwa Ensaba and his spiritual followers did.

Now, then, because we have generated enlightenment mind, let us offer a prayer as a way of beginning to carry out the unsurpassed activities of the Conquerors' sons. Let us pray for an end to the various individual sufferings that are experienced by all the six classes of sentient beings who inhabit this universe reaching to the limitless ends of space. Let us also pray that we may establish all sentient beings in the unsurpassed state of perfect

[13]T: *rtzol bcas kyi myong ba*. See Part Two, Appendix F, p. 330.

[14]T: *bshar sgom*. See Part One, Day Six, note 92, and Part Two, Appendix F, p. 328.

[15]That is, the body of instructions and teaching system established by Je Tsongkapa.

[16]T: *rtzol med kyi myong ba*. See Part Two, Appendix F, p. 330.

enlightenment. We shall do this by reciting the prayer found in *Engaging in Bodhisattva Activities*.

This practice is not one that my own precious guru traditionally followed. However, it was done formerly, at the time of the Great Throne Holder[17] and his spiritual sons. I am restoring this noble tradition, because I believe that it will serve a great and extraordinary purpose. Therefore, we shall now recite this prayer with an undistracted mind. As we do so, I shall also explain the meaning of the verses.

(Kyabje Rinpoche then led us in a recitation of the dedication chapter[18] of the great work *Engaging in Bodhisattva Activities*. Following that, the session concluded with the presentation of a mandala offering of appreciation, the recitation of a *mönlam* prayer, and the chanting of auspicious verses. In this way, our precious guru completed the great act of kindness in which he revealed to us the essence of the entire Buddhist teaching—that noble system known as the Stages of the Path to Enlightenment—and kept it from disappearing during this final era of the Buddha's doctrine. And, in so doing, he clearly and in a most excellent manner illuminated the great lamp of knowledge that dispels all the darkness of the three realms.)

[17]T: *Khri chen*. "Throne Holder" is a reference to the line of official lineage holders of the Gelukpa tradition. This is likely a reference to Trichen Losang Yeshe Tenba Rabgye (T: *Blo bzang ye shes bstan pa rab rgyas*, fl. early nineteenth century).

[18]This is the tenth and final chapter, which consists of 58 verses.

Concluding verses

Having destroyed samsara with the sword of loving-kindness
and compassion,
He[19] rose to become a Master Vajraholder of the Sugata's
teaching.
By proclaiming the Conquerors' excellent deeds with his
unlimited great wisdom,
He aroused all beings from their bed of darkened slumber.

This supreme seal of compassion and emptiness is
a spring-like essence
That increases ultimate happiness as the hare-marked one[20]
enriches the inner oceans.
I honor again this Lord of all spiritual lineages—who opens
my mind fully
As the sun causes a lotus to bloom—by holding him atop
my head as a crown.

A hundred thousand gems of this Savior's oral instruction,
Which satisfy all the wishes of samsara and nirvana,
Fill this visible and tangible treasure chest[21]
So that the fortunate may take them as precious jewels
for the heart.

This well-arranged and multilevel collection of teachings
Is a great spectacle overcoming all that opposes omniscience.
Through its words and knowledge of unrivaled great splendor,
May you enter the supreme vehicle according to the nature
of your faculties.[22]

[19]That is, Kyabje Pabongka Rinpoche. These concluding verses were composed by Kyabje Trijang Rinpoche.

[20]T: *ri bong mtsan ma*. In Indian culture, the moon is said to display the outline of a hare.

[21]A reference to this text, *Liberation in Our Hands*.

[22]The Tibetan weaves into the lines of this verse the phrase "all the teachings are realized to be free of contradiction" (T: *bstan pa thams cad 'gal med du rtogs pa*), which describes the first of the four great attributes of the Lamrim teaching. See Part One, Day Three, pp. 68–71.

The myriad excellent sayings of the Muni are a precious
treasure for all beings.
With the mind that perceives them as the most supreme
of instructions,
One is able to enjoy the spectacle that reveals all things
in their highest form.
This is truly the path that pleases the Conquerors.[23]

The sound of the drum that was beaten to mark victory
over the four demons
And proclaimed the Muni's profound underlying thought
has been recorded unerringly
In this message that bestows with ease the two ultimate aims,
Thereby enabling many followers to traverse the path
so difficult to find.[24]

Where could a path more exalted than this one be found?
It clearly reveals to beings that in the great sea of conduct
unsullied by misdeeds
There lies a spiritual lineage that ripens the essence of the path,
A dependent origination that is not self-existent and does not
arise or pass away.[25]

If you can see that all the wishing gems combined do not equal
This human form so difficult to acquire, and that instead
of enjoying the spectacle
Of this life's common aims you should pursue the
ultimate goal of supreme happiness,
Who would practice anything other than this supreme
path?

[23]The Tibetan of this verse contains the phrase "All the scriptures are recognized as personal instruction" (T: *gsung rab ma lus gdams ngag tu shar ba*), the second of the Lamrim's four great attributes. See Part One, Day Three, pp. 72–77.

[24]This verse contains the phrase "The Conqueror's underlying thought is easily comprehended" (T: *rgyal ba'i dgongs pa bde blag tu rnyed pa*), the third great attribute. See Part One, Day Three, pp. 77–78.

[25]This verse contains the phrase "Great misdeeds are terminated spontaneously" (T: *nyes spyod chen po rang 'gags su 'gro ba*), the fourth great attribute. See Part One, Day Three, pp. 78–80.

Therefore, those who seek liberation should not
Proudly regard a mistaken path as supreme.
Pursue instead this nourishing essence that combines all
instructions into one;
You can be sure that all your wishes will be satisfied.

The mass of virtue gained from creating this work is
the River Ganges;
It is a pearl necklace as lovely as the moon;
And an ornament as long as the fence that encircles
the world.
Through this limitless wonder that dependent origination
magically produced,

May the soothing moon of the Conqueror's immaculate
doctrine—
A crown jewel to be worn atop the head by gods and men
That brings great splendor to those white lotuses of
fortunate disciples—
Dispel forever all the torment of the three realms.

May this noble Genden system[26]—a repository of
treasure creating endless waves
Of teaching and practice that reach to the ends of space,
And an ocean upon which golden lotus flowers bloom—
Remain for a very long time to come.

May Tenzin Gyatso,[27] that lord of mountains who rises
to the heights of samsara and nirvana,
And whose atoms are the gems of all the Conquerors'
wisdom, love, and power,
Remain immutably firm for hundreds of kalpas,
And may his activities shine brightly like the sun and
moon that are his earrings.

[26]The phrase "noble Genden system" (T: *dge ldan lugs bzang*) refers to the tradition established by Je Tsongkapa.

[27]That is, the Fourteenth Dalai Lama.

The splendor of vast delight found in the three timers'[28]
city
Has descended upon this land[29] like clouds during the rainy
season of a golden age.
May this prosperity that forms a canopy across the sky
of merit
Pour down in a nectar-like rain of happiness and
well-being.

May we, too, traverse the path of the supreme vehicle
With the strength of a powerful eagle,
By relying, properly and unceasingly, upon our supremely
kind guru
With the priceless drop inside the crown of our head.

In short, may all beings that reach to the ends of space
Quickly complete the noble activities of the perfections
And achieve, at the foot of the lord of trees, the ten powers
Of the glorious state of adamantine enlightenment.

ଓ ଓ ଓ ଓ

[28]See Day Fourteen, note 101.

[29]Tibet.

Colophon

This teaching was delivered in the courtyard of the Chusang Hermitage[30] in the Iron Bird Year of the fifteenth Rabjung cycle (1921) by our Root Lama, the Omnipotent Lord Dorjechang Pabongkapa, whose kindness is unrivalled, who is the sole embodiment of all the wisdom, love, power, and activities of all the Conquerors of the three times and their spiritual sons, and whose name I utter purposefully as the glorious, exalted and most holy Jampa Tenzin Trinley Gyatso. Motivated by compassion and using inconceivably great skillful means, he enabled me and other ignorant beings like me to enjoy the good fortune of experiencing the supreme Mahayana vehicle.

The event was sponsored by Hlajam[31] Yangzom Tsering, wife of the Kungo[32] of the Hla-lu Gatsel Estate and a person of unparalleled faith and devotion, who expressed the wish that the virtue gained from the teaching be dedicated to the benefit of two deceased Gung-level officials, Jikme Namgyel and Puntsok Rabgye.

Our kind teacher ripened our minds by giving an extensive and profound practical instruction that combined the explanations of three works: (1) the *Quick Path*, an explicit instruction on the stages of the path to enlightenment; (2) *Mañjughosha's Oral Instruction*, including the instructions from both the central and southern lineages; and (3) the *Seven-Point Instruction on Mind Training*, which was taught in conjunction with the instructions on enlightenment mind.

While I, a common and dull-witted person, was enjoying the great opportunity to experience this profound and extensive nectar of speech, Ratö Dragyab Dongkong Trulku Rinpoche had been recording a somewhat informal transcript of each day's teachings. This lama had gone over his notes with our Supreme Holy Lama as far as the fourth preliminary practice and finished adding to and revising them up through the explanations for visualizing the merit field. However, because the activities that our precious Lama carried out on behalf of all beings were as vast as space, this review effort did not continue beyond this point and remained unfinished. Thinking it would serve to promote the activities of our kind Lama and Spiritual Father, I had long held a strong aspiration to complete the editing of this material. A great many fellow disciples who were born from the speech of

[30]T: *Chu bzang ri khrod*. See Part One, Prologue, note 7.

[31]T: *Hla ljam*. General honorific used to refer to the wives of Tibetan noblemen.

[32]T: *sKu ngo*. General honorific used to refer to Tibetan noblemen of rank in the Tibetan government.

our precious Lord—including lamas who bear the responsibility for preserving the Buddha's teaching and *geshes* from all around who teach the great treatises—had also urged me on numerous occasions to complete this task.

The next step was to use the just-mentioned transcript as the root text and then consult all the various other authoritative records of Lamrim teachings that our Lama Dorje Chang had given at different times, in order to carefully examine all his excellent instructions and arrange them into proper order. However, as I myself was caught up in a continuous chain of distractions and did not have the leisure to do so, I asked Gelong Losang Dorje, a secretary/scribe from the Denma region who served our holy Lama for many years, to review the available manuscripts that I had collected and rearrange the explanations among the appropriate topics. Not only was he unrivalled in the way that he honored Kyabje Rinpoche by faithfully carrying out his instructions, but, as Ananda with Buddha Shakyamuni, he also personally had attended most of his teachings. Ignoring the hardship of this lengthy task, Losang Dorje did an excellent job of assisting me in this project.

For my part, whenever I had a spare moment, I went over the manuscript carefully, making slight corrections or deletions in those places where the text did not correspond exactly with our Lama's actual teaching and, in those cases where I thought it appropriate, adding oral instruction from my own knowledge that did not appear in the recorded material.

The effort put forth in compiling this collection of teachings was done with the wish that it might serve as a substitute for our supremely kind Lama's speech and therefore benefit all who use it. This Supreme Lord, who took care of me from the time that I was seven or eight years old, always did so with a great sense of joy. As such, this lowest of his disciples was raised and nurtured by the unsurpassed blessings of his compassion.

Though considered the reincarnation of Lama Yongzin Ganden Trijang, I, Losang Yeshe Tenzin Gyatso, am just a lazy individual lacking any real dharma, as my words are contradicted by my practice. Nonetheless, I did complete this work on a very auspicious Saturday governed by the third lunar mansion Rohini, the 15th day of the tenth lunar month in the Fire Bird Year of the sixteenth Rabjung cycle (1957). May it help the precious teaching on the Stages of the Path to Enlightenment to flourish, thrive, and last in all places, times, and circumstances!

APPENDIX G

AN OUTLINE FOR A PRACTICAL INSTRUCTION BASED ON THE "EASY PATH" OR THE "QUICK PATH," TWO EXPLICIT INSTRUCTIONS ON THE STAGES OF THE PATH TO ENLIGHTENMENT[1]

I make obeisance to and take refuge at the feet of the exalted holy guru, who is endowed with great nonapprehending compassion. May he protect me with his great loving-kindness at all times and in all circumstances.

I. The greatness of the originator, presented in order to demonstrate the authoritative source of the dharma
   A. How Atisha took birth into an excellent family
   B. How Atisha attained knowledge
   C. How Atisha, after attaining knowledge, acted on behalf of the teaching
      1. His activities in India
      2. His activities in Tibet
II. The greatness of the dharma, presented in order to generate respect for the instruction
   A. All the teachings are realized to be free of contradiction
   B. All the scriptures are recognized as personal instruction
   C. The Conqueror's underlying thought is easily comprehended
   D. Great misdeeds are terminated spontaneously
III. The method of both listening to and teaching this dharma, which possesses the two attributes of greatness
   A. The correct manner of listening to dharma
      1. Contemplating the benefits of listening to dharma
      2. Generating reverence for the dharma and the dharma teacher
      3. The actual manner of listening to dharma
         a. Abandoning the three detrimental attitudes, which are like defects of a vessel
         b. Observing the beneficial attitudes of the six conceptions

[1]This outline indicates the number and order of topics that Kyabje Pabongka Rinpoche determined were appropriate when giving a "practical instruction" (T: *nyams khrid*, see Day One, p. 25) on the two works mentioned. In Bibliography see listing under author's name for *Byang chub lam gyi rim pa'i dmar khrid bde myur gyi thog nas nyams khrid stzal skabs kyi sa bcad.*

- B. The correct manner of teaching dharma
  - 1. Recalling the benefits of teaching dharma
  - 2. Generating reverence for the Master and the dharma
  - 3. Thoughts and actions to be employed in teaching
  - 4. Differentiating between those who are suitable to be taught and those who are not
- C. Concluding activities to be performed by both teachers and listeners—namely, dedicating the virtue resulting both from teaching and hearing dharma to the goal of perfect enlightenment

IV. The method of leading the student by means of the actual instruction
- A. The root of the path—how to serve a spiritual teacher
  - 1. What to do during meditation periods
    - a. Preliminary activities: the six preliminary practices
    - b. Main practice
      - i. The advantages of properly serving a spiritual teacher
        - 1) We will be closer to Buddhahood
        - 2) We will please the Conquerors
        - 3) Demons and evil companions will not be able to harm us
        - 4) Our mental afflictions and bad deeds will automatically come to an end
        - 5) All our realizations of the paths and their levels will develop further
        - 6) We will never lack a spiritual teacher in all our future lives
        - 7) We will not fall into the lower states
        - 8) We will achieve all temporary and ultimate aims effortlessly
      - ii. The disadvantages of not serving, and of improperly serving, a spiritual teacher
        - 1) In scorning our guru, we scorn all the Conquerors
        - 2) To become angry with our guru destroys so much virtue that we will have to remain in the hells for as many kalpas as the number of instants that the anger lasted
        - 3) Though we practice the Mantrayana, we will not attain the supreme goal
        - 4) Even if we try to practice tantra diligently, it will be as if we were striving to be born in the hells
        - 5) We will generate no new knowledge and lose what knowledge we may have developed previously

6) We will be afflicted in this life by illnesses and other adversities
7) In future lives we will wander endlessly in the lower states
8) We will be without a spiritual teacher in all our future lives

iii. Serving a spiritual teacher through thought
1) The root practice of cultivating faith
a) Why we should regard our guru as a Buddha
b) Why it is possible to regard our guru as a Buddha
c) How to regard our guru as a Buddha
i) Vajradhara affirmed that our guru is a Buddha
ii) A guru is the agent for all Buddhas' activities
iii) Even nowadays Buddhas and Bodhisattvas are acting on behalf of all sentient beings
iv) Our perceptions are unreliable
2) Generating respect by recalling the spiritual teacher's kindness
a) The guru is more kind than the Buddhas
b) His kindness of teaching dharma
c) His kindness of blessing our minds
d) His kindness of using material objects to gather disciples

iv. Serving a spiritual teacher through action
1) Offering him material things
2) Showing him honor and respect
3) Following his instructions exactly

c. Conclusion

2. What to do between meditation periods

B. How to practice the stages for training the mind once we have served a spiritual teacher
1. An admonition to derive value from a human form that has leisure
a. Identifying leisure and fortune
b. Contemplating the great value of leisure and fortune
c. Contemplating the difficulty of acquiring leisure and fortune
2. The methods of deriving value from a human form possessing leisure and fortune
a. Training the mind in the levels of the path that are held in common with persons of lesser capacity
i. Generating an attitude of concern for future lives

1) Recalling death in the sense that we do not remain long in this life
    a) The disadvantages of failing to recall death
        i) The disadvantage that we will fail to recall dharma
        ii) The disadvantage that, although we might recall dharma, we will fail to practice it
        iii) The disadvantage that, even though we might attempt to practice dharma, we will not do so correctly
        iv) The disadvantage that our practice will lack intensity
        v) The disadvantage that we will develop a bad character
        vi) The disadvantage that we will have to die in a state of regret
    b) The advantages of recalling death
        i) The advantage of bringing great value to our practice
        ii) The advantage of bringing great power to our practice
        iii) The advantage of being important at the beginning
        iv) The advantage of being important in the middle
        v) The advantage of being important at the end
        vi) The advantage that we will be able to face death with joy and happiness
    c) The actual method of recalling death
        i) Meditating on the set of nine points relating to death
            (1) Contemplating the certainty of death
                (a) Contemplating that the Lord of Death is certain to appear and cannot be turned back by any means
                (b) Contemplating that our life spans cannot be increased and that they are constantly growing shorter
                (c) Contemplating the certainty of death in the sense that we do not have much time to practice, even during the time that we remain alive

- (2) Contemplating the uncertainty of the time of death
  - (a) The life span of a person in the Jambudvipa is uncertain in a general sense and also, in particular, because this is a degenerate age
  - (b) The time of death is uncertain because the factors that contribute to death are many and because those that sustain life are few
  - (c) The time of death is uncertain because our bodies are extremely fragile
- (3) Contemplating that when we die nothing except the dharma can benefit us
  - (a) Our wealth is of no help
  - (b) Our family and friends are of no help
  - (c) Even our bodies are of no help

ii) Meditating on the nature of death

2) Contemplating the nature of future lives in terms of the happiness and suffering that the two basic types of beings experience
- a) Contemplating the suffering of hell beings
  - i) Contemplating the suffering of the great hells
  - ii) Contemplating the suffering of the adjacent hell regions
  - iii) Contemplating the suffering of the cold hells
  - iv) Contemplating the suffering of the partial hells
- b) Contemplating the suffering of hungry ghosts
  - i) Contemplating the suffering of heat and cold
  - ii) Contemplating the suffering of hunger and thirst
  - iii) Contemplating the suffering of weariness and fear
- c) Contemplating the suffering of animals
  - i) The suffering of eating one another
  - ii) The suffering of being dull and ignorant
  - iii) The suffering of heat and cold
  - iv) The suffering of hunger and thirst
  - v) The suffering of exploitation

- ii. Pursuing the methods for achieving happiness in future lives
    - 1) Taking refuge: the sacred door by which the teaching is entered
        - a) The causes that form the basis for taking refuge
        - b) The object in which we take refuge
            - i) Identifying the object of refuge
            - ii) The reasons why this is a worthy object of refuge
        - c) The measure for determining that we have taken refuge properly
            - i) Taking refuge after learning the qualities of each aspect of the Triple Gem
            - ii) Taking refuge after learning the distinctions within the Triple Gem
            - iii) Taking refuge by professing faith in the Triple Gem
            - iv) Taking refuge by disavowing faith in other religions
        - d) The benefits of taking refuge
            - i) We will become Buddhists
            - ii) Taking refuge serves as a foundation for all the vows
            - iii) We will remove karmic obscurations accumulated in the past
            - iv) We will easily accumulate extensive merit
            - v) We will avoid both human and nonhuman harm
            - vi) We will avoid falling into the lower states
            - vii) We will easily achieve all our goals
            - viii) We will quickly achieve Buddhahood
        - e) The precepts to be observed by those who take refuge
            - i) Individual precepts
                - (1) Negative precepts
                - (2) Affirmative precepts
            - ii) General precepts
                - (1) Recall the virtues of the Triple Gem and take refuge in them again and again
                - (2) Recall how the Triple Gem benefits you and offer them the choice part of anything you eat
                - (3) Encourage others to take refuge

- (4) Recall the benefits of taking refuge and do so three times each morning and each night
- (5) Undertake an activity only after placing your trust in the Triple Gem
- (6) Don't abandon the Triple Gem, whether to save your life or merely as a joke

2) The root of happiness: generating the faith of believing in karma and its results
   - a) Contemplating karma and its results in general
     - i) The actual method of contemplating karma and its results in general
       - (1) Karma is certain
       - (2) Karma becomes magnified greatly
       - (3) We cannot meet with a karma that we did not perform
       - (4) A karma that we did perform does not lose its power to bear fruit
     - ii) Contemplating several classifications of karma and its results
       - (1) Contemplating the black karmic paths
         - (a) The actual presentation of the black karmic paths
         - (b) A presentation of their varying degrees of gravity
         - (c) The results of the black karmic paths
           - (i) Maturation results
           - (ii) Corresponding results
           - (iii) Governing results
       - (2) Contemplating the white karmic paths
         - (a) The actual presentation of the white karmic paths
         - (b) The results of the white karmic paths
       - (3) An incidental presentation of several types of powerful deeds
   - b) Contemplating a specific teaching on karma and its results
     - i) The maturation qualities
     - ii) The function of the maturation qualities
     - iii) How to pursue the causes of the maturation qualities

c) How to perform virtuous actions and avoid non-virtuous ones, once we have contemplated the principles of karma

b. Training the mind in the levels of the path that are held in common with persons of moderate capacity
  i. Developing the aspiration to achieve liberation
    1) Contemplating the general suffering in samsara
      a) The defect of being uncertain
      b) The defect of providing no satisfaction
      c) The defect of having to discard one's body again and again
      d) The defect of having to be reborn again and again
      e) The defect of having to fall from a high position to a low one again and again
      f) The defect of having no companion
    2) Contemplating the specific types of suffering in samsara
      a) Contemplating the suffering of the lower states
      b) Contemplating the suffering of the higher states
        i) Contemplating the suffering of humans
          (1) Contemplating the suffering of birth
          (2) Contemplating the suffering of old age
          (3) Contemplating the suffering of illness
          (4) Contemplating the suffering of death
          (5) Contemplating the suffering of being separated from things that we like
          (6) Contemplating the suffering of meeting with disagreeable things
          (7) Contemplating the suffering of seeking, but not being able to acquire, the things that we desire
        ii) Contemplating the suffering of demigods
        iii) Contemplating the suffering of gods
  ii. Establishing the nature of the path that leads to liberation
    1) Contemplating the origin of suffering and the process by which samsara is perpetuated
      a) How the mental afflictions arise
        i) Identifying the mental afflictions
        ii) The order in which the mental afflictions arise
        iii) The causes of the mental afflictions
        iv) The disadvantages of the mental afflictions

b) How the mental afflictions cause us to accumulate karma
c) How we die and are reborn
i) How death occurs
ii) How death is followed by entrance into the intermediate state
iii) How the rebirth occurs at conception
2) The actual explanation of the path that leads to liberation
a) The type of human form that we need to escape from samsara
b) The type of path that we must practice to escape from samsara
c. Training the mind in the levels of the path that relate to persons of great capacity
i. Establishing that enlightenment mind is the sole means of entering the Mahayana path, along with a presentation of its benefits
1) Generating enlightenment mind is the sole means of entering the Mahayana path
2) We will be called a Conqueror's son
3) We will surpass the Listeners and Solitary Realizers by virtue of our spiritual lineage
4) We will become the supreme object to which offerings should be made
5) We will easily accumulate extensive merit
6) We will quickly purify ourselves of bad karma and mental obscurations
7) We will achieve whatever goals we seek
8) We become invulnerable to harms and obstacles
9) We will quickly complete all the paths and their levels
10) We will become a field that produces every form of well-being and happiness for sentient beings
ii. How to generate enlightenment mind
1) The actual stages for training oneself in enlightenment mind
a) Training one's mind with the Sevenfold Instruction of Cause and Effect.
i) Equanimity
ii) Recognizing all sentient beings as our mothers
iii) Recalling their kindness
iv) Repaying their kindness

v) The loving-kindness that regards all sentient beings as dear
vi) Compassion
vii) Extraordinary intention
viii) Enlightenment mind
b) Training one's mind with the instruction called Equality and Exchange of Self and Others
2) The ritual method of adopting enlightenment mind
a) The method for gaining the vow that has not been taken previously
b) The method for preserving the vow so that it will not degenerate once it has been taken
iii. How to train oneself in the Bodhisattva activities once enlightenment mind has been generated
1) How to ripen one's own mind by training oneself in the six perfections
a) A general discussion of how to train oneself in all of the perfections
i) How to train oneself in generosity
ii) How to train oneself in ethics
iii) How to train oneself in patience
iv) How to train oneself in effort
v) How to train oneself in concentration
vi) How to train oneself in wisdom
b) A specific discussion of how to train oneself in the last two perfections
i) How to train oneself in quiescence, which is the essence of one-pointed meditation
(1) Cultivating the requisites for achieving quiescence
(2) The actual method of achieving quiescence: how to cultivate the eight remedial factors that overcome the five faults
(3) How to attain the nine levels of mental stability on the basis of this instruction
(4) How to attain the nine levels by means of the six powers
(5) The four kinds of attention that are applied in cultivating quiescence
(6) How the actual state of quiescence arises on the basis of this practice

- ii) How to train oneself in insight, which is the essence of wisdom
  - (1) Establishing the insubstantiality of the self
    - (a) How to cultivate the space-like realization during a state of mental composure
      - (i) The key point of determining the object to be refuted
      - (ii) The key point of determining the range of logical possibilities
      - (iii) The key point of determining that the self cannot be identical with the heaps in a truly existent sense
      - (iv) The key point of determining that the self cannot be distinct from the heaps in a truly existent sense
    - (b) How to cultivate the realization that the self resembles an illusion, during the period after one arises from meditation
  - (2) Establishing the insubstantiality of phenomena
    - (a) Establishing that composed entities are not inherently existent
      - (i) Establishing that form is not inherently existent
      - (ii) Establishing that mental entities are not inherently existent
      - (iii) Establishing that unassociated compositional factors are not inherently existent
    - (b) Establishing that uncomposed entities are not inherently existent
  - (3) The method of developing insight
- c) How to train oneself in the Vajrayana path
- 2) How to ripen others' minds by training oneself in the four methods of gathering a following

APPENDIX H

THE ROOT TEXT
OF THE MAHAYANA TEACHING ENTITLED:
THE SEVEN-POINT INSTRUCTION
ON MIND TRAINING

I prostrate to great compassion.

The greatness of the originator, presented in order to demonstrate the authoritative source of the dharma

This instruction, which is the Essence of Immortality
Nectar,
Has come down in a lineage from the Suvarnadvipa Guru.

The greatness of the dharma teaching, presented in order to generate respect for the instruction

Similar to a diamond, the sun, and a medicinal tree;
Thus should the meaning of the text be understood.
It transforms the rise of the five degeneracy factors
Into elements of the path that leads to enlightenment.

The method of leading the student by means of the actual instruction. Section one: The preliminary teachings that form the foundation of the instructions

Begin by training yourself in the preliminary teachings.

Section two: The main instruction of training oneself in the two forms of enlightenment mind—ultimate enlightenment mind and conventional enlightenment mind

Most of the early editions present the exercise of training oneself in ultimate enlightenment mind first. The view expressed in this edition is that there is an important reason for placing it later in the text. In doing so, I am following the tradition established by the great Jamgön Lama Tsongkapa. This view is also reflected in numerous works, such as the Mind Training Like the Rays of the Sun, Ornament of Losang's View, Essence of the Nectar of Immortality, *and the edition of the root text compiled by Keutsang Jamyang Mönlam.*

Training oneself in conventional enlightenment mind:

> All blame rests with one.
> Meditate on the great kindness of all beings.
> Cultivate alternately the two of Giving and Taking.
> The order for taking should start with yourself.
> Let these two practices ride on your breath.
> There are three objects, three poisons, and three virtue-roots.
> An abbreviated instruction for the period after meditation
> Is to remind yourself of the practice
> By reciting it aloud during all your activities.

Training oneself in ultimate enlightenment mind:

> When you have gained proficiency, practice the secret instruction.
> Regard all entities as like objects in a dream.
> Analyse the unoriginated nature of mind.
> Allow the antidote to be self-liberating.
> Place the mind in the all-encompassing essence of the path.
> Between meditation periods, regard beings as illusory.

Section three: transforming unfavorable circumstances into elements of the path to enlightenment

When the world and its inhabitants have become filled
with evil,
Transform unfavorable circumstances into the path
to enlightenment.
Immediately apply your practice to whatever you happen
to encounter.
The supreme form of spiritual training is one that includes
the four actions.

Section four: a summary of what to practice over one's entire lifetime

A summary of the instruction's essence
Is to devote yourself to the five strengths.
The Mahayana instruction for transference is to practice
These very five strengths and give special importance to
your body position.

Section five: explaining the measure for determining that you have mastered the Mind Training practices

All dharma is based on one underlying thought.
Heed the more important of the two witnesses.
Always maintain a happy mind.
The measure of mastery is for self-cherishing mind to
have been overcome.
The signs of mastery are the five greatnesses.
Mastery is when you can practice even if distracted.

Section six: the pledges to be observed

Always train yourself in the three general principles.
Change your aspirations but remain natural.
Do not mention others' flaws.
Never think adversely of others.
First strive to remove your worst mental affliction.
Give up all expectation of reward.
Avoid poisonous food.
Don't be steadfast.
Don't engage in bitter quarreling.

Don't wait along a back road.
Don't strike a vulnerable point.
Don't place a *dzo*'s load onto an ox.
Don't practice perversely as if performing mundane rituals.
Don't try to be the fastest.
Don't turn a god into a demon.
Don't seek misery as a means to happiness.

Section seven: a presentation of the precepts that practitioners of the mind training instructions should observe

Do all yoga practice with one thought.
Respond with one thought when overwhelmed by obstacles.
Two actions are for the beginning and the end.
Be patient no matter which of the two you encounter.
Protect the two even at the cost of your life.
Train yourself in the three that are difficult.
Take up the three principal causes.
Meditate on the three in an undiminished form.
Maintain the three you should never be without.
Train yourself impartially toward all objects.
Cherish everything with a practice that is heartfelt
and all-encompassing.
Train yourself constantly toward special objects.
Don't let your practice depend on conditions.
This time practice what is most important.
Don't do mistaken activities.
Don't practice sporadically.
Train in a way that cuts through indecision.
Free yourself using deliberation and reflection.
Don't be conceited.
Don't be resentful.
Don't be fickle.
Don't yearn to be thanked.

The teachings are concluded with a verse expressing the feeling of security that is gained by having attained enlightenment mind:

Motivated by the many aspirations that I had,
I ignored hardships and words of disapproval
To receive instructions that overcome belief in a self.
Now I am ready to die with no feelings of regret.

Among the writings of teachers from both the Old and New Kadampa traditions there are a great many commentaries on the Seven-Point Mind Training Instruction, *as well as numerous versions of the root text. However, the order in which the instructions are presented varies significantly in these texts. Even the wording and corpus of the instructions differ from edition to edition. Some editions of the root text do not correspond to the outlines for teaching the instructions that are presented in different commentaries. The wording of other editions does not correspond to more popular versions in which some of the instructions have been preserved. Therefore, because of my long-held wish to compile an edition of the root text that conforms with the views expressed in such works as the* Mind Training Like the Rays of the Sun, *the* Ornament of Losang's View, *and the* Essence of the Nectar of Immortality, *which form part of the teaching tradition that we follow and that was established by the great Jamgön Lama Tsongkapa, and in response to a request by Puntsok Palden, a devoted practitioner of the Lamrim teachings, which was accompanied by the traditional offerings, I, a monk recognized as a tulku who carries the name of Pabongka, composed this edition of the root text and embellished it with an outline of the topics after a careful study of numerous editions of the root text and many commentaries. It was completed in the Wood Boar Year (1935) at the Gelukpa monastery known as Jampa Ling, which is located in the district of Chamdo. May the welfare of all beings be greatly enhanced!*

BIBLIOGRAPHY

The bibliography is divided into four sections, of which only the first, "Canonical Works," lists the entries by title. The other three sections (with a few exceptions) are arranged by author or translator. The order follows the roman alphabet, with both Tibetan authors and titles presented according to the capitalized "main" letter of the first word.

Wherever a Sanskrit edition is known to have survived, we have listed that first. To accommodate readers with little or no facility in either Tibetan or Sanskrit, we have also tried to include information for any English translations that may be available. Therefore, as many as three editions may appear for a number of entries: first the original Sanskrit, followed by Tibetan and English translations.

For works in the Kangyur, folio numbers (abbreviated "f." or "ff." as appropriate) refer to the Lhasa edition. The listings for works found in the Tengyur refer to the Cone edition. Almost all of the native Tibetan works are contained in the collections created through the Special Foreign Currency/Public Law 480 program administered by the Library of Congress. Where these editions have page numbers in Arabic numerals, they are cited with the abbreviation "pp." We have also provided the reference numbers for works that appear in the well-known catalogues published by Tohoku University.

Please note the following abbreviations:

Kg.	Kangyur; woodblock print of the Lhasa edition housed at First Kalmuk Buddhist Temple, Howell, New Jersey, USA
Tg.	Tengyur; microfiche of the Cone edition distributed by the Institute for Advanced Studies of World Religions, Carmel, New York, USA
Toh.	Tohoku catalogue numbers from *A Complete Catalogue of the Tibetan Buddhist Canons* (#1–#4569) and *A Catalogue of the Tohoku University Collection of Tibetan Works on Buddhism* (#5001–#7083); see separate listings below in last section of Bibliography.

Canonical works

Aṣṭasāhasrikāprajñāpāramitā. In Buddhist Sanskrit Texts No. 4. Darbanga, India: Mithila Institute, 1960, pp. 1–261. Tibetan Translation: (*'Phags pa*) *Shes rab kyi pha rol tu phyin pa brgyad stong pa*. In *Sher phyin bsdus pa* section of Kg., vol. 1 (*ka*) (Toh. #12). English translation in *The Perfection of Wisdom in Eight Thousand Lines & Its Verse Summary*. Tr. Edward Conze. Bolinas: Four Seasons Foundation, 1973, pp. 75–300.

(*'Phags pa*) *Byams pas zhus pa'i le'u zhes bya ba theg pa chen po'i mdo*. (Tibetan translation of *Āryamaitreyaparipṛcchāparivartanāmamahāyānasūtram*). In *dKon brtzegs* section of Kg., vol. 6 (*cha*), ff. 189a–207a (Toh. #85).

(*'Phags pa*) *Chos yang dag par sdud pa zhes bya ba theg par chen po'i mdo* (Tibetan translation of *Āryadharmasamgītināmamahāyāna-sūtram*). In *mDo mang* section of Kg., vol. 19 (*dza*), ff. 1a–154a (Toh. #238).

(*'Phags pa*) *Dam pa'i chos dran pa nye bar bzhag pa* (Tibetan translation of *Āryasaddharmasmṛtyupasthānasūtram*). In *mDo mang* section of Kg., vol. 22 (*za*), ff. 171a–end through vol. 25 (*ra*), ff. 1a–356a (Toh. #287).

Daśabhūmikasūtram. Buddhist Sanskrit Texts No. 7. Darbanga, India: Mithila Institute, 1958. Tibetan translation: *Sa bcu pa'i mdo* (Ch. 30 of *Sangs rgyas phal po che zhes bya ba shin tu rgyas pa chen po'i mdo*) In *Phal chen* section of Kg., vol. 3 (*ga*), ff. 67a–234b (Toh. #44). English translation in *Flower Ornament Scripture*. Tr. Thomas Cleary. Boston: Shambhala Publications, 1984, Ch. 26, pp. 695–811.

(*'Phags pa*) *Des pas zhus pa zhes bya ba theg pa chen po'i mdo* (Tibetan translation of *Āryasuratapariprcchānāmamahāyānasūtram*). In *dKon brtzegs* section of Kg., vol. 5 (*ca*), ff. 319a–339a (Toh. #71). English translation in *A Treasury of Mahayana Sūtras*, Ch. 13 "Bodhisattva Surata's Discourse," University Park: The Pennsylvania State University Press, 1983, pp. 243–255.

Divyāvadānam. Buddhist Sanskrit Texts, No. 20. Darbanga, India: Mithila Institute, 1959.

'Dul ba gzhi. See listing for Tibetan translation of *Vinayavastu*.

'Dul ba rnam par 'byed pa (Tibetan translation of *Vinayavibhaṅgaḥ*). In *'Dul ba* section of Kg., vol. 5 (*ca*), f. 21a–vol. 8 (*nya*), f. 328 (Toh. #3).

mDzangs blun zhes bya ba'i mdo (Tibetan translation of *Damamūkasūtram*). In *mDo mang* section of Kg., vol. 28 (*sa*), ff. 207b–476b (Toh.

#341). English translation: *Sutra of the Wise and the Foolish*. Tr. Stanley B. Frye. Dharamsala: Library of Tibetan Works & Archives, 1981.

(*'Phags pa*) *dGa' bo mngal na gnas pa bstan pa zhes bya ba theg pa chen po'i mdo* (Tibetan translation of *Āryanandagarbhāvakrāntinirdeśaḥ*). In *dKon brtzegs* section of Kg., vol. 3 (*ga*), ff. 399b-448a (Toh. #57).

Gaṇḍavyūhasūtram. Buddhist Sanskrit Texts No. 5. Darbanga, India: Mithila Institute, 1960. Tibetan translation: *sDong po bkod pa'i mdo* (also *sDong po brgyan pa'i mdo*). In *Phal chen* section of Kg. (final chapter of sutra, vol. 5 (*ca*), ff. 24a–vol. 6 (*cha*) (Toh. #44). English translation: *Entry into the Realm of Reality*. Tr. Thomas Cleary. Boston: Shambhala Publications, 1989.

dGe slong la rab tu gces pa'i mdo (Tibetan translation of *Bhikṣupriyasūtram*). In *mDo mang* section of Kg., vol. 26 (*la*), ff. 193b–196a (Toh. #302).

(*'Phags pa*) *'Jam dpal gyi sangs rgyas kyi shing gi yon tan bkod pa zhes bya ba theg pa chen po'i mdo* (Tibetan translation of *Mañjuśrībuddhakṣetraguṇavyūhālaṃkārasūtram*). In *dKon brtzegs* section of Kg., vol. 4 (*nga*), ff. 1-85a (Toh. #59). English translation in *A Treasury of Mahāyāna Sūtras*, Ch. 10 "The Prediction of Mañjuśrī's Attainment of Buddhahood." University Park: Pennsylvania State University Press, 1983, pp. 164–188.

Karuṇāpuṇḍarīkanāmamahāyānasūtram. 2 vols. Ed. by I. Yamada. London: University of London, 1968. Tibetan translation: (*'Phags pa*) *sNying rje chen po'i padma dkar po zhes bya ba theg pa chen po'i mdo*. In *mDo mang* section of Kg., vol. 6 (*cha*), ff. 86a–209b (Toh. #111).

Kāśyapaparivartaḥ. Ed. A. von Staël-Holstein. Shanghai: Commercial Press, 1926. Tibetan translation: (*'Phags pa*) *'Od srung gi le'u shes bya ba theg pa chen po'i mdo* In *dKon brtzegs* section of Kg., vol. 6 (*cha*) ff. 211a–260b (Toh. #87). English translation in *A Treasury of Mahāyāna Sūtras*, Ch. 20 "The Sūtra of Assembled Treasures." University Park: Pennsylvania State University Press, 1983, pp. 387–414.

(*'Phags pa*) *Klu'i rgyal po ma dros pas zhus pa zhes bya ba theg pa chen po'i mdo*. (Tibetan translation of *Āryānavataptanāgarājaparipṛcchānāmamahāyānasūtram*). In *mDo mang* section of Kg., vol. 12 (*na*), ff. 314a–383a (Toh. #156).

Lankāvatārasūtram. Buddhist Sanskrit Texts No. 3. Darbanga, India: Mithila Institute, 1963. Tibetan translation: (*'Phags pa*) *Lang kar gshegs pa'i mdo*. In *mDo mang* section of Kg., vol. 5 (*ca*), ff. 87b–307a (Toh. #107).

Lalitavistaraḥ. Buddhist Sanskrit Texts No. 1. Darbanga, India: Mithila Institute, 1958. Tibetan translation: (*'Phags pa*) *rGya cher rol pa zhes bya ba theg pa chen po'i mdo*. In *mDo mang* section of Kg., vol. 2 (*kha*), ff. 1–352a (Toh. #95). English translation: *The Voice of the Buddha* (2 vols.). Berkeley: Dharma Publishing, 1983.

(*'Phags pa*) *Ma skyes dgra'i 'gyod pa bsal ba zhes bya ba theg pa chen po'i mdo* (Tibetan Translation of *Āryājātaśatrukaukṛttyavinodananāma-mahāyānasūtram*). In *mDo mang* section of Kg., vol. 12 (*ma*), ff. 313a–413a (Toh. #216).

Mahākarmavibhaṅgaḥ. In *Mahāyāna Sūtra Saṃgraha*, Buddhist Sanskrit Texts No. 17. Dharbanga, India: Mithila Institute, 1961, pp. 176–220. Tibetan translation: There are two works in the Lhasa Kg. entitled *Las rnam par 'byed pa*. While both cover the same general topics, they vary somewhat in the order and detail of their presentations. Neither one corresponds exactly to the Sanskrit text. They are found in *mDo mang* section of Kg., vol. 26 (*la*), ff. 425b–455a and ff. 455b–490b (Toh. #338).

(*Ārya*) *Mañjuśrīmūlakalpaḥ*. In vol. 2 of Buddhist Sanskrit Texts No. 18. Darbanga, India: Mithila Institute, 1964. Tibetan translation: (*'Phags pa*) *'Jam dpal gyi rtza ba'i rgyud*. In *rGyud* section of Kg., vol. 10 (*tha*), ff. 53b–448b (Toh. #543).

(*'Phags pa*) *sNying rje chen po'i padma dkar po zhes bya ba theg pa chen po'i mdo*. See listing for Tibetan translation of (*Ārya*) *Karuṇā-puṇḍarīkanāmamahāyānasūtram*.

Prātimokṣasūtram. ed. Banerjee. In *Indian Historical Quarterly*, Calcutta, 1953. Tibetan translation: *So sor thar pa'i mdo*. In *'Dul ba* section of Kg., vol. 5 (*ca*), ff. 1b–30a (Toh. #2).

Ratnaguṇasaṃcayagāthā. In *Mahāyāna Sūtra Saṃgraha*, Buddhist Sanskrit Texts No. 17. Darbanga, India: Mithila Institute, 1960, pp. 352–398. Tibetan translation: (*'Phags pa*) *Shes rab kyi pha rol tu phyin pa sdud pa tsigs su bcad pa*. In *Sher phyin sna tsogs* section of Kg., vol. 1 (*ka*), ff. 189–215a (Toh. #13). English translation in *The Perfection of Wisdom in Eight Thousand Lines & Its Verse Summary*. Tr. Edward Conze. Bolinas: Four Seasons Foundation, 1973, pp. 1–73.

(*'Phags pa*) *Rin po che'i phung po zhes bya ba theg pa chen po'i mdo* (Tibetan translation of [*Ārya*] *Ratnarāśināmamahāyānasūtram*. In *dKon brtzegs* section of Kg., vol. 6 (*cha*), ff. 260b–298b (Toh. #88). English translation in *A Treasury of Mahāyāna Sūtras*, Ch. 16 "Abiding in Good and Noble Deportment." University Park: Pennsylvania State University Press, 1983, pp. 280–312.

Śālistambhasūtram. In Buddhist Sanskrit Texts No. 17, pp. 100–106. Darbanga, India: Mithila Institute, 1961. Tibetan translation: (*'Phags pa*) *Sā lu'i ljang pa zhes bya ba theg pa chen po'i mdo*. In *mDo mang* section of Tg., vol. 16 (*ma*), ff. 180a–192a (Toh. # 210). English translation in: *The Śālistamba Sūtra*. Tr. N. Ross Reat. New Delhi: Motilal Banarsidass, 1993.

Samādhirājasūtram. Buddhist Sanskrit Texts No. 2. Darbanga, India: Mithila Institute, 1961. Tibetan translation: (*'Phags pa chos thams cad kyi rang bzhin mnyam pa nyid rnam par spros pa*) *Ting nge 'dzin gyi rgyal po zhes bya ba theg pa chen po'i mdo*. In *mDo mang* section of Kg., vol. 9 (*ta*), ff. 1–269b (Toh. #127).

Sangs rgyas phal po che zhes bya ba shin tu rgyas pa chen po'i mdo (Tibetan translation of *Buddhāvataṃsakanāmamahāvaipulyasūtram*). In *Phal chen* section of Kg., 6 vols. (*ka–cha*) (Toh. #44). English translation: *The Flower Ornament Scripture*. Tr. Thomas Cleary. Boston: Shambhala Publications, 1984.

Shes rab kyi pha rol tu phyin pa stong phrag nyi shu lnga pa (Tibetan translation of *Pañcaviṃśatisāhasrikāprajñāpāramitā*). In *Nyi khri* section of Kg., vols. 1–3 (*ka–ga*) (Toh. #9). English translation: Significant portions of a reworked version of this sutra, as well as sections from the versions in 100,000 and 18,000 lines, are found in *The Large Sutra on Perfect Wisdom*. Tr. and ed. by Edward Conze. Berkeley: University of California Press, 1975.

Sukhāvatīvyūhaḥ (long and short versions). In *Mahāyāna Sūtra Saṃgraha* Buddhist Sanskrit Texts No. 17. Darbanga, India: Mithila Institute, 1961. pp. 221–253. Tibetan translation: (long version) (*'Phags pa*) *'Od dpag med kyi bkod pa zhes bya ba theg pa chen po'i mdo*. In *dKon brtzegs* section of Kg., vol. 1 (*ka*), ff. 367a–418 (Toh. #49). English translation (long version) in *A Treasury of Mahāyāna Sūtras* Ch. 18 "The Land of Utmost Bliss." University Park: Pennsylvania State University Press, 1983, pp. 339–360.

Suvarṇaprabhāsottamasūtram. Buddhist Sanskrit Texts No. 8. Darbanga, India: Mithila Institute, 1967. Tibetan translation: *gSer 'od dam pa mdo sde'i dbang po'i rgyal po*. In *rGyud* section of Kg., vol. 11 (*da*), ff. 215b–405b (Toh. #556). English translation: *The Sutra of Golden Light*

(Sacred Books of the Buddhists No. 27). Tr. R.E. Emmerick. London: Luzac, 1970.

Thabs mkhas pa chen po sangs rgyas drin lan bsab pa'i mdo (Translated from Chinese; Sanskit title uncertain). In *mDo mang* section of Kg., vol. 29 (*aa*), ff. 135b-314a (Toh. #353).

Tsul khrims yang dag par ldan pa'i mdo (Tibetan translation of *Śīla-saṃyuktasūtram*). In *mDo mang* section of Kg., vol. 26 (*la*), ff. 196a–197a (Toh. #303).

Udānavargaḥ. Ed. Franz Bernhard. Gottingen: Vandehoeck & Ruprecht, 1965. Tibetan translation: *Ched du brjod pa'i tsoms*. In *mDo mang* section of Kg., vol. 26 (*la*), ff. 320b–387b (Toh. #326). English translation: *Udānavarga*. Tr. W. Woodville Rockhill. 1884; reprinted Amsterdam: Oriental Press, 1975.

(*Mūlasarvāstivāda*) *Vinayavastu*. Buddhist Sanskrit Texts No. 16 (2 vols.). Darbanga, India: Mithila Institute, 1970. Tibetan translation: *'Dul ba gzhi*. In *'Dul ba* section of Kg., vols. 1–4 (*ka–nga*) (Toh. #1).

Indian treatises

Āryadeva. *bsTan bcos bzhi brgya pa zhes bya ba'i tsig le'ur byas pa* (Tibetan translation of *Catuḥśatakaśāstrakārikā*). In *dBu ma* section of Tg., vol. 18 (*tsa*), ff. 1b–21b (Toh. #3846).

Āryaśūra. *Jātakamālā*. Buddhist Sanskrit Texts No. 21. Darbanga, India: Mithila Institute, 1960. Tibetan translation: *sKyes pa'i rabs kyi rgyud*. In *sKyes rabs* section of Tg., vol. 89 (*hu*), ff. 1–135a (Toh. #4150). English translation: *The Jātakamālā*. Tr. J.S. Speyer. Reprint edition, Delhi: Motilal Banarsidass, 1971.

__________. *Pāramitāsamāsam*. Ed. Alfonsa Ferrari. In *Annali Lateranensi*, vol. X. The Vatican: Pontificio Museo Missionario Etnologico, 1946, pp. 19–60. Tibetan translation: *Pha rol tu phyin pa bsdus pa*. In *dBu ma* section of Tg., vol. 32 (*khi*), ff. 219b–239a (Toh. #3944).

Asaṅga. *Abhidharmasamuccayaḥ*. Ed. Prahlad Pradhan. Shantiniketan, India: Visva-Bharati, 1950. Tibetan translation: *Chos mngon pa kun las btus pa*. In *Sems tzam* section of Tg., vol. 55 (*ri*), ff. 44a–120a (Toh. #4049).

__________. *Bodhisattvabhūmiḥ*. Tibetan Sanskrit Works Series Vol. VII. Ed. Nalinaksha Dutt. Patna: K.P. Jayaswal Research Institute, 1978.

Tibetan translation: (*rNal 'byor spyod pa'i sa las*) *Byang chub sems dpa'i sa*. In *Sems tzam* section of Tg., vol. 50 (*wi*), ff. 1a–215a (Toh. #4037).

_________. *rNam par gtan la dbab pa bsdu ba*. (Tibetan translation of *Viniścayasaṃgrahaṇī*). In *Sems tzam* section of Tg., vol. 51 (*zhi*), f. 1a–vol. 52 (*zi*), f. 128b (Toh. #4038).

_________. *Śrāvakabhūmiḥ*. Tibetan Sanskrit Works Series Vol. XIV. Ed. Karunesha Shukla. Patna: K.P. Jayaswal Research Institute, 1973. Tibetan translation: (*rNal 'byor spyod pa'i sa las*) *Nyan thos kyi sa*. In *Sems tzam* section of Tg., vol. 49 (*dzi*), 201ff. (Toh. #4036).

_________. *Yogācārabhūmiḥ* (incomplete). Parts 1-5 are in *The Yogācārabhūmi of Ācārya Asaṅga*. ed. Vidhushekhara Bhattacharya. Calcutta: University of Calcutta, 1957, pp. 1-232. Parts 8, 9, 11, and 14 are in *Buddhist Insight*, Delhi: Motilal Banarsidass, 1984, pp. 327–331 and pp. 333–352. See separate listings for *Śrāvakabhūmiḥ* (part 13) and *Bodhisattvabhūmiḥ* (part 15). Tibetan translation: Parts 1-12, referred to as *Sa mang po pa*, in *Sems tzam* section of Tg., vol. 48 (*tsi*), ff. 1–285 (Toh. #4035).

Aśvaghoṣa. *Mya ngan bsal ba* (Tibetan translation of *Śokavinodanam*). In *sPring yig* section of Tg., vol. 94 (*nge*), ff. 33a–34b (Toh. #4177).

Atiśa (Dīpaṃkara Śrījñāna). *Bodhipathapradīpaḥ* (restored from Tibetan by Losang Norbu Shastri; also contains Tibetan, Hindi, and English texts), Bibliotheca Indo-Tibetica Series VII, revised 2nd edition. Sarnath, India: Central Institute of Higher Tibetan Studies, 1994. Tibetan translation: *Byang chub lam gyi sgron ma*. In *dBu ma* section of Tg., vol. 32 (*khi*), ff. 242a–245a (Toh. #3947). English translation in *Bodhipathapradīpaḥ* (see above).

_________. *bDen pa gnyis la 'jug pa* (Tibetan translation of *Satyadvaya-avatāraḥ*). In *dBu ma* section of Tg., vol 30 (*a*), ff. 71b–73a (Toh. #3902).

Bhavya. *dBu ma'i snying po'i tsig le'ur byas pa* (Tibetan translation of *Madhyamakahṛdayakārikā*). In *dBu ma* section of Tg., vol 19 (*dza*), ff. 1a–41a (Toh. #3855).

Blo sbyong brgya rtza. A collection of Mind Training works compiled by dKon mchog rgyal mtsan (a number of which are translations of works by Indian pandits). Dharamsala, India: Shes rig par khang, 1973.

Bodhibhadra. *Ting nge 'dzin gyi tsogs kyi le'u* (Tibetan translation of *Samādhisambhāraparivartaḥ*). In *dBu ma* section of Tg., vol 23 (*ki*), ff. 81b–93a (Toh. #3924).

Candragomī. *Byang chub sems dpa'i sdom pa nyi shu pa.* (Tibetan translation of *Bodhisattvasaṃvaraviṃśakaḥ*). In *Sem tzam* section of Tg., vol. 59 (*hi*), ff. 167a–168a (Toh. #4081). English translation in: *Candragomin's Twenty Verses on the Bodhisattva Vow.* Tr. Mark Tatz. Dharamsala, India: Library of Tibetan Works & Archives, 1982.

_________. *bShags pa'i bstod pa* (Tibetan translation of *Deśanāstavaḥ*). In *bsTod pa* section of Tg., vol. 209 (*ka*), ff. 236b–239b (Toh. #1159).

_________. *Śiṣyalekhaḥ*. Ed. by J. P. Minayeff. In *Zapiski* (notes) of the Imperial Russian Archaeological Society, Oriental Section, Vol. IV, pp. 29–52. St. Petersburg: Imperial Russian Archaeological Society, 1889. Tibetan translation: *Slob ma la springs pa'i spring yig*. In *sPring yig* section of Tg., vol. 94 (*nge*), ff. 46b–53a (Toh. #4183).

Candrakīrti. *dBu ma la 'jug pa* (Tibetan translation of *Madhyamakaavatāraḥ*) In *dBu ma* section of Tg., vol. 23 (*'a*), ff. 198a–216a (Toh. #3860).

_________. *Byang chub sems dpa'i rnal 'byor spyod pa bzhi brgya pa'i rgya cher 'grel pa.* (Tibetan translation of *Bodhisattvayogācāracatuḥśatakaṭīkā*) In *dBu ma* section of Tg., vol. 24 (*ya*), ff. 29a–264b (Toh. #3865).

_________. *Mūlamadhyamakavṛttiprasannapadā* (*Prasannapadā*). In *Madhyamakaśāstra of Nāgārjuna*, Buddhist Sanskrit Texts No. 10. Darbanga, India: Mithila Institute, 1960, pp. 1–259. Tibetan translation: *dBu ma rtza ba'i 'grel pa tsig gsal ba zhes bya ba.* In *dBu ma* section of Tg., vol. 23 (*'a*), ff. 1a–197a (Toh. #3860).

Dharmakīrti. *Pramāṇavārttikam.* In *Pramāṇavārttika The Kārikās with Manorathanandi's Vṛtti.* Varanasi: Bauddha Bharati, 1968. Tibetan translation: *Tsad ma rnam 'grel hyi tsig le'ur byas pa.* In *Tsad ma* section of Tg., vol. 95 (*ce*), ff. 95b–151a (Toh. #4210).

Dharmarakṣita. *bTzan dug nags su rma bya rgyu ba* (*rMa bya dug 'joms*). In *Blo sbyong brgya rtza*, pp. 111–121.

_________. *dGra bo gnad la dbab pa blo sbyong tson cha'i 'khor lo.* In *Blo sbyong brgya rtza*, pp. 96–110. English translation: *The Wheel of Sharp Weapons.* Tr. Geshe Ngawang Dhargyey et al. Revised edition. Dharamsala, India: Library of Tibetan Works and Archives, 1981.

Haribhadra. *Abhisamayālaṃkārālokaḥ*. In *Aṣṭasāhasrikā Prajñāpāramitā*, Buddhist Sanskrit Texts No. 4. Darbanga, India: Mithila Institute, 1960, pp. 267–558. Tibetan translation: (*'Phags pa shes rab kyi pha rol tu phyin pa brgyad stong pa'i bshad pa*) *mNGon par rtogs pa'i rgyan gyi snang ba*. In *Shes phyin* section of Tg., vol. 6 (*cha*), ff. 1–360a (Toh. #3791).

_________. *Shes rab kyi pha rol tu phyin pa stong phrag nyi shu lnga pa* (Tibetan translation of the *Pañcaviṃśatisāhasrikāprajñāpāramitā* sutra, arranged so as to identify the specific passages of the sutra that correspond to the topics of Maitreya Nātha's *Ornament of Realizations* [S: *Abhisamayālaṃkāraḥ*]). In *Shes phyin* section of Tg., vols. 3–5 (*ga–ca*) (Toh. #3790).

'Jig rten gzhag pa (Tibetan translation of *Lokaprajñāptiḥ*; a collection of teachings on Abhidharma said to have been compiled by Maudgalyāyana). In *mNgon pa* section of Tg., vol. 60 (*i*), ff. 1b–94a (Toh. # 4086).

Kamalaśīla. *Dvitīyabhāvanākramaḥ*. In *Bhāvanākramaḥ*, Bibliotheca Indo-Tibetica Series IX (Sanskrit restoration). Sarnath, India: Central Institute of Higher Tibetan Studies, 1997, pp. 231–252. Tibetan translation: *bsGom pa'i rim pa bar ba* (Tibetan translation of the second *Bhāvanakramaḥ*). In *dBu ma* section of Tg., vol. 31 (*ki*), ff. 42b–56b (Toh. #3916).

Kṣemendra. *Bodhisattvāvadānakalpalatā*. Buddhist Sanskrit Texts Nos. 22, 23. Darbanga, India: Mithila Institute, 1959. Tibetan translation: *Byang chub sems dba'i rtogs pa brjod pa dpag bsam gyi 'khri shing*. In *'khri shing* section of Tg., vols. 91, 92 (*ke, khe*) (Toh. #4155).

Maitreya Nātha. *Abhisamayālaṃkāraḥ*. (Sanskrit & Tibetan texts) Ed. T. Stcherbatsky and E.E. Obermiller, Leningrad: Bibliotheca Buddhica, 1929. Tibetan translation: (*Shes rab kyi pha rol tu phyin pa'i man ngag gi bstan bcos*) *mNgon par rtogs pa'i rgyan zhes bya ba'i tsig le'ur byas pa*. In *Shes phyin* section of Tg., vol. 1 (*ka*), ff. 1b–13a (Toh. #3786). English translation: *Abhisamaya Alaṃkāra*. Tr. Edward Conze. Rome: Serie Orientale Roma, 1954.

_________. *Madhyāntavibhāgakārikā*. Contained in *Madhyānta Vibhāga Śāstra*. Ed. by Ramchandra Pandeya. Delhi: Motilal Banarsidass, 1971. Tibetan translation: *dBus dang mtha' rnam par 'byed pa'i tsig le'ur byas pa*. In *Sems tzam* section Tg., vol. 44 (*phi*), ff. 37a–42a (Toh. #4021).

_________. *Mahāyānasūtrālaṃkāraḥ*. In Buddhist Sanskrit Texts No. 13. Darbanga, India: Mithila Institute, 1970. Tibetan translation: *Theg pa chen po mdo sde'i rgyan zhes bya ba'i tsig le'ur byas pa*. In *Sems tzam* section Tg., vol. 44 (*phi*), ff. 1–37a (Toh. #4020).

_________. *Mahāyānottaratantraśāstram* (*Ratnagotra Vibhāga*). In *Ratnagotravibhāga Mahāyānottaratantraśāstra*. Ed. E.H. Johnston. Patna: Bihar Research Society, 1950. Tibetan translation: *Theg pa chen po rgyud bla ma'i bstan bcos*. In *Sems tzam* section of Tg., vol. 44 (*phi*), ff. 51a–69a (Toh. #4024). English translation in *The Sublime Science of the Great Vehicle to Salvation*. Tr. E.E. Obermiller. In Acta Orientalia Vol. IX, 1931.

Mātṛceṭa. *Varṇārhavarṇastotram*. Ed. D.R. Shackleton Bailey. Sanskrit not complete, includes English translation and Tibetan (ch. 5–12 only). Bulletin of the School of Oriental Studies 1950, Part I (ch. 1–4) pp. 671–701; Part II (ch. 5–12), pp. 947–1003. Tibetan translation: *Sangs rgyas bcom ldan 'das la bstod pa bsngags par 'os pa bsngags pa las bstod par mi nus par bstod pa* (*bsngags 'os bsngags bstod*) In *bsTod pa* section of Tg., vol. 209 (*ka*), ff. 96b–116a (Toh. #1138).

Nāgārjuna. *mDo kun las btus pa*. (Tibetan translation of *Sūtra-samuccayaḥ*). In *dBu ma* section of Tg., vol. 31 (*ki*), ff. 151a–218a (Toh. #3934).

_________. *Mūlamadhyamakakārikā*. In *Madhyamakaśāstra of Nāgārjuna*, Buddhist Sanskrit Texts No. 10. Darbanga, India: Mithila Institute, 1960. Tibetan translation: *dBu ma rtza ba'i tsig le'ur byas pa shes rab ces bya ba*. In *dBu ma* section of Tg., vol. 17 (*tza*), ff. 1a–19a (Toh. #3824). English translation in *Emptiness—A Study in Religious Meaning*. Tr. Streng, F.J. Nashville, New York: Abingdon Press, 1967, pp. 183–220.

_________. *Ratnāvalī* (incomplete text). In *Nāgārjuna's Ratnavalī*, ed. Michael Hahn. Bonn: Indica et Tibetica Verlag, 1982. Tibetan translation: *rGyal po la gtam bya ba rin po che'i phreng ba*. In *sKyes rabs* section of Tg., vol. 93 (*ge*), ff. 116a–135a (Toh. #4158). English translation in *The Precious Garland and the Precious Song of the Four Mindfulnesses*. Tr. Jeffrey Hopkins and Lati Rinpoche with Anne Klein. New York: Harper and Row, 1975.

_________. *bShes pa'i spring yig* (Tibetan translation of *Suhṛllekhaḥ*). In *sPring yig* section of Tg., vol. 94 (*nge*), ff. 40b–46b (Toh. #4182). English translation with commentary in *Nāgārjuna's Letter*. Tr. Sermey

Khensur Lobsang Tharchin & Artemus B. Engle. Dharamsala, India: Library of Tibetan Works & Archives, 1979.

_________. *Śūnyatāsaptatiḥ*. In *Śūnyatāsaptatiḥ with Auto-Commentary* Bibliotheca Indo-Tibetica Series VIII (Sanskrit restoration). Sarnath, India: Central Institute of Higher Tibetan Studies, 1996, pp. 3–66. Tibetan translation: *sTong pa nyid bdun cu pa'i tsig le'ur byas pa*. In *dBu ma* section of Tg., vol. 17 (*tza*), ff. 24a–27a (Toh. #3827).

_________. *rTen cing 'brel bar 'byung ba'i snying po'i tsig le'ur byas pa* (Tibetan translation of *Pratītyasamutpādahṛdayakārikā*). In *mDo 'grel* section of Tg., vol. 17 (*tza*), ff. 144a–144b (Toh. #4001).

Śāntideva. *Bodhicaryāvatāraḥ*. (Sanskrit and Tibetan texts) Ed. Vidushekhara Bhattacharya. Calcutta: The Asiatic Society, 1960. Tibetan translation: *Byang chub sems dpa'i spyod pa la 'jug pa*. In *dBu ma* section of Tg., vol. 26 (*la*), ff. 1–39a (Toh. #3871). English translation: *A Guide to the Bodhisattva's Way of Life*. Tr. Stephen Batchelor. Dharamsala: Library of Tibetan Works & Archives, 1979.

_________. *Śikṣāsamuccayaḥ*. Buddhist Sanskrit Texts No. 11. Darbanga, India: Mithila Institute, 1960. Tibetan Translation: *bSlab pa kun las btus pa*. In *dBu ma* section of Tg., vol. 32 (*khi*), ff. 3a–396b (Toh. #3940). English translation: *Śikshā Samuccaya, A Compendium of Buddhist Doctrine*. Tr. Cecil Bendall and W.H.D. Rouse. Reprint edition. Delhi: Motilal Banarsidass, 1971.

Sthiramati. *mDo sde rgyan gyi 'grel bshad* (Tibetan translation of *Mahāyānasūtrālaṃkāravṛttibhāṣyam*). In *Sems tzam* section of Tg., vols. 46 (*mi*) and 47 (*tzi*) (Toh. #4034).

Suvarṇadvīpa Guru (aka Dharmakīrti). *mTha' 'khob 'dul ba'i chos*. In *Blo sbyong brgya rtza* (see listing under title), pp. 136–137.

Vasubandhu. *Abhidharmakośakārikā*. Ed. G.V. Gokhale. Journal of the Royal Asiatic Society. Bombay, vol. 22, 1946. Tibetan translation: *Chos mngon pa mdzod kyi tsig le'ur byas pa*. In *mNgon pa* section of Tg., vol. 61 (*ku*), ff. 1–25a (Toh. #4089). English translation in *Abhidharmakośabhāṣyam* (4 vols.). Tr. Leo M. Pruden. Berkeley: Asian Humanities Press, 1988.

_________. *Abhidharmakośabhāṣyam*. Ed. Prahlad Pradhan. Patna: K. P. Jayaswal Research Institute, 1975. Tibetan translation: *Chos mngon pa'i mdzod kyi bshad pa*. In *mNgon pa* section of Tg., vol. 61 (*ku*), ff. 25a to end (Toh. #4090). English translation: *Abhidharmakośa-*

bhāṣyam (4 vols.). Tr. Leo M. Pruden. Berkeley: Asian Humanities Press, 1988.

_________. *'Dod pa'i yon tan lnga'i nye dmigs bshad pa* (Tibetan translation of *Pañcakāmaguṇopālambhanirdeśaḥ*). In *sPring yig* section of Tg. vol. 94 (*nge*), ff. 39a–39b (Toh. #4180).

_________. *Tsogs kyi gtam* (Tibetan translation of *Saṃbhāraparikathā*). In *sKyes rabs* section of Tg., vol. 93 (*ge*), ff. 182a–183b (Toh. # 4166).

_________. *Yon tan bdun yongs su brjod pa'i gtam*. (Tibetan translation of *Saptaguṇaparivadanakathā*). In *Spring yig* section of Tg., vol. 93 (*ge*), ff. 117a–117b (Toh. #4163).

(Ārya) Vimuktisena. *mNgon par rtogs pa'i rgyan gyi 'grel pa* (Tibetan translation of *Abhisamayālaṃkāravṛtti*) (Sanskrit of the first chapter only is available in *L'Abhisamayālaṃkāravṛtti di Ārya Vimuktisena: Primo Abhisamaya*, Rome: Istituto Italiano per il Medio ed Estremo Oriente, 1967). In *Shes phyin* section of Tg., vol. 1 (*ka*), ff. 14a–223a (Toh. #3787).

Yaśomitra. *Sphuṭārthābhidharmakośavyākhyā* (4 vols). Ed. by Swami Dwarikadas Shastri. Varanasi: Bauddha Bharati, 1970. Tibetan translation: *Chos mngon pa' mdzod kyi 'grel bshad*. In *mNgon pa* section of Tg., vols. 63 (*gu*) and 64 (*ngu*) (Toh. #4092).

Tibetan works

bKa' gdams kyi skyes bu dam pa rnams kyi gsung bgros thor bu (*bKa' gdams thor bu*). Handwritten photo-offset edition. Dharamsala, India: Shes rig par khang, n.d.

(Tā la'i bla ma sku 'phreng bdun pa) Blo bzang bskal bzang rgya mtso. *'Phags pa thugs rje chen po la bstod cing gsol ba 'debs pa phan bde'i char 'bebs*. In vol. 2 of *The Collected Works (gsuṅ 'bum) of the Seventh Dalai Lama Blo-bzaṅ-bskal-bzaṅ-rgya-mtsho* (13 vols.). Gangtok: Dodrup Sangye, 1975–1983, pp. 304–310. This work appears in a collection of praises and supplications entitled *Bla ma dang sangs rgyas byang sems sogs la bstod cing gsol ba 'debs pa dang de dang 'brel ba'i brtan bzhugs kyi rim pa phyogs gcig tu bsgrigs pa dge legs nyin mor byed pa'i snang ba* (Toh. # 5841).

_________. *Sems gting nas skyo ba'i snang glu*. In vol. 1 of *Collected Works*, p. 484. This work is item #17 in a collection of eighteen poems entitled *Blo sbyong dang 'brel ba'i gdams pa dang snyan mgur gyi rim pa phyogs gcig tu bkod pa don ldan tsangs pa'i sgra dbyangs* (Toh. #5847).

(Paṇ chen) Blo bzang chos kyi rgyal mtsan. *Bla ma mchod pa'i cho ga*. In vol. 1 (*ka*) of the *Collected Works (gsuṅ 'bum) of Blo-bsan-chos-kyi-rgyal-mthan, the First Paṇ-chen Bla-ma of bKra-śis lhun po* (5 vols.). New Delhi: Mongolian Lama Gurudeva, 1973, pp. 777–797 (Toh. # 5892).

__________. *Bar do 'phrang sgrol gyi gsol 'debs*. In vol. 5 (*ca*) of *Collected Works*, pp 73–76. This work appears in a collection of miscellaneous works entitled *Paṇ chen thams cad mkhyen pa chen po'i gsung thor bu ba phyogs gcig tu bsdebs pa* (Toh. #5977).

__________. *Byang chub lam gyi rim pa'i dmar khrid thams cad mkhyen par bgrod pa'i bde lam* (*bDe lam*). In vol. 4 (*nga*) of *Collected Works*, pp. 365–429 (Toh. #5944).

__________. *dGe ldan bka' brgyud rin po che'i phyag chen rtza ba rGyal ba'i gzhung lam*. In vol. 4 (*nga*) of *Collected Works*, pp 81–92. (Toh. #5939).

__________. *dGe ldan bka' brgyud rin po che'i bka' srol phyag chen rtza ba rgyas par bshad pa Yang gsal sgron me*. In vol. 4 (*nga*) of *Collected Works*, pp. 93–154. (Toh. #5940).

(Ke'u tsang) Blo bzang 'jam dbyangs smon lam. *Byang chub lam gyi rim pa chung ngu'i zin bris blo gsal rgya mtso'i 'jug ngogs*. In vol. 2 (*kha*) of *The Collected Works of Keu-tsaṅ Sprul-sku-Blo-bzaṅ 'jam-dbyaṅs-smon-lam* (2 vols.). Dharamsala: Library of Tibetan Works and Archives, 1984, pp. 425–805 (Toh. #6516).

(Paṇ chen) Blo bzang ye shes. *Byang chub lam gyi rim pa'i dmar khrid thams cad mkhyen par bgrod pa'i myur lam* (*Myur lam dmar khrid*). Modern folio style reprint, n.p., n.d. (Toh. #6980).

Blo bzang ye shes bstan 'dzin rgya mtso (sKyabs rje Yongs 'dzin Khri byang rin po che). *Theg chen gso sbyong gi sdom pa len pa'i cho ga nag 'gros su bkod pa Byang chen khang bzang 'dzegs pa'i them skas*. Wood block text [India] n.p., n.d.

Blo sbyong brgya rtza. A collection of Mind Training works (T: *Blo sbyong*) compiled by dKon mchog rgyal mtsan. Dharamsala: Shes rig par khang, 1973.

Bu ston Rin chen grub. *bDe bar gshegs pa'i bstan pa'i gsal byed chos kyi 'byung gnas gsung rab rin po che'i mdzod* (*Bu ston chos 'byung*). In vol. 24 (*ya*) of *The Collected Works of Bu-ston* (28 vols.). New Delhi: International Academy of Indian Culture, 1966, pp. 633–1055 (Toh. #5197). English translation: *History of Buddhism by Bu-ston*. Tr. E. E. Obermiller. Originally published Heidelberg: O. Harrassowitz, 1931. Reprint edition Tokyo: Suzuki Research Foundation.

(A kya Yongs 'dzin) dByangs can dga' ba'i blo gros. *Theg pa chen po'i blo sbyong nyi ma'i 'od zer gyi brda don*. In vol. 2 of *The Collected Works of A-kya Yoṅs 'dzin* (2 vols.). New Delhi: Gurudeva Lama, 1971, pp. 122–134.

lCang skya rol pa'i rdo rje (bLo bzang bstan pa'i sgron me). *lTa mgur a ma ngos 'dzin*. In *Lam gyi gtzo bo rnam gsum dang de'i 'grel pa, lta mgur a ma ngos 'dzin dang de'i 'grel pa, rmog lcog gsung mgur rnams*, pp. 9–12. Sarnath, India: Pleasure of Elegant Sayings Press, n.d.

mChad ka wa Ye shes rdo rje. (*Theg pa chen po*) *Blo sbyong don bdun ma'i rtza ba*. Ed. Pha bong kha pa (Rin po che) Byams pa bstan 'dzin 'phrin las rgya mtso. In vol. 5 (*ca*) of his *Collected Works*, pp. 480–485.

(Glang ri thang pa) rDo rje seng ge. *Blo sbyong tsig brgyad ma*. In *Legs par bshad pa bka' gdams rin po che'i gsung gi gces btus nor bu'i bang mdzod*, pp. 334–336.

(*Bla ma'i rnal 'byor*) *dGa' ldan lha brgya ma*. In *Chos spyod zhal 'don nyer mkho phyogs bsdebs*. Varanasi, India: Wa nā mtho slob dge ldan spyi las khang, 1979, pp. 11–14 (Toh. #6620). English translation with commentary in *A Commentary of Guru Yoga & Offering of the Mandala*. Sermey Khensur Lobsang Tharchin. Reprint edition Ithaca: Snow Lion Press, 1987.

lHa 'bri sgang pa. *bKa' gdams kyi man ngag be'u bum sngon po'i 'grel pa* (*Be'u bum sngon po'i 'grel pa*). Bir, India: T. Tsondu Senghe, 1976.

(Dvags po bla ma rin po che) 'Jam dpal lhun grub. *Byang chub lam gyi rim pa'i dmar khrid myur lam gyi sngon 'gro'i ngag 'don gyi rim pa khyer bde bklag chog skal bzang mgrin rgyan* (*sByor chos sKal bzang mgrin rgyan*) Modern folio–style reprint, [India:] n.p., n.d.

mKhas grub rje (dGe legs dpal bzang). *rJe btsun bla ma tzong kha pa chen po'i ngo mtsar rmad du byung ba'i rnam par thar pa dad pa'i 'jug ngogs*. In vol. 1 (*ka*) of *The Collected Works of the Incomparable Lord Tsongkhapa blo bzang grags pa* (18 vols.). New Delhi: Mongolian Lama Guru Deva, 1978–1983, pp. 5–146 (Toh. #5259).

__________. *dPal ldan bla ma dam pa rje btzun tzong kha pa chen po nyid kyi rnam par thar pa mdo tzam zhig brjod pa'i sgo nas gsol ba 'debs pa'i tsigs su bcad pa* (*dPal ldan sa gsum ma*). In vol. 9 (*ta*) of the *Collected Works of the Lord mkhas-grub Rje Dge-legs dpal bzaṅ-po* (12 vols.) (item #2 in *gSung 'bum thor bu*). New Delhi: Mongolian Lama Guru Deva, 1980, pp. 477–482 (Toh. #5500). English translation in *Life & Teachings of Tsong Khapa*. Ed. Robert Thurman. Dharamsala, India: Library of Tibetan Works & Archives, 1982, pp. 232–237.

__________. *Shes rab kyi pha rol tu phyin pa'i man ngag gi bstan bcos mngon par rtogs pa'i rgyan gyi 'grel pa don gsal ba'i rnam bshad rtogs dka'i snang ba.* In vol. 1 (*ka*) of *Collected Works*, pp. 731–1179 (Toh. #5461).

(rJe Gung thang pa) dKon mchog bstan pa'i sgron me. *Blo bzang rgyal bstan ma.* In *Zhal 'don gces btus*, a prayer book published by the Shes rig par khang, Dharamsala, India, pp. 547–550.

__________. *mDo sngags kyi gzhung la slob gnyer byed tsul gyi bslab bya nor bu'i gling du bgrod pa'i lam yig sogs bslab bya sna tsogs kyi skor.* In vol. 4 (*nga*) of *The Collected Works of Guṅ-thaṅ dkon-mchog-bstan-pa'i sgron-me* (10 vols.). New Delhi: Ngawang Gelek Demo, 1972–1979, pp. 51–116.

__________. *Mi rtag bsgom tsul gyi bslab bya.* In vol. 4 (*nga*) of *Collected Works*, pp. 117–121.

__________. *Nyams myong rgan po'i 'bel gtam yid 'byung dmar khrid.* In vol. 9 (*ta*) of *Collected Works*, pp. 283–291.

(Sa skya Paṇḍita) Kun dga' rgyal mtsan. *sDom pa gsum gyi rab tu dbye ba.* In vol. 5 of *The Complete Works of the Great Masters of the Sa Skya Sect of Tibetan Buddhism*, pp. 297–320. Tokyo: The Toyo Bunko, 1968.

Legs par bshad pa bka' gdams rin po che'i gsung gi gces btus nor bu'i bang mdzod (*bKa' gdams bces btus*). Compiled by Yeshe don grub bstan pa'i rgyal mtsan. Delhi: D. Tsondu Senghe, 1985 (Toh. #6971).

(rGyal mchog lnga pa) Ngag dbang blo bzang rgya mtso. *Byang chub lam gyi rim pa'i khrid yig 'jam pa'i dbyangs kyi zhal lung* (*'Jam dpal zhal lung*). Photo offset reprint of *rMe ru Phun Tsogs Gling* woodblock edition. Dharamsala, India: Namgyal Monastery, 1989 (Toh. #5637).

dNgul chu Dharma bhadra. *Blo sbyong don bdun ma'i zin bris rgyal sras snying nor.* In vol. 6 (*cha*) of the *Collected Works (gsuṅ-'bum) of Dṅgul-chu Dharma-bhadra* (6 vols.). New Delhi: Champa Oser, 1973–1976 (Toh. #6426), pp. 195–381.

mNyam med rJe btzun Tzong kha pa chen pos mdzad pa'i byang chub lam rim chen mo'i dka' ba'i gnad rnams mchan bu bzhi'i sgo nas legs par bshad pa theg chen lam gyi gsal sgron (*Lam rim mchan bzhi sbrags ma*) (2 vols.). New Delhi: Chos-'phel-legs-ldan, 1972.

(sKyabs rje) Pha bong kha pa (Rin po che) Byams pa bstan 'dzin 'phrin las rgya mtso (sKyabs rje bDe chen snying po). Newly compiled edition of (*Theg pa chen po*) *Blo sbyong don bdun ma'i rtza ba*. In vol. 5 of *The Collected Works of Pha-boṅ-kha-pa* (11 vols), pp. 303–317. New Delhi: Chophel Legdan, 1973.

__________. *Byang chub lam gyi rim pa'i dmar khrid bde myur gyi thog nas nyams khrid stzal skabs kyi sa bcad*. In vol. 5 (*ca*) of *Collected Works*, pp. 303–317.

__________. *rDo rje 'chang pha bong kha pa dpal bzang pos lam gtzo'i zab khrid stzal skabs kyi gsung bshad zin bris lam bzang sgo 'byed* (*Lam gtzo'i zab khrid gsung bshad kyi zin bris*). In vol. 8 (*nya*) of *Collected Works*, pp. 375–455. English translation: *The Principal Teachings of Buddhism*. Tr. Sermey Khensur Lobsang Tharchin & Geshe Michael Roach. Howell, New Jersey: Mahayana Sutra & Tantra Press, 1988.

__________. *rNam grol lag bcangs su gtod pa'i man ngag zab mo tsang la ma nor ba mtsungs med chos kyi rgyal po'i thugs bcud byang chub lam gyi rim pa'i nyams khrid kyi zin bris gsung rab kun gyi bcud bsdus gdams ngag bdud rtzi'i snying po* (*rNam grol lag bcangs*). vol. 11 (*da*) of *Collected Works*.

(dGe bshes Dol pa dMar zhur pa) Shes rab rgya mtso. *Be'u bum sngong po*. Verses contained in *bKa' gdams kyi man ngag be'u bum sngon po'i 'grel pa* (see lHa 'bri sgang pa).

sTag tsang Lo tzā ba Shes rab rin chen rgyal mtsan. *Dad pa'i padma rgyas par byed pa'i bstod tsig gi nyi ma*. In *Three Texts Reflection the Views of Pha-boṅ-kha-pa bde-chen-sñiṅ-po on the Questions of Heresies and Intersectarian Relations in Tibet*. New Delhi: Ngawang Topgay, 1977, pp. 217–234.

(mKhas grub) bsTan pa dar rgyas. *bsTan bcos chen po dbu ma la 'jug pa'i spyi don rnam bshad dgongs pa rab gsal gyi dgongs pa gsal bar byed pa'i blo gsal sgron me* (*dBu ma spyi don*). Reprint edition. New Delhi: Geshe Lobsang Tharchin, 1980.

__________. *bsTan bcos mngon par rtogs pa'i rgyan rtza 'grel gyi spyi don rnam bshad snying po rgyan gyi snang ba* (*Phar phyin spyi don*). Reprint edition. New Delhi: Sermey Khensur Lobsang Tharchin, 1980.

(rGyal sras) Thogs med bzang po dpal. *rGyal ba'i sras kyi lag len so bdun ma*. Gangtok: Namgyal Institute of Tibetology, 1972. English Translation: *The Thirty-Seven Practices of All Buddhas' Sons*. Dharamsala, India: Library of Tibetan Works and Archives, 1973.

gTzang smyon He ru ka. *rJe btzun mi la ras pa'i rnam thar rgyas par phye ba mgur 'bum* (*Mi la ras pa'i mgur 'bum*). n.p., n.d. English translation: *The Hundred Thousand Songs of Milarepa* (2 vols.) (Toh. # 7047). Tr. Garma C.C. Chang. Shambhala: Boulder, 1977.

(rJe) Tzong kha pa (Blo bzang grags pa'i dpal). *Bla na med pa rin po che gsum gyi gtam gyi sbyor ba*. In vol. 2 (*kha*) of *Collected Works* (item #60, *bKa' 'bum thor bu*), pp. 313–316 (Toh. #5275).

_________. *dBu ma la 'jug pa'i rgya cher bshad pa dgongs pa rab gsal*. In vol. 16 (*ma*) of *Collected Works*, pp. 3–535 (Toh. # 5408).

_________. *Byang chub lam gyi rim pa chen mo* (*Lam rim chen mo*). Vol. 13 (*pa*) of *The Collected Works of the Incomparable Lord Tsongkhapa blo bzang grags pa* (18 vols.). New Delhi: Mongolian Lama Guru Deva, 1978–1983 (Toh. #5392).

_________. *Byang chub lam gyi rim pa'i nyams len gyi rnam gzhag mdor bsdus te brjed byang du bya ba* (also known as *Lam rim bsdus don* and as *Nyams mgur*). In vol. 2 (*kha*) of *Collected Works* (item #59, *bKa' 'bum thor bu*), pp. 308–313 (Toh. #5275). English translation in *Life & Teachings of Tsong Khapa*. Ed. Robert Thurman. Dharamsala, India: Library of Tibetan Works & Archives, 1982, pp. 59–66.

_________. *Byang chub sems dpa'i tsul khrims kyi rnam bshad byang chub gzhung lam*. In vol. 1 (*ka*) of *Collected Works*, pp. 513–728 (Toh. #5271).

_________. *Byin rlabs nyer 'jug* (*sKabs gsum pa*). In vol. 2 (*kha*) of *Collected Works* (item #14, *bKa' 'bum thor bu*), pp. 222–225 (Toh. #5275).

_________. *bDe ba can gyi zhing du skye ba 'dzin pa'i smon lam zhing mchog sgo 'byed*. In vol. 2 (*kha*) of *Collected Works* (item #69 of *bKa' 'bum thor bu*), pp. 367–397 (Toh. #5275).

_________. *sKyes bu gsum gyi nyams su blang bya'i byang chub lam gyi rim pa chung ba* (*Lam rim chung ngu*). In vol. 14 (*pha*) of *Collected Works*, pp. 4–406 (Toh. #5393).

_________. *Lam gyi gtzo bo rnam gsum*. In vol. 2 (*kha*) of *Collected Works* (item #85, *bKa' 'bum thor bu*), pp. 584–586 (Toh. #5275).

English translation with commentary in *The Principal Teachings of Buddhism*. Tr. Sermey Khensur Lobsang Tharchin & Geshe Michael Roach. Howell, New Jersey: Mahayana Sutra & Tantra Press, 1988.

_________. *Lam mchog sgo 'byed*. In vol. 2 of *Collected Works* (item #1 of *bKa' 'bum thor bu*), pp. 202–206 (Toh. #5275).

_________. *Sangs rgyas bcom ldan 'das 'jig rten thams cad kyi ma 'dris pa'i mdza' bshes chen po ston pa bla na med pa la zab mo rten cing 'brel bar 'byung ba gsung ba'i sgo nas bstod pa legs bshad snying po* (*rTen 'brel bstod pa*). In vol. 2 of *Collected Works* (item #15 of *bKa' 'bum thor bu*), pp. 225–231 (Toh. #5275). English translation in *Life & Teachings of Tsong Khapa*. Ed. Robert Thurman. Dharamsala, India: Library of Tibetan Works & Archives, 1982, pp. 99–107.

_________. *Zhu lan sman mchog bdud rtzi'i 'phreng ba*. In vol. 1 (*ka*) of *Collected Works*, pp. 289–314 (Toh. #5268). English translation in *Life & Teachings of Tsong Khapa*. Ed. Robert Thurman. Dharamsala, India: Library of Tibetan Works & Archives, 1982, pp. 213–230.

(Tse mchog gling yongs 'dzin) Ye shes rgyal mtsan. *Byang chub lam gyi rim pa'i bla ma brgyud pa'i rnam thar rgyal bstan mdzes pa'i rgyan mchog phul byung nor bu'i phreng ba* (*Lam rim bla ma brgyud pa'i rnam thar*) 2 vols. Reprinted as *Lives of the Teachers of the Lam-rim Precepts*. New Delhi: Ngawang Gelek Demo, 1970 (Toh. #5985).

_________. *dGa ldan phyag rgya chen po'i khrid yig lam bzang gsal ba'i sgron me*. In vol. 22 of *The Collected Works of Tshe mchog gliṅ Yoṅs-'dzin Ye-śes-rgyal-mtshan* (25 vols), pp. 201–450. New Delhi: Tibet House Library, 1974–1977 (Toh. #6127).

_________. *Theg chen blo sbyong gi khrid yig bdud rtzi'i snying po*. In vol. 19 of *Collected Works*, pp. 1–343 (Toh. #6091).

_________. *Theg pa chen po'i blo sbyong gi khrid yig lo bzang dgongs rgyan*. Vol. 25 of *Collected Works* (Toh. #6148).

Reference materials and other English language works

A Catalogue of the Tohoku University Collection of Tibetan Works on Buddhism. Ed. Y. Kanakura et al. Sendai, Japan: Tohoku Imperial University, 1953.

A Complete Catalogue of the Tibetan Buddhist Canons. Ed. Hakuju Ui et al. Sendai, Japan: Tohoku Imperial University, 1934.

Chattopadhaya, Alaka. *Atīśa and Tibet*. Reprint ed. New Delhi: Motilal Banarsidass, 1981.

History of Buddhism by Bu-ston. Tr. E.E. Obermiller. Originally published Heidelberg: O. Harrassowitz, 1931. Reprint edition Tokyo: Suzuki Research Foundation.

Roerich, George N. *The Blue Annals*. Translation of Gö Lotsawa's *Deb ther sngon po*. Reprint edition New Delhi: Motilal Banarsidass, 1976.

Tāranātha's History of Buddhism in India. Tr. Lama Chimpa and Alaka Chattopadhyaya. Simla, India: Indian Institute of Advanced Study, 1970.

Tharchin, Sermey Khensur Lobsang. *Achieving Bodhichitta*. Howell, New Jersey: Mahayana Sutra & Tantra Press, 1999.

_________. *A Commentary on Guru Yoga & Offering of the Mandala*. Reprint edition. Ithaca: Snow Lion Press, 1987.

_________. *Six Session Guru Yoga*. Howell, New Jersey: Mahayana Sutra & Tantra Press, 1999.

Tharchin, Sermey Khensur Lobsang with Judith Chiarelli et. al. *King Udrayana and The Wheel of Life*. Howell, New Jersey: Mahayana Sutra & Tantra Press, 1984.

INDEX OF ENGLISH AND ANGLICISED WORDS

cessations, the two, 299
analyitic, 299n
nonanalytic, 299n
Chanakya, 105
Chandrakirti, 53, 155, 196, 270, 272, 273
Chandraprabha, 164
Changkya Rölbey Dorje, 104, 281
Chapter on the Requisites for One-pointed Concentration, 233n
Charvaka, 56n. *See also* Lokayata.
Chekawa Yeshe Dorje, Geshe 152, 153, 191, 205
Chen-ngawa, 14. *See also* Tsultrim Bar.
cherishing others, 161–166
Chinese Ritual for Overcoming Obstacles, 121
Chittamatra, 106, 205. *See also* Mind Only School.
chö or "ego-cutting" practice, 160n
Chöding Hermitage, 289
Chudamani, 164
chülen, 107
Chusang Hermitage, 313, 324
Chushur, 105
classes of beings, the six, 3, 3n
Classification of the Three Vows, 265n
cognitional teaching, 87
Collection of Jewel-like Qualities, 207
Collection of Uplifting Sayings, 16n
Commentary to the Blue Manual, 29n, 83n
Commentary to the Four Hundred Verses, 275
Commentary to the Ornament of Realizations, 49n
Commentary to the Treasury of Higher Learning, 2n, 30n, 34n, 49n, 55n, 70n, 132n, 154n, 299n
Compendium of Elucidations, 22n, 27n
Compendium of Higher Learning, 66, 244, 247, 247n, 254n, 298n
Compendium of the Perfections, 100n, 243n
Compendium of Training, 49n, 138, 172n, 212n, 213
completion stage. *See* Anuttarayoga Tantra.
Confession of Transgressions Sutra, 185
Conversation with an Experienced Old Man, 24n, 25n, 26n
corrective factors, the eight, 240
craving and grasping, 46, 69

Dalai Lama, the Fifth, 5n, 18n
Dalai Lama, the Seventh, 17n, 18n. *See also* Losang Kelsang Gyatso.
Declaration on the Accumulations, 36
degeneracies, the five, 154, 205
deliberation, 204, 256
Dependent Origination, the Twelve Limbs of, 73–82
Desi Sang-gye Gyatso, 18, 252
desire, 48–50
Dharani Spell that Settles Legal Disputes, 121
dharma activities, the ten, 194
dharma heap(s), 109n
eighty-four thousand, 109

INDEX OF TIBETAN WORDS

INDEX OF SANSKRIT WORDS

remember our
1. Precious human life.

Very important

Life is impermanent

time of death uncertain

Nothing can help only dharma practice.

dharma is the protection of your mind.

dharma practice is all day -

We are living our Karma

happy, unhappiness

and we keep accumulating it.

Real refuge is dharma.

understanding Samsara will reduce your attachments.

our minds are always under the power of Karma & delusion